Multilingual Memories

Advances in Sociolinguistics Series

Series Editor: Tommaso M. Milani

Since the emergence of sociolinguistics as a new field of enquiry in the late 1960s, research into the relationship between language and society has advanced almost beyond recognition. In particular, the past decade has witnessed the considerable influence of theories drawn from outside of sociolinguistics itself. Thus, rather than see language as a mere reflection of society, recent work has been increasingly inspired by ideas drawn from social, cultural and political theory that have emphasized the constitutive role played by language/discourse in all areas of social life. The *Advances in Sociolinguistics* series seeks to provide a snapshot of the current diversity of the field of sociolinguistics and the blurring of the boundaries between sociolinguistics and other domains of study concerned with the role of language in society.

Becoming a Citizen: Linguistic Trials and Negotiations in the UK, Kamran Khan

Discourses of Endangerment: Ideology and Interest in the Defence of Languages, Edited by Alexandre Duchêne and Monica Heller

Globalization and Language in Contact: Scale, Migration, and Communicative Practices, Edited by James Collins

Globalization of Language and Culture in Asia, Edited by Viniti Vaish

Language, Culture and Identity: An Ethnolinguistic Perspective, Philip Riley

Language Ideologies and Media Discourse: Texts, Practices, Politics, Edited by Sally Johnson and Tommaso M. Milani

Language Ideologies and the Globalization of 'Standard' Spanish, Darren Paffey

Language in the Media: Representations, Identities, Ideologies, Edited by Sally Johnson and Astrid Ensslin

Language and Power: An Introduction to Institutional Discourse, Andrea Mayr

Language Testing, Migration and Citizenship, Edited by Guus Extra, Massimiliano Spotti and Piet Van Avermaet

Linguistic Minorities and Modernity, 2nd Edition: A Sociolinguistic Ethnography, Monica Heller

Making Sense of People and Place in Linguistic Landscapes, Edited by Amiena Peck, Christopher Stroud and Quentin Williams

Multilingual Encounters in Europe's Institutional Spaces, Edited by Johann Unger, Michał Krzyżanowski and Ruth Wodak

Multilingualism: A Critical Perspective, Adrian Blackledge and Angela Creese

Negotiating and Contesting Identities in Linguistic Landscapes, Edited by Robert Blackwood, Elizabeth Lanza and Hirut Woldemariam

Remix Multilingualism: Hip-Hop, Ethnography and Performing Marginalized Voice, Quentin Williams

Semiotic Landscapes: Language, Image, Space, Adam Jaworski and Crispin Thurlow

The Languages of Global Hip-Hop, Edited by Marina Terkourafi

The Language of Newspapers: Socio-Historical Perspectives, Martin Conboy

The Languages of Urban Africa, Edited by Fiona Mc Laughlin

The Sociolinguistics of Identity, Edited by Tope Omoniyi

The Tyranny of Writing: Ideologies of the Written Word, Edited by Constanze Weth and Kasper Juffermans

Voices in the Media: Performing Linguistic Otherness, Gaëlle Planchenault

Multilingual Memories

Monuments, Museums and the Linguistic Landscape

Edited by
Robert Blackwood and John Macalister

BLOOMSBURY ACADEMIC
LONDON • NEW YORK • OXFORD • NEW DELHI • SYDNEY

BLOOMSBURY ACADEMIC
Bloomsbury Publishing Plc
50 Bedford Square, London, WC1B 3DP, UK
1385 Broadway, New York, NY 10018, USA
29 Earlsfort Terrace, Dublin 2, Ireland

BLOOMSBURY, BLOOMSBURY ACADEMIC and the Diana logo are trademarks of Bloomsbury Publishing Plc

First published in Great Britain 2020
This paperback edition published in 2021

Copyright © Robert Blackwood, John Macalister and Contributors, 2020

Robert Blackwood and John Macalister have asserted their right under the Copyright, Designs and Patents Act, 1988, to be identified as Editors of this work.

For legal purposes the Acknowledgements on p. xvii constitute an extension of this copyright page.

Cover illustration © Martin O'Neill

All rights reserved. No part of this publication may be reproduced or transmitted in any form or by any means, electronic or mechanical, including photocopying, recording, or any information storage or retrieval system, without prior permission in writing from the publishers.

Bloomsbury Publishing Plc does not have any control over, or responsibility for, any third-party websites referred to or in this book. All internet addresses given in this book were correct at the time of going to press. The author and publisher regret any inconvenience caused if addresses have changed or sites have ceased to exist, but can accept no responsibility for any such changes.

A catalogue record for this book is available from the British Library.

A catalog record for this book is available from the Library of Congress.

ISBN: HB: 978-1-3500-7125-4
PB: 978-1-3502-5400-8
ePDF: 978-1-3500-7126-1
eBook: 978-1-3500-7127-8

Series: Advances in Sociolinguistics

Typeset by Integra Software Services Pvt. Ltd.

To find out more about our authors and books visit www.bloomsbury.com and sign up for our newsletters.

Contents

List of Figures	ix
Tables	xii
List of Contributors	xiii
Acknowledgements	xvii

Introduction *Robert Blackwood and John Macalister* 1

Part 1 Monuments

1 Forging a Nation: Commemorating the Great War *John Macalister* 13
2 Montreal's Black Rock: The Forgotten Grave of the Irish Typhus Victims *Patricia Lamarre* 35
3 *La fraternité franco-marocaine* Remembered in France and in Morocco – Multilingual Memorials and *patrimoine national* *Dawn Marley* 63

Part 2 Museums

4 Multilingual Memories: Artefactual Materiality of Erasure and Downscaling in Linguistic and Semiotic Landscapes of Livingstone Town, Zambia *Hambaba Jimaima and Felix Banda* 89
5 'Twa Tongues': Modern Scots and English in the Robert Burns Birthplace Museum *Robert Blackwood and James Costa* 113
6 Multiple 'Ways of Telling' in the LL at the Second World War Japanese American Internment Camp Memorial Cemetery in Rohwer, Arkansas *Rebecca Todd Garvin and Yasushi Onodera* 135
7 Sarajevo's War Childhood Museum: A Social Semiotic Analysis of 'Combi-Memorials' as Spatial Texts *Maida Kosatica* 161

Part 3 Memories

8 Remembering in Order to Forget: Scaled Memories of Slavery in the Linguistic Landscape of Rio de Janeiro *Branca Falabella Fabrício and Rodrigo Borba* 187

9   Cast in Iron: Remembering the Past in Penang *John Macalister and Teresa Ong* 213
10 Instances of Emplaced Memory: The Case of Alghero/L'Alguer *Stefania Tufi* 237
11 Appropriation and Re-appropriation: The Memorial as a Palimpsest *Christian Bendl* 263

Conclusions 285
Index 294

List of Figures

1.1	The Cenotaph in the 1930s; the Parliamentary precinct, then separated from the memorial by a road, is in the background. Source: Crown Studios Collection	18
1.2	The Cenotaph today; the lions and plaques are later additions, as is the paving creating a pocket park and a physical link to the Parliamentary precinct	19
1.3	Map of Pukeahu. © Government of New Zealand	20
1.4	Red sandstone pillar with black granite inset, part of the Australian memorial at Pukeahu	21
1.5	A whakatauki on the southern wall of Pukeahu	25
1.6	Other languages on the periphery	27
2.1	The fever ships waiting below Grosse-Île. Illustration B. Duchesne. Source: Parks Canada	38
2.2	Lithograph of the fever sheds in the 1850s. Credit: McCord Museum	40
2.3	The Black Rock in its island	49
2.4	The blessing of the blue-collar workers. Credit: Montreal Irish Monument Park Foundation	53
2.5	The Liberal Party poster at the Black Rock. Credit: Montreal Irish Monument Park Foundation	54
3.1	The monument to Franco-Moroccan friendship	68
3.2	The South Face, with the message from Foch	70
3.3	The South Face, with the message from Lyautey	71
3.4	Left-hand side of the North Face	73
3.5	The monument to the glory of the Mixed Moroccan Goumiers	80
4.1	The statue of Livingstone outside of Livingstone Museum	96
4.2	Local languages naming herbal relics	102
4.3	The Livingstone Museum external sign	104
4.4	The juxtaposition of Mosi-oa-tunya, Victoria Falls and Shuungu namutitima	105
4.5	The statue of David Livingstone in the falls area	106

List of Figures

5.1	A road sign including the stylized detail of Nasmyth's portrait of Burns	125
5.2	Instruction in English in the toilets at the RBBM	126
5.3	The main exhibition space's entry panel	127
5.4	Lines from Burns's poems inside the Burns's cottage	129
6.1	Placement of memorial objects in the Rohwer Relocation Camp Cemetery	145
6.2	Orientational marker (Item #1) on the east side of the cemetery	147
6.3	Front and side views of the 'Tank' monument (Item #3)	149
6.4	The Japanese inscription on the Obelisk, Item #5	151
6.5	A gravestone (Item #7)	152
7.1	War Childhood Museum, entrance and façade, Sarajevo, 2017	166
7.2	Illuminated artefacts creating shadows	175
7.3	'Adidas hat'	177
7.4	Bulletproof vest	179
8.1	The Valongo Wharf memorial	199
8.2	Bilingual plaque in the Valongo Wharf memorial	200
8.3	Graffiti at Pedra do Sal	204
8.4	New Blacks Institute and skeletal remains of Josefina Bakhita	207
9.1	Jimmy Choo. Local information: Muntri Street, Buffer Zone, George Town World Heritage Site. Site information: This is the place where the famous shoe designer Jimmy Choo started his apprenticeship	221
9.2	Labourer to trader. Local information: Chowrasta Market, Buffer Zone, George Town World Heritage Site. Site information: The early convict labourers were reputed to have built most of the government buildings in Penang. Some ex-convicts became petty traders and were the core group who started the Chowrasta Market	223
9.3	Kopi O. Local information: Kimberley Street, Buffer Zone, George Town World Heritage Site. Site information: [none provided]	225
9.4	Win Win. Local information: Muntri Street, Buffer Zone, George Town World Heritage Site. Site information: Muntri Street was named after the Orang Kaya Menteri of Larut, Perak, Ngah Ibrahim. The tin merchants of Penang worked very closely with Ngah Ibrahim as Larut District was one of the major suppliers of tin at that time	226
9.5	Escape. Location information: UNESCO World Heritage Site, Core Zone. Site information: The local Chinese say the rich men who lived on Muntri Street kept their mistresses here, hence the name 'Ai Cheng Hang' [or Love Lane]	228

9.6	Learn Hokkien	229
10.1	Via Roma – Italian-only sign	248
10.2	Example of spatial de-structuration: Muntada del Campanil/ Via Roma	249
10.3	Example of inaccurate reconstruction of successive street names	250
10.4	*Lo Portal Nou* (New Gate)	252
10.5	Monolingual Catalan sign (literally Road of the Old Post Office) coexisting with Italian sign	253
10.6	Bilingual sign displaying the Alguerese translation only of *Piazza/Placa* (Square)	254
11.1	Aerial view of the *Heldenplatz* (structural map) © OpenStreetMap contributors	272
11.2	Inscription on the Outer Castle Gate	273
11.3	Entering the Crypt at the Outer Castle Gate	276
11.4	The wreath-laying ceremony (26 October 2017). Source: Ulrike Hütter	278

Tables

1.1	Contrasting values in Pukeahu and the Cenotaph	29
4.1	Linguistic impressions in LL of Livingstone Museum and Victoria Falls area	99
6.1	List of memorial monuments analysed	145
9.1	Languages on signs close to *Escape*	232
10.1	Language use in Alghero as reported in Oppo (2007)	242
10.2	Language use in Alghero as reported in Generalitat de Catalunya (2008)	242
10.3	Language use in Alghero as reported in Generalitat de Catalunya (2015)	242
10.4	Breakdown of signs according to language combination	251

List of Contributors

Felix Banda is a Senior Professor in the Linguistics Department, University of the Western Cape, South Africa. His research interests include sociolinguistics, linguistic landscapes, language practices in society and education, Bantu linguistics, multimodality, critical media and material culture of migration studies. His recent publications include a co-edited monograph *A Unified Standard Orthography of South-Central African Languages* (2015), and articles 'Linguistic Landscapes and the Sociolinguistics of Language Vitality in Multilingual Contexts of Zambia' (*Multilingua* 36(5), 595–625, with Hambaba Jimaima, 2017) and 'Language Policy and Orthographic Harmonization across Linguistic, Ethnic and National Boundaries in Southern Africa' (*Language Policy* 15, 257–275, 2017).

Christian Bendl is a doctoral university assistant at the Department of Linguistics, University of Vienna, Austria. He has worked as scientific collaborator in the projects 'INPUT: Investigating Parental and Other Caretakers' Utterances to Kindergarten' (PI: Prof. Wolfgang Dressler) and 'My Literacies. Approaches to Literacies in Multimodal and Multilingual Contexts – The View of the Child' (PI: Dr Nadja Kerschhofer-Puhalo). In his doctoral thesis, he discusses the Viennese *Heldenplatz* as discursively constituted by contextualizations of space-time (supervized by Prof. Jürgen Spitzmüller and Prof. Brigitta Busch). Other areas of research are (right-wing) protest movements and doctor-patient communication in homeopathic consultations (MA thesis).

Robert Blackwood is Professor of French Sociolinguistics at the University of Liverpool, UK, and currently editor of the journal *Linguistic Landscape* with Elana Shohamy. He is the author of a number of articles and book chapters on language policy and regional language revitalization in France, including work on the linguistic landscape. He is the author of *The State, the Activists, and the Islander: Language Policy on Corsica* (Springer, 2008) and co-author with Stefania Tufi of *The Linguistic Landscape of the Mediterranean: French and Italian Coastal Cities* (Palgrave Macmillan, 2015). He also explores questions of French digital discourse.

Rodrigo Borba is Professor of Socio/Applied Linguistics at the Federal University of Rio de Janeiro, Brazil. He has been a visiting research fellow at King's College London, University of Birmingham (UK) and Oxford University. His research interests lie within the remit of interdisciplinary work on language in society with a special focus on gender and sexuality. He has published extensively on the areas of language and gender, queer linguistics, interactional sociolinguistics and linguistic landscapes. His work has appeared on high-profile venues such as *Journal of Sociolinguistics, International Journal of the Sociology of Language, The Handbook of Language and Sexuality* (Oxford University Press) and *Making Sense of People and Place in Linguistic Landscapes* (Bloomsbury).

James Costa is Senior Lecturer in Sociolinguistics at Université de la Sorbonne nouvelle in Paris, France. In his work, he tries to reproblematize the social implications and consequences of language revitalization in Provence and Scotland. While at the University of Oslo, he questioned the consequences of the absence of standardization in the case of Scots in Scotland. The main focus of his work is on social relations and on how those shape and are shaped by linguistic regimes such as standardization.

Branca Falabella Fabrício is Associate Professor in Applied Linguistics at the Federal University of Rio de Janeiro, Brazil, being a researcher of the Brazilian National Research Council (CNPq). She has been a research fellow at King's College London. Her research interests comprise queer literacies, performative approaches to language and processes of socialization, text trajectories on the web, online interactions and semiotic-discursive landscapes. Her recent academic production includes articles to be published in *Discourse, Context and Media* and *Gender and Language* and book chapters in *The Handbook of Language and Sexuality* (Oxford University Press) and *The Handbook of Discourse Studies* (Cambridge University Press).

Rebecca Todd Garvin is an Associate Professor in the Department of English and World Languages at Arkansas Tech University, Russellville, Arkansas, United States. Her published research includes emotional responses to the linguistic landscape, educational sites and schoolscapes, and utilizing creative genres in second language writing. Her current interests are in migration and multilingualism in North America, memorials and reconstructions of history in the linguistic landscape. She currently serves on the editorial board of the journal *Linguistic Landscape*.

Hambaba Jimaima holds a PhD in linguistics from the University of the Western Cape, Cape Town, South Africa. He is a lecturer and Head of Department, Department of Literature and Languages in the School of Humanities and Social Sciences at the University of Zambia. His research interests revolve around semiotics, sociolinguistics, syntax and the extended view of multimodality, predicated on language production and consumption in the public spaces. His recent publications include 'Linguistic Landscapes and the Sociolinguistics of Language Vitality in Multilingual Contexts of Zambia', *Multilingua*, De Gruyter Mouton vol 36/5: 595–626, 2017 (with Felix Banda) and 'Semiotic Ecology of Linguistic Landscapes in Rural Zambia', *Journal of Sociolinguistics* 19/5: 643–670, 2015 (with Felix Banda).

Maida Kosatica is an affiliated researcher in the Department of English at the University of Bern, Switzerland. She received her PhD in Sociolinguistics from the University of Bern with a doctoral dissertation on the discourses of remembering in post-war contexts. Her research interests include discursive and multimodal approaches to violence, suffering and remembering, historical traumas, visual communication and social semiotics. In her current project, she focuses on the visual-discursive politics of empathy realized through the mass-mediatized representation of children's suffering.

Patricia Lamarre is Full Professor in the Faculty of Education at the University of Montreal. Canada. She is a research member at the CRIEM (*Centre de recherches interdisciplinaires en études montréalaises*) at McGill University and at the CEETUM (*Centre d'études ethniques des universités montréalaises*). Her areas of expertise are urban sociolinguistics, the language practices of young Montrealers and bilingualism/plurilingualism in Quebec. Her current research is on the mobility of young Francophones in Western Canada. She has published in the *International Journal of the Sociology of Language, Canadian Ethnic Studies, Langue et société* and *Francophonies d'Amérique*.

John Macalister is Professor of Applied Linguistics at Victoria University of Wellington, New Zealand. His most recent co-edited book was *Family Language Policies in a Multilingual World: Opportunities, Challenges, and Consequences* (with S. Hadi Mirvahedi; published by Routledge in 2017) and his earlier work on linguistic landscapes in New Zealand and Timor Leste has appeared in the journals *Multilingua* and *Language Problems & Language Planning*.

Dawn Marley is Principal Teaching Fellow at the University of Surrey, UK, where she has taught French for twenty-five years. Throughout her career she has been interested in the relationship between France and Morocco, and the way this plays out through language. Her work on attitudes towards French in Morocco developed into an interest in the role of French in the linguistic landscape of the country. She teaches on wider sociolinguistics issues and in 2017 co-wrote the second edition of *The French-Speaking World: A Practical Introduction to Sociolinguistic Issues* (Routledge).

Teresa Wai See Ong is an early-career researcher at Griffith University, Australia, having been awarded her PhD in 2019. Her main areas of interest are language maintenance and language shift, and linguistic landscape. Her PhD thesis employed an ecological approach to examine the relationship between national language policy and language maintenance pertaining to Chinese community languages in Malaysia. She is currently working on projects related to linguistic landscapes in Singapore and Malaysia.

Yasushi Onodera is Associate Dean for International and Multicultural Student Services at Arkansas Tech University, United States. He overseas global education programmes and student support services to international students, having previously worked at a British telecommunications company in Tokyo, Japan; the Consulate General of Japan in Auckland, New Zealand; a business consultation firm in Kuala Lumpur, Malaysia; and a consumer division of an American bank in Japan. He holds a bachelor's degree in economics from State University of New York at Buffalo, and a master's degree in education and human development from the George Washington University.

Stefania Tufi is Senior Lecturer in Italian Studies at the University of Liverpool, UK. Her research falls within sociolinguistics and has focused on aspects such as social dialectology, minority languages (including migrant languages) and plurilingual repertoires. An ongoing research interest is represented by the relationship between language and space (the Linguistic Landscape), and in particular the linguistic construction of transnational spaces of agency and belonging. Her publications include a co-authored monograph *The Linguistic Landscape of the Mediterranean – French and Italian Coastal Cities* (with Robert Blackwood), and she is currently completing a longitudinal study on the linguistic landscape of Naples.

Acknowledgements

As with any other edited volume, this book has emerged after a series of conversations, collaborations and contributions.

At the earliest stages, exchanges with Brigitta Busch, Elizabeth Lanza and Unn Røyneland were fundamental in establishing preliminary parameters and focusing some of the thinking around multilingualism and memorials. We are conscious that, in this volume, we cross over into a well-established and highly respected field of scholarship; and in problematizing the relationship between memory studies and multilingualism, we are grateful in particular to Charles Forsdick and Kate Marsh who generously and supportively commented on what we very grandly refer to as the position piece that underpinned the initial endeavour.

Several contributions in this volume were first aired at the twenty-first Sociolinguistics Symposium in Murcia in 2016, and we recognize here the contribution made to this project by those who attended and engaged with our panel.

It was in Murcia that a conversation with Andrew Wardell at Bloomsbury Academic led to the proposal for this volume, and we would like to thank Andrew for his enthusiasm and backing since the very start. Also at Bloomsbury Academic, at different stages of the project, we have been supported by Helen Saunders and Becky Holland, to whom we express our thanks for their patience. Equally, we are grateful to Tommaso Milani – the Series Editor – and the anonymous reviewers of the proposal for their very insightful comments and engagement with what we have been trying to do.

Peer review has enhanced this volume considerably and, on behalf of all the contributors, we would like to thank Gilles Baro, Charles Forsdick, Ben Ireland, Kate Marsh, Tommaso Milani, Matthew Philpotts, Marenka Thompson and Karyn Wilson Costa for their careful and considered readings of the chapters, and the truly invaluable feedback they provided.

Writing and editing this volume have been a pleasure, and for this we thank the authors for their enthusiastic and cheerful approach to working together.

Finally, we would like to record our grateful thanks to those who, on a personal level, have supported, endured and encouraged this project. In particular, Robert would like to thank Jude, Luke and Julia.

Liverpool and Wellington, December 2018.

Introduction

Robert Blackwood and John Macalister

Although memory studies looms large in much scholarship now undertaken in the humanities and social sciences, the extent to which multilingualism – and in particular visible, public multilingualism – plays a part in these debates has not been exploited to its full potential. Linguistic Landscape (henceforth LL) research has begun to engage critically with memory, memorialization and multilingualism[1] and this volume both develops existing lines of enquiry and opens up new avenues of research which draw on cross-disciplinary expertise from sociolinguistics, semiotics, sociology, pedagogy and language policy to inform wider discussions. From the conception of this volume, we have placed language (in the broadest understanding of the term) at the heart of the debate in order to ask to what extent multilingualism legitimizes memory and memorialization. That memory is affective and meaningful is uncontested, but we have set out here to explore how language – and in particular multilingualism – contributes to the inevitable partiality of public memorials. In the following chapters, drawing on a diverse corpus that includes monuments, historic buildings, museums, statues and plaques, we consider the very specific contribution LL research makes to the study of the interface of memorialization and multilingualism.

As a starting point, it is helpful to establish how we understand the 'multilingual memories' in the title of this collection. Rather than exploring multilingualism as a psychological function or faculty of the brain, we consider memorials in the public space which, to differing degrees, engage with the multilingual realities of the communities that commission, construct and challenge them. These memorials are referred to as 'memory places' by Blair et al. (2010: 24), although their definition is applied to war memorials, and in this chapter, the contributors expand the scope of such places to include a cemetery, street signs, a monumental boulder, several museums, sculptures and a public square in addition to the more conventional war memorial. The existing scholarship on reading monuments and memorials is vast, and the claim we stake in this volume is the urgency to extend the research to include – if not privilege – language and languages as found in, on and around these memory places. Our approach has been inspired in part by Abousnnouga and Machin's landmark 2013 *The Language of War Monuments* and their systematic approach to the critical analysis of war memorials. They consider not only the memorials (and their iconography and representations) and the materialities of these memory places, but also cultural influences on monument design and political contexts. The axis we foreground in this volume is language, and in particular the relationships between named languages found at these memory places. All of the contributors here contend with the ways in which multilingualism is memorialized at memory places where language(s) was/were not the primary motivation for the memorials themselves.

It is almost axiomatic to state that memorials are used (and exploited) to emplace an ideology in the public space. This is not merely the symbolic construction of the public space (Ben-Rafael et al. 2006), but also the articulation of a specific attitude and approach to multilingualism. As Shohamy and Waksman (2010: 254) assert, memorials are anchored in specific political ecologies, and these extend to the attitudes of those with power towards multilingualism and the relationship between languages within a given community's repertoire. Those in a position to present their ideologies through memorials find that their privilege and power are neither guaranteed nor eternal, meaning that successive political systems and regimes modify, elaborate or deny earlier public memories. Woldemariam (2016: 288) concludes that monuments simultaneously 'promote but also […] counter-speak and contest national history', which we argue includes beliefs towards named languages as much as towards multilingualism as a phenomenon. She echoes Train (2016: 227) who argues that public memory 'is not a once-told tale. Rather it is memorized and co-memorized by recursive tellings by tellers in the same and different spaces, places, and times'. In this volume, we extend this understanding to how multilingualism is memorialized at different times and in very different places. The oldest memory places examined in this volume date back to the nineteenth century, while the most recent were opened in the second decade of the twenty-first century. Regimes of language vary considerably, and through this volume we tentatively identify commonalities in multilingual memory places.

A key context for all of the chapters in this volume is the existence of multilingualism as a lived reality across the globe, in direct challenge to the assertion that monolingual communities (let alone states) exist. If we accept Connerton's assumption (1989: 3) that the shared memories found in memorials 'legitimate a present social order' as much as they commemorate some kind of event, the contributors here investigate a range of experiences of multilingualism to understand better how the activation of memory through monuments reflects attitudes towards monolingualism, minority languages or languages actively marginalized by communities, and not only at the time of the monuments' production. To this end, we explore shared memories as articulated through public memorials as not merely a reflection of common identities, but also the embodiment of shared emotions. As Blair et al. (2010: 7) conclude, 'public memory embraces events, people, objects, and places that it deems worthy of preservation, based on some kind of emotional attachment' and collectively we present this volume as a new perspective for appreciating monuments as a nexus for affect, signification and language choice. Simultaneously, we discuss how the relationship between languages on monuments and memorials is in and of itself 'a means of social construction' (Abousnnouga and Machin 2013: 29).

Ben-Rafael (2016: 208) in his introduction to a special issue devoted to memory in the LL highlights the viewpoints that researchers privilege in their approach to these memorials:

> Some may view the same memorials through the lenses of ethnolinguistic-vitality theory while others question their geosemiotic contextualization or their visual non-linguistic aspects. Still others study memorials from a historical-narrative perspective while their colleagues are more interested in political or sociological angles.

In this volume, each of these starting points is exploited, oftentimes in conjunction with each other, enriching the collective contribution of this volume with a broad range of critical readings of memorials. One of the significant perspectives that are addressed by our examination of multilingual memorialization is the inherent multiplicity of messages conveyed by the museums, monuments and memorial plaques. By their very nature as (irregularly) multilingual texts, the corpora studied here – and, in particular, the messages they are designed to articulate – are, as Blair et al. (1991: 269) note, multivalent, multiple and frequently conflicting. The audiences addressed by the memorials in this volume have a range of repertoires, including monolinguals, those able to 'read' several languages, and those whose languages are omitted. In part, therefore, we return to the typology for reading signs first proposed by Reh (2004: 8) and subsequently critiqued, where the multilingualism of memorials is uneven, and at the very least overlaps, duplicates, or is fragmentary. If we accept that memorials convey messages, these messages when glossed by texts in different languages inevitably demand multiple readings.

A recurrent theme in memory studies is the dialectic of memory and forgetfulness, although Blair et al. (2010: 18) note that 'the remembering-forgetting dialectic has been employed as a stand-in or simplistic restatement of the problem of representation in public memory studies. In other words, a failure to represent a particular content publicly is not a necessary, or even provisional, sign of forgetting'. With a shared understanding that forgetting can be framed as the obverse of memory, we consider absence and omission as the actualized reality of forgetting in the public space, which for Train (2016: 226) 'entails public learning to forget the histories of past conquest and violence in the interest of a supposed national and cultural unity shared by "all"'. In this volume, we develop this further by considering explicitly the absence and presence of a range of named languages from memorials where individuals and communities identified with these languages are written into or erased from prominent articulations of ideologies. Connerton (2008) identifies a typology of forgetting, with the intention of demonstrating that the act of omission is not necessarily a failing or imperfection but is often actively embraced for potentially valid reasons. From the perspective of this project, memorials have the potential to erase linguistic diversity as much as they can entextualize multilingualism, and this process – that Lou (2016: 219) reminds us 'illuminates contextualization as a dialectic process' – invites audiences to engage with the phenomenon of multilingualism as much as with that which is memorialized.

Trauma and violence are often invoked in discussions of public memory; as Radstone and Schwarz (2010: 3) comment:

> In the afterlife of collectively experienced catastrophes – slavery, the Holocaust, and many genocides; wars, and ecological disasters; forced migration and the fact of becoming a refugee or an "illegal"; the damage done to the self by acts of sexual violence and by torture – the medium of memory has seemed to offer the possibility not only that an element of selfhood can be reconstituted, but also that a public, political language can be fashioned in which these experiences, and others like them, can be communicated to others.

It is the medium of this communication to others, both in terms of language as discrete codes and language as a system, that we seek to explore here. Some – but not all – of the memorials explored here address violence, and the extent to which multilingualism is deployed, overlooked or fetishized in order to respond to violence varies. In the long-standing tradition of sanitizing – or, to use Abousnnouga and Machin's verbs of choice – obscuring and silencing (Abousnnouga and Machin 2013: 2) violence, we look in this volume at older monuments, such as the early twentieth-century memorials from Morocco, New Zealand and the United States, as well as much more recent memory places in Bosnia-Herzegovina and Brazil. Not all of the memory places evoke painful memories, such as the birthplace museum of Scottish poet Robert Burns and the street signs in the Sardinian town of Alghero.

By drawing on research already exploited in LL studies, we take as sites of enquiry the range of 'realms of memory' identified by Nora (1984: 28–29), namely 'museums, archives, cemeteries, festivals, anniversaries, treaties, depositions, monuments, sanctuaries, fraternal orders' – although we acknowledge here the privileging of Western understandings of memory in Nora's list. With a number of different approaches, including multimodal discourse analysis, code preferences, interaction orders and indexicality (as identified by Scollon and Scollon 2003), we seek to identify, in the words of Abousnnouga and Machin (2013) '*what kinds* of discourses […] are disseminated, legitimized and naturalized in society and also *how* they are disseminated' (original emphasis) from an explicitly multilingual perspective.

We have arranged the chapters in this volume according to the three kinds of memory places, although we acknowledge from the outset the porosity of the borders between some of these categories. The first section considers what we have defined as *Monuments*, and it opens with John Macalister's examination of two memorials in Wellington, New Zealand: the 1931 Cenotaph and the 2015 Pukeahu National War Memorial Park. He investigates the interplay between linguistic and non-linguistic elements in these two memory places, with a specific focus on the ways in which national identity is constructed at two points separated by almost a century. Of particular interest are the ways in which remembering the past is shaped by twenty-first-century attitudes at Pukeahu in comparison with the Cenotaph from an earlier era. Patricia Lamarre shifts the attention to another older memory place, this time in the city centre of Montreal, Canada, and in particular a monument that marks a neglected and disputed cemetery which is also connected to heritage buildings further down the river. The Black Rock, a 10-foot boulder raised in memory of the Famine Irish who died of typhus in the middle of the nineteenth century, has a complex history and has been contested since its original erection. Lamarre traces the struggles over symbolic and material space in Montreal, as well exploring the extent to which the discourses which surround memorialization are multivocal and subject to prevailing but shifting ideologies. The third monument discussed is part of a corpus of memorials that relate to Morocco's involvement in the First and Second World Wars, and Dawn Marley investigates the use of French and Arabic in memorialization as the relationship between France and Morocco evolves. With particular emphasis on Landowski's *Monument to Franco-Moroccan Friendship*, Marley draws parallels between the imbalance in language use on the monuments and the power dynamic between the two countries. Landowski's monument is particularly interesting in that it was erected in Morocco but subsequently transported to France after the North African kingdom's independence.

The focus of the second section moves to *Museums*, with contributions from Africa, Europe and North America. Hambaba Jimaima and Felix Banda scrutinize the semiotic processes at play in Livingstone, Zambia, in particular at the Livingstone Museum and Mosi-oa-tunya/the Victoria Falls. Drawing on what they describe as artefactual materialities, Jimaima and Banda examine the selective narration of the glocal histories of the sites, where there is a striking imbalance between the representation of voices and narratives from the local populations and the European colonizers in southern Africa. They contend that the museum is a prime site for the production and consumption of a skewed narration of the area's past and present, where dominant foreign histories have obscured and even illegitimized local memories. Robert Blackwood and James Costa continue the exploration of the LL of museums, questioning whether the absence of a standard form and the concomitant lack of state recognition can ever go hand in hand with the normalization of minority language use. In south-east Scotland, UK, the Robert Burns Birthplace Museum was opened to commemorate the life and work of the eighteenth-century poet who wrote mainly in Scots, a non-standardized language of Scotland. Despite the intentions of the museum's managers, Blackwood and Costa find that English remains the main language of communication in the museum, with Scots assigned a mostly symbolic role. Rebecca T. Garvin and Yasushi Onodera highlight another almost forgotten site, namely a cemetery and memorial centre for US-Japanese internees during the Second World War. In Arkansas, USA, this once-neglected memory place has been renovated, and Garvin and Onodera, from a diachronic perspective, analyse the orientation of the cemetery in conjunction with memorial objects and multimodal literacies. This they undertake in order to investigate the individual and national identities of Americans of Japanese heritage who both saw active service but were also interned by the US authorities. In Sarajevo, Bosnia-Herzegovina, Maida Kosatica offers a close reading of the War Childhood Museum as an interior semiotic landscape. She argues that the museum, framed as a 'combi-memorial', challenges the traditional discourses of remembering by producing self-reflectional and participatory remembrance realized through an appeal for emphatic and critical perspectives on loss and suffering. This new way of representing the 1992–1995 Bosnian War defies established meanings and conventional memorial topographies.

The final section of the volume is devoted to what we refer to as *Memories* with contributions tackling complex sites in Asia, Europe and South America. In Rio de Janeiro, Brazil, Branca Falabella Fabrício and Rodrigo Borba examine the LL of Valongo Wharf, the landing point for slaves transported from Africa. They explore how memories of destruction, survival and resistance are communicated in the port area by analysing the LL through the sociolinguistic notions of scale and indexicality. Falabella Fabrício and Borba seek in their chapter to understand how the LL around what is known as 'Little Africa' performatively constructs the waterfront quarter at the intersection of a slavery past and Rio's allegedly cosmopolitan present. In a world where so many memory places are associated with suffering and death, the iron rod sculptures of Georgetown, Penang in Malaysia discussed by John Macalister and Teresa Ong offer a more light-hearted take on remembering the past. These sculptures are located on walls in the historic heart of the city and recall events from the past; Macalister and Ong question the extent to which the multiple languages of Malaysia contribute to the memories of the past chosen to be conveyed through the sculptures. Furthermore, they explore the potential for these sculptures to relate to the wider LL and the local language ecology. Stefania Tufi discusses the issues of spatial and linguistic organization of memory using a sample of multilingual street signs in Alghero/L'Alguer, a Catalan enclave in north-western Sardinia, Italy. Within a dynamic view of memory as performative cultural practice, Tufi considers multilingual street names as an enactment of memory acts constituting fluid memorial intertext. From this perspective, she argues that they enable the construction of a hypertext which is able to return not only the physicality of three-dimensional space, but also a fourth element – time. In the last chapter, Christian Bendl forensically examines a single act of commemoration at what he explains is a multilayered memorial at the *Heldenplatz* ('Heroes' Square) in Vienna, Austria. The long history of the *Heldenplatz* has meant that changing meanings about this place, its historic events and even certain actors turn a monumental square into a multifaceted 'spatial palimpsest' with buried, unseen or highlighted discourses. In a short concluding chapter, we seek to draw together the commonalities from across this disparate range of studies.

Note

1 Inter alia, we note the contributions made by Shohamy and Waksman (2009, 2010), Abousnnouga and Machin (2010, 2013), Ben-Rafael (2016), Lou (2016), Train (2016), Guilat and Espinosa-Ramírez (2016), Woldemariam (2016), Huebner and Phoocharoensil (2017).

References

Abousnnouga, G. and D. Machin (2010), 'War Monuments and the Changing Discourses of Nation and Soldiery', in A. Jaworski and C. Thurlow (eds), *Semiotic Landscapes: Language, Image, Space*, 219–240, London: Bloomsbury.

Abousnnouga, G. and D. Machin (2013), *The Language of War Monuments*. London: Bloomsbury.

Ben-Rafael, E. (2016), 'Introduction', *Linguistic Landscape*, 2 (3): 207–210.

Ben-Rafael, E., E. Shohamy, M. H. Amara and N. Trumper-Hecht (2006), 'Linguistic Landscape as Symbolic Construction of the Public Space: The Case of Israel', *International Journal of Multilingualism*, 3: 7–30.

Blair, C., G. Dickinson and B. L. Ott (2010), 'Introduction: Rhetoric/Meaning/Place', in G. Dickinson, C. Blair and B. L. Ott (eds), *Places of Public Memory: The Rhetoric of Museums and Memorials*, 1–54, Tuscaloosa: University of Alabama Press.

Blair, C., M. S. Jeppeson and E. Pucci, Jr. (1991), 'Public Memorializing in Postmodernity: The Vietnams Veterans Memorial as Prototype', *Quarterly Journal of Speech*, 77 (3): 263–288.

Connerton, P. (1989), *How Societies Remember*, Cambridge: CUP.

Connerton, P. (2008), 'Seven Types of forgetting', *Memory Studies*, 1 (1): 59–71.

Guilat, Y. and A. Espinosa-Ramírez (2016), 'The Historical Memory Law and Its Role in Redesigning Semiotic Cityscapes in Spain: A Case Study from Granada', *Linguistic Landscape*, 2 (3): 247–274.

Huebner, T. and S. Phoocharoensil (2017), 'Monument as Semiotic Landscape: The Contests Historiography of a National Tragedy', *Linguistic Landscape*, 3 (2): 101–121.

Lou, J. J. (2016), 'Shop Sign as Monument: The Discursive Recontextualization of a Neon Sign', *Linguistic Landscape*, 2 (3): 211–222.

Nora, P. (1984), 'Entre Mémoire et Histoire: la problématique des lieux', in P. Nora (ed.), *Les Lieux de Mémoire*, 23–43, Paris: Gallimard.

Radstone, S. and B. Schwarz (2010), 'Introduction: Mapping Memory', in S. Radstone and B. Schwarz (eds), *Memory: Histories, Theories, Debates*, 1–9, New York: Fordham University Press.

Reh, M. (2004), 'Multilingual Writing: A Reader-oriented Typology – With Examples from Lira Municipality (Uganda)', *International Journal of the Sociology of Language*, 170: 1–41.

Scollon, R. and S. W. Scollon (2003), *Discourses in Place: Language in the Material World*, Abingdon, Oxon: Routledge.

Shohamy, E. and S. Waksman (2009), 'Linguistic Landscape as an Ecological Arena: Modalities, Meanings, Negotiations, Education', in E. Shohamy and D. Gorter (eds), *Linguistic Landscape: Expanding the Scenery*, 313–331, London: Routledge.

Shohamy, E. and S. Waksman (2010), 'Building the Nation, Writing the Past: History and Textuality at the *Ha'apala* Memorial in Tel Aviv-Jaffa', in A. Jaworski and C. Thurlow (eds), *Semiotic Landscapes: Language, Image, Space*, 241–255, London: Bloomsbury.

Train, R. W. (2016), 'Connecting Visual Presents to Archival Pasts in Multilingual California: Towards Historical Depth in Linguistic Landscape', *Linguistic Landscape*, 2 (3): 223–246.

Woldemariam, H. (2016), 'Linguistic Landscape as Standing Historical Testimony of the Struggle against Colonization in Ethiopia', *Linguistic Landscape*, 2 (3): 275–290.

Part One

Monuments

1

Forging a Nation: Commemorating the Great War

John Macalister

Introduction

In April 2015, the New Zealand government opened Pukeahu National War Memorial Park in Wellington, the capital city. The official opening was timed to coincide with the 100th anniversary of the Gallipoli campaign, a disastrous military operation during the First World War that in contemporary commentary is often described as a key event in forging a sense of New Zealand's national identity.

The First World War began fewer than seventy-five years after the signing of the Treaty of Waitangi in 1840, which is generally viewed today as the nation's founding document. While English speakers had been present in New Zealand in the form of whalers, sealers, traders and missionaries in the decades before 1840, this treaty signed between the British Crown and Māori chiefs laid the basis for systematic colonization. Within twenty years the Māori population was in the minority, and the New Zealand Wars of the 1860s resulted in the confiscation of around 1 million hectares of Māori land, laying the foundations for generations of grievance that began to be addressed only from the 1970s, when the Waitangi Tribunal was set up as a permanent commission of inquiry into actions by the Crown, such as land confiscation, that breached the Treaty of Waitangi. The establishment of the Tribunal was recognition that the Treaty carried legal weight.

Confiscated land was not the only source of grievance. By the time the Waitangi Tribunal was established, Māori language loss was a real concern. For, while the language began from a position of strength and dominance in 1840 it was followed 'by an extended period of bilingualism, increasingly unidirectional'

(Benton 1991: 14) with 'the process of language change [beginning] in earnest in the 1930s, although [the] results did not really become discernible until the 1950s, when the large numbers of people who had learned Māori as a second language in childhood were succeeded by a new generation with many monoglot English speakers' (ibid: 17). Various factors have been mentioned as contributing to this shift, including broadcasting, inter-marriage and economic changes (such as the end of subsistence farming as a viable lifestyle; Benton 1981: 15), but overall the important probable causes are seen to have been urbanization and education (Benton 1991: 18). In terms of education, much has been made of the role of schools, and particularly the native schools, in contributing to the shift from Māori to English. Thus, for example, Benton (ibid.) writes that 'punishment for speaking Māori at school had been widespread up until this time [the 1930s]', and Fishman (1991: 242) writes of 'public schools as well as church schools, that not only typically taught no Māori at all but that punished ("strapped") Māori children for speaking Māori to each other on the school grounds'. While there is no dispute that such punishment did occur, it is also clear that the situation as regards the use of Māori in schools was variable:

> At one extreme was draconian assimilation; at the other were close relations between school and marae, along with good education, and the encouragement of Māori identity and arts, if not language. Even the language issue has ambiguities. Often, Māori themselves wanted their children taught English because they realised that this gave them independent access to global knowledge. ... Urbanisation from 1945 did much more damage to the Māori language than did the Native Schools. (Belich 2001: 203–204)

Regardless, however, of the causes, the movement for te reo Māori was towards language loss, language death. Realization of the situation led to the establishment of the first kohanga reo (a 'language nest' for pre-school children) in 1981, and a Māori Language Commission in 1987. With these and other initiatives a commitment to the preservation of te reo Māori was made.

As a result of these developments in the final quarter of the twentieth century, national identity in modern New Zealand is typically framed in bilingual and bicultural terms, recognizing the 1840 Treaty of Waitangi. Key elements of this framing of national identity are the relationship between Māori and government, and recognition of the Māori language which is one of two official languages, the other being New Zealand Sign Language. At the same time, census data suggests that New Zealand is becoming increasingly multilingual and multicultural, although this has not been reflected in local linguistic landscape (henceforth LL) studies to date (Macalister 2010).

Pukeahu can be read as an officially sanctioned expression of national identity. This chapter investigates the interplay between linguistic and non-linguistic elements in this landscape and the messages of inclusiveness it is designed to convey. Of particular focus are the way in which remembering the past is shaped by twenty-first-century attitudes and the way this contrasts with a similar memorial from an earlier era, the Wellington Cenotaph.

Literature review

LL research has become a fairly well-established field in a relatively short period of time, with a number of books and a dedicated journal contributing to its development. In essence, LL began as a quantitative study, counting signs in a defined area with a view to getting insight into multilingualism in that neighbourhood. Increasingly, however, researchers have challenged that characterization, with one example of such a challenge being Shohamy and Waksman (2009)'s 'radical' notion of extending the boundaries of LL research, taking it beyond the quantitative. They illustrated this with an examination of the *Haʾapala* memorial in Tel Aviv and framed it within thinking of the LL as an educational resource – 'The main idea is the need for students to be aware and *notice* the multiple layers of meanings displayed in the public space' (Shohamy and Waksman 2009: 327–328, original emphasis). Their discussion of the memorial focuses on five sources of meaning and information: the geographical location, placement and design; the photographs and their titles; the written texts; the multilingualism; the people in the place.

Perhaps their suggestion of extending the boundaries of LL research was not as radical as it may at first appear when we consider research developments in other, related fields. Blair et al. (2010), for instance, argue that the application of rhetoric – defined as 'the study of discourses, events, objects, and practices that attends to their character as meaningful, legible, partisan, and consequential' (p. 2) – allows interrogation beyond the linguistic level. Similarly, Jaworski and Thurlow (2010) seek to 'complicate' LL research by introducing the idea of semiotic landscapes, or 'the interplay between language, visual discourse, and the spatial practices and dimensions of culture' (p. 1). All of these approaches take LL research beyond the quantitative and the mono-modal and have influenced the approach adopted in this study of Pukeahu and the Cenotaph.

The site Shohamy and Waksman considered could be called a 'memory place' (Blair et al. 2010: 24), and one type of 'memory place' that was of interest to Blair, Dickinson and Ott in their introductory discussion of public memory places was war monuments. The ways in which the messages, the remembering of such monuments, are constructed have received attention elsewhere. For example, Bodnar (2010) focused on the ways in which one particular battle in the Philippines during the Second World War was commemorated in local and national monuments. The battle was, in fact, a military defeat for the American and Filipino troops, and in the local monuments Bodnar found 'a strong resistance to forgetting the pain and the tragedy' (2010: 147) whereas the national 'works diligently to forget much of what it promises to commemorate' (2010: 143). In another comparative study, Abousnnouga and Machin (2010) undertook a synchronic examination of eight war monuments and found both similarities and differences in English monuments over time. Changes they identified included a shift from the ideal to the real, and towards the abstract, making use of 'complex references and cultural heritage markers', but some features remained the same, not least the portrayal of militarism and warfare as 'acceptable parts of our societies' conduct' (Abousnnouga and Machin 2010: 238). Change is also identified in the role of the Shrine of Remembrance in Melbourne, Australia, as it accommodates the demands of commemoration, education and tourism (Sumartojo 2017).

In New Zealand, monuments to war seem to form part of the landscape. Indeed, memory of wars is preserved in more than monuments; it can also be seen in the names of, as examples, libraries, hospitals and bridges. As Maclean and Phillips (1990: 9) explained in the introduction to a book on New Zealand war memorials, they 'were simply part of the accepted fabric of our life' and at first 'did not seem worthy of examination – they were merely part of our world, like football fields, or lamp-posts or supermarkets'. These monuments memorialize many different wars, from the nineteenth-century New Zealand Wars, through the South African War at the turn of the last century to more recent conflicts, and including both First and Second World Wars. The focus here is on two monuments that primarily commemorate the First World War.

The conflict that began in 1914 had a tremendous impact on New Zealand. At the time the country had a population of around 1.1 million and of that almost 10 per cent, around 100,000, served abroad in the armed forces. Nearly one in five of these, mainly young, men did not return. In addition to the 18,000 dead, over 40,000 were wounded (WW100 n.d.). There was no community, and very few families, who were not affected in some way.

Memorialization began early. Maclean and Phillips (1990: 69) describe the origins of the first monument.

> Barely a fortnight after the evacuation from Gallipoli and with the New Zealand soldiers yet to endure almost three years of death and injury on the western front, a Māori, L. T. Busby of Pukepoto in the far north, wrote to the minister of defence, James Allen, in hesitant English to say that the local community had decided to put up a war memorial.

Despite some resistance, the community persisted and in a little over two months from Busby's letter in January 1916, the memorial was unveiled. It would be the first of many.

Busby's memorial was a local one. The two memorials, built in the capital city at different times, discussed in this chapter are not local but constructed for, respectively, a province and a nation. They are examined to understand how war is being remembered and the ways in which this remembering reflects ideas of national identity. From this examination, elements of disjuncture between the intended and the experienced interpretation of these memory places emerge.

Methodology

The data gathered for this study was generated at approximately the same time, mid-afternoon, on two separate days, two days apart, in summer 2016. On both occasions the approach was similar; the sites were explored and their layout sketched, linguistic and non-linguistic elements were noted and photographed. The five sources of information and meaning identified by Shohamy and Waksman (2009) were all included. Once the sites were mapped in this way, time was taken to sit and observe how people interacted with the places. This included my own reactions, both then and later, and these reactions are incorporated in the discussion below. These were monuments in my home city and, as a Wellingtonian, I had known the older of these two sites all my life; or rather, as this study revealed, I discovered the older site was familiar but not necessarily 'known'. Subsequently, my understanding of these two sites further evolved through developing two conference presentations, and audience reaction.

In the following sections, I begin by describing the two sites and follow this with an analysis of, first, the Cenotaph, then Pukeahu. I follow this by identifying and discussing the similarities and differences between them.

Orienting to the sites

Work on the Wellington Cenotaph began in the years after the First World War, to commemorate the service and sacrifice of men and women from the Wellington province. It was unveiled on Anzac Day 1931, and for decades it was the site for remembrance, and at times protest, activities. Over time, however, it has changed; from being a triangular island bounded by three roads (Figure 1.1), it is now a pocket park, connected to Parliament grounds (Figure 1.2). It has changed in appearance, too. Subsequent wars have seen the addition of two large octagonal plagues, and perhaps most strikingly the addition after the Second World War of two large bronze lions flanking the steps leading up to the memorial, at which time bronze friezes were also added. These changes are a reminder, then, that 'memory places themselves have histories' (Blair et al. 2010: 30).

Pukeahu, by contrast, is a work in progress. At the time this study was carried out, areas of the park were still under development.[1] Not only is it a far newer site than the Cenotaph, it is considerably larger, and it was conceived of, by the

Figure 1.1 The Cenotaph in the 1930s; the Parliamentary precinct, then separated from the memorial by a road, is in the background (Source: Crown Studios Collection, Ref: 1/1-032755-F. Alexander Turnbull Library, Wellington, New Zealand. Reproduced with kind permission).

Figure 1.2 The Cenotaph today; the lions and plaques are later additions, as is the paving creating a pocket park and a physical link to the Parliamentary precinct.

central government, as a national site of remembrance. As described by the Ministry of Culture and Heritage:

> The Pukeahu National War Memorial Park is the national place for New Zealanders to remember and reflect on this country's experience of war, military conflict and peacekeeping, and how that experience shapes our ideals and sense of national identity.[2]

The involvement of government in the design of the park points to the fact that Pukeahu is an exercise in heritage politics, where decisions are made about what to select for inclusion. As Abdelhay et al. (2016) explain when discussing the historic heart of Jeddah, inclusion requires passing 'through a set of regulatory conditions and criteria to be selected as part of the heritage record' and as a result some elements of heritage become 'part of the nationally shared memory while others would be erased'. Unusually perhaps, the design of Pukeahu was the creation of a new space, extending and adding meaning to an existing space; the design was not 'complicated' by what was already there, allowing greater scope to fulfil the design brief.

A further difference between Pukeahu and the Cenotaph is that Pukeahu is multiply signposted so that there is a sense of entering onto a site no matter which way one approaches. Pukeahu, then, is among the more recent memory places that are 'often positioned as tourist/learning sites' (Abousnnouga and Machin 2010: 238). It is a destination, a place to visit, rather than a place to walk by.

To orient to the site, it is necessary to imagine a rectangular park running west to east, from Taranaki Street on the west to Tory Street on the east (see Figure 1.3). The northern boundary borders the city; to the south and overlooking the site are the pre-existing National War Memorial that is dominated by a towering carillon and the former New Zealand Dominion Museum building, both dating from the 1930s. Pukeahu is built above a road that was undergrounded as the first phase of the project; this road tunnel was given the name Arras, to commemorate the work of New Zealand tunnellers beneath the French town of Arras during the First World War, and is lined with stylized red poppies. It is fair to say that Pukeahu is freighted with, sometimes fairly obvious, symbolism.

At the heart of the park, the space that is the real destination, the southern side appears to be more indigenous in orientation, the northern more international. The northern side is dominated by the red sandstone pillars of the Australian memorial (Figure 1.4), with gum trees planted among the pillars. The trees and

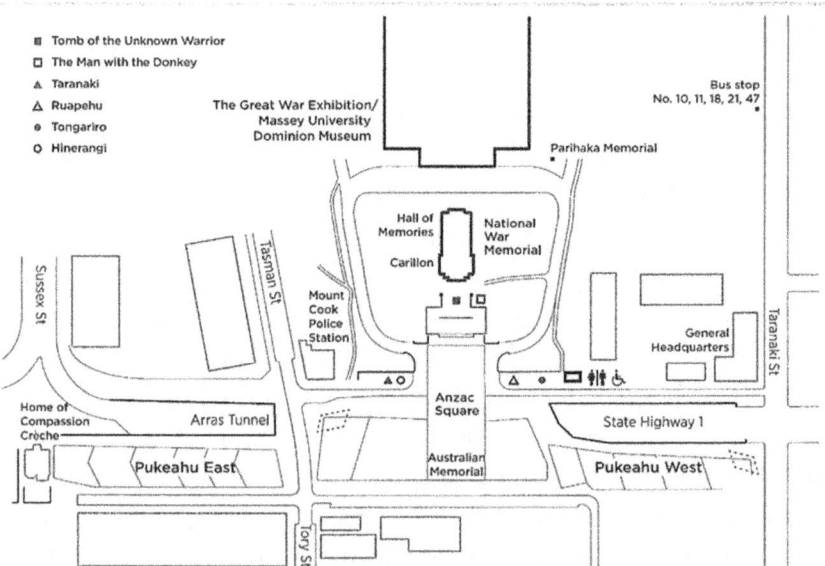

Figure 1.3 Map of Pukeahu. Source: https://mch.govt.nz/pukeahu/park.

Figure 1.4 Red sandstone pillar with black granite inset, part of the Australian memorial at Pukeahu. Note the reflection of the Carillon below the word ANZAC.

the sandstone reference Australia, and a plaque informs the visitor that this memorial was opened in April 2015, a few days before ANZAC Day, by both the New Zealand and Australian prime ministers.

As these brief descriptions have perhaps made clear, language is not immediately central to these monuments. There is little doubt that the creators of public memory in both sites are 'relying on material and/or symbolic supports' (Blair et al. 2010: 10) to convey meaning. For, even at Pukeahu where there are many signs intended to guide and aid interpretation of the site, it is not the linguistic but the non-linguistic, the visual, that visitors see and through which they can interpret without much recourse to the linguistic. In other words, language plays a role, but it is not what the viewer, the visitor notices first.

Reading the Cenotaph

The bronze lions that were a later addition to the Cenotaph are perhaps what catches the passer-by's attention and may serve as a starting point for reading the memorial. Such lions are not unique to Wellington and may perhaps bring to mind the more famous, and far larger, bronze lions at the foot of Nelson's Column in Trafalgar Square, London. This would seem to be consistent with other elements of the Cenotaph: the swags carved in the lintel above the entrance to the reliquary chapel, the sheaves and geometric design carved towards the top of the tower, the clipped mane of the horse (which, indeed, turns out to be Pegasus) that forms part of the statue surmounting the memorial. In these elements, the monument appears to be evoking (the British) Empire and Greek classicism.

The Cenotaph also has a strong narrative element. This was so when it was first constructed, for bas-relief stone friezes adorn the front, on either side of the entrance to the reliquary chapel. These tell the story of recruiting and enlisting, the transition from civilian to military life, with supportive children, women and older men, waving them on, or forward. The inclusion of a couple of dogs and a kitten makes going off to war seem normal, safe, even a little cosy. This, at least, is my reading of the friezes. An alternative reading is offered by an official website that explains, 'The detailing of the stone reliefs on the base of the memorial call attention to the disillusionment felt at the commencement of the "Great War"' (Wellington Heritage 2015).

Further narrative elements were added through the eight plaques added after the Second World War; each shows a different branch of the services in action.

In the New Zealand Army Nursing Services plaque, for instance, a female nurse raises a wounded man in a well-made bed so that he can drink from the cup she holds; their heads almost touch; it is an almost tender scene.

Interspersed between these plaques are nine shields, each with a named virtue or value, some with an obvious military bias, above. Some would seem to be required in war; others to be things to be preserved or protected by going to war. The nine virtues are: Peace, Honour, Purity, Wisdom, Amity, Valour, Sacrifice, Security and Justice. These shields may complement the narrative told through the plaques.

A final narrative element is the statue atop the tower, horse and horseman, he reaching heavenwards. To me, this has always seemed an odd, even discordant element of the Cenotaph. I had often seen it from below and from afar, and the rider's falling backwards, his outstretched arm seemed to be despairing, perhaps a prelude to death. Only during the course of this research did I discover that the horse was Pegasus, that the statue has a name, The Will to Peace, and according to the official programme booklet (cited on https://nzhistory.govt.nz/media/photos/wellington-cenotaph) it has the following intended meaning:

> Pegasus spurning underfoot the victor's spoils of war and rising into the heavens, enables his rider to emerge from the deluge of blood and tears, and to receive the great spiritual assurance of peace.

Regardless of how one reads the statue, it is the structural and decorative elements that convey the meaning of the monument, with language in a largely supporting role and added at a later date, as in the naming of the shields. Where language is used, it is always English.

In summary, then, the Cenotaph speaks of a monolingual and monocultural New Zealand, a New Zealand with strong ties to Britain. It is located centrally, close to buildings of power – Parliamentary buildings, courts, the old Government Building. But it has become a place that people pass as they go to and from work, to and from the railway station or bus terminus. It is unmarked, unsignposted, unexplained.

Reading Pukeahu

Unlike the Cenotaph, Pukeahu is not centrally located; it is at the outer edge of the central city, where commercial activity begins to give way to residential. As has been observed elsewhere, 'the primary action the rhetoric of the memory place invites is the performance of traveling to and traversing it' (Blair et al. 2010: 26). On the day on which I visited for this project there was a mix of human interaction with the site. There were people passing through, a security officer and people using the park as a resting place – two men drinking alcohol, two boys with skateboards sitting on a lawn. But there were also people visiting the site because it was a memorial, most obviously a group of young adult tourists with a guide.

Although not as centrally located as the Cenotaph, Pukeahu is also associated with buildings of power, but of a very different nature from those in the parliamentary precinct. These are buildings and sites of memory on the southern side of the park – the National War Memorial and Carillon, the Tomb of the Unknown Warrior, the former Dominion Museum Building. Inside the former museum, the Great War Exhibition is on display and this is not the sole reinforcement of the positioning of Pukeahu as a tourism/learning site; an arresting billboard advertising an exhibition at Te Papa (or, in full, The Museum of New Zealand Te Papa Tongarewa) about Gallipoli is one of two large billboards clearly visible to the north of the park.

Although much that is immediately on view as the visitor enters Pukeahu has obvious symbolic meaning, it also contains, as has been observed elsewhere in contemporary memory sites, 'complex references and cultural heritage markers' (Abousnnouga and Machin 2010: 238), many of which would be hidden from the casual visitor. Furthermore, the site reads differently in different places.

On the northern side of the central square, the Australian memorial yields meaning without too much effort, and with the assistance of numerous interpretation plaques. It stands as a testament to the trans-Tasman relationship and was opened by the then prime ministers of the two nations. Fifteen red sandstone pillars rise, and on some, etched into vertical black granite insets, are the names of fields of engagement, from Flanders and Gallipoli during the First World War to more recent engagements under UN auspices in East Timor and Afghanistan, and the word ANZAC (Figure 1.4). On other pillars, art works have been etched into the black granite. Interpretation stones reveal that these are both Māori and Aboriginal art works; the Māori art works reference concepts from tikanga Māori: whanaungatanga, rangatiratanga, manakitanga, wairuatanga, kaitiakitanga, orangatanga, mauritanga (see Table 1.1). These concepts are explained on the interpretation stones, in English, with occasional use of Māori words among the English. There are also a couple of words of Aboriginal origin injected into the explanation of the Aboriginal art works. These linguistic contributions to the landscape, however, are not immediately obvious. Their presence would not be noted unless the visitor took the time to stop and read the interpretation stones. Indeed, the reflective surface of the black granite makes them hard to read on a fine day.

Among the sandstone pillars gum trees have been planted, in an obvious reference to Australia; almost as obvious is that the red sandstone is supposed to recall the red earth, the deserts of Australia. Elsewhere in the park, the plantings are clearly symbolic – the red-flowered pohutukawa, the yellow-flowered kowhai and olive trees, those last perhaps recalling military engagements in Crete and elsewhere during the Second World War. However, obvious symbolism aside, the plantings struck me as well-chosen, for in future years this will be a well-treed park, providing shade for visitors and habitat for birdlife.

If the northern side is outward-looking, the southern side is inward in focus, indigenous in orientation. Here it is that the Māori language is immediately visible, through three *whakatauki*, or sayings, on walls (Figure 1.5). They are offered without translation, and it is debatable whether they are meaningful to most visitors. Also here is a statue, the sole human representation in the central square of Pukeahu. It is in the form of a Māori woman wearing headscarf and cloak, but where the face should be is only an empty black hole. The statue is offered without interpretation; the sole language accompanying it is the artist's signature on the base. To me, this is a haunting, almost discordant feature of the memory place; it does not fit neatly into the design and symmetries of the whole.

Figure 1.5 A whakatauki on the southern wall of Pukeahu (English translation: Peace across the land).

However, through delving into the 'complex references and cultural heritage markers' much more meaning is revealed (Nicholas 2015). To take just one component of this section of the park, the statue:

> The main element in this bronze sculpture by Darcy Nicholas is the kākahu (cloak). The symbols of the sun, moon, stars and mountains tell the story of family, home and guardianship.
>
> The top of the kākahu represents the land. The tassels are tears for those lost in the tribal and colonial wars, and wars across the world. The poutama designs on the cloak are symbolic of the pathways our soldiers took in their journey to the spirit world. Some of the pathways are deliberately broken to represent the harshness of war.
>
> *Hinerangi* faces the Tomb of the Unknown Warrior, and the mountain Aoraki (Mt Cook) in the South Island. In Māori tradition, when people of significance pass on, their spirit traverses the ancestral hills and mountains to pay homage to those remaining in the physical world before returning and departing in the north.

While dominant here, the Māori language also has a presence elsewhere in the park, appearing as it typically does in New Zealand, as words and phrases within English language texts (Macalister 2006), such as on the interpretation stones of the Australian memorial. It is also present as the primary text (i.e. on the left-hand side (Scollon and Scollon 2003: 120)) on the unveiling plaque for Pukeahu, the sole example of a bilingual text. However, the bilingualism of this plaque is not balanced; the information about the opening of the park, on the bottom of the plaque, is only in English.[3] The Māori language is also, of course, present in many places as the name of the park. Indeed, the official styling often appears as Pukeahu | National War Memorial Park; one is not a translation of the other, however. Pukeahu is the name of the small hill atop which the former Dominion Museum Building sits. The use of the Māori name, however, is part of an ongoing process in contemporary New Zealand of recognizing and using the place names that were in use when, and before, Europeans arrived. No twenty-first-century politician is likely to stand up and say, 'But what is the use of using Māori names which only a few can pronounce. Take Otahuhu, for instance. That place would be better named "Glover"' (spoken by an MP named Glover in 1910, cited in Macalister 2007).

In summary, then, and by contrast with the Cenotaph, this memory place speaks of a bilingual and bicultural New Zealand, of a partnership between Māori and non-Māori, and a country that is outward-looking and, in partnership with Australia, that contributes internationally to making and maintaining peace (through military intervention).

Comparing Pukeahu and the Cenotaph

Despite the different statements of national identity made by Pukeahu and the Cenotaph, outlined above, they also share a number of similarities. Indeed, many of the similarities turn out to be absences, which may be regarded as acts of forgetting, although it is important to remember that 'We cannot … infer the fact of forgetting from the fact of silence' (Blair et al. 2010: 18).

From a contemporary perspective the striking absence from the Cenotaph is any mention of the Māori people, or use of the Māori language or elements of Māori design. This is not the case at Pukeahu, but also striking there is the absence of any New Zealand people other than Māori and Pakeha (or European New Zealanders, whose presence is manifest through the use of English). Pacific and pan-Asian peoples, after all, make up almost 20 per cent of the population. This absence is brought home by a sign in a window of the former Mount Cook Police Barracks on the Buckle Street south approach; it is a sign in Chinese and English (Figure 1.6). Its presence there is a reminder that the new New Zealand – multilingual, multicultural – is absent from Pukeahu. Indeed, it should be mentioned that New Zealand Sign Language, one of the country's two official languages, has no presence there either.[4]

Another shared absence is the depiction of real people. At Pukeahu, depictions of people are absent; the closest to one is the Nicholas statue mentioned earlier. At the Cenotaph, idealized depictions are part of the narrative as described above. These depictions were part of the original monument, in the friezes to left

Figure 1.6 Other languages on the periphery.

and right of the reliquary chapel, and also in the plaques added after the Second World War. Hand in hand with this absence is the absence of names of the dead; perhaps this is unsurprising given that these were intended as provincial and national monuments, rather than local ones; the names would have been too many. Yet, there is a similarity here with the Iwo Jima monument in Washington D.C., which records the names of battles and arenas of engagement in the Second World War but not soldiers, thus managing 'to evoke the memory of one of the bloodiest battles of the Pacific war without any hint that there was an enormous loss of life on the island' (Bodnar 2010: 141).

A caveat to this statement about the depiction of people, however, is that on the approach to Pukeahu from Taranaki Street south, there is an eye-catching display of black-and-white photographs of soldiers taken prior to departing for the First World War. Eleven such portraits and one interpretation panel fill the windows of the former General Headquarters building. Only one of these portraits is of a named Māori man. He is young, handsome and although described as a private has an officer-like appearance, with a rattan cane flexed over his knees. These portraits look more like art objects than evocations of (local) loss; the Nicholas statue, while also undeniably an art object, may have more affective power: as one journalist wrote, 'The statue, Hinerangi, by Darcy Nicholas, is a poignant reminder of the grief and hope of those who stayed behind during times of conflict' (Francis 2015: 30).

The depiction, or not, of people leads to a further similarity between the two sites, the absence of the idea that war is about loss, death, killing. A partial exception to this may be the bronze falling bombs added later to the Cenotaph; the depiction of military hardware on such monuments is not unknown and, it has been claimed, while 'not directly convey[ing] a sense of atrocities or suffering' does 'represent an effort to resist a rhetoric of tradition that aspires ultimately to forget much of what a war was about' (Bodnar 2010: 155). If that is the case, the bombs on the Cenotaph – and the Nicholas statue – seem almost accidental, not quite in keeping with the dominant message of these memory sites. Nowhere is the question asked: was the loss worth it?

But as well as similarities there are differences. Some of these have been mentioned already – the ways in which people interact with the sites, for instance, and the role of language. Table 1.1 compares the language used to refer to values at the two memorials. It is not just in the choice of language that they differ. As the glosses on the Māori words suggest, at Pukeahu the emphasis is less militaristic; it is on relationships between people, and between people and the land.

Table 1.1 Contrasting values in Pukeahu and the Cenotaph

Cenotaph	Pukeahu	Gloss
Peace	Whanaungatanga	Whanaunga = relatives; this recognizes connections and relationships
Honour		
Purity	Rangatiratanga	Rangatira = chief; this recognizes rights to being and self-determination
Wisdom		
Amity	Manakitanga	The offering of hospitality which includes welcoming, acknowledging and respecting others
Valour		
Sacrifice	Wairuatanga	Wairua = spirit; this recognizes the spirit that sustains relationships between people and place
Security		
Justice	Kaitiakitanga	Kaitiaki = guardian; this recognizes the responsibilities involved in sustaining cultural and environmental relationships
	Orangatanga	This involves the health and well-being of a community
	Mauritanga	Mauri = the life force; this recognizing life and its vital and dynamic essence

Another difference is that Pukeahu speaks of partnerships. The first is the partnership between Māori and Pakeha, or European New Zealanders, the second that between New Zealand and Australia. The first also addresses issues of reconciliation between Māori and Pakeha, of compensation and recognition of the past and of past wrongs done to Māori. This will not be obvious to all who visit, and is largely conveyed through 'complex references and cultural heritage markers', such as the tassels on the kākahu of *Hinerangi*. Indeed, perhaps the most interesting single observation that arises from this scrutiny of Pukeahu is that parts of the park are addressing different audiences.

A further difference arises from the fact that the Cenotaph has an eighty-plus years history. For Wellingtonians going about their daily lives it has become an 'accepted fabric of our life' and not 'worthy of examination', as Maclean and Phillips noted of war memorials in New Zealand more generally (1990: 9). Yet, when examined, it reveals layers of meaning added over time. At least four layers can be readily identified, marking changes from its inauguration to the present day. These changes link to changes in the world – to other wars, to the functioning of the city, to shifts in thinking about national identity. From being a striking, relatively unadorned monument in 1931 it gained embellishment, both linguistic (but only English language) and non-linguistic after the Second World War. This change reinforced rather than challenged the original meaning of the memorial. Later it lost its physical separation from its near environment, becoming a pocket park, and perhaps thereby losing some of its mana as a monument. Once physically connected, it also became linked to wider concerns in New Zealand society; in 2015 a sculpture was installed on the pavement that connects the Cenotaph to the near environment. A plaque set in the pavement tells the viewer that the sculpture marks the Waipiro stream. Named *Walk the Line*, it takes the form of a meandering line of small green medallions set into the paving stones, evoking the bed of the now-undergrounded stream. The medallions are pounamu, or greenstone, a form of jade. In this way the life and the landscape of the Māori who lived in the area prior to European settlement are commemorated. Although not strictly part of the Cenotaph, it forms part of the context in which the memorial must be read.⁵ By the addition of *Walk the Line* to this landscape the bilingual and bicultural New Zealand that is so clearly expressed at Pukeahu is referenced here.

A further layer of meaning is created by what Scollon and Scollon (2003: 146) call transgressive signs, 'a sign which is in place but which is in some way unauthorized'. At the Cenotaph was a fading wreath accompanied by a printed sheet encased in a plastic sleeve; the heading on the printed page read 'For the forgotten Armenian's [*sic*] – those we left behind' and after three columns of text, all in English, ended with a 'Call upon the Government to recognise the Armenian genocide of WW1'. This wreath and the accompanying text were the evidence of an earlier protest action. Though a temporary sign they recalled the history of protest actions that have taken place at this site over the years, and thus of contestation. Public memory, Blair et al. (2010: 9) remind us, is 'partial, partisan, and thus frequently contested'.

As a memorial place still in the process of creation, Pukeahu does not have the same layered history as the Cenotaph, or not in the same way. Through its location and relationship to buildings from an earlier era – the National War Memorial and Carillon, the Tomb of the Unknown Warrior, the former Dominion Museum Building – it is placed in a setting where some of the same history is evoked. Furthermore, on a wall of the General Headquarters building, faded painted signs can be discerned and one at least faintly read. It may in fact be the shadow of two former signs, as some of the letters appear to have a degree of overlap. Whether originally one sign or two, today the viewer reads 'Health Education Branch New Zealand Military Forces' along with information about opening hours and is reminded that the history of the place is tied to military history.

Concluding thoughts

The different ways in which national identity is constructed and conveyed multimodally in the two memorials built roughly eighty years apart would come as little surprise to most New Zealanders. The differences are consistent with what most know about changes in how we think about who we are as a nation. This is captured in the imagining of New Zealand's post-contact history as forming three phases, with a phase of 'recolonization' from the 1880s to the 1960s during which there were 'a renewal and reshaping of links between colony and metropolis' (Belich 2001: 29) followed by a phase of 'decolonization', of which a defining characteristic is 'the disconnection from Britain' (Belich 2001: 426). The ties to Britain are clear at the Cenotaph, but peripheral at Pukeahu. The recognition of New Zealand today as a bilingual and bicultural society is evident at Pukeahu. The park is an expression of national identity, reinforced through emphasizing links with Australia and commemorating military and peace-keeping involvement in many parts of the world. As new elements have been added to the park, the messages it conveys have been expanded. In the future, it is certain that Pukeahu will be used in ways unplanned, and evolve, and continue to have layers of meaning added to it as the nation changes just as has happened with the Cenotaph. Quite possibly a more inclusive expression of identity will emerge, one that recognizes the Asian and Pacific peoples in New Zealand.

Yet, for all that these memory places are a result of a design process and through the act of construction have gained an official imprimatur, the ways in which people experience them, the meaning they take from them, cannot be fully controlled. Intended meanings, such as those attached to the statue *Hinerangi* at Pukeahu, may not be accessible to the visitor, possibly through the lack of the requisite linguistic or cultural resources. Similarly, the visitor's own reading of elements of a memory place – the friezes at the Cenotaph, for instance – may differ from those intended, or officially provided. This is a useful reminder that memory places, that linguistic landscapes are multilayered, multi-voiced and rewarding sites of discovery.

Notes

1 On a recent visit, new additions to the park included a Turkish memorial, a British memorial that was condemned by a leading local artist as 'the most malevolently mangled piece of messaging ever' (Backlash on memorial 2017) and a horizontal French memorial balanced by a vertical twin, with Māori being used on the latter. In linguistic terms, the French memorial introduces the French language to Pukeahu.
2 http://www.mch.govt.nz/pukeahu/park.

3 On a recent visit to Pukeahu, one instance of parallel text bilingualism was found. This was on one side of the brass interpretation sign associated with the recently installed French memorial. The French poem was translated in both Māori and English.
4 Braille, however, was found at Pukeahu in the form of instructions on the inside and outside of public lavatories installed on the site.
5 Speakers are also inset into the pavement, so that the soundscape of a running stream has also been created. This, however, was not audible on the afternoon the data for this study was generated.

References

Abdelhay, A., M. Ahmed and E. Mohamed (2016), 'The Semiotic Landscaping of Heritage: Al-Manṭiqa al-Tarikhiyya in Jeddah', *Linguistic Landscape*, 2 (1): 52–79.

Abousnnouga, G. and D. Machin (2010), 'War Monuments and the Changing Discourses of Nation and Soldiery', in A. Jaworski and C. Thurlow (eds), *Semiotic Landscapes: Language, Image and Space*, 219–240, London: Continuum.

Backlash on memorial (2017), *The Dominion Post*, 29 July: A3.

Belich, J. (2001), *Paradise Reforged: A History of the New Zealanders from the 1880s to the Year 2000*, Auckland: Allen Lane/Penguin Press.

Benton, R. A. (1981), *The Flight of the Amokura: Oceanic Languages and Formal Education in the South Pacific*, Wellington: New Zealand Council for Educational Research.

Benton, R. A. (1991), *The Maori Language: Dying or Reviving?* Honolulu, Hawaii: East-West Center Association Working Paper, 28.

Blair, C., G. Dickinson and B. L. Ott (2010), 'Introduction: Rhetoric/Meaning/Place', in G. Dickinson, C. Blair and B. L. Ott (eds), *Places of Public Memory: The Rhetoric of Museums and Memorials*, 1–54, Tuscaloosa: University of Alabama Press.

Bodnar, J. (2010), 'Bad Dreams about the Good War: Bataan', in G. Dickinson, C. Blair and B. L. Ott (eds), *Places of Public Memory: The Rhetoric of Museums and Memorials*, 139–159, Tuscaloosa: University of Alabama Press.

Fishman, J. A. (1991), *Reversing Language Shift: Theoretical and Empirical Foundations of Assistance to Threatened Languages*, Clevedon: Multilingual Matters Ltd.

Francis, H. (2015), 'Pukeahu', *Landscape Architecture New Zealand* (Winter): 28–33.

Jaworski, A. and C. Thurlow (2010), 'Introducing Semiotic Landscapes', in A. Jaworski and C. Thurlow (eds), *Semiotic Landscapes: Language, Image, Space*, 1–40, London & New York: Continuum.

Macalister, J. (2006), 'The Maori Presence in the New Zealand English lexicon, 1850–2000: Evidence from a Corpus-based Study', *English World-Wide*, 27 (1): 1–24.

Macalister, J. (2007), '"That Place Would Be Better Named Glover": Establishing and Contesting Identity through the (re)naming of Places', *Wellington Working Papers in Linguistics*, 18: 49–61.

Macalister, J. (2010), 'Emerging Voices or Linguistic Silence?: Examining a New Zealand Linguistic Landscape', *Multilingua*, 29: 55–75.

Maclean, C. and J. Phillips (1990), *The Sorrow & The Pride: New Zealand War Memorials*, Wellington, NZ: GP Books.

Nicholas, D. (2015), *Pukeahu National War Memorial Park*. Available online: http://mch.govt.nz/pukeahu/park/significant-sites/nga-tapuwae (accessed 9 January 2019).

Scollon, R. and S. W. Scollon (2003), *Discourses in Place: Language in the Material World*, London: Routledge.

Shohamy, E. and S. Waksman (2009), 'Linguistic Landscape as an Ecological Arena: Modalities, Meanings, Negotiations, Education', in E. Shohamy and D. Gorter (eds), *Linguistic Landscape: Expanding the Scenery*, 313–331, London: Routledge.

Sumartojo, S. (2017), 'Local Complications: ANZAC Commemoration, Education and Tourism at Melbourne's Shrine of Remembrance', in J. Wallis and D. C. Harvey (eds), *Commemorative Spaces of the First World War: Historical Geographies at the Centenary*, 156–172, London & New York: Routledge.

Wellington Heritage (2015, 25 September 2017), *Wellington Cenotaph*. Available online: http://wellingtoncityheritage.org.nz/buildings/objects/31-cenotaph?q (accessed 9 January 2019).

WW100. (n.d.), *History Guide*. Available online: https://ww100.govt.nz/history-guide (accessed 9 January 2019).

2

Montreal's Black Rock: The Forgotten Grave of the Irish Typhus Victims

Patricia Lamarre

Introduction

Questions of remembering and forgetting were powerfully evoked by a Canadian journalist recently when she asked: 'What if thousands of people lay dying on Montreal's waterfront? What if some of the city's best doctors, nurses, members of the clergy and the mayor were caring for the sick newcomers at the risk of their own lives? What if the dead were being buried in hastily dug trenches next to the makeshift hospital, piled three coffins deep? What if the death toll rose to the equivalent of 12 per cent of the city's population? You'd think a city couldn't forget a thing like that' (Scott 2017b). This chapter reveals the background behind these questions and explores how Montreal responded when 'what if' was actually taking place on the city's riverfront.

There are over a hundred monuments to the Irish Famine victims in the world today, most of them set in a memorial space (Mark-Fitzgerald 2018). Canada's most important memorial to the Famine is the quarantine station on Grosse-Île, below Quebec City, a historical site since 1996. Toronto, New York, Boston and Philadelphia have all created spaces to memorialize Famine victims, but Montreal, where the crisis was felt at its hardest, has not. There is only the Black Rock, a primitive 10-foot boulder marking the forgotten graves of the typhus victims, the very first memorial in the world to the Irish Famine, sitting grimly in its no-man's-land between two busy arteries, virtually inaccessible.

When I first considered writing about the Black Rock,[1] I felt it offered a powerful way of examining erasure,[2] symbolic competition, and space and language in the city. Sociolinguistics, I thought, needs to pay attention to what is, but also what isn't in the linguistic landscape (henceforth LL). I was also truly puzzled that such an important event as the arrival of over 70,000 Irish famine victims in 1847 (known as Black '47), when Montreal itself was a city of only 50,000, was so little known by most Montrealers.

As Blackwood and Macalister propose in the introduction to this book, sociolinguistics brings new tools to research on memorialization, in this case, what discourse around memorialization reveals about ideology, social hierarchies and competition. My first interest as a sociolinguist lies in what gets ascribed to commemoration and what this reveals about people's struggles for symbolic space. At the more specific level of text in the LL, my focus is on what does not get recognized in the textscape (Sebba 2010) of a city, and consequently, in the narrative of places like Montreal and Quebec. Omission reveals as much as any text. In the same vein, unilingual texts also reveal erasure, speaking to power in cities like Montreal, that are anything but unilingual. Researching this paper, however, provided me with new things to think about. The more I learned about the history of Black '47 and the Black Rock, the more I realized that it tells the story of Montreal, of social class, religion, language and ethnicity, played out in struggles over memorial space, which are highly symbolic and often politicized. These struggles for symbolic recognition intersect and compete with industrial and urban development, government interests and plans for the use of physical space. The Black Rock is very much about the role of 'heritage elites' (McMahon 2007), those who can determine what gets recognized, and subsequently, what is included in the narrative of place. What is particular to this story is that there has been a major change in who the heritage elites are in Montreal and this is reflected in the language of commemorative texts, but also in the discourses and tropes drawn upon to build support for a memorial. It's an evocative and grim story and I can't help but agree with the *Société historique de la Pointe-St-Charles* (2018) that: 'The "Irish Rock", the simplest of monuments to be found in Montreal, is also, in many respects, the most moving'.[3]

From Montreal, colony within a colony, to *Montréal Français*

In the nineteenth century, Montreal was the industrial and financial centre of Quebec and Canada, and the language of business was English. Montreal was also home to most of Quebec's English-speaking population and French Canadians had yet to move from rural areas to work in the city's factories and within the city. The two language groups lived basically in parallel and largely separate worlds. It was not until the 1960s, Quebec's Quiet Revolution, a period of intense sociopolitical and sociocultural change, that a new French-speaking middle and professional class, claiming majority status in the province, made Montreal the battle ground over language (McRoberts 1993). Marking these efforts is Quebec's *Charte de la langue française*, Bill 101, which affirms the place of French in five domains, one of which is the LL.[4] In Quebec, it is clear to all that the sign law, making French the most important language of public and commercial signage, is about symbolic space in Montreal and designed to send a clear message that *'ici, ça se passe en français'* ('here things are done in French') (Lamarre 2014). Further changes to the 'linguistic face' (Bourhis and Landry 2002) of the city were also undertaken, with streets and squares renamed to erase a colonial past (e.g. Dorchester Boulevard became Boulevard René Levesque). Levine (1997) calls this period the reconquest of Montreal, during which Montreal was re-imagined from a multicultural English-dominant city to *Montréal français*, where it would be possible to live and work in French. In the imagining of this French-dominant Montreal, and in the recounting of Quebec's past and the economic divide between Francophones and a wealthy English-speaking elite, what is often erased is the history of poor English-speaking Montreal, the lower city, home to working-class Irish Roman Catholics, many of them descendants of the Famine Irish. What is also forgotten is the role that Montrealers, of all denominational and language backgrounds, played in bringing help to the Irish who arrived sick and dying of typhus and starvation on the riverfront in 1847.

Black Forty-Seven (1847)

They came for a new life and found a grave – Don Pidgeon

Two years into the Irish Famine, nearly 80,000 Irish immigrants sailed into the mouth of the St Lawrence River,[5] when Montreal numbered barely 50,000 (Kinealy et al. 2015). Starvation and the inability to pay rent to absentee landlords forced Irish tenant farmers to accept small sums of money to abandon their farms and emigrate. The choice was to starve or leave and they chose survival, but, as Kinealy et al. point out, many would not survive. While Irish emigration to North America was not new,[6] the great Famine provoked a massive exodus of destitute families, crammed into the holds of lumber ships not intended for passengers, in which typhus fever quickly flourished (McGowan 2009).[7] The flotilla of 'fever ships' sailing into the mouth of the St Lawrence in 1847 carried Ireland's most desperate and wretched.

Where the St Lawrence narrows below Quebec City, a quarantine station had been constructed on Grosse-Île (O'Gallagher and Masson-Dompierre 1995) to handle an earlier epidemic of cholera.[8] Rumours reached Quebec in the spring of the vast wave of Irish soon to sail up the St Lawrence and some preparation had been made,[9] but no one foresaw the size of the fleet of ships or that everyone of those ships would be carrying the fever. Grosse-Île, with under 200 beds, was totally inadequate to deal with the sick and dying Irish about to arrive.[10] The first 'Famine ship' docked in May, as the ice broke, followed by more ships arriving each day, lining up for miles down the St Lawrence (Gallagher 1936). Over 400 ships would come through and many buried on Grosse-Île had died aboard (see Figure 2.1) (Charbonneau 1995).

Figure 2.1 The fever ships waiting below Grosse-Île. Illustration B. Duchesne. Credit: Parks Canada.

The job of the quarantine master was to disembark the sick and quickly send the healthy on, but many of those who looked well in Grosse-Île would be ill or dead from typhus before arriving in the port of Montreal. Those quarantined were further separated: men from women, children from adults, Catholics from Protestants. The medical emergency quickly became a social emergency, with families already dealing with deaths during the crossing, now dealing with the separation of family members.

The fever sheds of Pointe-Du-Moulin

Montreal was even less prepared to handle the crisis than Grosse-Île (Charest-Auger 2012). While different levels of government were figuring out who would take charge, a very real drama was unfolding fast on the waterfront.[11] Montreal's mayor, John Easton Mills, a Protestant American, played an important leadership role in calming the city's population and bringing help to the typhus victims, as did Montreal's Roman Catholic Bishop, Mgr Bourget. Both would be struck down by the typhus which Mills did not survive.

Prior to 1847, as Montreal moved into its industrial era, sheds had been built on the Lachine Canal to house immigrants working on its construction and many were Irish from earlier waves of immigration. These became the initial sheds used to house the sick and dying (Figure 2.2); however, there was no one to care for them (Charest-Auger 2012). Into this void stepped religious congregations. The first to go to the succour of the Irish were the Sulpician priests, but news of the drama on the waterfront quickly reached 'les sœurs grises', the Grey Nuns, Sisters of Charity, who rushed to care for the typhus victims, knowing they risked death. A journal written by the Grey Sisters (Sisters of Charity 1847: 3) provides a first-hand account of that summer and what they found on the docks that first day in early June:

> Good God! What a spectacle. Hundreds of people, most of them lying naked on planks, pell mell, men, women and children, sick, moribund and cadavers; all of this confusion hit the eyes at once.

Over the summer, three congregations of Sisters of Charity would become 'Canada's first responders' (*The Famine Irish and Canada's First Responders* 2017). While Roman Catholic priests and Anglican clergymen cared for the souls of those on the waterfront, saying mass and giving the last sacraments, the Grey Nuns, mostly French-Canadian, cared for the bodies of the sick and dying

Figure 2.2 Lithograph of the fever sheds in the 1850s. Credit: McCord Museum.

(Charest-Auger 2012). Doctors, mostly Anglo-Protestant, also joined the rank of first responders in the Sheds. Faced with the typhus emergency, Montreal's different denominational and linguistic groups pulled together to provide help.

A seemingly never-ending flow of Irish arrived that summer, with caregivers and the sick struggling with heat and torrential rains. Twenty-two huge sheds were eventually built. Two were destined for Protestant Irish from Derry also hit by the Famine. In reality, their numbers were small and Protestant sheds were mainly filled with Catholics. By July, the average number of deaths per day stood at twenty; by the end of August, thirty. The dead were quickly buried in mass trenches, but no records were kept of their exact location. Over the summer came those separated at Grosse-Île: children looking for parents, parents looking for children, spouses looking for each other.

By the end of June, with almost all of their members sick and exhausted, the Grey Nuns were obliged to let other Sisters of Charity take over in caring for the ill.[12] When the Grey Nuns went back to the sheds in September, tensions between Catholics and Protestants had become apparent, taking shape around administrative issues, but also around what had become a competition for the conversion of souls of the dying and the orphaned (Charest-Auger 2013).

No linguistic tensions were recorded in the annals written by the Grey Nuns that summer, but denominational ones, so important in nineteenth-century Montreal, had emerged.

When fall set in, the epidemic wound down, but many, still convalescent, spent the winter in the dismal sheds. When the sheds closed in April, no more funds or foods were provided by the administration and it was the Roman Catholic bishop, Mgr Bourget, who continued to provide funding and the Grey Nuns care. As the medical emergency lessened, the social emergency remained. Religious congregations, in particular French-speaking and Roman Catholic, took charge of the children left in the wake of Black '47, opening orphanages. As administrative pressure grew and funding was cut, homes needed to be found. Mgr Bourget coordinated the adoption of over one thousand orphans into rural French-Catholic families. Many of the adopted would forget their Irish ancestry as they became part of Quebec's Francophone population, whereas the Famine Irish who stayed on in Montreal became part of the city's English-speaking population.

Of the tragedy that unfolded in Montreal in 1847, the Grey Nuns wrote in their annals (Grey Nuns 1847: 1–2), 'this dreadful time leaves its memory written indelibly in the hearts of all the citizens of this city'.[13] This has not been the case. The heroism of the Grey Nuns and of Montrealers in 1847 is as forgotten today as the story of the Famine Irish they cared for.

Raising the Black Rock and commemorating the famine victims[14]

In the decade following 1847, no efforts were made to commemorate those buried in unmarked graves. Many of the Famine Irish had moved on. Those who stayed were living in the lower industrial part of the city, close to where the fever sheds had been erected. Hired as unskilled labourers, many were working on a bridge being built by a British company. Some were actually housed in the old fever sheds (King 2016),[15] a dark reminder of what had taken place a decade earlier. As the riverfront rapidly turned into a major industrial area, concern that the graves of their countrymen would be forgotten created a need to commemorate the burial grounds. In 1859, workmen received permission to raise the Black Rock, a 30-ton boulder, possibly dredged from the St Lawrence riverbed during bridge building operations. On the boulder was chiselled this dedication, written only in English and with no mention of the fact that most of those buried were Irish Catholics fleeing the Famine:

> To preserve from desecration the remains of 6000 immigrants who died of ship fever A.D.1847–8 this stone is erected by the workmen of Messrs. Peto, Brassey and Betts employed in the construction of the Victoria Bridge A.D.1859.

It is a reflection of Montreal in the nineteenth century that the dedication was only in English, as was the commemorative event which followed. The boulder was, in effect, inaugurated and appropriated by representatives of the Anglo-Protestant elite of Montreal. It was perhaps not surprising that a British company would organize a dedication ceremony with the Anglican Church and that the land would eventually be given by that company to the Anglican Bishop, rather than the Roman Catholic Church or a poor Irish parish. What remains difficult to understand is that no Roman Catholic representatives were invited to the ceremony, either French or English-speaking, although nearly all the typhus victims buried there were Catholic, and despite the role played by the Sisters of Charity and Roman Catholic priests in tending them, many of whom died. While there had been some Protestant–Catholic tension in the sheds during the crisis (Charest-Auger 2012), the absence of Catholic representatives at this event 'revealed the growing animus between Catholics and Protestants in Montreal' (McMahon 2007: 47). Furthermore, Irish Protestants, many of whom had come to Canada prior to the famine, were not keen on being associated with destitute typhus victims. Nor were they keen on giving attention to a monument that could lend support to rising Irish nationalism, which described the Famine as a deliberate genocide of the Irish by the British. Memorializing the Famine had, in the decade following Black '47, become politicized, revealing tensions within the Irish community between Protestants and Catholics, but also between Irish Catholic radical nationalists and other Irish Catholics (McMahon 2007). It also revealed social class differences, with the more established Irish hoping to distance themselves from the memory of the wretched Famine Irish. Those most interested in remembering the Famine were the working-class poor of St Ann Parish. But even within this community, there were conflicting feelings about the Rock and about what should be remembered about the past. According to McMahon (2007), memorialization of Black '47 also had the potential to aggravate tensions between French Canadian and Irish Catholics, at that time negotiating the boundaries of parishes, with Irish parishes determined to stay separate from French Catholic ones. During these negotiations, when Mgr Bourget reminded the Irish of the assistance brought by Francophone Roman Catholics to the typhus victims, his remarks were met with anger.[16]

The Rock, neglected marker of the graves of the typhus victims, sat in a tangle of grass and weeds near the riverfront. It was only in 1870 that a first visit to the rock was organized for a priest from Ireland, who commented not on the unilingualism of the dedication – at the time this was taken for a given – but rather that there was no mention that the immigrants buried there were Irish Famine victims (Buckley 1889: 65). It took until the formation of a chapter of the Ancient Order of the Hibernians (AOH) in 1895 for attention to be drawn to the neglect of the memorial. Initially, the AOH was a militant and nationalist association which drew on the famine and the typhus outbreak as powerful symbolic events to invoke support for the cause of Irish independence. Since their mandate was to maintain a sense of history and tradition in the Irish diaspora, the AOH claimed the role of guardians of the memorial, a role they eventually won and keep to this day. The AOH approached the Anglican archdeacon, asking to be allowed to erect a cross, and to fence and landscape the plot. They were refused by the Anglican trustees, who underlined that there was more than one denomination buried there. To the Anglican elite, the Black Rock was not an Irish Catholic Famine memorial and had not been intended as such in the ceremony organized in 1859.

The Famine Jubilee, two years later in 1897, marking the fiftieth anniversary of Black '47, heightened attention on the lack of a memorial to the Irish Famine. The Jubilee was the first major commemorative event in Montreal, with 25,000 Irish Montrealers participating. This time, the Roman Catholic Archbishop Bruchesi led the procession to the Rock, followed by prominent Irish Catholic leaders, judges and politicians. Many of the speeches drew heavily on nationalist tropes and the Famine Irish were described as 'martyrs to their faith and their nationality'. Recognition of courage was also extended to the priests, nuns and French Catholic families who had responded to the crisis. The speeches talked of the strength of the Irish when faced with adversity, but also the need for a memorial to their predecessors. To rectify this, the site of the Black Rock needed to be transferred from the Anglican Church to the Catholic Church and the cemetery properly consecrated. The struggle between Irish Catholics and Anglican trustees intensified.

According to McMahon (2007), not all Irish Catholics appreciated the rough crudeness of the boulder calling it that 'primitive rock'. Some would have preferred a memorial of bronze and polished marble, like those being erected all across Montreal in the late nineteenth century, in a flurry of memorialization to the city's two dominant ethnic groups (French Catholics and Anglo-Protestants) (McMahon 2007). Meanwhile, the Grand Trunk Railway (GTR) had become interested in obtaining the Black Rock plot to expand development. It established a committee to verify that the site was indeed a real burial ground, upsetting

Irish Catholics who saw this as a violation of the site and its sanctity. Propelled into action, key representatives met to prevent the transfer of the plot from its Anglican trustees to the GTR. This did not reflect consensus in the community as some felt that the bones needed a more dignified resting place and should be moved to the Cote-des-Neiges cemetery or to St Patrick Square in the St Ann Parish where survivors of the 'scourge' still worshiped.

The fate of the Rock was decided early one morning, when workmen were sent to move it onto a flat car and down a train track to St Patrick (King 2016: 11). The GTR had gone ahead and taken things into their own hands. While some Irish Catholics would have accepted the opportunity to build a different memorial, the move mostly generated strong feelings about the Rock, giving it the attention it had not had for over half a century. By being displaced, the Black Rock acquired new significance, adding to the sense that the Famine Irish, and also their descendants a half century later, had suffered yet again indignity. A petition was sent to the Anglican bishop and Montreal's city council, asking that the GTR be required to return the Rock to its original site. The Rock became at this point a monument not only to the Irish of Montreal, but also to the Irish across the country as local and national pressure grew to have it restored to the burial site of the typhus victims. The Anglican bishop eventually notified the GTR that it had to return the monument and that it had illegally trespassed and interfered with property. Refuting that the site was even a cemetery (King 2016: 11), the GTR had laid three tracks over the burial ground and was using part of the plot as a dumping ground. The Anglican bishop, however, insisted that the land should remain undeveloped, as it marked a 'very sad and important event in the history of the country' (McMahon 2007: 52). Reassured that the Anglican bishop was determined to have the Rock returned to its site, Irish Catholics little appreciated being told by the GTR that the plot was not a cemetery, nor did they appreciate having to go through Anglican trustees to protect a monument and a burial ground they considered their own (McMahon 2007: 52).

The Famine had become, by this time, a powerful symbolic event for Irish Catholics. Rumours began to circulate that a local Irish politician had collaborated with the GTR and this betrayal of the Famine Irish would bring him down. His rivals plastered the Rock with posters charging him with its displacement from the burial site and when they won the election, they covered the rock again with crêpe paper. The Rock was now ascribed with political and social meanings constructed in a different time from when it was raised, indexing stakes within local and Irish diaspora politics, as well as the place of Irish Catholics in Montreal's social hierarchy. Its displacement to St Patrick Square echoed the displacement of the Irish in the 1840s, but also served as a reminder that Irish Catholics lacked the status in the social structure of Montreal to protect the graves of their own (McMahon 2007). Debates and conflicts about the Black Rock, which sat for ten more years in St Patrick Square, were in English, the language of Montreal's Irish population, Anglicans and the Anglophone industrial elite.

Grosse-Île as a site of memorialization had caught the attention of Irish Catholic societies by this time and plans to erect a Celtic cross were made. Times were changing, as was the status of the Irish in Canada. In 1909, during the ceremonies held at the old quarantine station with Irish representatives from across the diaspora, the president of the AOH drew attention to how bad the typhus outbreak had been in Montreal, the neglect of the Black Rock and how a greedy corporation had laid tracks across the graves of the dead. This provided new energy for efforts to restore the Rock to its original site and a petition was sent to the Railway Commission to deny GTR's application for the land. The petition met with support from Montreal's city council, and the Railway Board of Commissioners began an investigation on whether the site was really a burial site and whether the property, still in Anglican trusteeship, could be sold to the GTR for commercial purposes. The land had become critical to plans to extend its yards and the GTR continued to claim that the site had never been a cemetery and that the graves of the typhus victims were located closer to the Wellington Basin. The Railway Board finally granted the GTR permission to expropriate the entire site, except for a plot of land that would be kept for the memorial. The GTR, under obligation, returned the Rock to what had become a very busy industrial area, surrounded by railroad yards, sheds and tracks, 15 feet from where it originally stood, to allow for construction of a road (King 2016: 11). To mark the return, a re-dedication ceremony was organized and local Irish representatives, as well as from Quebec City, Ottawa and the United States, attended the walk to the rock. In his speech, the AOH president emphasized the callousness displayed by authorities but followed with a tribute to the people of Montreal: Catholic, Protestant, French, English and Irish, who had all come to the help of the typhus victims. The movement to return the Rock was no longer only about a duty to remember typhus victims but had also become a political struggle to protect what had become an important Irish monument. In the late nineteenth and twentieth centuries, both Anglo-Protestant and French-Canadian elites left the Irish, a politically and economically disadvantaged group, out of the 'public contest to shape the city's collective memories. Returning the rock to its site did not signal a shift in the agendas of the "heritage elites"' (McMahon 2007), who decided what was historically significant in the city.

By the twentieth century, the Irish were increasingly recognized as Canadians and in the eyes of French Catholics, 'les Irlandais' had become English Canadians and their past, part of Anglo-Canadian history (Charest-Auger 2012). But their strong ties to Ireland became problematic during the First World War as Irish Catholics found themselves juggling loyalty to Canada and support for Irish independence. In the early 1920s, the war over, annual commemorative walks to the Stone became more important, with processions of different Irish societies, pipers and mounted police, prayers and addresses.

In 1942, workers came across coffins in trenches not far from the Rock (Sirois 1942). This discovery renewed attention to the Black Rock and vindicated those who had argued that the stone's site was indeed an unmarked cemetery. Its authenticity no longer questioned, approval was sought from Anglican authorities (still proprietors of the memorial land) and from the Canadian National Railway (CNR), which replaced the GTR in 1923, to re-establish the sanctity of the Black Rock site and to rebury the dead, discovered in old trenches, below the monument. The Anglican bishop agreed, stating that the discovery of bones is what had motivated his predecessors to establish the site in 1859. Anglicans and the CNR, recognizing the significance of the site for Irish Catholics in Montreal, nevertheless underlined that some of the typhus victims had been Protestant. So an interdenominational reinterment event was 'orchestrated', ensuring that by the time the Catholic procession made their way from St Ann's Church, the Anglican service on the site would be coming to a close (McMahon 2007). Catholics and Protestants then joined in a civil commemorative ceremony. By 1942, the Irish clearly saw themselves as pioneers and patriots of Canada and had supported the war effort (even if Ireland itself stayed out of the war).[17] At the 1942 reinterment ceremony, while the Irish in Montreal were using the past to reconstitute themselves as Canadian patriots in the present and positioning themselves within the national development of Canada, the High Commissioner of Ireland was also present with his own agenda, claiming the dead buried near the Black Rock as Ireland's own, martyrs in the great destiny of the Irish 'race'. The ceremony marked reinterment and remembrance but was also an occasion, in what McMahon (2007) calls a multivocal orchestration, to ascribe various meanings to a monument and a historical event. Until this point, multivocal struggles over the memorial took place in English, within Montreal's English-speaking community, nevertheless marked by denominational and social class tensions. There were no efforts to build support among French-speaking Roman Catholics, reflecting the growing importance of language within social division in Montreal at the time.

McMahon's careful historical analysis of the history of the Black Rock from 1859 to 1942 shows the complexity surrounding memorialization, as the Irish contended with changing and sometimes conflicting popular memories and political priorities, vying for prominence within their own community. They furthermore had to negotiate with the industrial powers and the GTR/CNR, as well as the Anglican elites of the city and various levels of government. How they have done this from the time of the raising of the Black Rock to the mid-twentieth century reveals not only tensions around their own changing forms of identification but also their rising mobility within the social hierarchies of Montreal and Canada, as well as their place in a powerful Irish diaspora. It also shows how, over time, the Irish population in Montreal became part of what Francophones understand as English Canada, which perhaps helps explain how the history of the Irish is so little present in today's narrative of Montréal and Québec.

The Black Rock from the mid-twentieth century to 2018

We can't stand in the middle of the road forever.

McMahon's historical analysis of the Black Rock ends in the mid-twentieth century, by which time the representation of the Irish population and their contribution to the making of Canada had taken the shape it retains to this day. This period marks, however, the end of an era and an important shift in the power dynamics of Quebec and Montreal. While Irish Catholics had previously had to negotiate with an Anglo-Protestant business elite and Anglican clergy in efforts to memorialize 1847, they would soon have to negotiate with a rising Francophone-Québécois elite. By the 1960s, the *révolution tranquille* was underway and once again the Black Rock would be an obstacle to major development plans in the city.

Displacing the Black Rock was once again considered in preparation for Expo '67, a world exposition, and Bridge Street needed to be widened. The Irish Stone Committee was quickly formed by community stakeholders to protect the Black Rock and representatives of Irish societies were invited to City Council meetings (King 2016: 13). But as in previous negotiations with development planners, plans would finally go ahead to the detriment of the Irish Memorial, albeit leaving the Rock undisturbed. Instead, Bridge Street would pass on either side of the small plot accorded the Black Rock in earlier negotiations with the GTR. The memorial plot would become a dividing meridian in a major artery and effectively inaccessible. To better protect the Rock in the future, a letter was sent by the St. Patrick's Society to the Historical Sites and Monument Board of Canada (HSMBC) to have the cemetery declared a historical site (King 2016). The Board never replied. Ten years later, when the City of Montreal attempted to buy the land from the Anglican Church to 'better maintain it', another letter of petition was sent to the HSMBC. This time, the board responded, rejecting the request for historical designation and stating that the Irish Famine was a disaster which precluded it from Parks Canada involvement. In 1982, the Anglican Church relinquished trusteeship of the Black Rock, selling the cemetery plot to the City of Montreal on the condition that human remains be 'disposed of in dignity' (King 2016).

It was in the turbulent years of the 1980s that a local group of leftist writers and poets wrote a manifesto in English appropriating the Black Rock[18] and its raw primitiveness, as a symbol of the poor and working-class Anglos of the lower city, once again revealing multivocal and competing representations attributed to the stone:

> Not a Bleeding Heart of Christ or the head of holy fool John the Baptist but a huge black rock like a bad tooth pulled out of the river and placed on the common grave by the working men that built the Victoria Bridge.

The Manifesto also drew attention to the erasure of the working-class Anglo poor:

> The unemployable poor that have no choice but to stay in the Montreal of the Eighties in a Quebec that doesn't officially recognize that there ever was an Anglo working class in this city. (Adams et al. 1982)

In the 1990s, with the Famine's 150th anniversary on the horizon, refurbishment and creation of monuments to the famine were underway around the world and local efforts were made to improve the site and commemorate the Famine. The United Irish Societies decorated the fence put up by the GTR with shamrocks (see Figure 2.3) and the city gave a nearby road the name '*rue des Irlandais*', marking in French the historical presence of the Irish but also the symbolic dominance of French in post-101 Montreal. The city also built a viewing area across from the Black Rock with a plaque to explain its significance. Far from being unilingual, the memorial text was in three languages, Irish, French, and English, in that order. Symbolically, that Irish comes first is significant, an important sign of recognition, given that Quebec's language legislation requires French be the first and most important language on signage.

Figure 2.3 The Black Rock in its island.

In 1992, the St. Patrick's Society proposed a memorial park, an 'Irish garden of remembrance' where the Black Rock is located. The HMSBC was again approached in 1995 but a committee of academics 'was not prepared to recommend the Black Stone monument to be of national historic significance'

(King 2016). In 2005, developers purchased the CNR yards close to the Rock, provoking new fears for the site. It was only in 2014, however, that the Montreal Irish Monument Park Foundation (MIMPF) was created. According to King, a key member of the Foundation, efforts to memorialize the graves of the typhus victims have always been hedged in by obstacles and politics, erasure and encroachment. Since Irish Catholics never owned the land, they have had to defend it over time through commemorative events, annual walks and 'persuasive political discourse' (King 2016: 15). With major commemorative events again on the horizon, efforts to give the Black Rock more importance in Montreal's heritage landscape intensified. In effect, 2017 marked not only Montreal's 375th anniversary, but also Canada's 150th. The Foundation drew on all opportunities to bring the lack of a memorial park to the attention of the public, this time reaching out in both languages to build support, sending letters to editors of local French and English language newspapers and media, and creating a bilingual website explaining the Rock. Letters were also sent to Irish diaspora newspapers, in efforts to gather support further afield. One of the arguments used to coax local support was that an Irish memorial park where the Black Rock stands has the potential to commodify the Rock within a global trend of Irish Famine commemoration, essentially becoming a 'tourist attraction for the millions of Irish in North America whose ancestors arrived and survived' ('An Irish Memorial Park at the Black Rock' 2014) a form of 'dark pilgrimage' tourism (Collins-Kreiner 2016). It was further argued that a park at the entrance to Montreal from Victoria Bridge would provide a much more attractive entryway into the city for arriving tourists and much-needed greenspace in Griffintown, currently under gentrification (Montreal Irish Monument Park Foundation 2018). But to win over Francophone Quebecers to their efforts for memorialization, the Foundation drew on a new persuasive strategy, drawing attention to a shared cultural and genetic background (roughly 40 per cent of Quebec's French population claims some Irish ancestry):

> When the Irish settled in urban areas, they became English. When they settled in rural areas, they became French-Canadian, retaining their Irish surnames but otherwise indistinguishable from everyone else ... it's a story of people becoming accepted into their new communities, people becoming new French-Canadians or Irish-Canadians. In a nutshell, it's a story of integration. (King 2016)

Always within efforts to build broader support for the project, the national president of the AOH expanded on who would be honoured by the park, describing the tragedy of 1847 as important to all Montrealers. The Rock was shifting symbolically from an Irish Catholic monument, to a monument for the Irish and for the many who came to their help. The Foundation also appealed to Canada's perception of itself as a country that welcomes refugees:

> Much as the tragedy of what took place in 1847 is an Irish story, the bigger story is the number of Montrealers – French, English, Protestant, Catholic, Jewish, that all came down to that site, that horrible site. It was mired in mud and sickness and disease, it was the hottest summer on record, yet all these people came from their homes and went down to see if they could help … Mohawks from Kahnawake contributed food, nuns and other volunteers nursed the ill and families adopted Irish orphans … Many caregivers died, including the then-mayor of Montreal, John Easton Mills … The story that we're hoping to preserve is one that Canada sticks to today. Look at the refugees that we accepted from Syria. The rest of the world was holding them at arms' length and we embraced them, just like we did the Irish in 1847. That's the story we want to preserve … (Scott 2017b)

Working with McGill architects to design a memorial park, this time it was Irish representatives who planned to move the Rock to a new site, where it would be more accessible. A large granite Celtic cross would be raised to replace the Rock in the traffic island, providing a clearer message to commuters driving over the place where so many Irish Famine are buried. The Foundation met with newly elected mayor Denis Coderre, who seemed genuinely interested in bringing support to the project, declaring that he was one-quarter Irish. Coderre promised to do everything possible to 'make it happen' and to be the 'political champion' of the memorial park (Scott 2017a). There were complications, however, as the actual land on which a memorial could be built turned out to be owned by the Old Port of Montreal, along with a federal agency, the Canada Lands Company. Meetings with these two agencies were organized in 2016 and hope continued to build. Mayor Coderre walked in the St Patrick's Day Parade, honoured as Grand Marshall (Scott 2017a) and in early summer he joined the annual walk to the Rock. The Irish government declared that it was prepared to contribute financially to the memorial park, as they had at other sites (such as Toronto's Ireland Park) and Prime Minister Justin Trudeau, who had campaigned on his vision of Canada as an open and welcoming society, backed the project, giving his support for this 'inclusive site for all citizens of Montreal' (Montreal Irish Memorial Park Foundation 2015).

Hopes were high that the project would be announced by Mayor Coderre in 2017, during the celebrations for Montreal's 375th anniversary. The area around the Black Rock where the proposed park would be built had become of interest, however, to the city as the site for a substation to provide electricity for the new light rail train. Coderre abandoned the Irish Memorial to ultimately back this project, and the Canada Lands Company sold the land near the Victoria Bridge to Hydro-Québec. The Irish Memorial Foundation members only found out about the electrical substation and the sale of the lands when Coderre made a formal announcement to which they were not invited. After five years of working on plans for a memorial park, this announcement came like a deathblow and a shock to those working within the Foundation. Jason King, former Montrealer and a historian in Dublin and adviser to the Irish Heritage Trust, called the news 'devastating':

> Every North American city where the famine Irish arrived in significant numbers has a major monument except Montreal … The paradox is that in Montreal, the Black Stone is the oldest famine memorial. It's also the most neglected and the least appreciated. (Scott 2017b)

The sale by Canada Lands obliged Hydro-Québec to erect a memorial to the Irish victims near the new substation and Hydro-Quebec signalled a willingness to do this. Coderre also continued to extend hopes for a memorial. During his re-election campaign, Coderre revisited the Rock, promising a new commemorative site that would be easily accessible and include an interpretive centre, but without inviting the Foundation's members to the announcement (Grillo 2017).

In the fall of 2017, workers started digging a series of holes at the substation site to check for soil contamination before new construction, a requirement by law. Victor Boyle, Canadian president of the AOH, organized to have a Montreal Irish Catholic Priest from St. Gabriel Parish at the site:

> The Good Father took a moment to bless the space, as well as the workers on the site and their task … We certainly have to take a moment to mention that the company doing these tests seems to be called GHD – likely a contractor for Hydro – and the guys working were absolutely terrific … They shut down their machinery so Father could give his blessing and mentioned that in all the years that they have done this work, they had never been blessed before and seemed pleased with the small ceremony. (Montreal Irish Memorial Park Foundation 2018)

One of the Francophone workers commented that his grandmother had been Irish and the photo of the blue-collar team being blessed on the site is an odd echo to the bridge workers who insisted on raising the Rock in 1859 (see Figure 2.4).

Figure 2.4 The blessing of the blue-collar workers. Credit: Montreal Irish Monument Park Foundation.

Coderre, however, was not re-elected, and in 2017 a new mayor, Valérie Plante, participated in the annual walk to the Rock. She had campaigned on greater recognition of diversity in Montreal and promised her support to the memorial park. At the present time, the memorial park project appears to be stalled and the Black Rock still sits in its meridian, inaccessible and unrecognized.

The fast rail project that upset the plans for a memorial park did offer, however, a new opportunity to claim a place in Montreal's urban landscape and history. A petition was launched, calling for a new transit station to be named *Station des Irlandais* to commemorate the lower city's Irish history. Those who worked to claim a space for an Irish past in Montreal have not given up, but there seems no end to the indignities the Black Rock has suffered since being raised. During the provincial election campaign in 2018, the Black Rock found itself once again being used within local politics when two major political parties mounted huge election signs on the Black Rock cemetery to catch commuter's attention. The signs provoked outrage among those who know what the Black Rock signifies, but most of the drivers crossing the bridge have no idea what the dark boulder in the meridian represents. The director of the Montreal Irish Monument Park Foundation issued a news release calling for the signs to be removed: 'This is indeed a cemetery, and both parties have dug into the ground

Figure 2.5 The Liberal Party poster at the Black Rock. Credit: Montreal Irish Monument Park Foundation.

in order to install their sign' (Riga 2018; Riga and Gauthier 2018). The Parti Québécois were the first to respond, saying their signs would be removed and offering their apologies. In contrast, the Liberals initially refused to move their sign, saying it is not directly on the memorial and that it did not obscure the view of the Black Rock. Later that day, a spokesperson for the Liberals confirmed that they, too, would remove their sign which read ironically '*pour faciliter la vie des travailleurs*' ('to bring support to workers'), oblivious to the history of the Irish workers who had raised the Black Rock to the memory of their dead countrymen (see Figure 2.5).

Conclusions

The dedication chiselled into the Black Rock remains to this day in English only, a testament, like other texts engraved in Montreal's cityscape, to when it was erected and English dominated in Montreal. In the nineteenth century, there seems to never have been any request or thought given to marking the graves of the typhus victims, who had emigrated from one British colony to another, with a commemorative text in Irish Gaelic, the first language of many who came across. It was not just the language of those who died on the riverfront that has been erased from the dedication through omission, but also their nationality, cultural and religious background. The plaque placed by the City of Montreal in the viewing centre in the 1990s testifies to an important shift in linguistic regime. Written in three languages, Irish, French, then English, it clearly recognizes that those buried there were Irish and that many were speakers of Irish Gaelic. Within current ideology in Quebec, language is considered the most important trait within collective and individual identity, and respect for linguistic background has been extended to Irish immigrants. Our focus on language in Quebec, however, sometimes leads us to forget that in the past, language was intertwined not only with social class, but denominational traits and that these traits were, at times, more important than language background – the role played by Francophone sisters and Mgr Bourget an obvious example. A change in linguistic regime, however, is clearly revealed in the naming of a street to mark the presence of an Irish community in the lower city. A sign of the times, it is in French only, as French is the language of public administrative signage. The unilingualism present in nineteenth-century Montreal has been replaced with a new unilingualism, with both regimes building on the premise of one nation/one language. To maintain this premise on which ideologies were built and continue to be built, the real linguistic diversity of the population is pushed to the side. A new regime is perhaps most powerfully revealed in the persuasive bilingual strategies used to build support for the Black Rock, which now include reaching out in French to a local French-speaking population. In the past, struggles over commemoration took place solely in English, within Montreal's English-speaking population. While the struggles themselves were not about language, the use of languages in the discourses surrounding debates reveals much.

When looking at the history of the Black Rock over time, what is most striking are its precarity and the difficulty it has had in being recognized as more than a rough tombstone, a 'primitive rock'. Never a planned and formal memorial erected by Montreal's heritage elites, struggles over the Black Rock reveal over and over again the marginal place occupied by Montreal's Irish Catholic working class in the narrative of Montreal as place, whether in Anglo-Protestant or in present-day Montréal. The Black Rock is, more than anything a dark reminder of a neglected part of Montreal's history, a monument with symbolic importance as much through what it stands for, as for what it has never truly been able to memorialize. From the moment it was lifted up in memory of the Irish typhus victims by workmen, the Rock has been caught up not only in the social and political history of Montreal but also in its industrial development, reflecting struggles between symbolic and material interests, and between working-class Irish Catholics and the heritage elites of Montreal within the evolving dynamic of the city. What is constant over time is that the Rock remains an obstacle to urban and industrial interests, and that efforts to protect it have always lost out to these interests. While the struggles over the coveted physical space on which the rock sits remain much the same, there is a shift in how arguments for memorial space are framed discursively, as well as the languages used to present arguments. Having won recognition over time as Canadians and as a population that had made considerable contributions to the development of Canada, Irish Montrealers now strive for recognition for their contributions to the development of *Montréal* and *Québec*. Struggles around the Black Rock are, in effect, divided into two periods. The first period covers the tail end of colonial administration in British North America to the emergence in the twentieth century of a Canadian nation and a Canadian identity made up of the many groups who immigrated here. The second period begins mid-twentieth century and is marked by the shift of power in Montreal from an Anglo-dominant to a French-dominant city. It is within these two distinct periods that the efforts of Irish Catholics to obtain recognition take place and that the strategies and symbolic stakes evoked during negotiations around the Black Rock are framed. In the first period, Irish Catholics negotiated in English with Anglo-Protestant elites to obtain guardianship of the Rock and defend the site from industrial and urban development interests. In the second period, post-*révolution tranquille*, they must negotiate with Montreal's Francophone elite, now very much in charge of municipal and provincial administrative structures. In the first period, McMahon's research (2007, 2010) shows how struggles over the Black Rock are not only about the past, but about claiming a place as Canadians. And if by the mid-twentieth century, recognition of the Irish in the making of Canada is no longer in question, recognition of an Irish past in Montreal and Quebec has not yet been won and shapes how negotiations for a memorial park for the Rock are presented in competition with new urban development plans. Over time, the importance of a memorial has been reframed and reframed again: from struggles for recognition that the Black Rock marks the grave of Irish Famine victims, to a marker of an Irish presence in Canada and in Canadian history, to a proposed new memorial that is inclusive, recognizing all of the groups present in the Sheds during the typhus and recognition that the Irish contributed not only to Canada (as in English Canada), but to Quebec – its development and culture, and also its genetic bloodline.

The erasure of the story of the Famine Irish and typhus is also the erasure of the courage of Montrealers in the nineteenth century, many of whom were Francophone. This erasure is not just from Montreal's memorial landscape, but also Montreal's narrative of place and memory of the past. As Ochs (2005) proposes, narratives 'bring the remembered past into the present and projected possible realities'. The Black Rock, a specific symbolic 'text' in Montreal's cityscape, is an unrecognized piece within a larger narrative, continuously being negotiated. Its omission from the larger narrative needs to be approached as a form of action. 'Erasure is a blunt word for a blunt process' (Seghal 2016) which begs the questions: 'Whose stories are taught and told? Whose suffering is recognized? Whose dead are mourned?' (Seghal 2016). In Montreal's textscape and in its discursive telling of itself, there is a blotting out of a horrendous piece of history, but also of the courage and local bravery of Montrealers when faced with a tragedy on the shores of the St Lawrence. While this text is primarily about struggles and competition, it seems important to remember that the story is also about cooperation in Montreal in a time of crisis, played out against the dark backdrop that provoked the Irish Famine. It's a grim mix of heroism and tragedy.

And it is not only an Irish past that is not recognized today, there are other pasts, other silences in the narrative of Montreal and Quebec. We have, among other things, our own dark story of colonization in *la Nouvelle France*, marked by epidemics spread among First Nations. No memorial stands to the many First Nations people who also died by the thousands in the St Lawrence River Valley from contact with white European settlers. There is a politics of remembrance in Quebec as elsewhere, memory regimes that by being voiced talk to who we are and who we were. But silence is also a form of language, a stance (Jaffe 2009), a statement within a LL, within a narrative, within representations of the past – and what is not said needs to be examined and answered by the question, why?

Notes

1 The Black Rock has many names in both English and French: '*le rocher noir*', '*le rocher irlandais*', the Fever Ship Monument, the Irish Rock, the Stone.
2 Erasure refers to actions and processes that render certain people and groups invisible. Thinking about erasure has evolved within the study of ideologies, which dismiss inconvenient facts (Irvine and Gal 2000).

3 My translation: 'Le "roc irlandais", le plus simple des monuments de Montréal, demeure aussi, à bien des égards, le plus émouvant'.
4 In the seventies, linguistic landscape was referred to in Quebec as 'visage linguistique', the linguistic face of the city (Bourhis and Landry 2002).
5 Historians agree that it is almost impossible to determine exactly how many died in the crossing and along the St Lawrence. Of the roughly 80,000 who sailed into the St Lawrence, over 7,000 are estimated to have died before reaching Montreal.
6 The United States was much less affected by the typhus epidemic, having put in place regulations to control Irish Famine immigration (Gallagher 1936).
7 The dead were committed to the sea by sailors, many reluctant to touch the infected bodies, unless paid to do so. They were right to be afraid. Sailors and shipcrew are among those that died in the crossings of Black '47 (Gallagher 1936).
8 Quebec City had been hit hard fifteen years earlier by the cholera epidemic, which also travelled up the seaway, carried over by immigrants from Europe. Cholera, unlike typhus, spread into the local population, killing many (Sévigny 1992).
9 Funding had been provided to improve quarantine facilities: two more medical assistants were hired and a steamship service planned to move immigrants between Grosse-Île and Quebec City and Montreal (Gallagher 1936).
10 German immigrants arrived aboard passenger ships and disembarked healthy during that summer, not decimated by the ship fever of the coffin ships (Charest-Auger 2012).
11 The Catholic bishop of Quebec City, Mgr Signay wrote to Irish congregations to warn them of conditions on arrival in Canada (Gallagher 1936).
12 All of the Grey Nuns attending caught typhus, seven of whom died. Of the sisters of Providence, twenty-seven caught typhus and four would die (Charest-Auger 2012).
13 '…cette funeste époque laissa un souvenir écrit en caractère indélible dans les coeurs de tous les citoyens de cette ville'.
14 In this section, I draw heavily on the historical research of Colin McMahon whose excellent historical study on the Fever Ship Monument examined three main commemorative events (1897, 1913, 1942). See bibliography for reference to his doctoral thesis *Ports of Recall: Memory of the Great Irish Famine in Liverpool and Montreal* (2010) and an article published in *Canadian Journal of Irish Studies* (2007).
15 According to King (2016), thousands of labourers were hired to build the bridge and approximately 500 were actually housed in the Sheds by the British company in charge of construction.
16 This was eventually taken to the Pope in Rome who decided that Irish Roman Catholic were to keep their parishes and run their schools (King 2016).
17 The only Commonwealth country to do so, creating tension and uneasy relations between Ireland and the allied powers as Ireland tried to assert its independence during the war years (McMahon 2007).
18 A Black Rock Theatre and Café were also created.

References

Adams, D. et al. (1982), 'The Black Rock Manifesto', *Canadian Journal of Political and Social Theory/Revue Canadienne de theorie politique et sociale*, 6 (1/2): 139–142.

'An Irish Memorial Park at the Black Rock' (2014), *Montreal Gazette*, 26 June. Available online: https://montrealgazette.com/opinion/opinion-an-irish-memorial-park-at-the-black-rock (accessed 20 December 2018).

Bourhis, R. and R. Landry (2002), La loi 101 et l'aménagement du paysage linguistique au Québec: 25 ans d'application de la Charte de la langue française. *Revue d'aménagement linguistique*. Automne hors-série, pp. 107–132.

Buckley, M. B. (1889), *Diary of a Tour in America*, Dublin: Sealy, Bryers & Walker.

Charbonneau, A. (1995), '1847: A Tragic Year at Grosse Île', *Parks Canada*. Available online: https://www.pc.gc.ca/en/lhn-nhs/qc/grosseile/decouvrir-discover/natcul1/b (accessed 20 December 2018).

Charest-Auger, M. (2012), 'La réaction montréalaise à l'épidémie de typhus de 1847', MA diss., Université du Québec à Montréal.

Charest-Auger, M. (2013), 'Prosélytisme et conflits religieux lors de l'épidémie de typhus à Montréal en 1847', *Cap-aux-diamants*, 11: 8–12.

Collins-Kreiner, N. (2016), 'Dark Tourism As/Is Pilgrimage', *Current Issues in Tourism*, 19 (12): 1185–1189.

Gallagher, J. A. (1936), 'The Irish Emigration of 1847 and Its Canadian Consequences', *CCHA Report*, 3: 43–57.

Grey Nuns (1847), *La terrible épidémie de 1847*. Available online: http://faminearchive.nuigalway.ie/docs/grey-nuns/GreyNunsFamineAnnalLaterriblede1847transcribed.pdf (accessed 20 December 2018).

Grillo, M. (2017), 'Plans Unveiled for Irish Commemoration Site in Montreal', *Global News*, 6 October. Available online: https://globalnews.ca/news/3790237/plans-unveiled-for-irish-commemoration-site-in-montreal/ (accessed 20 December 2018).

Irvine, Judith T. and S. Gal (2000), 'Language Ideology and linguistic differentiation.' In P.V. Kroskrity (ed). Regimes of language ideologies, polities and identities. Santa Fe: School of American Research Press, 35–84.

Jaffe, A. (2009). 'Introduction', in A. Jaffe (ed.), *Stance: Sociolinguistic Perspectives*, 3–28, Oxford Studies in Sociolinguistics.

Kinealy, C. with P. Fitzgerald and G. Moran (eds) (2015), *Irish Hunger and Migration. Memory, Myth and Memorialization*, Hamden, CT: Quinnipiac University Press.

King, D. (2016), 'Montreal's Irish Famine Cemetery: Commemoration Struggles from 1847 to the Present'. Available online: http://www.montrealirishmonument.com/sites/default/files/MontrealsIrishFamineCemetery.pdf (accessed 20 December 2018).

Lamarre, P. (2014), 'Bilingual Winks and Bilingual Wordplay in Montreal's Linguistic Landscape', *International Journal of the Sociology of Language*, 228: 131–151.

Levine, M. (1997), *The Reconquest of Montreal: Language Policy and Social Change in a Bilingual City*, Philadelphia, PA: Temple University Press.

Mark-Fitzgerald, E. (2018), 'Canada', *Irish Famine Memorials*. Available online: https://irishfaminememorials.com/canada/ (accessed 20 December 2018).

McGowan, M. (2009), *Death or Canada: The Irish Famine. Migration to Toronto, 1847*, Toronto: Novalis.

McMahon, C. (2007), 'Montreal's Ship Fever Monument: An Irish Famine Memorial in the Making', *The Canadian Journal of Irish Studies*, 33 (1): 48–60.

McMahon, C. (2010), 'Ports of Recall: Memory of the Great Irish Famine in Liverpool and Montreal', PhD thesis, York University, Toronto.

McRoberts, K. (1993), *Quebec: Social Change and Political Crisis*. Toronto: McClelland and Stewart.

Montreal Irish Monument Park Foundation (2015), 'Mr. Justin Trudeau & Walk to the Rock'. Available online: http://www.montrealirishmonument.com/node/49 (accessed 20 December 2018).

Montreal Irish Monument Park Foundation (2018), 'Mission'. Available online: http://www.montrealirishmonument.com/mission (accessed 20 December 2018).

O'Gallagher M. and R. Masson-Dompierre (1995), *Eyewitness Grosse isle 1847*, Sainte-Foy: Livres Carraig.

Ochs, E. (2005), 'Narrative Lessons', in A. Duranti (ed.), *A Companion to Linguistic Anthropology*, 269–289, Malden, MA: Blackwell.

Riga, A. (2018), 'Quebec Election Blog September 11: Irish Denounce Campaign Signs in Black Rock Cemetery', *Montreal Gazette*, 11 September. Available online: https://montrealgazette.com/news/quebec/live-quebec-election-blog-charts-explain-legaults-nationalist-shift-on-immigration-french-language (accessed 20 December 2018).

Riga, A. and P. Gauthier (2018), 'Quebec Election: Liberals Apologize for Election Sign in Black Rock Cemetery', *Montreal Gazette*, 12 September. Available online: https://montrealgazette.com/news/local-news/quebec-election-liberals-apologize-for-election-sign-in-black-rock-cemetery (accessed 20 December 2018).

Scott, M. (2017a), 'Black Rock Memorial Park: Irish Community Feels Betrayed', *Montreal Gazette*. 25 May 2017. Available online: https://montrealgazette.com/news/local-news/black-rock-folo (accessed 20 December 2018).

Scott, M. (2017b), 'Montreal, Refugees and the Irish Famine of 1847', *Montreal Gazette*, 12 August 2017. Available online: https://montrealgazette.com/feature/montreal-refugees-and-the-irish-famine-of-1847 (accessed 20 December 2018).

Sebba, M. (2010), 'Discourses in Transit', in A. Jaworski and C. Thurlow (eds), *Semiotic Landscapes: Language, Image, Space*, 59–76, London: Bloomsbury.

Sehgal, P. (2016), 'Fighting Erasure', *The New York Times Magazine*, 2 February. Available online: https://www.nytimes.com/2016/02/07/magazine/the-painful-consequences-of-erasure.html (accessed 20 December 2018).

Sévigny, A. (1992), 'La Grosse-Île: quarantaine et immigration à Québec (1832–1937)', *Le Cahier des dix*, 47: 9–338.

Sirois, J. (1942), 'Victims of 1847 Typhus Horror to Be Buried Anew Here.' *Montreal Gazette*, 31 October. Available online: https://news.google.com/newspapers?nid=194

6&dat=19421031&id=VQMuAAAAIBAJ&sjid=wZgFAAAAIBAJ&pg=5486,5989857&hl=fr (accessed 20 December 2018).

Sisters of Charity (1847), *Ancien Journal*, translated by J-F. Bernard. Available online: http://faminearchive.nuigalway.ie/docs/grey-nuns/GreyNunsFamineAnnalAncienJournalVolumeI.1847.pdf (accessed 20 December 2018).

Société historique de la Pointe-St-Charles (SHPSC) (2018), 'Gardien du pont Victoria: le roc irlandais'. Available online: http://www.shpsc.org/Roc_Irlandais.pdf (accessed 20 December 2018).

The Famine Irish and Canada's First Responders (2017), [Film] Dir. Kevin Moynihan, Canada: KM Productions.

3

La fraternité franco-marocaine Remembered in France and in Morocco – Multilingual Memorials and *patrimoine national*

Dawn Marley

Introduction

The starting point for this chapter will be the monument originally known as the 'Monument to Victory and Peace' and later renamed as the 'Monument to Franco-Moroccan Friendship'. This statue by Paul Landowski, created shortly after the First World War, carries text in French and in Arabic, primarily celebrating the heroism of the Moroccan troops who fought alongside the French in the First World War. While this monument is of particular interest for a number of reasons, not least the large amount of text in two languages, it is far from being the only one to commemorate Moroccan involvement in French wars. There are numerous war memorials for Moroccans in France, most of which bear inscriptions in French and Arabic. Some date from the same era as the Landowski monument, some from shortly after the Second World War and others were produced much more recently. This chapter will examine the wording on a number of these monuments, beginning with the Landowski monument, and consider what they might tell us about the evolving relationship between the two countries, and what impact they may have had and continue to have on both French and Moroccan remembering of past events. The analysis will focus on the wording, and the parity or disparity between the two languages, but will also consider the nature and location of the monuments and the potential impact on those who look at them and read the inscriptions, using some of the elements of geosemiotics (Scollon and Scollon 2003).

Before looking in detail at the monuments themselves, the chapter will provide some historical context, explaining the particular relationship between

France and Morocco at the time of the First World War and in subsequent years. This will be followed by a brief discussion of the potential social and cultural meanings to be found in war memorials.

France and Morocco: A shared history

The Protectorate (1912–1956)

France and Morocco have a shared history, which started officially only just before the First World War. Although France had had a colonizing interest in Morocco since the turn of the twentieth century, the Protectorate was officially declared in 1912, and at the outbreak of war in 1914 the 'pacification' was far from complete. Morocco was the third North African state to come under French rule, Algeria having become a French colony in 1830 and Tunisia a Protectorate in 1881. Unlike these neighbours, Morocco had never been under Ottoman rule, and at the turn of the twentieth century was a sovereign nation, with a monarchy tracing its origins to the seventeenth century. In the early nineteenth century the country was in many respects still a closed medieval kingdom (Ganiage 1994: 77), which attracted the interest of several European powers in the course of the century. By the early twentieth century, failed attempts to reform and modernize, wars and a series of natural disasters had led to the gradual breakdown of the State, and from the turn of the twentieth century France and other European powers became increasingly involved in Moroccan affairs. Finally in 1912 a French Protectorate was set up in most of Morocco, while Spain kept possession of a large area in the south of the country and Tangier became an international zone (Ganiage 1994: 395). General (later Marshall) Lyautey, appointed as governor, represented France in both civil and military capacities and devoted himself to reforming the Sharifian Empire, as Morocco was also known, and subjugating the people, who had risen up in protest at the French Protectorate.

The First World War: *La Division marocaine*

When war broke out, Lyautey was asked to return two-thirds of the troops engaged in Morocco and it was suggested that he should reduce his efforts to gain control over the country. Lyautey did not take up this suggestion; he sent back to France all the regiments requested, but then carried on with his plan to maintain and expand French control of Morocco (Ganiage 1994: 409). This he succeeded in doing, while the so-called *Division marocaine*, made up of French and 'colonial' troops – Tunisians, Algerians and even some Moroccans – went off to distinguish themselves on the battle fields of Europe. In fact this division was the most decorated in the French army, being the only division in which every single regiment wears the *fourragère rouge*[1] (Trouillard 2015).

The *Division marocaine* was far from being the only 'colonial' division in the French army; at the outbreak of the First World War, there were several regiments of *'tirailleurs', 'spahis'*[2] *'méharistes'* and other *'indigènes'* from across North Africa. These regiments, together with others from sub-Saharan Africa, made up the *'Armée d'Afrique'*, whose headquarters were in Algiers. Although this paper will focus on the Franco-Moroccan link, it is impossible to look at this issue without also mentioning other 'colonial' links.

Involvement in the Second World War

By the time the Second World War broke out, the French Protectorate of Morocco was an integral part of the French colonial empire, and the Sultan Mohamed V announced that Morocco would fight alongside France. Indeed Morocco would become an important strategic base for the French Resistance, as those forces joining General de Gaulle had no base in metropolitan France. It was during this war that the Moroccan troops known as *goums mixtes marocains* (GMM), created by Lyautey in the early days of the Protectorate, would achieve military success, most notably in the battle of Garigliano and the landings in Provence (Association La Koumia, n.d.), but also in North Africa and the Far East. They were to be decorated for their achievements in battle, although they were not subsequently recognized in the same way as their French counterparts.

The meaning of war memorials

It is a basic principle in Linguistic Landscape research that 'messages in the public space are never neutral, they always display connections to social structure, power and hierarchies' (Blommaert 2013: 40). War memorials send a multimodal message, through imagery as well as text, which can be read in a number of ways, depending on the attitude of the onlooker towards the war being commemorated. There is an assumption in Britain and France that the message is obvious, as these memorials fit into a national narrative which is rarely queried. In the British context, the War Memorials Trust (2017) states that war memorials are important because 'they act as historical touchstones [...] The sacrifices made by so many for freedom needs to be remembered and war memorials play a vital role in ensuring that continues.' Although there are war memorials dating back many centuries, it was only after the First World War that France, like Britain, experienced a vast programme of memorial building. Moreover, it was the first time that such monuments would honour ordinary people and be more about remembrance of loss than celebration of victory. As the War Memorials Trust (n.d.) notes, the sheer numbers of casualties among British troops and the ban on repatriation of the dead meant that every community was affected, and the memorials gave a focus for the grief and loss. A similar wave of monument building occurred in France at the same era, for the same reasons; France had lost 10 per cent of the male population, and the country needed to be convinced that the bloodshed had been worthwhile. According to the French *Ministère des Armées* (2014), the purpose of building memorials was not only to remember those who never came back from the war, but to honour them and, in engraving their names on the monuments, to give them some of the glory due to those who had sacrificed their lives for France. This explanation of war memorials focusing on concepts of 'honour' and 'remembrance' may seem natural and 'common sense' to most people who look at them, yet Aboussnouga and Machin (2013: 29) point out that they have also 'played their part in recontextualising warfare and conflict as a natural and inevitable practice of contemporary societies, concealing actual processes, causes and consequences'. Aboussnouga and Machin (2013) develop the idea that war monuments, through their idealized images, present a particular version of war, focusing minds on the nobility of sacrifice for one's country rather than the waste of human life. They refer to the sociopolitical climate in post-war Britain, and the perceived need to convince the working class that the loss of so many lives had not been in vain. They contend that 'it may be that nationalism, communicated by the wide-scale commissioning of commemorative war monuments, became the mechanism by which the elites attempted to reconcile with the average citizen' (Aboussnouga and Machin 2013: 82).

If the British and French working classes felt betrayed by their governments, which had led them into a war which certainly produced no benefits for them, it could be assumed that the working classes in the colonies felt even more betrayed. The elite classes across France's colonial empire had believed they should support France in this war, in recognition of the benefits of French civilization. In Morocco, the colonial authorities and local elite were complicit in a form of 'ideological coercion' which attracted young men into signing up in the belief that they would be taking part in a 'holy war' (Maghraoui 2004: 10). However, after the colonies had lost thousands of young men to a cause that was not their own, those who survived were not even awarded the pensions and other marks of gratitude that were offered to French veterans. Among the African intellectual elite the concept of the '*dette du sang*' ('blood debt') developed: the idea that France owed citizenship to those Africans who had fought in the trenches (Dewitte 1991). Moreover, the barbaric nature of this war led to disillusionment with French 'civilization' and contributed to the growth of independence movements (Dewitte 1991).

Although France did not reward colonial troops in the way they might have hoped or expected, it did recognize them in war memorials. Aldrich (2005: 108) has suggested that 'commemoration of colonial troops seemed a legitimate expression of gratitude' and was also evidence that those troops were attached to France, being ready to die for the 'national' cause. The following analysis will consider how the use of both French and Arabic on monuments speaks to the power relations between France and Morocco, at the time of the First World War, and in the century that has followed.

Analysis of specific monuments

Landowski's Monument to Victory and Peace or to Franco-Moroccan friendship

At the end of the First World War, Paul Landowski was commissioned by the *Association casablancaise des vétérans* (the Casablanca Veteran Association) to produce a monument, originally known as the 'Monument to Victory and Peace', in honour of Moroccan soldiers who died during the First World War. Landowski was a well-known humanist sculptor, whose work includes numerous sculptures in Paris, across France and around the world. His best-known work is probably the statue of Christ the Redeemer above Rio de Janeiro, Brazil, completed in 1931, but his collaboration on this project came after many years of fame in France. He had seen active service during the First World War and afterwards was commissioned to produce a number of war memorials, in France and in various parts of the French colonial empire, including Morocco.

This statue was originally installed in the *Place centrale* in Casablanca, Morocco, in 1924, having been produced in France in 1921 and transported to Morocco. In 1924, Lyautey had been drawn into the Rif War, supporting the

Spanish against Abd El-Krim's Berber forces in the North of the country, and was anxious to present Franco-Moroccan relations in a good light. This statue thus had a dual role, not only commemorating the Moroccan soldiers who had given their lives for France during the war, but also celebrating the wider collaboration between French and Moroccans. In his speech Lyautey noted that the monument symbolized above all the 'union of the two races' and thus highlighted the idea that the French Protectorate was a collaboration between two friendly countries, rather than a colonial domination (Alexandre and Neiger 2014).

Whatever Moroccans may have thought of the monument in 1924, after Independence in 1956 it was decided that it was no longer appropriate for it to remain in Casablanca. In common with a number of monuments in former colonies, most notably Algeria, it was 'repatriated'; in 1961 it was taken down and in 1965 reinstalled in the town of Senlis in Northern France, former location of Spahi regiments. It was at this point that it was renamed the 'Monument to Franco-Moroccan Friendship', dropping the reference to war and 'pacification'. It now stands in an open space on the edge of this peaceful small town, where the Spahi Museum serves as a further reminder of the historic link with Morocco (see Figure 3.1). It is beyond the scope of this paper to consider the artistic

Figure 3.1 The monument to Franco-Moroccan friendship.

merit of the sculpture, but it is worth noting that it does in fact represent this friendship, as it consists of a Moroccan *spahi* shaking hands with a French cavalryman, both seated on horseback. As Lyautey noted, it thus symbolizes the comradeship between these brothers in arms and could be seen as a fitting image of the relationship between the two countries.

The focus of this chapter is not the images but the wording on the monument. The base carries text in French and in Arabic, celebrating the heroism of the Moroccan troops who fought alongside the French in the First World War, as well as their support for Lyautey's 'pacification' of Morocco (Alexandre and Neiger 2014). What is immediately striking about the text is the lack of parity between the two languages: although the monument is ostensibly for and about the Moroccan soldiers who fought for France, the text is mainly in French, as the following description and analysis will demonstrate.

There is rather a lot of writing on the base, most of it in French, but a small amount in Arabic. Since the monument was commissioned by French 'veterans' primarily for the French community in the Protectorate of Morocco, the use of French is unsurprising. The presence of a small amount of Arabic text could be seen as symbolic, since it was not at that time the language of the administration, and thus symbolizes the fact that the Moroccan soldiers are in fact Arabic speakers (Scollon and Scollon 2003:133). Nevertheless, it is also worth noting that in terms of 'space semiotics' (Scollon and Scollon 2003: 120), the placing of the Arabic code sends a slightly mixed message. Assuming that 'preferred code' is placed top, left and centre, the Arabic text on one side could be taken as the 'preferred code', since it features above the French, but as the 'non-preferred code' on the other side, as it features on the margins, with French text in the centre.

It is easy to find out the details of the French wording, since it is reproduced on various websites, listed at the end of this chapter. What follows here is a summary.

- The **East face** notes the date of the monument being unveiled in Casablanca and its removal to Senlis; it lists the regiments who left Morocco to fight in the First World War.
- The **West face** gives details of action in Belgium, La Marne, L'Artois.
- The **North face** gives details of action in Champagne, Verdun, La Somme.
- The **South face** is perhaps the most interesting, appearing to be a personal message from Foch and Lyautey, as follows (my translation and my italics):

Officers, non-commissioned officers and soldiers, after having resolutely stopped the enemy, you attacked them without respite, with unbounded faith and energy. *You won the greatest battle in History and saved the most sacred cause, the Freedom of the world. Be proud.* You have adorned your flags with immortal glory. May posterity grant you recognition. Maréchal Foch (Figure 3.2).

While in France your brothers in arms were bringing Alsace-Lorraine back to the motherland, you in Morocco not only maintained the hold France had in 1914 *but significantly increased the pacified zone.* You demonstrated endurance, bravery, self-denial and discipline, of which I am the witness and the guarantor. Maréchal Lyautey[3] (Figure 3.3).

These messages make it clear that the monument is a tribute to the men, both French and African, who gave up their lives for the cause of freedom, but who also helped to 'pacify' Morocco, and bring the two countries closer together. The language used is typical of war memorials, focusing on the 'immortal glory' and the 'most sacred cause, the freedom of the world', rather than any reference to the pain and suffering that they or their families have endured. There is also the euphemism of the 'pacified zone', common in colonial discourse: Lyautey in effect thanks those who contributed to completing the French takeover of Morocco,

Figure 3.2 The South Face, with the message from Foch.

Figure 3.3 The South Face, with the message from Lyautey.

while Moroccan soldiers were helping to liberate France. The connections to social structures and power could not be clearer. The French reader can take away the comforting message that French and Moroccans have worked together to bring about peace in both countries. The Moroccan, who cannot read the French, will be excluded from the message completely. The message is already exclusionary, since it celebrates the 'pacification' of Morocco, but the use of French rather than Arabic to convey the message reinforces it.

The Arabic is a very different matter. There are far fewer words in Arabic – just two short inscriptions on the South end and another two on the North, so it is immediately clear that they do not represent a translation of the French wording, and it might be assumed that they represent rather a token towards the Moroccans represented by the statue. In the descriptions in French the Arabic inscriptions are simply noted as *écriture arabe* (Arabic writing) with no attempt to decipher or explain. This may be seen as normal, given that those recording the wording in French are unable to read Arabic, but it is also telling that they have not taken the trouble to find out what the words mean, indicating perhaps a language ideology that sees only French as worthy of inclusion. However, closer inspection reveals that it would be difficult even for a competent Arabic reader to decipher the words.

At the first glance these inscriptions look more like graffiti than official engraving, and when studied closely it is clear that the person who engraved these words could not actually read what he was writing, as the letters are not properly formed. This suggests that a French engraver was simply asked to copy Arabic words written out for him. For example, at one point there are probably two letters together, one of which has one dot below it, the next two. On the monument this looks like one letter with three dots, thus changing the sound and meaning of the word completely. Perhaps it should come as no surprise that in the early 1920s nobody checked that this part of the monument was correctly executed, particularly as the French also has an error and an omission (a place name is misspelled, and one sentence is incomplete, with the names of regiments missing). On the other hand, it could be interpreted as a lack of real concern for the memory of the colonial troops who died fighting for a cause that was not their own. It is therefore difficult to decipher the words, but they appear to read as follows[4]:

- On the **South face**, to the right of the bas-relief (Figure 3.3), the words of the *shahada*, the Muslim declaration of faith, appear across the top (i.e. I testify that there is no God but God and Mohammed is His prophet). This is accessible simply because there are enough recognizable elements to assume safely the whole. The double *l* in the word Allah is not correctly formed; the same is true of the name Mohammed (the *h* is not properly formed and *d* appears as *w*). To the left, it appears to say 'Allah has mercy on [illegible] who are fighting for freedom'.
- On the **North face**, the words appear to spell out two rather cryptic sentences, both using imperatives, perhaps proverbs. Both are difficult to read due to incorrectly formed letters, but are likely to mean something like 'Engrave on stones with gold water' and 'Write on sand things that are not important' (Figure 3.4).

What do these inscriptions tell us about the way these events are recorded and remembered? Clearly it was not a Moroccan decision to go to war in Europe. The *Division marocaine* was only so called because soldiers from already conquered African nations were already in Morocco helping the French to 'pacify' the country. The extensive writing in French demonstrates the importance the French nation attached to honouring its glorious dead. The Arabic wording appears to be something of an afterthought, although its location in relation to the French suggests that its inclusion was planned. However, the fact that

Figure 3.4 Left-hand side of the North Face.

it was not thought necessary to ask an Arabic-speaking engraver to add these inscriptions, and that they do not translate the French, suggests that they are more about appearing to show respect rather than fulfilling a language need.

Although the monument was designed to be on display in Morocco, the inscriptions were clearly not aimed at the local population. The monument was claiming 'victory and peace' not only in Europe, but also in Morocco, and could be seen as a symbol of French victory over Morocco as much as Moroccan involvement in France's war. The Arabic inscriptions might be perceived as a gracious gesture by the French, or simply not noticed. It could be assumed that most French nationals would not look closely at these inscriptions, as they would have no way of knowing what, if anything, the words represent.

The decision to move the monument to France after Independence (in 1956) is indicative of the fact that remembering the First World War is intrinsically linked to remembering the onset of the colonial era. It is understandable that in the immediate aftermath of the colonial era, Morocco would prefer not to have a monument to the sacrifices Moroccans made for the colonizing power. The careless nature of the engraving of Arabic words on the monument means that, had it stayed in Morocco, today's literate population might have been puzzled and angered or possibly amused by it. The disparity between the two languages could be interpreted as evidence not only of French arrogance, but of lack of linguistic competence and cultural insight. The significance of the Arabic text could be viewed quite differently in the new location. It now clearly symbolizes 'Morocco', as it is in a geographical location where French is the unmarked code, and where Arabic would be out of place

The monument is not listed as one of the historic monuments in the Commune of Senlis (communes.com n.d.), presumably since it is not historically related to the town, but does feature in documentation about the First World War, as one of the many war memorials across Northern France. The Arabic wording is never referred to beyond noting that it exists.

Other monuments from this era also carry French and Arabic inscriptions but are very different to the Landowski monument. We will consider some of these, followed by later monuments, and note some interesting differences in some cases.

Monument à la Division marocaine

There is a monument specifically in honour of the *Division marocaine*, inaugurated in 1925, within the Canadian National Memorial Park at Vimy Ridge. It is a small monument, overshadowed by the vast memorial to the victory by Canadian troops in 1917. Although it was the Canadians who took the Ridge from the Germans in 1917, the *Division marocaine* came close to doing so two years earlier and only failed due to lack of reinforcements. This monument is generally overlooked by the many visitors who come to see the Canadian memorial, in the same way that the Moroccan role in the war has been overlooked.

As with the Landowski memorial, the words in French are clear and easily found online on numerous websites, whereas the Arabic is limited to one line, which is quite difficult to read. The French begins with the usual words, and the motto of the Division:

> To the dead
> Of the *Division marocaine*
> Without fear – without pity.[5]

This is followed by a brief description of the events of 9–11 May 1915, when the *Division marocaine* managed, for the first time, to break the enemy line. It is dedicated to the memory of the men, officers and soldiers, who 'fell gloriously' on those three days.

The Arabic simply translates the line 'sans peur –sans pitié', the motto of the *Division*. In terms of code preference (Scollon and Scollon 2003: 120), there is no question that French is the preferred code, as the Arabic text is not only very small, it appears to the right, beneath the title, all in French, in much larger typeface. As with the Landowski monument, it can be assumed that there was a lack of ability when it came to producing text in Arabic, coupled with a lack of interest in doing so. The monument was not created for Moroccan families to mourn their dead, rather for France to acknowledge that colonial troops had been present alongside the French. It is apparent that the Moroccans who 'fell' were not the most important people; only the two colonels are named, and the Arabic words seem to be a token gesture to the fact that among the 'fallen' were Arabic speakers. This public space is primarily for French or English speakers, due to the Canadian memorial, and the Arabic is meaningless to them. As in the case of the Landowski monument, the use of Arabic can be seen to symbolize the Moroccan element.

In addition to these memorials, there are large numbers of Muslim war graves, also with bilingual inscriptions. Although these are not, strictly speaking, war memorials, they are a poignant physical reminder of war deaths and, since they bear bilingual inscriptions, are worth considering in this context.

Muslim war graves – 'lieux de mémoire'

After the war, Muslim graves were brought together in designated areas within national cemeteries, such as the one in Douaumont in Lorraine (NE France). Originally they had wooden headstones, which were replaced in the 1930s by cement stones, engraved with the Islamic star and crescent, and the words approximating to 'this is the grave of the deceased' in Arabic script. Beneath this is a metal plaque where the name, rank and regiment, the words '*mort pour la France*' and the date of death, all feature in French.

Even during the war, efforts were made to respect Muslim burial traditions; as early as December 1914 ministerial guidance was given on how to bury Muslims, and to mark Muslim graves with a headstone turned towards Mecca (Ministère de la Défense, n.d.). This, together with the use of Arabic on the headstones, can certainly be interpreted as a desire to acknowledge and honour Moroccan and other Muslim involvement in the war. This appears to be borne out by evidence that this desire to follow Muslim rites around death and burial precedes the war (Renard 2014). Indeed, as Renard (2014) points out, graves rather than mosques were the first evidence of a Muslim presence in France in the nineteenth century. Maghraoui (2004: 10, 12), however, has noted that the French used Islam and in particular the concept of 'holy war' to recruit Moroccans to the French army during the First World War, suggesting that the French authorities were well aware of the tenets and practices of Islam, and made use of them for less benign purposes.

These war graves also create '*lieux de mémoire*' which can be a place of shared remembrance for French and Moroccans. Although the Arabic wording is minimal, its prominence, together with the shape of the headstones, suggests that the identity of Muslim war dead is being respected. According to Renard (2014), these stelae were modelled on those seen in Algeria, and the authenticity of the writing and decoration owed a great deal to a certain Etienne Dinet, an artist who had converted to Islam. It would appear from this that the French authorities took seriously the need to use the correct language when it came to individual graves, in a way that it seemed not to do for the far more public war monuments.

In more recent times, monuments to commemorate Moroccan or other Muslim participation in the First World War have been produced. These monuments were produced long after the end of the colonial era, and very much as an act of public acknowledgement of the debt France owed to her former colonies. The following sections analyse how this is reflected in terms of the use of French and Arabic.

Douaumont, Lorraine

In June 2006, to mark the 90th anniversary of the battle of Verdun, a monument in honour of Muslim soldiers was unveiled in Douaumont in Lorraine (NE France). The then-President Jacques Chirac unveiled the monument, a Moorish-style building, some seventy years after memorials had been built for Christian and Jewish soldiers, proclaiming that the battle of Verdun represented France, 'in all its diversity'. The design of the building is significant from a geosemiotic perspective, as it symbolizes the Muslim world in general and the Maghreb in particular for the French gaze.

Chirac named two Senegalese soldiers who had demonstrated exceptional bravery and noted that 70,000 men from the former French Empire died for France in the course of the war, before going on to claim that all those who died at Verdun were motivated not by nationalism or hatred of the enemy, but by love of their country and republican values (Présidence de la République 2006). While this last point may be debatable, the general idea that Muslim soldiers died alongside French soldiers for noble ideals is very much in line with the sentiments expressed on the Landowski monument. The reason for the memorial was to end the injustice of having no Muslim memorial worthy of the name. Ninety years after the battle, France was anxious to acknowledge publicly the sacrifice that so many North Africans made, and to honour the Muslim dead in the same way as the Christian and Jewish dead. For this reason the memorial was fully funded by the state. This illustrates perfectly Aldrich's observation (2005: 2): 'In the celebration, commemoration and "instrumentalisation" of history, different regimes and groups espouse varying versions of that past, and they embody their versions in monuments.' The unveiling of this monument came at a time when the French government was acknowledging that war pensions for these soldiers had been shamefully out of line with those of French veterans and was rectifying the historical injustice. At the same time a far wider audience was being made aware of the North African involvement in the Second World War as a result of Rachid Bouchareb's film *Indigènes* (Days of Glory), starring Moroccan actor Jamel Debbouze. The president of the French Council of Muslims and rector of the Paris Mosque, Dalil Boubakeur, stated that it was here, on the battle fields of the First World War, that French Islam was born. He suggested that it is important, at a time when young French people are wondering about their identity, that they should know that their ancestors took part in defending the country (L'Obs 2006).

Although the memorial is built on a big scale, the actual monument is very simple, and bears only a few words, just one sentence in each language, first in Arabic, then in French. The fact that the Arabic text features above the French, and the letters appear to be bigger, would suggest that Arabic is the preferred code. However, in geosemiotic terms, the Arabic text can still be seen as symbolizing the Muslim soldiers, since the location of the monument, in France, makes French the default language of the monument. Furthermore, the two sentences are not identical. The French translates as 'To the Muslim soldiers who died for France', while the Arabic wording is identical to that found on the war graves, and translates roughly as 'This is the grave of the deceased [one person]'. Moreover, while the Arabic writing is not as incoherent as that on the Landowski monument, it still looks as if it was produced by someone who was not very competent at writing in Arabic. They look very much as if they have been copied by someone who did not understand them. In this case it may be that the wording was simply copied from the war graves. This disparity between the two languages seems to suggest that even though the French government was making a very public statement of recognition towards those Muslim soldiers, they nonetheless did not feel it necessary to ensure that the Arabic lettering was produced accurately or that it actually had the same or similar meaning to the French. The paternalistic attitudes of the 1920s are no longer expressed in France but the lack of interest in the language (and therefore culture) of the Muslims who died for France appears to be unchanged. The message appears to be one of gratitude and respect, but for anyone who can read the Arabic words, it is a rather odd message.

Grande Mosquée de Paris

The Verdun monument was followed four years later by a plaque in the Grande Mosquée de Paris. It was inaugurated on Armistice Day (11th November) 2010, in honour of Muslim soldiers who died for France in the two world wars. The rector of the Mosque, Dalil Boubakeur, who had expressed his belief in the importance of this act of remembering at Verdun in 2006, claimed that this plaque represented the final stone in the building of the Mosque (Gruot 1994). Unlike the other memorials under consideration, this is not really public, as it is inside a mosque, and therefore the question of who it is addressed to, and who is included or excluded by the language, is rather different. In fact the memorial consists of two plaques, one in French and one in Arabic. The words in French read simply 'To the Muslim soldiers who died for France', followed by the dates of the two world wars, and the Arabic plaque contains exactly the same words. Given its location, inside a mosque, it is only to be expected that the Arabic wording would be perfectly produced, to at least the same high standard as the French, since Arabic is the holy language of Islam, and those who enter the mosque are likely to be able to read it. In this case, it would be the non-Arabic speaker who would be excluded, being unable to ascertain whether or not the Arabic corresponds to the French. The wording is short and simple, with no reference to glory or victory, just an acknowledgement of the ultimate sacrifice paid by Muslims for France. The total parity here makes it impossible to say that one language is the 'preferred code', particularly given the fact that French works from left to right, and Arabic from right to left, so the conventions on right and left could be seen as redundant.

The Mosque was opened in 1926, so it is interesting that it was only in 2010 that this memorial was created. As with the Douaumont memorial, it could be said that a new generation sees the past differently; while earlier generations of Muslims in France might have preferred to forget the involvement of colonial troops in the First World War, current generations may feel it is important that their ancestors died for France. Thus, the use of the two languages is symbolic of the fact that they are French Muslims, for whom French is the language of their everyday lives, while Arabic is the language of their religion and their ancestors, who died for France.

Place Denys Cochin – A Moroccan monument in Paris

The final and most recent monument under consideration is rather different to the others in another way. It owes its existence not to the French State, but to the *Association La Koumia*, a voluntary organization which exists to commemorate the *goumiers marocains* before, during and after the First World War. In fact this association has been responsible for a number of other monuments honouring the *goumiers* in Morocco and in France, but this appears to be the only one with French and Arabic inscriptions (Association La Koumia, n.d.). This monument was unveiled on 13 October 2015 in the Place Denys Cochin, near the *Hôtel national des Invalides* in Paris.[6] It commemorates the Moroccans who took part in the Second World War, and also the 1939 call of the then Sultan of Morocco, Mohammed V, to support France in the war. The monument is very visibly Moroccan, using shapes and images which are easily recognizable as symbols of Morocco. The monument is shaped like doors in traditional Moroccan buildings, while the background images relate to the Association La Koumia, most notably the traditional Moroccan dagger, known as a *koumia*, which bears the letters GMM, for *goums mixtes marocains*, the name of the regiments formed in Morocco from the earliest days of the French Protectorate (Association La Koumia, n.d.). Thus, the monument can be read as symbolizing Morocco before even looking at the text (see Figure 3.5).

This monument carries quite a large amount of text, first in French, then in Arabic. Where it differs significantly from all the others under consideration is in the quantity of Arabic, roughly equal to the quantity of French. At each point on the memorial there is French text followed by Arabic text. The headline reads 'To the glory of the *goums mixtes marocains*'. This is followed by an expanded version: 'To the glory of the *goums mixtes marocains*, created at the instigation of Maréchal Lyautey' and then goes on to pay tribute to all those who were killed in action. It notes the epic scale of their bravery and sacrifices in Morocco, France, and in the Far East, and then lists the scenes of their days of glory: Morocco, Tunisia, Sicily, Corsica, Italy, France, Germany, Indochina and AFN (*Afrique Française du Nord* – French North Africa). Finally it notes '*Zidou l'gouddam*: forward, was their motto'.

Figure 3.5 The monument to the glory of the Mixed Moroccan Goumiers.

Lower down, and in smaller print, is a section detailing the date of the unveiling and those who were present, again first in French then in Arabic.

This monument is the only one to give Arabic the same weighting as French and can therefore be perceived as being fully inclusive, as accessible to Arabic speakers as to French speakers. Nevertheless, the words themselves perpetuate the ideas expressed on earlier monuments, expressing gratitude to Moroccans who sacrificed themselves so that France could be free. It also refers to the fact that they fought under *'chefs prestigieux'* – the French officers. It is worth noting that although La Koumia exists to commemorate the Moroccan troops, their base is in Boulogne-Billancourt, in the suburbs of Paris, and the names that appear on the website are all French, suggesting that it is French veterans, rather than Moroccans, who oversee the commemoration.

Remembering in France and in Morocco

This brings us to consider how the war dead are remembered, in France and in Morocco. In France there are significant archives documenting the contribution of Morocco to the First World War (ECPAD n.d.), not only in terms of the bravery and loyalty of the combatants, but also in the way that Moroccan resources contributed to the war effort. As the analysis of monuments has suggested, the French may not always have acknowledged Moroccan and other colonial participation in the war effort as fully as it might have done. Nevertheless, a brief online search reveals countless references on French websites and publications. The renewed interest may in part be due to the general renewed interest in the First World War over the past four years, but is also part of a wider revisiting of France's colonial past. Aldrich (2005: 19) suggests that for several decades during and after the painful period of decolonization, France wanted to hide and forget its colonial past. Now that that era is in the distant past, the memories can be recalled, to be viewed in a new, critical light. The unveiling of the monument in Douaumont is a clear example of this, as is the unveiling of plaques in the *Grande mosquée*. Both represent a recognition that men from North Africa fought and died for a country they had no reason to love, but which has become home to their descendants. The use of Arabic is purely symbolic in the former, and essential in the latter, highlighting that those men were Muslims, for whom Arabic is a sacred language, even for those who cannot read it.

On the Moroccan side, however, it appears to be the case that these veterans are largely forgotten. There is an excellent online resource, created between 2002 and 2006 by a team at the Lycée Lyautey in Casablanca (Touron and Riera n.d.). It is based on two projects, entitled « Le souvenir des deux guerres mondiales au Maroc » and « 1914–1918/1939–1945 – Récits et images de guerre – Mémoire partagée ». The two teachers leading the projects also co-authored a book, *Ana! Frères d'armes marocains dans les deux guerres mondiales*. A new and bigger edition of the book was launched in 2014, to celebrate the 100th commemoration of the outbreak of war (AEFE 2014). Although Moroccan officials were present at the relaunch of the book, it was two French nationals who led the project and wrote the book. As with the Association La Koumia, it appears to be the French rather than the Moroccans who are keen to keep alive the memories of Moroccan involvement in the wars.

A shared history?

This chapter of history was initiated by the French and its memory is kept alive by the French. As mentioned above, it is only in recent years that the French have shown a greater willingness to remember explicitly the participation of Moroccans and others in the two world wars. The references to shared experiences are perhaps perceived as more necessary and meaningful in an age when a significant part of the population in metropolitan France is of North African origin. The fact that the population has changed, and that wider sensibilities and attitudes have changed, means that monuments may now be seen in a different way. The use of Arabic may be purely symbolic, and in some cases quite unreadable, but there appears to be a desire to include Moroccans in the collective memory, or at least to be seen to do so.

In Morocco, on the other hand, '*patrimoine national*' (national heritage) on the whole fails to acknowledge the French era of its history. In a list of '*Monuments, sites et zones classés "patrimoine national"*' there are twenty-one listings for Rabat-Salé, but only one of these dates from the era of the French Protectorate: the *Cinéma Royal*. Most towns have no French buildings or monuments listed, apart from Tangier, where a number of hotels are listed. This may simply reflect a general lack of interest in historical buildings; while French colonial buildings in Morocco are generally rather run-down and not looked after, the same could be said of some heritage sites dating from antiquity, such as Chellah in Rabat, or Volubilis, near Meknes. While France is struggling to come to terms with a more diverse population, and to find ways of including everyone in the national narrative, Morocco is dealing with a young and growing population, subject to a wider range of influences than ever before, and is looking forward not back. In the 1920s fewer Moroccans were literate, so the use of Arabic was very much a gesture. In more recent times, most literate Moroccans are also literate in French, and therefore the Arabic is still in a sense a gesture. Literacy in French is of course a direct result of the Protectorate and that period of shared history, in which Morocco and France were unequal partners.

Notes

1 The colour of the Légion d'honneur, indicating six to eight citations (Ministère des Armées 2016).
2 Historically, the Spahi had been a cavalry regiment in the French army, drawn from the populations of France's North African territories.
3 Officiers, sous-officiers et soldats, après avoir résolument arrêté l'ennemi, vous l'avez, pendant des mois, avec une foi et une énergie inlassable, attaqué sans répit. *Vous avez gagné la plus grande bataille de l'Histoire et sauvé la cause la plus sacrée: la Liberté du monde. Soyez fiers.* D'une gloire immortelle, vous avez paré vos drapeaux. La postérité vous garde sa reconnaissance, 12 novembre 1918, GQGA M^{al} Foch. Alors qu'en France, vos compagnons d'armes rendaient l'Alsace-Lorraine à la patrie, vous lui avez, au Maroc, non seulement gardé la situation acquise en 1914 *mais vous y avez largement étendu la zone pacifiée.* Vous avez fait preuve d'une endurance, d'une vaillance, d'une abnégation et d'un esprit de discipline dont je suis le témoin et le garant. M^{al} Lyautey.
4 I am deeply indebted to Zitouni Ould-Dada, for having read and deciphered this and all other Arabic texts under consideration in this chapter.
5 AUX MORTS
   DE LA DIVISION MAROCAINE
   SANS PEUR – SANS PITIÉ
6 This building, whose dome is one of the most recognized in the Paris skyline, was originally a military hospital, built in the seventeenth century to house the veterans of Louis XIV's wars.

References

Aboussnouga, G. and D. Machin (2013), *The Language of War Monuments*, London: Bloomsbury.

AEFE (2014), 'Réédition de l'ouvrage du lycée Lyautey de Casablanca «Ana ! Frères d'armes marocains dans les deux guerres mondiales »'. Available online: http://www.aefe.fr/vie-du-reseau/toute-lactualite/reedition-de-louvrage-du-lycee-lyautey-de-casablanca-ana-freres-darmes-marocains-dans-les-deux (accessed 7 December 2018).

Aldrich, R. (2005), *Vestiges of the Colonial Empire in France: Monuments, Museums, and Colonial Memories*, Basingstoke: Palgrave Macmillan.

Alexandre, N. and E. Neiger (2014), 'Le Monument à la Victoire et à la Paix de Paul Landowski. Une découverte récente à Casablanca'. Available online: https://lakoumia.fr/monuments-et-lieux-de-memoire (accessed 7 December 2018).

Blommaert, J. (2013), *Ethnography, Superdiversity and Linguistic Landscapes. Chronicles of Complexity*, Bristol: Multilingual Matters.

Communes.com (n.d.), 'Les Monuments Historiques de la Ville de Senlis (60300)'. Available online: http://www.communes.com/picardie/oise/senlis_60300/monuments.html (accessed 7 December 2018).

Dewitte Ph. (1991), 'La dette du sang', *Hommes et Migrations*, 1148: 8–11.

ECPAD (n.d.), 'Le Maroc et la première guerre mondiale dans les collections de l'ECPAD'. Available online: http://centenaire.org/sites/default/files/references-files/maroc.pdf (accessed 7 December 2018).

Ganiage, J. (1994), *Histoire contemporaine du Maghreb de 1830 à nos jours*, Paris: Fayard.

Gruot, B. (1994), 'Une plaque en hommage aux soldats musulmans morts pour la France inaugurée à la Grande Mosquée de Paris, Ministère de la Défense'. Available online: https://www.defense.gouv.fr/english/actualites/articles/une-plaque-en-hommage-aux-soldats-musulmans-morts-pour-la-france-inauguree-a-la-grande-mosquee-de-paris (accessed 7 December 2018).

L'Obs (2006), 'Chirac inaugure un mémorial musulman'. Available online: https://www.nouvelobs.com/societe/20060625.OBS3012/chirac-inaugure-un-memorial-musulman.html (accessed 7 December 2018).

Maghraoui, D. (2004), 'The 'grande guerre sainte': Moroccan Colonial Troops and Workers in The First World War', *Journal of North African Studies*, 9 (1): 1–21.

Ministère des Armées (2014), 'Les monuments aux morts'. Available online: https://www.defense.gouv.fr/memoire/memoire/sepultures-et-monuments-aux-morts/les-monuments-aux-morts (accessed 7 December 2018).

Ministère des Armées (2016), 'La fourragère à l'honneur'. Available online: http://www.defense.gouv.fr/terre/actu-terre/la-fourragere-a-l-honneur (accessed 7 December 2018).

Ministère de la Défense (n.d.), 'Chemins de mémoire, Les soldats nord-africains. 1914–18. Monuments et sépultures'. Available online: http://www.cheminsdememoire.gouv.fr/fr/les-soldats-nord-africains-1914-1918 (accessed 7 December 2018).

Présidence de la République (2006), 'Allocution de M. Jacques CHIRAC, Président de la République, à l'occasion du 90ème anniversaire de la bataille de Verdun'. Available online: http://www.jacqueschirac-asso.fr/archives-elysee.fr/elysee/elysee.fr/francais/interventions/discours_et_declarations/2006/juin/fi000721.html (accessed 7 December 2018).

Renard, Michel (2014), 'L'armée française et la religion musulmane durant la Grande Guerre (1914–1920)'. Available online: http://etudescoloniales.canalblog.com/archives/2014/08/23/30279901.html (accessed 7 December 2018).

Scollon, R. and S.W. Scollon (2003), *Discourses in Place: Language in the Material World*, London: Routledge, Taylor & Francis.

Touron, C. and J.-P. Riera (n.d.), 'Le site du souvenir des deux guerres mondiales au Maroc'. Available online: http://lyceelya.cluster006.ovh.net/marocomb/index.php?lng=fr (accessed 13 March 2018).

Trouillard, S. (2015), 'Grande Guerre : la Division marocaine qui n'avait de marocaine que le nom, France 24'. Available online: http://www.france24.com/fr/20150509-premiere-guerre-mondiale-division-marocaine-vimy-crete-tirailleurs-algeriens-tunisiens-legions-etrangeres-artois (accessed 7 December 2018).

War Memorials Trust (n.d.), 'History of War Memorials'. Available online: http://www.learnaboutwarmemorials.org/uploads/publications/105.pdf (accessed 7 December 2018).

War Memorials Trust (2017), 'Why Are War Memorials Important?' Available online: http://www.warmemorials.org/uploads/publications/64.pdf (accessed 7 December 2018).

Part Two

Museums

4

Multilingual Memories: Artefactual Materiality of Erasure and Downscaling in Linguistic and Semiotic Landscapes of Livingstone Town, Zambia

Hambaba Jimaima and Felix Banda

Introduction

In discussing multilingual memories, this chapter focuses on two Zambian sites which embody history and multilingual memory: the Livingstone Museum and the Victoria Falls area. Both these sites are situated in Livingstone district, a tourist capital of Zambia. As will become apparent in the discussion which follows, the Livingstone Museum is named after the Scottish missionary, David Livingstone. The Victoria Falls is one of the Seven Wonders of the World, and first sighted, from the Eurocentric perspective, by Livingstone in 1855, who named it after Queen Victoria of England.

The Victoria Falls sits right between the Zambia-Zimbabwe border, each claiming their side as the vastest and providing the best view. In a sense, both countries draw for their foreign exchange earnings from the proceeds of tourism which these spaces afford. The co-ownership of the Victoria Falls by Zambia and Zimbabwe later led to the co-hosting of the United Nations World Tourism Conference in 2013. This explains in part how the space is communally owned and yet a special natural heritage to the two states. However, this notwithstanding, each country appropriates its own historical and sociocultural narratives to these commonly held spaces just as each country attracts its own tourists. The chapter focuses on the falls from the Zambian side.

It is important to underscore the fact that the geopolitical and historical significance of what would become known as the Victoria Falls predates the arrival of David Livingstone. The locals speaking related and not-so-related languages – the majority of whom are the modern-day Toka-Leya (Tonga) – claim that they are the indigenous ethnic group to have had uninterrupted interaction with the falls until the colonial epoch which would extend from the tail-end of the nineteenth century to the turn of the twentieth century. As Muwati (2015: 28) reports concerning the Tonga of Zimbabwe that are separated from their fellow Tonga of Zambia by the Zambezi river, the falls were familiar places of play and festivity to the indigenous Tonga people. He further evinces the apparent 'utilitarian relationship between the Tonga and their natural ecology' in which the river provided them with means of survival while they, in turn, revered the river as the embodiment of the deity (Muwati 2015: 29). All this would later be disrupted at the dawn of colonialism and would lead to relocation of the indigenous communities from these pristine spaces of ancestral history and heritage (Muwati 2015: 28). The view that 'relocation … engenders conceptual erasure' (Muwati 2015: 28) extends to our theorization which holds that 'selective remembering' accentuates the erasure of collective historicity by which a community should be identified. For, as Schacter (2001: 5) contends, 'The sin of bias reflects the powerful influences of our current knowledge and beliefs on how we remember our past. We often edit or entirely rewrite our previous experiences – unknowingly and unconsciously – in light of what we now know or believe.' Therefore, the disruptive nature of colonialism, undergirded by the exploration work of David Livingstone, forces us to interrogate the extent to which these environs of memorization, history and commemoration have maintained their multilingual historicity. The realization that since the arrival of David Livingstone at what would become Zambia gave rise to two plausible histories and narratives – local and global – further necessitates an examination of how the criss-crossing histories of the local and the global actors are (re-)narrated, (re-)produced and consumed in the broader context of multilingual memory.

Against this background, we set out to show how the linguistic labels together with the extended taxonomy of artefactual materialities in and around the Livingstone Museum and the precincts of the Victoria Falls are used to offer narratives about the histories and memories of both the local and the global actors. Using the notion of material culture of multilingualism as advanced by Aronin and Ó Laoire (2012), we explore the LL/semiotic landscapes and cultural artefacts emplaced in the two sites so often understood as places of historical and memorial narratives and objective voices of the local pre- and post-history. Taking every artefact in place as semiotic – that is meaning-making material – we assess the degree of representation of the criss-crossing histories of the local and the global. In this connection, we underpin the exclusionary nature of the accentuated and often magnified global materiality over the sparingly represented local material culture of multilingualism and multiculturalism in these sites of history and memory. We take as objects of study and analysis the sculptures of David Livingstone, as well as personal effects (coat, umbrella) and weaponry placed in Livingstone Museum as the epitome of globality. In similar breath, the dwarfed and normally obscure murals and drawings of African hunters, together with the natural materialities, have been understood as typifying localness. The emphasis on English over what are often called local languages further heightens the degree and extent of the erasure and the assumed fixity and stability of the local histories, as well as the diminishing linguistic capital of the local languages. Seen from this perspective, the chapter problematizes the multilingual and historical trajectory of the Livingstone Museum and the Victoria Falls during the pre- and post-contact phenomenon of the local and global histories. In what follows, the LL and the material culture of multilingualism are presented.

Linguistic/semiotic landscapes and the material culture of multilingualism and multiculturalism

In contextualizing our undertaking in the broader context of linguistic/semiotic landscapes, we turn to Stroud and Mpendukana's (2009) material ethnography for the very reason that their work avails much in foregrounding agency and voice. This is predicated on the fact that material ethnography overcomes many shortcomings witnessed in quantitative approaches of the earlier LL conceptualization. For, in these earlier works (e.g. Landry and Bourhis 1997, Backhaus 2006, 2007), the written language in public space was the focus of study and analysis. The focus on language on the signage indirectly minimized the potential of the voices and narratives embedded in the artefactual materialities (Banda and Jimaima 2015). The insistence on counting languages in order to account for multilingualism meant that a great many voices instantiated by unscripted material culture in place were muted. As Banda and Jimaima (2017) point out, in many parts of Africa, languages thrive through word of mouth even though they are not on scripted signage or have an official orthography. Apparently, despite the call to 'expand the scenery' as epitomized in Ben-Rafael et al. (2009), the expansion of linguistic/semiotic landscapes studies seems to have been skewed towards qualitative methods. Banda and Jimaima (2015) call for extending the taxonomy of signage amenable to study for meaning-making to include those used in Africa and elsewhere, such as mounds, trees and other non-human-made signs. Stroud and Mpendukana's (2009) conceptualization of material ethnography, as well as Blommaert and Haung's (2010) discussion of material ethnography, heralded an important turn in redirecting research towards the material condition in a qualitatively driven project, despite relying on the conventional, written signage. However, Banda and Jimaima (2015) in what they call oral linguascaping go further to suggest that in rural (and even urban) areas of Africa people rely on the spoken language and not the written language for sign-making and consumption.

Stroud and Mpendukana (2009) remind us that sites rely on their materiality to co-construct their LL and that the narratives borne by some of the signs have long-established trajectories as they are merely revoiced through the processes of resemiotization and intertextuality. As a result of the overarching economic imbalances observable on the landscape of Khayelitsha, a township 28 km southeast of the central business district of Cape Town, a dichotomy is visualized, namely, sites of luxury and sites of necessity (Stroud and Mpendukana 2009). In framing their material ethnography, Stroud and Mpendukana (2009: 364–365) argue for a sociolinguistics of multilingualism in which space is constructed as 'flows, processes and social practices', thereby showing 'how constructs of space are constrained by material conditions of production, and informed by associated phenomenological sensibilities of mobility and gaze'. By conceding that the construction of space is subject to the material conditions, Stroud and Mpendukana (2009) forge a material ethnography which has the potential of articulating multiple stories occasioned by the constraints of the material condition of a given place. This explains why they conclude that Khayelitsha is a delineated space with two sites: site of luxury and site of necessity. This is consistent with their view that a material ethnography should be seen as the 'social circulation of linguistic forms across commercial signage for ongoing processes of *enregisterment*, the process whereby speech practices become consolidated as repertoires of socially recognized register of forms' (2009: 364). Given their focus, there is little attempt to include as part of their object of study the material culture of multilingualism and multiculturalism. The materiality they bring to the fore is restricted to those with the written language, predicated on Scollon and Scollon's (2003) notion of emplacement, especially inscription.

We believe that the use of the notion 'material ethnography' should presuppose something beyond the conventional graphemes and emplaced billboards, warning signs, traffic signs and other signs which are analysed in these works. For Blommaert and Haung (2010), they take London's Chinatown and the warning sign written in Chinese as their point of departure to discursively produce a qualitative account for place- and meaning-making. In particular, their study makes a significant contribution to the overall framing of a material ethnography as it foregrounds the subjective narration of space. Their study helps to bring into the spotlight the consumer for whom certain signs are emplaced and the specific story they are deployed in these specific spaces to narrate. In this regard, as Banda et al. (2018) suggest the need to go beyond the written text so that the oral narration rather the written language becomes as significant as an object of study.

As a result of the limited use of this robust and potentially productive notion of material ethnography in earlier works, we turn to Aronin and Ó Laoire's (2012) notion of material culture of multilingualism. In their theorization, Aronin and Ó Laoire exploit the full potential of material ethnography by turning to the material culture of multilingualism in which objects, artefacts and things with which people interact are seen to possess unparalleled narratives and meaning. In essence, the mundane and everyday life objects such as portraits, souvenirs on store shelves, food and clothes can all be active voices in the LL. Framed following this theorization, Banda and Jimaima (2015) observe how the interplay between social actors and ecological features such as abandoned structures, skylines, trees, rivers and unscripted signs extend the taxonomy of the signs in the LL which is orally dominated. They argue that rather than seeing the material condition of the rural communities of Zambia as restricting the production and consumption of the LL, as well as the meaning potential of the signs, including the ones which are not scripted, the material condition in these spaces leads to unlimited creativity in which actors reinvent and extend the meaning potential of any available materiality when engaged in any exchange. This is primarily so because, as Kress (2010) reminds us, signs arise from the environment in which they are used by the social actors who share knowledge of the sociocultural history. Seen from this perspective, the material culture ascribed to by a community is readily consumable by that culture without any constraint. This is why Pennycook (2009) concedes that people are makers and consumers of the LL. Thus, as argued by Banda and Jimaima (2015), LL should not exclude trees, mounds and environmental conditions, and the oral language, which social actors deploy to make their extended meanings alive.

Therefore, there is no end to what would constitute signage in LL studies especially in the broader context of a material ethnography and material culture of multilingualism. For example, Waksman and Shohamy (2010) add as LL items poems, historical anecdotes, old photographs and drawings to underpin the connection between the city of Tel Aviv-Jaffa and the Zionist ideology, as well as history. Waksman and Shohamy's (2010) work brings into the spotlight an 'associative line' between the artefacts of the past and the present LL environment in which memorization and commemoration are acted out. The use of historical photographs and drawings can be read alongside Connerton's (1989) theorization in '*How Societies Remember*' in which he foregrounds the dialectics of forgetting and remembering in forging a present social order. He alludes to two aspects of memory: social memory and commemorative memory. In both kinds of memory, he shows how the past social order is foisted on the present social order. Invariably, collective memory continues to be undergirded by a shared historical memory – one arising from the social memory. This chapter places a high premium on the ideas of Connerton (1989) in as far as multilingual memory is concerned, especially in sites designed as places of memorization, remembrance and history. He asserts:

> Our experience of the present very largely depends upon our knowledge of the past. We experience our present world in a context which is causally connected with past events and objects, and hence with reference to events and objects which we are not experiencing when we are experiencing the present … because past factors tend to influence, or distort, our experience of the present. (Connerton 1989: 2)

The contribution which Connerton (1989) makes to the discussion framed in this chapter relates to how the past persistently superimposes its frames and memory on the present events and imaginings. Furthermore, Connerton's mention of distortions of the present as a result of the past events and objects that come to bear on the present implicates the extent to which spaces of historical significance can faithfully narrate their history and memory when the past and present histories collide. For he avers that 'our images of the past commonly serve to legitimate a present social order' (Connerton 1989: 3). This assumption is theoretically informative and insightful in discussing the multilingual imaginings of the postcolonial Zambia in and around the Livingstone museum and the Victoria Falls area. As discussed below, the semiotic ecology captured in these two sites orients towards historical figures and artefactual materialities of foreignness. The superimposition of such historical material onto the present historical narratives has been largely informed by Connerton's view.

By applying the semiotic ecology to the general theorization of semiotic/linguistic landscapes, Banda and Jimaima (2015) not only propose an extended taxonomy of signs amenable to use for meaning-making, but they also attempt to read into these signs (trees, mounds, rivers, skylines) pliable meanings which different consumers assign to them at different times during the production and consumption of the LL. The pliability of the semiotic ecology is largely co-articulated by resemiotization and oral remediation partly due to the fact that these ecological features, as opposed to conventional signs, do not have written languages on them. However, in Africa and many parts of the global south, scripted signs are often in English, Portuguese, French, and other former colonial languages, which local people do not understand let alone read. Thus, social actors consume them from an oral perspective as points of reference as they traverse the landscape (e.g. you'll see a big tree to your left just before the stream, Banda and Jimaima 2015: 652, 654). The potential of unscripted signs in meaning-making is also apparent. For there is no end point to the use to which these signs can be put – as meeting points, reference points, boundary markers or adverts – turning sign/place-making into a creative and productive endeavour both for locals and for newcomers to these spaces.

Admittedly, the unregulated physical activities by social actors and effects of gentrification on the environment mean that the act of meaning-making in these environs is perpetually evolving and reinvented. Banda and Jimaima (2015) report that in an event where a tree which was once used as a reference point is cut, locals still reinvent new ways of referring to the sign such as the 'stump'; and others deploy memory (i.e. where there used to be a big tree). Thus, the material condition, rather than inhibiting the process of meaning-making, enhances it. It magnifies the creative ways in which the locals extend the taxonomy of signs as well as subjecting the old, displaced or removed to a process of metamorphosis in which case the signs pick up new ways of definition and configuration. The idea that signs or material culture live on despite some changes that may occur in their life time is well accounted for in visual history and generally in visual studies. Appadurai (1996) records how things/objects change roles. He argues that objects slip in and out of different forms, shapes and roles. This ability entails that signs – material culture including artefactual materiality – have a life independent of their makers (cf. Mitchell 2005). This implies that artefacts would have their own narratives, occasioned by their own voice and positioning. The analysis section below dwells much on this thought and builds its argument on the anthropomorphic power of agency willed to objects/artefacts once emplaced. In what follows, we contextualize the study area and the methodology.

Methodology and contextualization

Typically known for their historical significance, and therefore memory and remembrance, the Livingstone Museum and the Victoria Falls area (situated in Livingstone town, which is a district in the southern province of Zambia) continue to attract both local and international tourists. The Livingstone Museum is the oldest museum in Zambia and was originally established as Livingstone Memorial Museum in 1934, after the Scottish missionary and explorer David Livingstone. It is important to note also that the Livingstone Museum is a national museum. The iconic nature of David Livingstone has left indelible imprints in the museum to the effect that there is a gallery exclusively dedicated to him in the museum called 'The David Livingstone Gallery', while outside the museum is his towering statue. Thus, his historicity can be felt from afar, even before one reaches these precincts. Other galleries in the Livingstone Museum include Natural History and Ethnography. These are equally important in as far as the local-global narratives are concerned. The outside of the museum is just as important as the inside as can be seen from Figure 4.1. For the presence of the Livingstone statue outside of the museum pre-empts the dominant narratives

Figure 4.1 The statue of Livingstone outside of Livingstone Museum.

and histories of the place. It holds memories and histories akin to the local, as well as the global.

The historical evolution through which the Livingstone Museum passed further accentuates the nature of the history associated with the museum as well as its actorhood. Consequently, this historical evolution has to a larger extent shaped the history which a twenty-first-century visitor to the museum would unconditionally read off the emplaced artefactual materialities. We note that without uncovering the motive behind the construction of these spaces of history and memory, it would be counterproductive to engage in uncovering the meanings, narratives and voices embedded in the cultural materialities. Thus, as Mufuzi (2011: 28) suggests, the historicity of the Livingstone Museum understood in the light of colonial hegemony and the desire to justify colonial rule offers the best explanation for the unbalanced display of the materiality in the museum. We build on this argument as we attempt to underpin the entrapment of Zambian history in coloniality as displayed in the Livingstone Museum. The shift in onomastics – from David Livingstone Memorial Museum to Rhodes-Livingstone Museum and finally to Livingstone Museum in 1966 – pre-empts the ideological manipulation, transformation and erasure, a theme we pick up in the analysis section below.

Named after Queen Victoria of England and from the European perspective first sighted by David Livingstone, the Victoria Falls is a natural wonder attracting thousands of tourists each year. Within its precincts are memorial sites, statues, souvenir shops and offices. These offer narratives which cannot be ignored. The local population, years before European exploration brought David Livingstone in 1855 to the shores of Zambezi River and to the hinterland of what would later be known as Zambia, had not only sighted the falls but had named it as Mosi-oa-tunya, 'the smoke that thunders' in Kololo, a language that would later give rise to the Lozi lingua franca after its enmeshment with the local Lui language around 1830. Arguably, the geographic as well as the topographical nature of the falls did not only resonate with the locals' desire for expression of worship but it would later be a centre of attraction for Western civilization beyond the colonial era, thanks to nineteenth-century European exploration. Provisionally, therefore, the Victoria Falls holds two important historical narratives: one skewed towards the local metaphysical world and the other skewed towards the European heritage of conquest and exploration. We will return to this in the analysis section.

Liu and Mwanza (2014) report that over 6,000 tourists visit the Victoria Falls every month on average. These statistics make a commentary not only on the beauty of the scenery but also on the sociocultural as well as the political-economic significance of the falls to the Zambian government and its people. In turn, the presence of the tourists in these precincts engenders this place with the sense of foreignness. Granted, as we shall later show, the presence of tourists overlays the place with sensibilities transcending locality and globality – a creation of glocal narratives that do not necessarily represent either the local or the global semiotic stalk but enmeshed historical and sociocultural trajectories. These narratives are embedded in statues, souvenir, signs, billboards, street signs and names of trees, which occupy the public spaces. It is these materialities which were collected as data in an ethnographic-driven methodology described below.

Thus, using photography, the material culture displayed in these two sites was collected and much insight into the meaning of the material culture was gained through interviews and observation. This explorative ethnography leaned on interpretive epistemology with the view that the objective truth lies not in the given collective and universal view of reality but in the constant subjective questioning and interpretation of the reality as it unfolds (cf. Mafofo and Banda 2014; Denzin 2010). The digital images of artefactual materialities were examined in order to listen to their stories as embedded in the materiality out of which they are sculptured, painted and drawn, as well as the manner of their positioning against the other emplaced artefacts. This interpretation benefited from observation during the ethnographic tour of the precincts. Interviews with curators, directors and consumers deepened the appreciation of the narratives and voice each of the artefacts provided. In total, eleven unstructured interviews were held. The interviews were conducted in English and in some cases Tonga, Nyanja and Bemba. We took 265 digital images of the material culture in Livingstone Museum and 226 digital images in the Victoria Falls area, making the total of 591 images as our dataset. The linguistic impressions on signs that had labels provide insight into the imbalances in representation but also the global voice overlaid on the local material culture of multilingualism and multiculturalism. The unscripted signs together with sculptures, statues and paintings (murals) offer individualized narratives and sociocultural trajectories and histories.

The linguistic and semiotic landscapes of the Victoria Falls and the Livingstone Museum are further problematized by the fact that 'the remembering-forgetting dialectic has been employed as a stand-in or simplistic restatement of the problem of representation in public memory studies. In other words, a failure to represent a particular content publicly is not a necessary, or even provisional, sign of forgetting' (Blair et al. 2010: 18), as well as a pointer to Connerton's (1989: 68) reminder that 'we ... cannot infer the fact of forgetting from the fact of silence'. In this connection, we ask: how do monuments, statues, relics, as well as linguistic appendages to these artefactual materialities in the selected research sites eschew narratives of multilingual historicity and memories? Does the absence of other Zambian languages other than the four on the LL of the historical sites such as the museum 'de-voice' sociocultural histories and memories of their speakers and multilingualism? Are we experiencing an imposed material culture of monolingualism?

The linguistic impressions: Silencing local historical linguistic heterogeneity

Historical sites or, indeed, repositories of history and memory of the people for which the sites are made and preserved mirror in no uncertain ways the way of life of the said group. On the linguistic front, this should not be at all ambiguous as signs, linguistic labels and artefactual materiality would necessarily be reflective of the sociocultural knowledge and history of the people out of whom they arise (cf. Kress 2010). In the data below, we show how the linguistic imprints on the LL of the two sites challenge this hypothesis by minimizing local languages in places which would otherwise be dominated by repositories of the Zambian sociocultural and political narratives and voice.

Table 4.1 captures in a very clear way how the LL is constructed in these two spaces against the heterogeneity which often typifies these enclaves. The 60 per cent English presence in the Livingstone Museum and 59 per cent for the Victoria Falls forge an interesting lopsided linguistic and language history of

Table 4.1 Linguistic impressions in LL of Livingstone Museum and Victoria Falls area

Language	Livingstone Museum	Victoria Falls area
English	60%	59%
English and local languages	30%	18%
Local languages	4.8% (Tonga, Bemba, Nyanja, Lozi)	18% (Tonga, Lozi and Nyanja)
Foreign languages	5.2%	5%
Total images	265	226

these areas. The labels in the museum accompanying the artefactual materiality are often positioned in favour of the visitors, normally those who are literate in English rather than those who read only the local languages. Thus, 60 per cent of English dominance tends to distort the rich linguistic and language history and memory of Zambia. Besides, out of the seventy-two languages said to be spoken in Zambia, only four at most can be found in the oldest museum, which is supposedly a home and repository of the Zambian heritage – in both tangible and intangible historical materialities. Given that fewer than 5 per cent of the signs feature local languages, and of the seventy-two languages of Zambia, only four appear in the LL, these spaces of history and memory offer an unbalanced and distorted view of the language situation. In fact, the only time one finds these four languages used on an artefact is to name flora in the Natural History Gallery, in cases where the curators could not find the English name for the plants named. For, as was revealed in an interview with one of the curators:

> For most relics collected, we did not know what they are called in English. We normally depend on communities where these relics are collected for names.

It would seem therefore that reading the museum from this perspective only provides a limited narration of local linguistic complexity and diversity which forms a larger part of the local oral linguascaping (Banda and Jimaima 2015; Banda et al. 2018).

It is instructive to note that the apparent silencing of the local linguistic history and memory is traceable back to the broader colonial linguistic and language policy governing the education system. Carmody (2004) reminds us that initially only three local languages were adopted for use in schools during the colonial rule, namely Bemba, Tonga and Nyanja. Later, Lozi was added for the western part of the country. These languages, as a result of their use and promulgation, went on to receive considerable orthographic standardization which eventually led to enhanced literacy practice among users compared to the non-official local languages (Nkolola-Wakumelo 2013). Interestingly, even after independence, the Zambian government modelled their education system on the colonial language policy except they added a further three languages: Kaonde, Luvale and Lunda. However, it would seem the historical linguistic heritage continues to permeate twenty-first-century language practices (Nkolola-Wakumelo 2013). But also, the fact that the Livingstone Museum is a colonial legacy means that the colonial linguistic history and memory has persisted to the present regardless. The curators revealed, during the ethnographic interviews, that the reason they did not include other local languages, such as Luvale, Kaonde and Lunda, was because they lacked the required linguistic competence in these languages. When asked why only four local languages were used to label the relics out of the seventy-two dialects, the following was the response:

> Most of these relics were collected by curators who speak these local languages from the communities that speak the languages they know. If you look at the relics with Tonga names, they were collected by a Tonga curator. The same is true about those in Nyanja, Bemba, and Lozi.

It was revealed that 'local people will give you the names of plants/artefacts; it is up to you, to the curator to find its scientific name and its English equivalent'. Given this response from the curator, it would seem that most curators in Livingstone Museum are from the four local language backgrounds, giving disadvantage to the other local languages. This is however not to deny the fact that some of the curators are practising multilinguals. Their linguistic competence in languages other than those they deem as native may not readily support the complex naming system of their second language. One of the respondents explained that in terms of the demographics, there were more Tonga and Lozi speakers working for the museum, and these workers spoke more than one language. However, the respondent was quick to remind us that these keepers, though practising multilinguals, did not have sufficient linguistic competence to write in languages other than Lozi or Tonga. This included the botanist who heads this section. The presence of speakers of other language speakers does not help the matter either.

Evidently, the imbalance in the narratives in relation to language hierarchies does not only involve English over the local languages but also the local languages over other indigenous languages. Thus, the forces distorting histories and the multilingual memories of the apparent linguistic heterogeneity and the complex language interplay in Zambia are not only foreign, that is, global-to-local but local-to-local as well. Invariably, the four local languages used to label relics in the Livingstone Museum obscure the multilingual nature of the landscape upon which the museum is built. Thus, we concede that there is a double silencing here, thanks to both local and global language hierarchies. As such, the languages preserved in these repositories of history and memorization by the mere fact that they are used to label the artefactual materialities offer a biased linguistic representation in which an accurate picture of localness is vaguely and partially mirrored. For example, the Kaonde, Luvale and Lunda voices are missing in these spaces, which positions them as 'outsiders' despite these spaces being open to all the seventy-two Zambian ethnic groups. As stated earlier, Livingstone Museum is a national museum; it is not a regional museum.

Thus, framing our argument from this point of view, it seems that the language and sociolinguistic situation in Zambia is still trapped and embroiled in a complex colonial history and is thereby fossilized. In this vein, Connerton (1989: 2) reminds us that 'our experience of the present very largely depends upon our knowledge of the past. We experience our present world in a context which is causally connected with past events and objects'. What Connerton (1989) brings to the fore is the idea that the past and the present are intricately interwoven and that it is hard to avoid the influence of the past during the uptake of the present sociocultural narratives in place. It would seem the past percolates through to the present so that the former practices are replicated in the present LL orchestration.

In Figure 4.2 are the four dominant local languages used to label the herbal relics in the Livingstone Museum. Figure 4.2 shows Nyanja, Tonga, Lozi and Bemba used to name the herbal materiality. In fact the larger part of the script, as can be seen in the two images, is in English. Thus, even when the four local languages are said to be visible in LL of the museum, they only serve to name and never to describe materiality. In turn, one could argue that the local languages hardly provide extended narratives which allow for engagement with the materialities in place. For example, English is used to provide a procedure on how the herbal is prepared, thus extending the narrative and discoursal leverage of a foreign language over the local semiotics whose historicity the precincts were founded on. In using English the connection between the herbs and the local people who use the medicines is lost.

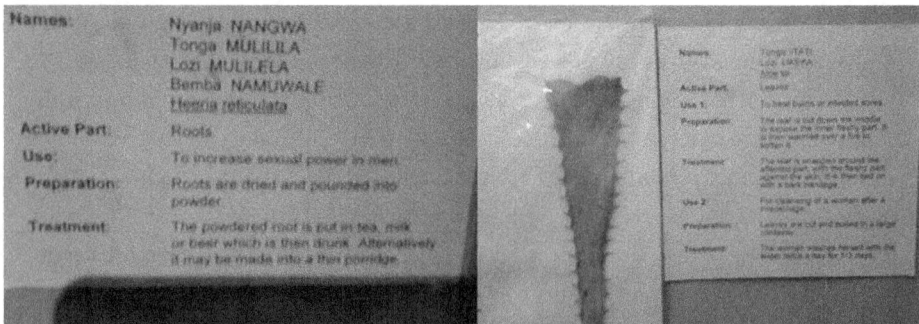

Figure 4.2 Local languages naming herbal relics.

The erasure of locality and downscaling of local historicity

Both the Livingstone Museum and the Victoria Falls are 'marked' by which we refer to the upscaling and global connotations these spaces have come to be associated with. As highlighted in the previous section, both these areas are local precincts of history and memory yet their 'markedness' obscures the sense of localness which invariably leads to the downscaling of the local historicity. First, we see the naming process of these heritage sites as the real cause of the erasure of the sense of localness and downscaling of local historicity. The name Livingstone Museum instantaneously shifts the historical trajectory from a local materiality to the foreign symbolization and actorhood. And so does Victoria in the name Victoria Falls. When we historicize the founding of the Livingstone Museum, it brings to the fore the forces behind the naming. For example, once the relics of David Livingstone were collected, they were donated to this newly opened museum which was later called David Livingstone Memorial Museum in 1934. Later, Rhodes's relics were added to the museum causing the change of name to Rhodes-Livingstone Museum in 1939. Notice that the addition of Cecil Rhodes's chattels occasioned a change in the name of the museum. Up until then, most of the relics in the museum represented the colonial hegemony and they offered a Scottish narrative about its civilization and supremacy. Contrariwise, once local artefactual materialities were later added to the museum, the initial name of the museum was not changed. The failure by those in authority to adjust the name in order to reflect the new additions accentuates the devoicing of the local artefactual materialities in which the local relic narratives, voice and meanings were completely downscaled. The apparent 'forgetting' to recognize the local materialities, so to speak, drawing on the dialectic of remembering-forgetting (Blair et al. 2010), forces us to argue for the erasure of locality as well as the downscaling of the local historicity. This is despite the museum's endowment with local material culture in the Ethnography Gallery, Archaeology Gallery and the History Gallery. We take the view that the failure to honour the local artefactual materialities cannot be summarized as mere forgetting; rather, it should be read as a deliberate refusal to give voice to the local materiality, predicated on selective memorization and remembering.

Despite the concrete sign on which the name of the museum is inscribed resonating with the sense of localness encapsulated in the accompanying local materialities of the hunters and the local wild life, the onomastics transport what

Figure 4.3 The Livingstone Museum external sign.

should have been the local space into imaginary global sensibilities. In this case, locality is ignored; hence local historicity is imbalanced if not obliterated by the forged sense of foreignness and unfamiliarity embodied in the name David Livingstone.

The meanings embedded in the foreign onomastics, in, for example, Figure 4.3 – that is, Livingstone Museum – conspicuously decentre the unpresented local relics while foregrounding and upscaling the Western materiality encapsulated in coloniality. In turn, the name Livingstone Museum displaces the entire establishment from the immediate semiotic flow and the locals for whom the place still exists. In the same vein, the naming of the falls – for which the locals already had a name – after Victoria, Queen of England, did not only lift the local geographic wonder from the local metaphysical world but also redefined the local space as foreign and British. This foreign narration of a local space dismantles the embedded local meanings and voices. In essence, the new name silenced local voices, identities and histories. Even if today the place is officially identified with two names, 'Mosi-oa-tunya' and 'Victoria', the degree to which the local name is used is limited. The local name does not usually appear in brochures and other promotion material. Thus, the local name has not been

Figure 4.4 The juxtaposition of Mosi-oa-tunya, Victoria Falls and Shuungu namutitima.

upscaled into the global tourist guides and advertisement. We argue that the attempt at reclaiming the falls as the local space through the juxtaposition of the two names as shown in Figure 4.4 falls short of the semiotic dynamism necessary to completely repossess the falls. It also does not help that the spaces within and around the falls are bedecked with foreign-owned establishments such as lodges and hotels to which very few locals have access.

In both instances, the name erases the history preceding the arrival of the Scottish explorer. The muffling of the local voices around the falls area is too apparent. The history of the local population – Toka-Leya, a dialect of Tonga – is actively embedded in the falls yet the name Victoria Falls or indeed the local Mosi-oa-tunya fails to historicize this early local engagement with the falls. Their local name – Shuungu namutitima – is never near the official municipal recognition. The unofficial use of this Toka-Leya name by a few Tonga/Toka-Leya speakers hardly provides a sustainable platform for deconstruction and reconstruction of their history and memory. In a sense, by imposing the foreign names on the immediate local population, there is a direct downscaling of the local historicity as there is an assumed prehistorical absence of their narratives and voices around the falls until the 1830s and 1850s, during which periods we see the arrival of the Kololo and David Livingstone, respectively. Reconstructively, however, the name Shuungu namutitima predates both the Kololo's and David Livingstone's naming of the falls. Following Shohamy (2006) we argue that those wielding much power seem to control the LL, and invariably the narratives and voices associated with the spaces. However, the superimposed narratives can hardly mute the historically embedded stories and cherished memories in place.

Materialities of erasure and imposition of foreignness

Apart from the onomastic considered above, the erasure and downscaling of local histories and memory is well narrated in the gigantic statues within the precincts of the Victoria Falls and the Livingstone Museum. Both these spaces are semiotically dislodged from locality by the domineering David Livingstone statue, sculpted from the same materiality, and taking the similar position, shape and size. See Figures 4.1 and 4.5.

The imposing nature of the statues in and around Livingstone Museum and Victoria Falls areas directly make a statement about ownership, remembrance and memory. In fact, Connerton (1989: 3) is on point when he argues that 'images of the past commonly serve to legitimate a present social order. It is an implicit rule that participants in any social order must presuppose a shared memory'. It would seem the colonial control of spaces, memory and who to remember are part of the collective – social memory. No wonder Connerton (1989: 1) is forthright on this matter: 'For it is surely the case that control of a society's memory largely conditions the hierarchy of power.' The point being made relates to the fact that those who are remembered as part of an important

Figure 4.5 The statue of David Livingstone in the falls area.

historical event remain upscaled while those who are forgotten suffer historical erasure and are permanently downscaled. It is the case therefore that coloniality plays out this game of upscaling and downscaling pretty well within the larger context of colonial and contemporary historicity. But then the two statues above seem to tell two different histories about the same historical figure, David Livingstone.

In attempting to unravel the extended narratives of the Livingstone statues in Figures 4.1 and 4.5, two specific narratives come to the fore: Livingstone as a missionary and Livingstone as an explorer, respectively. For in Figure 4.5, a statue emplaced in the Victoria Falls area, David Livingstone is shown to be carrying a Bible, which is emblematic of Christianity. In contrast, Figure 4.1, a statue at the Livingstone Museum, depicts David Livingstone as an explorer, thanks to the sheathed dagger on his left side and the staff in his hand. Both these 'instruments', so to speak, betoken power, subjugation and, at the very worst, the harbinger of colonialism. We take the view that as an explorer, David Livingstone felt justified to claim ownership of the falls since he positioned himself as the first person to have sighted the falls. No wonder he quickly named it after the Queen of England, Victoria. Therefore, it is compelling to sense elements of governmentality and control in the whole enterprise of the naming of the falls after Queen Victoria when one reads the Livingstone statue as typifying exploration work. Furthermore, when the two statues are juxtaposed, it is not surprising to witness the contradiction in the representation of David Livingstone: for history remembers him as both a missionary and an explorer (Ross 2002). In fact, on the statue in the Victoria Falls areas are inscribed these words: 'Christianity, Commerce and Civilization'. The three terms capture subtle contradictions in not only for what David Livingstone should be remembered but also the kind of history which is forged about missionaries such as David Livingstone in the broader context of colonial hegemony. For, in many instances, missionaries have been constructed as vanguards of European imperialism in Africa. Despite the apparent ambivalence in the tales of the two statues of Livingstone, in historicizing the artefactual materialities of David Livingstone and Cecil Rhodes in the Livingstone Museum, there are those that concede that David Livingstone represents only one history: the history of liberation and Christianity, as can be gleaned from this interview:

> Curator: 'You know Livingstone was a missionary while Rhodes was the mastermind behind colonialism. We associate anything good to missionaries such as education, hospitals and end of slavery. The same cannot be said about Cecil Rhodes. His name reminds us of colonialism and the oppression of

Africans. We have respect for David Livingstone, as you can see this town is named after him, so is this museum'. (Jimaima 2016: 249)

Summary and conclusion

Clearly, we are witnessing a selective remembrance of our once-upon-a-time holistic history. First, the remembrance is largely shaped by what colonial hegemony stipulated and handed down to postcolonial government. The case of the Livingstone Museum is illustrative of this blueprint if one considers the multilingual nature of the space. As aptly demonstrated above, the prominence of the four local languages in the museum is largely modelled after the indelible colonial blueprint which gave currency and capital only to these four languages during the colonial period. As observed by Nkolola-Wakumelo (2013), the regionalization of languages, which took effect during the colonial period, found its expression in the postcolonial language policy that led to the selection and legitimization of the seven regional languages in Zambia out of the seventy-two dialects. Thus, the LL of the Livingstone Museum is largely a mirror of coloniality, hence a type of local erasure of local materiality using colonial governmentality and hegemonic manipulation.

Furthermore, the co-construction of space by the use of local and global semiotic materials is very illuminating on the subject of erasure and marginalization. As Shohamy (2006: 110) rightly observes, 'The presence (or absence) of specific language items, displayed in specific languages, in a specific manner, sends direct and indirect messages with regards to the centrality versus the marginality of certain languages in society.' In the broader context of our discussion, Shohamy's assertion underpins the view that this chapter holds: the decentring of local materialities while centring the global ones. The ubiquitous spread of signage in English and the more Western-oriented artefactual materialities and sensibilities in and around these environs of what one would have assumed to be embodiments of (multilingual) memory and history provides a counter-narrative and, therefore, goes against the normative expectation that local spaces would embody local materialities. On this issue, Karp (1991: 16) is quite instructive as he reminds us that 'exotic objects displayed in museums are there only because of Western imperialism and colonial appropriation, and that the only story such objects can tell is the history of their status as trophies of imperial conquest'. Karp (1991) may sound rather harsh and blunt. However, the reality he attempts to present can easily be seen in the analysis provided above because Bronner (1985: 131) informs us that artefacts are 'a mirror of culture, a code from which the researcher can infer beliefs, attitudes, and values' owing to the fact that 'artefacts are active voices' always telling their own stories, histories and memory. In this connection, if we take the view that artefacts are a mirror of culture, the culture represented by the artefacts in Livingstone Museum and the Victoria Falls area should then be seen to be a mirror of foreign culture and history. It would be thus misleading to anticipate an accurate representation of local multilingual memory and history in these two study areas.

The foregoing assertion is fortified by Connerton's (1989) construct that conflates remembering and forgetting in discussing social order. For he reminds us that the past comes to bear on the future; the images of the past have potential to directly shape the present representation of the social order. The data presented, statistical and pictorial, corroborates the assertion Connerton (1989) makes; the view that the language situation fostered in the colonial period is seen to permeate the postcolonial period. Seen from this perspective, the language practices of the precolonial Zambia have been foisted on the present language practices. In turn, there has been institutionalized 'forgetfulness', one which attempts to ignore the multilingual nature of Zambia. It is important to repeat that Zambia has about seventy-two dialects reducible to twenty-six language clusters. All these languages had their own agency and voice in precolonial Zambia as languages of play, acculturation/socialization and socio-political-economy. However, the language policy of the colonial period which only recognized four out of the seventy-two dialects present in the LL of Zambia foisted on the postcolonial Zambia linguistic practises a similar policy. Today, apart from the four languages recognized by the colonial administration, only three have been granted the status of regional official languages. The fact that in both sites local memory is decentred confirms that the institutions which should have fostered a balanced representation of the multilingual historicity of Zambia have rather elected to selectively remember their own history. On this note, Armah's (2006: 196) call becomes relevant: he reminds us 'of the fact that memory, enduring memory, is a social acquisition [in that] a society that wishes to remember its values must work out deliberate ways of countering the normal, inertial slide into forgetfulness'. Thus, the multilingual memories framed in this chapter evince 'a community conducting dialogue with its history (both past and present) culture and expressing an unyielding desire to recontour the present and the future' (Muwati 2015: 24). Unlike Muwati (2015: 24) we go beyond conceding to the idea that 'remembering [should be] seen as a way of commemorating the past and celebrating victory over obstacles and colonial conquest'; rather, remembering should foster a faithful and balanced re-narration of history despite the persistent intersection of the past and present.

Finally, while the history which this chapter has attempted to discuss is one skewed towards erasure and downscaling of local historicity and multilingual memory, the ubiquitous spread and flow of foreign materialities force us to acknowledge elements of localization of what would seem foreign at first sight. For the fact that the name Livingstone has been maintained as an official name for Livingstone district and Livingstone Museum and the name 'Victoria' for the falls, respectively, demonstrates that there is a plausible enmeshment of the global materialities with the local semiotic environment, thanks to translocal and transnational mobility (Oakes and Schein 2006; Hedberg and Carmo 2012). We acknowledge that Zambia is not a passive recipient of these foreign semiotic symbols. As seen in the reappropriation of the name Livingstone to both the museum and the district, Zambia has actively reinvented the semiotic potential of this name. In fact, it is not uncommon to encounter people whose remembrance of the name Livingstone does not invoke the sensibilities of colonialism. The daily uptake of the name Livingstone in the narration of Zambian municipalities has erased the sense of foreignness with which the name potentially aligns. As noted elsewhere (Pennycook 2010; Banda et al. 2018: 67), the 'appropriation of global and local semiotic material in the construction of localised spatialities, that is, localised narratives of place' is realized in the broader context of translocal spatiality.

References

Appadurai, A. (1996), *Modernity at Large: Cultural Dimensions of Globalization*, Minneapolis: University of Minnesota Press.

Armah, A. K. (2006), *The Eloquence of the Scribes: A Memoire on the Sources and Resources of African Literature*, Popenguine: Per Ankh.

Aronin, L. and M. Ó Laoire (2012), 'The Material Culture of Multilingualism. Moving beyond the Linguistic Landscape', *International Journal of Multilingualism*, 10 (3): 225–235.

Backhaus, P. (2006), 'Multilingualism in Tokyo: A Look into the Linguistic Landscape', *International Journal of Multilingualism*, 3 (1): 52–66.

Backhaus, P. (2007), *Linguistic Landscapes: A Comparative Study of Urban Multilingualism in Tokyo*, Clevedon: Multilingual Matters.

Banda, F. and H. Jimaima (2015), 'The Semiotic Ecology of Linguistic Landscapes in Rural Zambia', *Journal of Sociolinguistics*, 19 (5): 643–670.

Banda, F. and H. Jimaima (2017), 'Linguistic Landscapes and the Sociolinguistics of Language Vitality in Multilingual Contexts of Zambia', *Multilingua*, 36 (5): 595–625.

Banda, F., H. Jimaima and L. Mokwena (2018), 'Semiotic Remediation of Chinese Signage in the Linguistic Landscape of Two Rural Areas of Zambia', in A. Sherris and E. Adami (eds), *Making Signs, Translanguaging Ethnographies: Exploring Urban, Rural and Educational Spaces*, 64–80, Bristol: Multilingual Matters.

Ben-Rafael, E. (2009), 'A Sociological Approach to the Study of Linguistic Landscapes', in E. Shohamy and D. Gorter (eds), *Linguistic Landscape: Expanding the Scenery*, 40–54, New York: Routledge.

Blair, C., G. Dickinson and B. L. Ott (2010), 'Introduction: Rhetoric/Meaning/Place', in G. Dickinson, C. Blair and B. L. Ott (eds), *Places of Public Memory: The Rhetoric of Museums and Memorials*, 1–54, Tuscaloosa: University of Alabama Press.

Blommaert, J. and A. Huang (2010), 'Semiotic and Spatial Scope: Towards a Materialist Semiotics', *Working Papers in Urban Language* and *Literacies 62*. Available online: https://www.kcl.ac.uk/sspp/departments/education/research/Research-Centres/ldc/publications/workingpapers/abstracts/WP062-Semiotic-and-spatial-scope-Towards-a-materialist-semiotics-Jan-Blommaert-.aspx (accessed 19 July 2018).

Bronner, S. J. (1985), 'Visible Proofs: Material Culture Study in American Flolkloristics', in T. J. Schlereth (ed.), *Material Culture: A Research Guide*, 127–153, Lawrence, KS: University of Press of Kansas.

Carmody, B. (2004), *The Evolution of Education in Zambia*, Lusaka: Bookworld Publishers.

Connerton, P. (1989), *How Societies Remember*, Cambridge: Cambridge University Press.

Denzin, N. (2010), 'On Elephants and Gold Standards', *Qualitative Research*, 10: 269–272.

Hedberg, C. and R. M. D. Carmon (2012), 'Introduction: Translocal Ruralism: Mobility and Connectivity in European Rural Spaces', in C. Hedberg and R. M. D. Carmon (eds), *Translocal Ruralism: Mobility and Connectivity in European Rural Spaces*, 1–12, London and New York: Springer.

Jimaima, H. (2016), 'The Social Structuring of Language and the Mobility of the Semiotic Resources across the Linguistic Landscapes of Zambia: A Multimodal Analysis', PhD thesis, University of the Western Cape, South Africa.

Karp, I. (1991), 'Culture and Representation', in I. Karp and D. L. Steven (ed.), *Exhibiting Cultures: The Poetics and Politics of Museum Display*, 1–17, Washington, DC and London: Smithsonian Institution Press.

Kress, G. (2010), *Multimodality: A Social Semiotic Approach to Contemporary Communication*, New York: Routledge.

Landry, R. and R. Y. Bourhis (1997), 'Linguistic Landscape and Ethnolinguistic Vitality an Empirical Study', *Journal of Language and Social Psychology*, 16 (1): 23–49.

Liu, B. and F. M. Mwanza (2014), 'Towards Sustainable Tourism Development in Zambia: Advancing Tourism Planning and Natural Resource Management in Livingstone (Mosi-oa-tunya) Area', *Journal of Service Science and Management*, 7: 30–45.

Mafofo, L. and F. Banda (2014), 'Accentuating Institutional Brands: A Multimodal Analysis of the Homepages of Selected South African Universities', *Southern African Linguistics and Applied Language Studies*, 32 (4): 417–432.

Mitchell, W. T. (2005), *What Do Pictures Want? The Lives and Loves of Images*, Chicago: University of Chicago Press.

Mufuzi, Friday (2011), 'Establishment of the Livingstone Museum and Its Role in Colonial Zambia', *Historia*, 56 (1): 26–41.

Muwati, I. (2015), 'Negotiating Space, Voice and Recognition: An Analysis of the 'District Song' of the Tonga People of Binga, Zimbabwe', *Muziki*, 12 (2): 22–36.

Nkolola-Wakumelo, M. (2013), 'A Critical Analysis of Zambia's Language in Education Policy: Challenges and Lessons Learned', in H. McIlwraith (ed.), *Multilingual Education in Africa: Lessons from the Juba Language in Education Conference*, 127–146, London: British Council.

Oakes, T. and L. Schein (2006), *Translocal China: Linkages, Identities and the Reimagining of Space*, London: Routledge.

Pennycook, A. (2009), 'Linguistic Landscapes and the Transgressive Semiotics of Graffiti', in E. Shohamy and D. Gorter (eds), *Linguistic Landscape: Expanding the Scenery*, 302–312, New York and London: Routledge.

Pennycook, A. (2010), 'Spatial Narrations', in A. Jaworski and C. Thurlow (eds), *Semiotic Landscapes: Language, Image, Space*, 137–150, London: Continuum.

Ross, A. C. (2002), *David Livingstone: Mission and Empire*, London: Hambledon.

Schacter, D. L. (2001), *The Seven Sins of Memory: How the Mind Forgets and Remembers*, Boston: Houghton Mifflin Company.

Scollon, R. and S. W. Scollon (2003), *Discourses in Place: Language in the Material World*, London: Routledge.

Shohamy, E. (2006), *Language Policy: Hidden Agendas and New Approaches*, New York: Routledge.

Stroud, C. and S. Mpendukana (2009), 'Towards a Material Ethnography of Linguistic Landscape: Multilingualism, Mobility and Space in a South African Township', *Journal of Sociolinguistics*, 13 (3): 363–386.

Waksman, S. and E. Shohamy (2010), 'Decorating the City of Tel Aviv-Jaffa for Its Centennial: Complementary Narratives via Linguistic Landscape', in E. Shahomy, E. Ben-Rafael and M. Barni (eds), *Linguistic Landscape in the City*, 57–73, Bristol: Multilingual Matters.

5

'Twa Tongues': Modern Scots and English in the Robert Burns Birthplace Museum

Robert Blackwood and James Costa

Introduction

The role of the contemporary museum is in transition. As Ravelli (1996: 368) notes, in recent memory, museums were expected to be the 'keeper of important information, and this information was delivered to and imposed upon largely passive visitors'. By the turn of the millennium, general expectations of museums were transformed, with their functions enumerated by Sirefman (1999: 297) to include 'cultural repository, dynamic civic space, popular entertainment centre, tool for urban revitalization'. Absent from this list, although prominent in much activity in museums and galleries today is the role of educator, and normally this involves some aspect of teaching, both children and adults, often around important issues and themes with significant currency. Within the domain of education, an under-explored line of enquiry is the extent to which the museum serves as a language teacher. Language saturates museums, with texts usually visible wherever the visitor turns; at the same time, the experience of museums from an explicitly linguistic perspective has shifted. Returning to Ravelli (1996: 369), she concludes that 'in today's museum environment, cultural and social information stands alongside the scientific, and the museum now plays the role of *facilitator*, drawing upon a broad range of knowledge, and providing the space for visitors to interact with this and *learn* from this in a variety of ways' (our emphasis). In this chapter, we explore the extent to which the Robert Burns Birthplace Museum (RBBM) facilitates the learning of a language – Scots, in this case – in an Anglophone context. In other words, we investigate the potential for a museum, which entextualizes multilingualism throughout its galleries, to inform about and even teach visitors a language with which they may or may not be already familiar.

We open this chapter with an overview of the Scots language and of the questions its use raises, with a specific focus on the debates most pertinent to the exploration of multilingualism in a new museum space in order to contextualize the findings. Briefly, we introduce the RBBM, in Ayrshire, western Scotland. We also identify relevant scholarship from museology and Linguistic Landscape (LL) research, which has informed our discussion of the RBBM. We approach the museum as a text, adopting a standard LL methodology to identify and record digitally all examples of Scots within the museum, as well as texts discussing ideologies of English and Scots as languages. Applying approaches from Multimodal Critical Discourse Analysis, the data is then analysed from the perspective of the terms used to discern the stances adopted by the museum's curators towards both Scots and English. We draw together the mains lines of enquiry to discern the potential for a museum space, such as the RBBM, to fulfil the range of functions from presenting multilingualism in an exhibition space to informally teaching a language to its visitors.

The Robert Burns birthplace museum

Robert Burns (1759–1796) occupies a special place in the Scottish national psyche, as national Bard and mythological figure, a venerated poet who wrote about rural life, love and Scotland (sometimes in proto-nationalist terms). The language he used was the one that his fellow Scottish Enlightenment literati were trying to eschew and despised for purposes other than poetry. He is also known throughout the world as the author of Auld Lang Syne. Yet, as Carol McGuirk points out, 'in his career path from acclaimed author of *Poems, Chiefly in the Scottish Dialect* (1786) to largely anonymous saviour of Scottish song, Burns does somehow mysteriously vanish into "Scotland". His status as a national icon has tended to obscure not only elements in his character, but also the nature of his literary achievement' (McGuirk 2007: 169). As a national icon, it was only fitting that Burns's birthplace be dedicated to the eternal memory of Scotland's literary beacon, despite the criticism and critique which he attracted during the Scottish (literary and linguistic) renaissance in the early twentieth century. Viewed as the eulogist of antiquated Scottish country life by the modernist writers of the Scottish renaissance, he was viewed ambiguously by Hugh MacDiarmid, one of the leading poets of the literary revival and a writer who tried to develop a standard, literary form of Scots, and who is said to have resorted to the rallying cry of 'Not Burns – Dunbar!' (Kay 2006: 55).¹

Burns's use of language(s) raises a number of sociolinguistic questions, however problematic it may be to interpret linguistic conflicts at a time when what we call 'languages', 'dialects' etc. were being defined. He wrote 'chiefly' in 'the Scottish dialect', as indicated in the title of his volume of poetry, but often resorted to English for the purpose of rhyme, and wrote his letters almost exclusively in English. The spelling system he uses departs from older, autochthonous spelling conventions and brings his language closer to English, from a visual perspective. For example, he uses the 'apologetic apostrophe' (e.g. <a'> for modern spelling <aa>, indicating a reliance on the English <all> and marking English as the proper, full, spelling). The fact that Scots was long excluded from Scottish schools except for the reading of Burns's poetry on 25 January, to mark the anniversary of his birth, also raises more contemporary questions as to the status of Scots in Scotland. Questioning the use of the Scots language at the museum is thus particularly cogent as it raises questions as to how Scots (and what forms of Scots) should be construed in contemporary Scotland as indexing nationality and heritage, and whether it should index new-found cultural and political confidence or merely past aspects of rural life in bygone times.

The RBBM is one of two Burns-related venues in the Ayrshire town of Alloway, just inland from Scotland's south-eastern coast. Centred around the two-roomed thatched clay cottage, constructed in 1757 by the poet's father, where Burns first lived, the RBBM was opened officially in January 2011 but admitted its first visitors in December 2010. The museum complex consists of a large gallery space designed for the permanent self-guided exhibition, plus a second, smaller space for temporary exhibitions. This main site, which also includes the obligatory gift shop and café, is linked to the other principal venue – Burns's cottage – by what is referred to as the Poet's Path. The restored cottage is where Burns lived with his family during his earliest years. Beyond the main site of the museum are other related venues, such as the cobblestone bridge over the River Doon, known as Brig o' Doon, and the ruined sixteenth-century church Alloway Auld Kirk, both of which appear in Burns's poem *Tam O' Shanter*. The RBBM, which took six years to build and cost in the region of £21m, is owned and managed by the National Trust for Scotland (NTS), a conservation organization which is responsible for over 100 historic properties and sites across Scotland. The RBBM is the NTS's most visited site and is seen as an important economic engine for the village of Alloway in Ayrshire where it stands. As a memorial to

Burns, the RBBM is the kind of museum that Williams (2007: 183) argues shows the visitor 'the best and brightest; those things held by famous hands, whether paintbrushes or swords'. In this sense, the RBBM is part of an older tradition of museology, rather than the memorial museums and dark tourism that have established themselves since the turn of the millennium.

Museums and Linguistic Landscape research

By the end of the last century, studies into museums and galleries were exploring the growth in the use of written texts in cultural institutions, recognizing that the presentation of artefacts by brief, often scientific, labels had been superseded by new approaches to designing exhibitions. As such, it is uncontroversial to consider museums and exhibitions as multimodal texts, and to examine them accordingly. Meaning-making takes place in a range of ways, from the architecture of the site, through the visuals of signage that names parts of the RBBM, to written texts on walls and in interactive displays. Ravelli (1996: 369) highlights the extent to which written texts in museum spaces perform a range of tasks, doing contextualizing and interpreting work, rather than their more traditional role of presuming levels of education and knowledge on the part of visitors, thereby rendering discursive explanations redundant. At the same time, as noted by San Roman (1992: 25), museums are also expected to act as 'reservoirs of natural and cultural heritage', communicating 'through objects, designs, lectures and other activities, non-tangible values of each society'. Language, therefore, does a considerable amount of work in museum and exhibition spaces, beyond the traditional role of giving a short written description of a given artefact. This tension between information-transfer and the scope for interpretation by the visitor has been debated in museology over the course of the twentieth century (Hein 2006: 340) but the extent to which language features in this discussion is, at best, marginal. Ravelli (2006) discusses comprehensively language and communication with museums, but she privileges the monolingual exhibition space, even within the exploration of multimodal discourse analysis. Elsewhere, Ravelli (2000) draws attention to intersemiosis, where meaning-making takes places across different sign systems, including language, images, architecture, design, and while we focus on language in particular within the RBBM, inevitably we have recourse to other sign systems, not least because these collectively contribute to the overall visitor experience.

Meanwhile, LL research has evolved significantly over its short lifespan; as a subfield of sociolinguistics, the exponential exploration of text, language, images and other resources in the public field can be dated back to at least 2006, and a Special Issue devoted to multilingualism, edited by Gorter (2006). It is fair to assert, therefore, that LL studies were initially rooted in the coexistence of multiple languages within given communities, even those – such as Backhaus' 2007 study of Tokyo – which are held to be largely monolingual. Given the emerging consensus that societies in general, and researchers in particular, now recognize multilingualism as a norm, and as the lived reality for most people, the potential for public writing – in its very broadest sense – to inform the complex connection between languages and people(s) is vast. This 'multilingual turn' (Conteh and Meier 2014) has been heralded by scholarship with LL studies, where researchers have taken an explicitly multilingual perspective in their examination of language in the public space. In particular, the tensions between ethnolinguistic groups vying to emplace discursive and other markers in public signage attest to the intensity and importance of the competition for visibility in our towns and cities. In turn, this underscores the significance of language conflict, revitalization and policy in informing the discussion. Ideologies are articulated onto public writing (which LL scholars refer to as a signs), which point to hierarchical relations between languages, their speakers and those with the agency to dictate the appearance of the public space. The role of language policies in the inclusion, exclusion or hierarchization of named languages has been explored elsewhere (Shohamy 2006, 2015; Dunlevy 2012), and in this chapter we address this question in a museum setting.

Kelly-Holmes and Pietikäinen (2016) adopt an explicitly LL approach for their study of language use in the Siida Museum devoted to Sámi culture in the Finnish town of Inari. There, they identify three distinct and simultaneously overlapping functions of language(s) as named, bounded constructs:

> Language is a major resource for enabling access to the museum and for directing visitors around the display for management of visitors [...]. Secondly, language is used for narrating the content of the museum and telling the story of Lapland's nature and Sámi culture. Thirdly, language itself is an object on display, as part of the content of the museum.

In the case of the RBBM, our particular interest is what Kelly-Holmes and Pietikäinen refer to as the third function, but which we consider to be its defunctionalization and its objectification. This we nuance by highlighting the potential for the museum to act as a space for language learning by virtue of language as an exhibited artefact.

If we turn our attention to education, within museology, it has long been recognized that the museum is not the same as the classroom, not least because its primary role is not to act as the space for active learning. However, Falk and Dierking (2000: 72–73) argue that museums have come to serve as the site for what they refer to as a 'learning-oriented entertainment experience'. Based on their research, they conclude that most museum visitors readily accept that fun and learning co-occur in museum spaces. Here, we make a distinction between the role of educating and that of learning; in its potential to enable language learning, the museum does not (necessarily) provide intellectual instruction to the visitor, nor does it offer training in language acquisition. Instead, amongst a range of other roles, the museum – and in particular the RBBM – is a memory site for language learning. We take inspiration at this point from both Malinowski (2015) and Trumper-Hecht (2010) before him, who adapt Lefebvre's (1991) triad of spaces, in particular in the light of the refocusing of language learning not merely as a social practice, but as a spatial practice (Malinowski 2015: 100).

The visitor's engagement with the Scots language is framed by the meaning-making processes staged by the museum's directors. Adapting Trumper-Hecht's reading of Lefebvre's 'conceived space' we see both the museum's policy documents and also the labels, information panels and signs around the museum as enxtextualizations of the museum directors' ideologies and preferred readings. In the light of Trumper-Hecht's (2010: 237) understanding of the 'perceived space' as 'the "physical" dimension of the LL, that is, the actual distribution of language on signs that can be observed and documented by camera', we seek in this chapter to draw on these differentiated understandings of space so as to investigate how the RBBM exploits multilingualism in order to yield meaning within the museum.

Scots: Ignorance, neglect and celebration

In 2013, a year before Scotland's inhabitants were asked whether Scotland should become an independent country or not, the Scottish government published a document entitled *Scotland's future*. The document addresses the various questions that citizens might ask about how the country would be governed once it became independent. Very little, however, was said about Scotland's potential future language policy. In fact, during the entire referendum period, language was never an issue. Even ballot papers were not bilingual in Gaelic, despite it being an official language in Scotland since 2005; such a measure had, in fact, been overtly opposed by the Scottish government. Language issues did, however, make it into the *Scotland's future* White Paper – the government report outlining proposals on this issue – in particular in chapter 9, 'Culture, Communications and Digital', which deals (in one paragraph) with Gaelic (only to reaffirm what was already in place). Yet interestingly, the paragraph on Gaelic is illustrated with two photographs: one of a statue of Robert Burns, and the other of the collection of poems by the same Robert Burns, a collection published in 1786 and entitled *Poems, Chiefly in the Scottish Dialect*. In other words, poems published not in Gaelic, but in something else.

This anecdote itself gives an idea of the status of Scots (as the said 'Scottish dialect' is now officially known in the country) in Scotland. Revered, yet ignored. Celebrated once a year, on the birthday of Scotland's national Bard on 25 January, even in schools where children still routinely get told off for speaking 'slang', the linguistic evolution of what Burns called 'Scottish dialect'. It was thus particularly interesting for us to analyse what the RBBM's language policy would be, how it would frame this ambiguous set of linguistic practices and to whom these practices would be addressed. First, precisely because of how ambiguous the status of Scots is, it would be pertinent to discuss briefly some of the debates that surround its very existence in Scotland.

There is little consensus on how Scots should be viewed, either among scholars or among the general population. In 2010, a government-commissioned survey found that 85 per cent of the sample spoke Scots, but 64 per cent of those people did not regard Scots as a language in the sense that they might call English or Greek a 'language':

> The majority of adults in the sample (64%) didn't think of Scots as a language, with around half of this group holding this view with conviction (34% of the total sample). However many of those who disagreed (30%) did so strongly (16% in total) highlighting the absence of any form of consensus on this issue. (TNS-BMRB 2010: 15)

Most school pupils, as well as many of their teachers, would thus call Scots 'slang' (Costa 2015). Furthermore, according to the 2011 National Census, some 30 per cent of the Scottish population declared some level of practice of Scots. Perhaps as many as 1.5 or 2 million people in Scotland can thus be said to use, or at least know, Scots. In literary and academic circles, several parallel debates were rife for several decades, first over the status of Scots as a language, a dialect or a collection of dialects. In the wake of early twentieth century modernism (Palmer McCulloch 2004), Scots was construed as a literary and societal issue by such poets as Hugh MacDiarmid and Edwin Muir, the former proposing a form of standardization which brought together several dialects and formalized spelling.

This attempt, which MacDiarmid terms 'synthetic Scots' and which was closely associated with the defence of Scottish independence, was soon derided and labelled 'plastic Scots', a reference to its purported artificiality (understood in terms of its lack of indexical ties with specific places) (Aitken 1980; McClure 1990). While standardization was subsequently abandoned, much works in literary, academic and educational circles have sought to construct Scots as a language on a par with English (Fitt 1998) and thus strengthen its position in education and government (Unger 2013).

Three positions (the third of which is more recent) seem to have become consensual among writers and scholars of Scots:

- Scots cannot be defined simply, and many perspectives should be allowed to coexist. As Iseabail Macleod, co-editor of the *Scots Thesaurus* (Macleod et al. 1999) and of several other Scots dictionaries, said in a 1997 interview to the *Scots Magazine*: 'Scots covers everything from dialects which the English – or even other Scots – wouldn't understand, to the way we're speaking just now, which is English with a Scottish Accent' (Dossena 2005: 15).
- Variation in form should be widely allowed. As James Robertson put it in his introduction to *A Tongue in Yer Heid*, a collection of short stories in Scots by various authors, commenting on the variety of forms used by each author:

  > There is a wide variety of approaches in these stories to problems of Scots orthography, and I have not sought to eliminate these. One argument against a standardisation of Scots spelling is that one of the language's very strengths lies in its flexibility and its less-than-respectable status: writers turn to it because it offers a refuge for linguistic individualism, anarchism, nomadism and hedonism. What has often been perceived as a fatal weakness may in fact be the secret of its resilience and survival against four hundred years of creeping Anglicisation. If there are inconsistencies – to adapt Walt Whitman – very well then, there are inconsistencies: the language contains multitudes. (Robertson 1994)

- A loose standard should perhaps be made available (McClure 1995). This position, which has always existed among some language advocates, re-emerged in 2016 after several incidents occurred involving Scots and the legitimacy of its usage. In particular, on 7 January 2016, *The National*, a daily newspaper published in Glasgow, published its front page in Scots only. It was immediately mocked, and Scots was largely viewed as a joke, the language of humour but not of serious news. As a consequence, Matthew Fitt, a celebrated Scots language author previously known for his opposition to standardization, soon reacted by saying the times were perhaps ripe for a standard to be proposed to avoid such reactions.

In other words, the absence of a recognizable and widely recognized standard form of Scots, which for historical reasons did not, or could not emerge at the time when other European vernaculars became standardized in the eighteenth century (Costa et al. 2018), largely confines the vernacular(s) in Scotland to indexically loaded uses, whether place-, class- or history-based (McClure 1984; Unger 2013; Costa 2015, 2018). Among those various types of indexicalities, the choices of the RBBM are of particular interest, given the prestigious indexical associations of Robert Burns in contemporary Scotland, and given the current debates over independence on the one hand and a possible wider role for Scots on the other.

Examining the RBBM

Scots in the conceived space of the RBBM

Inevitably, discussions of policy invoke questions of power and of politics, and the opening of the RBBM coincided with intensification of the debate around devolution and independence for Scotland, which led to the milestone of the 2014 referendum. The development of language policy for the RBBM at this time reminds us of Luke's (2002: xiv) conclusion that 'museum exhibits may not change public policies, but they can change other larger values and practices that will transform policy'. To this end, considering the 'conceived space' of the RBBM plays a part in the wider debate around the place for Scots in Scottish life, as articulated by the stancetaking adopted by the museum's curators and directors, as well as by the NTS. Our adaption of Trumper-Hecht's (2010: 237) reading of 'conceived space' opens with the scrutinizing of the RBBM's publicly available language policy, which not only explicitly presents the stance adopted by the museum but also identifies the ideologies that underpin the visual arrangement of language within the exhibition spaces. Furthermore, it proposes a strategy for developing the site's multilingual appearance. A second level of the RBBM's conceived space is the opening information panel in the main exhibition space, which presents to the visiting public the museum's stance towards multilingualism in general and the public display of Scots in particular. The 'Robert Burns Birthplace Museum Scots Language Strategy', published in the name of the NTS, sets out the guiding principles of the RBBM and is an invaluable document for the analysis of the museum as a conceived space. This Scots Language Strategy explicitly engages with the notion of the 'perceived space' (which we discuss more fully below) in its preamble, which identifies the strategy's aim to 'strengthen Scots within the Museum setting' (2016: 1). In this position paper, the RBBM discerns three guiding principles for the acquisition, use and development of Scots – the three pillars of the Scottish Government's 'Scots Language Policy' (2015). These three principles (National Trust for Scotland 2016: 4) are:

1. Ensuring that visitors continue to have access to use and learn from our collection (physically and online) of Burns-related material and the Scots Language contained therein.
2. Maintain the high standards of Scots Language provision already in place in interpretive media and ensure that commitment to Scots-based interpretation is enshrined throughout any developmental changes in future.
3. To continue and expand our education programmes be they formal – for schools and tertiary institutions; adult learners; volunteers or outreach customers – or through informal programming such as events and family provision.

More significantly from the perspective of this chapter, the museum's Scots Language Strategy then confirms the RBBM's desire to go beyond symbolic tokenism in the use of Scots on the grounds that the RBBM is 'as much about language as it is about the man who once used that language' (National Trust for Scotland 2016: 4). In a sleight of hand, the RBBM elides the distinction between language as a system of communication, and Scots as a formally named, immutable language, as if the two are interchangeable. The ideological positioning of this text overlooks the debates and controversies noted above and appropriates the traditional discourse of single, bound and often standardized languages. Our purpose here is not to critique the stance adopted by the RBBM but to highlight the extent to which the complexities of Scots, including its variation and its value on the linguistic market, are passed over. For the RBBM, the positions adopted by scholars and language activists (highlighted above) are overlooked and twenty-first-century reimagining of nineteenth-century Scottish nationalist language ideologies is applied to Scots.

The role of the museum as a language teacher is also addressed in this policy document, which appropriates the metalanguage of education to refer to 'General Learning Outcomes' for the RBBM, identifying the museum as a site of learning, and reinforcing the assertion that language learning is a spatial practice. The museum's Scots Language Policy commits to providing visitors with the opportunities 'to enhance their knowledge and understanding' of Scots, to read and speak in Scots through 'reciting Burn's poetry' and to acquire Scots vocabulary. This decision to assume the role of language teacher is confirmed by the subsequent coordination between learning outcomes and the specific teaching strategies, including the deployment of audio recordings in Scots, text provision and the use of an introductory panel (to which we return below). Hooper-Greenhill (2007: 29) distinguishes between specific and generic learning outcomes, identifying the former with 'particular skills, attitudes or knowledge', while the latter 'consist of broad general categories'. In the case of the RBBM, the educational purpose of the museum straddles the divide, with the general enhancement of knowledge and understanding echoing directly one of Hooper-Greenhill's examples of a generic learning outcome, while the acquisition of Scots vocabulary is a specific learning outcome. This tension is replicated in the perceived space of the RBBM, discussed below.

In terms of the potential for the museum to be a fully bilingual site, the Scots Language Policy confirms that duplicating translations (Reh 2004: 8) for the entire exhibition were considered by the RBBM but rejected for both practical and psychological reasons. The document notes that space in the museum is restricted, and that 'a well of text would be too off-putting on a psychological level'. It is not clear what would be disconcerting to the mental or emotional state of visitors by the enactment of complete translation of all information into Scots; the RBBM's Scots Language Policy offers no evidence for this claim. Nevertheless, the NTS as the named authors of the Scots Language Policy have concluded, there is an optimum amount of language that should appear within a given museum – the RBBM in this case – and that this threshold would be crossed were the texts across the complex to be consistently bilingual.

As part of the process of presenting labels and signs to the visitor, the driving force according to the Scots Language Policy document is to 'maximise access'. The RBBM concluded that, in addition to some use of Scots in interactive displays, 'object labels and explanatory text' are presented in English. The status of English as a language of wider communication, therefore, trumps the explicit aim of emphasizing language as an artefact as much as Robert Burns as a poet and writer. The RBBM reflected on its approach to presenting the space to the visitor, and elected to do so primarily in English, with certain panels and some interactive displays also produced in Scots.

In this conceived space, therefore, we can discern a tension between the ideological positioning in relation to Scots, and the planned emplacement of the language in the precincts of the museum. A clear stance towards Scots is taken, even to the extent of acknowledging the potential for tokenism in the use of the language in somewhere like the RBBM. At the same time, the value of English on the linguistic market, and its potential reach to visitors from a range of backgrounds, is recognized. As a conceived space, the RBBM is a multilingual venue, in that more than one recognized code is emplaced for consumption by visitors. However, this multilingualism is muted, and explicitly so: providing extensive information in two languages is deemed, at best, aesthetically inelegant, and at worst visually disturbing and distressing. The RBBM does not suggest that wide-ranging use of Scots in particular is problematic; rather, the problem is that too much text is 'off-putting' and that space for Scots is to be sacrificed.

Scots in the perceived space of the RBBM

At this stage, it is useful to recall the specific perspective we intend to explore within the museum, namely the use of language as an exhibited artefact through which visitors are invited to acquire Scots, or at the very least learn a few words of Scots. From the very first encounter with the RBBM, the visitor is faced with an irregularly multilingual space. The museum is named in English, not in Scots, and the physical approach to the site along the roads of Ayrshire draws on imagery related to Burns, notably the famous portrait of the poet omits Scots. A simplified and stylized version of Alexander Nasmyth's 1787 portrait of Burns is a widely used semiotic resource, both around the RBBM and across Scotland more widely, to index the poet and, indirectly, the Scots language (Figure 5.1). In this respect, Burns's image can be understood to stand in lieu of Scots. The role of Burns as a cultural giant inevitably inflects the multilingual dimension of the RBBM, not least because he is primarily associated – as recognized by the RBBM in the first information panel inside the museum – with the Scots language. For many, Burns embodies Scots, and so the material culture closely identified with him is presented in Scots.

The Scots language is at times emphasized, and at other times de-emphasized within the RBBM, with its saturation most acute in the Burns's cottage, more often in a symbolic and aesthetic way than in terms of functional guidance for visitors. The walls are decorated with Scots-language inscriptions, as well

Figure 5.1 A road sign including the stylized detail of Nasmyth's portrait of Burns.

as English-language captions; pieces of furniture, from the milking stool in the byre to the dining room chair, are also used as props onto which poetic texts are emplaced. When we consider the use of Scots as the first function enumerated by Kelly-Holmes and Pietikäinen (2016: 29), namely the resource for ensuring the flow of visitors through the site, the language disappears from view. Scots is wholly absent from the directional and informational signage within the RBBM, including instructions in the toilets, directions around the site and temporary texts in the exhibition spaces, a point to which we return below. This absence is not as a result of a national language policy that bars languages other than English from fulfilling this communicative role. In Wales, another country but equally part of the UK, such signage appears in both Welsh and English, meaning that individuals are warned in Welsh that the water from the taps can be very hot, or instructed in Welsh not to smoke within 50 metres of the front door. However, within a museum dedicated to the pre-eminent Scots language writer and poet, Scots is not deployed to manage the visitor experience (Figure 5.2).

When we approach the potential for the Scots language to serve as an artefact on display, there is evidence of an approach that creates space for Scots. The RBBM explicitly tackles the issue of multilingualism within a museum space

Figure 5.2 Instruction in English in the toilets at the RBBM.

in one of the first information panels inside the exhibition space, on what is known as the entry panel (Figure 5.3). Entitled *Twa Tongues* and opening with an excerpt of a 1792 letter from Burns to George Thomson, in English, the poet politely asserts his right to write with 'at least a sprinkling of our native tongue'. The information in the panel then sets out the ideological positioning of the RBBM's management, referring to Scots as a language 'that still forms an important part of the lives of many people across Scotland'. From this credo, the purpose of creating a multilingual museum is then expressly articulated with the hope that visitors (re)introduced to terms in Scots 'will take some of them with [them] as life-long companions'. Using Ravelli's typology of genres of museum texts, this entry panel stands as both an 'Exposition', designed to change visitors' opinions, and as a 'Directive', which is intended to influence their actions and behaviours (2006: 22). Not only does this text, which except for its title is solely in English, challenge ideologies about Scots assumed to be in wide circulation, but it also seeks to encourage language acquisition, even if limited to a few words. The framing of the RBBM's stance as aspirational reflects the limits of museums in discharging their educational role. The RBBM cannot force visitors to acquire a few words of Scots, or to deploy them once they

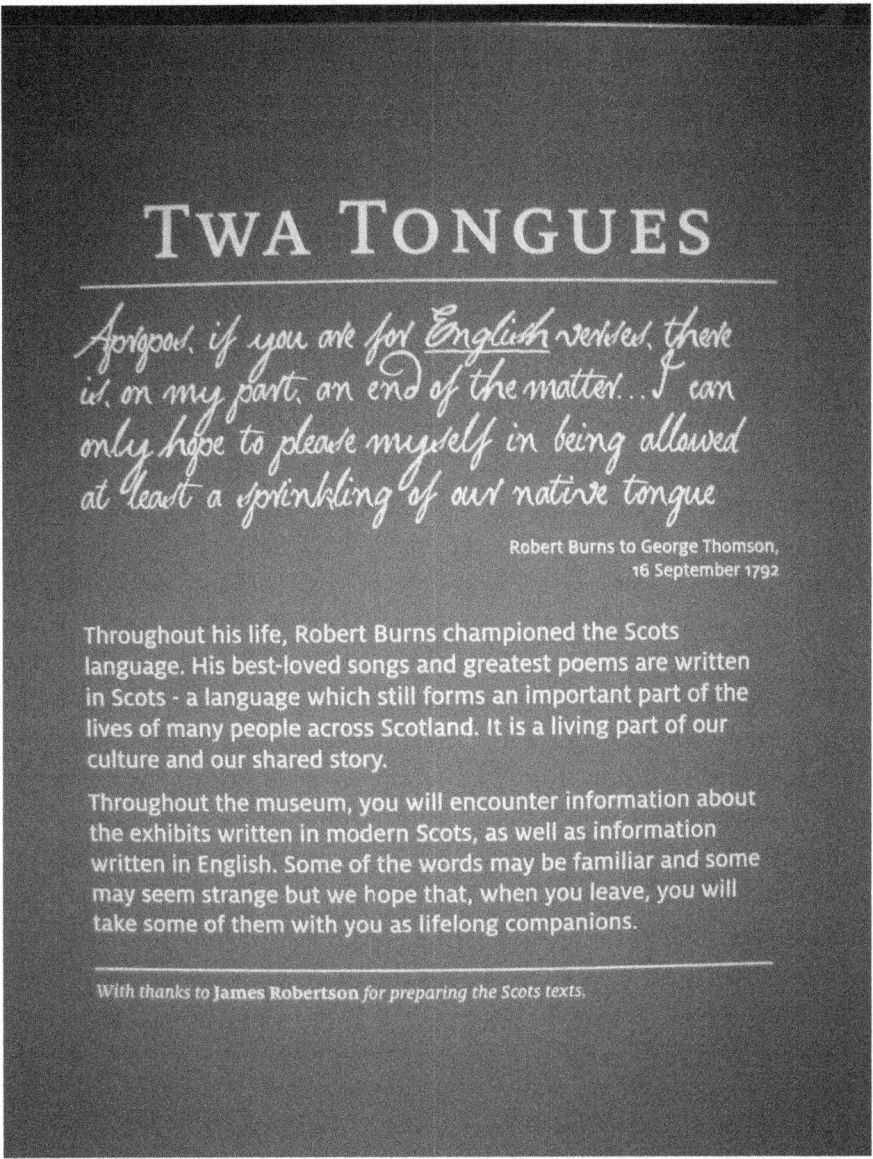

Figure 5.3 The main exhibition space's entry panel.

have left the museum space. Falk and Dierking (2000: 84), when discussing the didactic potential for museums, situate agency firmly in the hands of visitors: 'Museums are learning settings in which visitors have the opportunity to exercise considerable choice over what they will learn, or, framed in another way, visitors have the opportunity to control their own learning'. As such, while the RBBM may well wish to influence visitors' language practices, it is essential to recall that the visitor chooses whether or not to engage with the educational role that the museum seeks to assume (as attested in its language policy documents as well as on this entry panel).

From the perspective of discourse analysis, the entry panel attests to the valorization, from the very start of the self-guided exhibition, of the Scots language by the RBBM. Through this prominent act of stancetaking (Du Bois 2007), the sign authors align the museum with Scots language activists and scholars, thereby disaligning from the majority view (discussed above) regarding the status of Scots. The information panel also suggests that the visitor might find some terms in Scots familiar, while other 'may seem strange'. The choice of the term 'strange' is interesting for two reasons. First, the word 'strange' exoticizes a method of communication with which a considerable majority of Scottish people, as per the 2010 government-commissioned survey, claim familiarity. Of course, the museum is open to and attracts visitors from outwith Scotland, and the panel addresses all, not just Scottish, visitors. Nevertheless, for a domestic audience, the selection of 'strange' establishes a sense of alterity that is not recognized by writers and scholars of Scots. Second, strangeness as a concept serves to differentiate, or distanciate (Blackwood 2004), Scots from its close relation English. This confirmation of the distance between Scots and English conveys distinction, refuting lazy criticisms of Scots as an imperfect form of English by highlighting the extent to which Scots is not a variety of English.

This point is explored further as the visitor moves through the exhibition space and encounters signage exclusively in Scots. An example to illustrate this approach is the line of Scots used to introduce a poem by Burns displayed in the RBBM. The sign reads 'Efter his faither's **daith**, Robert wrote this sentimental poem depictin the life o an 18th-century peasant **fermer** and his faimly' (original emphasis). The two terms in bold are translated in a gloss presented as a footnote to the text thus: '**daith**, death; **fermer**, farmer'. The extent to which a translation for these two expressions, or any of the terms in this line, is needed is debatable, which diminishes the suggestion on entering the main exhibition space that examples of the Scots language used to inform the visitor might 'seem strange'. Although 'strangeness' is relative, it is doubtful that someone able to read the majority of the text would struggle to understand 'daith' and 'fermer', given their closeness to standard English. The process of translating selected terms from the Scots information panels continues throughout the self-guided exhibition, with terms such as 'ainly' ('only'), 'wark' ('work'), 'hairst' ('harvest'), 'cried' ('called') and 'sune' ('soon') translated. Decontextualized, these terms are sufficiently distinct from English to require a gloss. In context, their meaning is less elusive: 'This wis Robert Burns's first composition, written when he wis **ainly** 14.' The act of highlighting and translating words in these Scots-language information panels is one process in the creation of a multilingual museum. The provision of a glossary of terms used in the display panels renders the space multilingual, an act whose significance is greater where there is ongoing disagreement over the distinctiveness of one language over another.

This practice is replicated in Burns's cottage, a few hundred metres away from the main exhibition spaces. Here, there are fewer long texts, and more examples of Burns's poetry, often displayed creatively (such as written in white cursive text on the black one-dimensional silhouette of a cow in the byre – Figure 5.4) with glossaries painted directly onto the wall. The glossaries appear in the same way that those in the exhibition are presented, but the texts to which they refer are not necessarily adjacent, and as such, they appear as free-standing vocabulary lists, using italics for the English, and roman letters for the Scots.

Figure 5.4 Lines from Burns's poems inside the Burns's cottage.

The other of the functions of language identified by Kelly-Holmes and Pietikäinen (2016: 29) is the narration of content in the museum, and within the RBBM, this is another example of uneven multilingualism. This point evokes the discussion above regarding the conflict between the desire on the part of the RBBM, as outlined in their Scots Language Policy document, to include as much Scots as possible on the one hand, and the limitations of space (and its conjected consequences) on the other hand. The life story of Burns, and the parallel discussion of the evolution of Scots, is largely outlined in English on information panels, with some also appearing in Scots. There is an imbalance in space accorded to each language here, and Scots is relegated to a role supplementing information provided extensively in English.

Discussion – Bridging the distance between the conceived and perceived spaces

Trying to triangulate the conceived and perceived spaces of the RBBM with the context of Scots in Scotland highlights interesting tensions. While this is not a quantitative LL examination of the museum in the traditional sense of some LL research, it is clear that the difference in the proportions of Scots and of English labels, signs and information panels is noteworthy. This preliminary survey underlines how the use of English is consistent throughout the RBBM, in particular for the first function identified by Kelly-Holmes and Pietikäinen (2016), which enables the visitor to move through the museum space and access the range of facilities on offer. In a museum that is saturated with the significance of language, it is the referential use of language that dominates, a place occupied by English, with Scots confined to an indexical usage. Signage pointing the visitor to the toilets or giving information on the opening times or forbidding smoking within the museum's precincts is provided in English, and often supplemented by widely recognized icons (Scollon and Scollon 2003: 26). Scots is absent from this role, and its emplacement is limited to the signage within the main self-guided exhibition space, and Burns's cottage. Without counting signs, it is still uncontroversial to contend that English dominates the perceived space of the RBBM.

A close reading of the documentation used to guide the arrangement of language in the museum suggests that the visitor might expect some sort of preordained semiotic order, even if the language practices of the NTS and the RBBM do not map exactly onto the stances taken in their policies and mission statements. What is particularly striking in the conception of the museum is that it seeks to go against the grain of the general representation of Scots in Scotland. According to the RBBM, to adapt a motto, Scots is for life, not just for 25 January. There is a clear, ideological commitment to lift Scots from its role as slang and valorize it through its emplacement in and usage throughout a museum. The RBBM seeks to create indexicalities of heritage and simultaneously – through the iconic association with Nasmyth's portrait of Burns, capturing him as eternally youthful – of modernity and fashionableness. When we enter the perceived space of the museum, these approaches fall short because of the ways in which Scots is reduced within the exhibition spaces. On the one hand, Scots is consistently affirmed as something of the past, rather than contemporary and cool. On the other hand, Scots is reduced to a mere set of words, thus implying that it is not a language. The use of glossaries performs the function of making boundaries between Scots and English, and thereby serves an important purpose, even if the visitor is able to understand the Scots text without the use of the lexicon. However, in reducing Scots to word lists, the RBBM unintentionally diminishes the status of Scots, breaking the complex communication system down into lexical items, one or two of which the visitor is invited to take away with them.

The aspirations of the NTS and the RBBM to create a multilingual museum which primarily honours the life of Robert Burns but which also valorizes Scots by emplacing it within the museum and teaching it to visitors are ambitious, yet they remain symbolic. By no measure achieving parity with English, Scots is given a meaningful place in a domain from which it has traditionally been absent (and excluded); moreover, this is a high domain of élite culture, which challenges long-held stereotypes about the appropriateness for Scots in cultural matters. At the same time, however, Scots is historicized and corralled into a specific role that keeps it out of the practicalities of access, flows and movement, and therefore reinforces old clichés. As a teacher of language, the RBBM provides vocabulary lists and short texts with contexts. What it does not do is demonstrate practical ways in which Scots can be used in daily life in a context of written culture.

Note

1 Dunbar was a sixteenth-century Makar (poet) who developed Scots as a language of illustrious poetry. See, for a quick overview, Alan Riach's paper in *The National*, 22 January 2016, reproduced here: http://eprints.gla.ac.uk/149713/1/149713.pdf.

References

Aitken, A. J. (1980), 'New Scots: The Problems', in J. D. McClure, A. J. Aitken and J. T. Low (eds), *The Scots Language: Planning for Modern Usage*, 45–66, Edinburgh: Ramsey Head Press.

Blakwood, R. J. (2004), 'Corsican Distanciation Strategies: Language Purification or Misguided Attempts to Reverse the Gallicisation Process?', *Multilingua*, 22 (3): 233–256.

Conteh, J. and G. Meier (eds) (2014), *The Multilingual Turn in Languages Education*, Bristol: Multilingual Matters.

Costa, J. (2015), 'Can Schools Dispense with Standard Language? Some Unintended Consequences of Introducing Scots in a Scottish Primary School', *Journal of Linguistic Anthropology*, 25 (1): 25–42.

Costa, J. (2018), 'On the Pros and Cons of Standardizing Scots: Notes from the North of a Small Island', in P. Lane, J, Costa and H. De Korne (eds), *Standardizing Minority Languages: Competing Ideologies of Authority and Authenticity in the Global Periphery*, 47–65, London: Routledge.

Costa, J, H. De Korne and P. Lane (2018), 'Introduction. Standardising Minority Languages: Reinventing Peripheral Languages in the 21st Century?', in P. Lane, J. Costa and H. De Korne (eds), *Standardizing Minority Languages: Competing Ideologies of Authority and Authenticity in the Global Periphery*, 1–23, London: Routledge.

Dossena, M. (2005), *Scotticisms in Grammar and Vocabulary*, Edinburgh: Birlinn.

Du Bois, J. (2007), 'The Stance Triangle', in R. Englebretson (ed.), *Stancetaking in Discourse: Subjectivity, Evaluation, Interaction*, 139–182, Amsterdam: John Benjamins.

Dunlevy, D. A. (2012), 'Linguistic Policy and Linguistic Choice: A Study of the Galician Linguistic Landscape', in C. Hélot, M. Barni, R. Janssens and C. Bagna (eds), *Linguistic Landscapes, Multilingualism and Social Change*, 53–68, Frankfurt: Peter Lang.

Falk, J. H. and L. D. Dierking (2000), *Learning from Museums: Visitor Experiences and the Making of Meaning*, New York: AltaMira Press.

Fitt, M. (1998), 'Socts Language in the Classroom: Viewpoint III', in L. Niven and R. Jackson (eds), *The Scots Language: Its Place in Education*, 93–98, Dundee: In House.

Hein, G. E. (2006), 'Museum Education', in S. MacDonald (ed.), *A Companion to Museum Studies*, 340–352, Oxford: Wiley Blackwell.

Hooper-Greenhill, E. (2007), *Museums and Education: Purpose, Pedagogy, Performance*, New York: Routledge.

Kay, B. (2006), *The Mither Tongue*, Edinburgh & London: Mainstream Publishing.

Kelly-Holmes, H. and S. Pietikäinen (2016), 'Language: A Challenging Resource in a Museum of Sámi Culture', *Scandinavian Journal of Hospitality and Tourism*, 16 (1): 24–41.

Lefebvre, H. (1991), *The Production of Space*, Oxford: Blackwell.
Luke, T. W. (2002), *Museum Politics: Power Plays at the Exhibition*, Minneapolis: University of Minnesota Press.
Macleod, I., P. Cairns, C. Macafee and R. Martin (eds) (1999), *Scots Thesaurus*, Edinburgh: Polygon & Scottish National Dictionary Association.
McClure, J. D. (1984), 'Lowland Scots: An Ambivalent National Tongue', *Multilingua*, 3 (3): 143–152.
McClure, J. D. (1990), 'The Synthesisers of Scots', in E. Haugen, J. D. McClure and D. S. Thomson (eds), *Minority Languages Today*, 91–99, Edinburgh: Edinburgh University Press.
McClure, J. D. (1995), *Scots and Its Literature*, Amsterdam & Philadelphia, PA: John Benjamins.
McGuirk, C. (2007), 'Writing Scotland: Robert Burns', in S. Manning, I. Brown, T. O. Clancy and M. Pittock (eds), *The Ediburgh History of Scottish Literature: Enlightenment, Britain and Empire (1707–1918)*, 169–177, Edinburgh: Edinburgh University Press.
Malinowski, D. (2015), 'Opening Spaces of Learning in the Linguistic Landscape', *Linguistic Landscape*, 1/2: 95–113.
National Trust for Scotland (2016), *Robert Burns Birthplace Museum Scots Language Strategy*, Edinburgh: National Trust for Scotland.
Palmer McCulloch, M. (2004), *Modernism and Nationalism: Literature and Society in Scotland 1918–1939*, Glasgow: ASLS.
Ravelli, L. J. (1996), 'Making Language Accessible: Successful Text Writing for Museum Visitors', *Linguistics and Education*, 8: 367–387.
Ravelli, L. J. (2000), 'Beyond Shopping: Constructing the Sydney Olympics in Three-Dimensional Text', *Text*, 20 (4): 489–515.
Ravelli, L. J. (2006), *Museum Texts: Communication Frameworks*, London: Routledge.
Reh, M. (2004), 'Multilingual Writing: A Reader-oriented Typology – With Examples from Lira Municipality (Uganda)', *International Journal of the Sociology of Language*, 170 (1): 1–41.
Robertson, J (ed.) (1994), *A Tongue in Yer Heid: A Selection of the Best Contemporary Short Stories in Scots*, Edinburgh: B&W Publishing.
San Roman, Lorena (1992), 'Politics and the Role of Museums in the Rescue of Identity', in P. Boyland (ed.), *Museums 2000: Politics, People, Professionals and Profit*, 25–31, London: Routledge.
Scollon, R. and S. W. Scollon (2003), *Discourses in Place: Language in the Material World*, Abingdon, Oxon: Routledge.
Shohamy, E. (2006), *Language Policy: Hidden Agendas and New Approaches*. New York, NY: Routledge.
Shohamy, E. (2015), 'LL Research as Expanding Language and Language Policy', *Linguistic Landscape: An International Journal*, ½: 152–171.

Sirefman, S. (1999), 'Formed and Forming: Contemporary Museum Architecture', *Daedalus*, 128 (3): 297–320.

TNS-BMRB (2010), *Public Attitudes towards the Scots Language*, Edinburgh: The Scottish Government.

Trumper-Hecht, N. (2010), 'Linguistic Landscape in Mixed Cities in Israel from the Perspective of "Walkers": The Case of Arabic', in E. Shohamy, E. Ben-Rafael and M. Barni (eds), *Linguistic Landscape in the City*, 235–251, Bristol: Multilingual Matters.

Unger, J. W. (2013), *The Discursive Construction of the Scots Language: Education, Politics and Everyday Life*, Amsterdam & Philadelphia, PA: John Benjamins.

Williams, P. (2007), *Memorial Museums: The Global Rush to Commemorate Atrocities*, Oxford: Berg Publishers.

6

Multiple 'Ways of Telling' in the LL at the Second World War Japanese American Internment Camp Memorial Cemetery in Rohwer, Arkansas

Rebecca Todd Garvin and Yasushi Onodera

Introduction

The existence of Second World War relocation centres for Japanese American citizens in Jerome and Rohwer, Arkansas, during the 1940s, came as a surprise to many – in particular, local Arkansans. Thanks to the insistence and efforts of former internees (such as George Takei), a local historian, state institutions and national organizations, the remembering of a very dark period in American history is now on exhibit, open for public viewing through multiple online sources and physical information sites. With recent grants and modern technology, the Japanese American Relocation Center and Memorial Cemetery in Rohwer were geospatially surveyed by the University of Arkansas at Little Rock. The cemetery – most salient, a war memorial – had been declared a National Historic Site in 1992 and was renovated under the direction of Arkansas State University in 2011. In April of 2013, an interpretive centre was opened in the old train depot at McGehee, Arkansas, with support from the Butler Center for Arkansas studies and history.

This chapter presents a systematic study of the linguistic landscape (LL) marking the Rohwer camp memorial cemetery that was first constructed in 1943 by the internee residents of the Second World War Japanese American Relocation Center. From the relocation camp's opening in 1942 until its closure in 1945, this cemetery functioned as both burial grounds for 128 internees who died there (Fremon 1996) and as a war memorial site for residents from the camp who fought for America and died on foreign soil. Utilizing the LL as an instrument of remembrance, the purpose of the study was to document onsite and then analyse all objects, signage and multilingual texts created and arranged to tell this story and memorialize the ones who suffered alienation and injustice, yet served America courageously during times of war. As a built environment (Wang and Heath 2011), the LL at the Rohwer Cemetery has undergone two, perhaps three, phases of construction by multiple stakeholders and participants over the past seventy-five years. In the second phase of development, the language, emplacement and the solidity of new monuments marked the site as a National War Memorial, legitimizing war and the 'idea of national unity in the face of evident exploitations and inequality' (Abousnnouga and Machin 2010: 220). The third, the most recent renovation stage of the cemetery the LL includes narratives of former camp residents and the 'postmemory generation' (Hirsch 2008), written only in English, addressing in large part generations with no memory of the trauma that American citizens of Japanese heritage experienced in Arkansas during the Second World War. In particular, it is our purpose in this chapter to bring to the forefront the multilingual texts inscribed by the original builders at this memorial site. The meanings, messages and discourses in the words and symbols represent Japanese culture and thought that have been glossed over in existing studies of the site and not closely read.

Since the relocation centre's closing in 1945, camp buildings were used for various community purposes but by the turn of this century all traces of the camp had vanished leaving only the monuments in cemetery which had been neglected for years. After a long period of 'forgetting' (Connerton 2008) various organizations and educational institutions (including Korematsu Institute 2011) are now working with compassion and accountability to raise public awareness of this forgotten injustice. Absence and omission of this story in Arkansas history had become reality; therefore, remembering to honour the memory and sacrifices of Japanese Americans who lived in the community and fought for the country during the Second World War was deferred. Opened in 2013, an interpretive centre museum in McGehee is located about 12 miles from Rohwer and exhibits a wide range of artefacts, created and used by Japanese American internees of Arkansas relocation centres. The museum artefacts are thoughtfully juxtaposed with conscience-probing questions. One such question posted in large font on the back wall of the Second World War Japanese-American Internment Museum in McGehee: 'Can we let this happen again?' – a question that still begs for critical dialogue about oppressive language and the mistreatment of marginalized immigrant citizens in the United States. In the last five years, there have been multiple exhibits in Little Rock, Arkansas, replete with photographs, government orders and documents, artefacts, interviews and internees' artworks and essays. Moreover, numerous websites and blogs with narrative stories from Japanese Americans who went 'against their will' to relocation centres across the United States may be accessed virtually. Combined efforts for remembering have been performed throughout the state.

Nonetheless, this study argues that a close material and textual analysis of the LL at the Rohwer Memorial Cemetery site may provide deeper insights and understandings of this traumatic experience in American history. The prismatic nature of LL methodology encourages researchers to closely examine and translate when necessary the languages, discourses and materiality (Abousnnouga and Machin 2010) of concrete literacy artefacts in context, in isolation and in interaction with other texts to note the aspects of extralinguistic reality, what De Fina (2000) described as context-reflecting and context-changing discourse practices.

With an ethnographic approach we consider the initial inscribers' intentions (Malinowski 2009), the complex processes of mapping form onto function (Blommaert 2005), as well as possible constraints on readership and interpretations (Garvin 2011; Szabó and Troyer 2017). The data was collected onsite in order to document the discourses in the LL and in particular, spatial practices, looking for obvious and subtle reflections of social relationships and sociocultural constructs (Bourdieu 1981; Foucault 2002).

In this study we focus on specific 'ways of telling' (Berger 1972; Berger and Mohr 1982) through multimodal literacies and multilingual texts at this memorial site – expressions of identity from Japanese American internees, representations of the interested stakeholders, and salient messages shaping collective memory. Our specific questions are: (1) what types of texts and material objects are present in this memorial LL? How are objects of memorialization emplaced and oriented in this physically defined cemetery space? (2) In what ways do the inscriptions (languages, icons and symbols) in this LL interact and contribute to deeper understandings of the experiences, identities and intentionality of initial inscribers? Who is telling the story? (3) In what ways does the renovated memorial cemetery in Rohwer contribute to dialogues of immigration, nationality and citizenship?

Japanese American internment in Arkansas

After Pearl Harbor, America declared war against Japan and engaged militarily in the Second World War. By February 1942, President Franklin D. Roosevelt was pressured to sign executive order 9066 to round up 'enemy aliens' and although '[t]he word "Japanese" never appeared in Roosevelt's executive order, yet from the beginning, Japanese were the order's only intended targets' (Fremon 1996: 33). By March, the president had established the War Relocation Authority (WRA) whose primary function was to relocate, maintain and supervise the Japanese American population. Many had been living comfortable and productive lives as Japanese born *Issei* (一世) and American born *Nisei* (二世), legal residents and citizens. Motivated by fear of invasion by Japan, ten sites were selected in remote areas in the western, southwestern and southern United States. With two weeks' notice, the US Government forced Americans of Japanese ancestry on the west coast to abandon businesses and homes and go to large confinement sites. Close to 120,000 Japanese Americans (64 per cent were American citizens) were confined from 1942 until 1945. The two easternmost relocation camps were in Arkansas, in Jerome (Chicot and Drew Counties) and in Rohwer (Desha County). For the state of Arkansas, 'This was the largest influx and incarceration of any racial or ethnic group in the state's history' (Encyclopedia of Arkansas History and Culture 2018). Until recently, this event had almost been erased from local memory.

The Second World War Japanese American Relocation Center in Rohwer was opened on 18 September 1942 and closed on 30 November 1945. The camp 'was situated in the marshy delta of the Mississippi River's floodplain which was originally tax-delinquent lands in dire need of clearing, leveling, and drainage' (Encyclopedia of Arkansas History and Culture 2018). The camp included 10,000 acres of land with 500 acres equipped with A-framed, numbered buildings, arranged into blocks and was home to approximately 8,500 internees during this time. Like a mini-city, the camp had a mess hall, canteens, recreational buildings, administrative buildings, WRA residences, a hospital, a warehouse and factory section, barracks for schools and a fire station; however, the residential buildings did not have plumbing or running water and used wood stoves for heat in the winter. The camp was surrounded by barbed wire and wooded areas with armed guards in towers strategically located.

While their families were interned under these horrible conditions, many residents of the Rohwer camp were conscripted into the US army to fight during the Second World War on foreign soil and died in service to the United States. In total, 33,000 Japanese American men volunteered or were drafted for active combat duty for the United States and were among the most decorated for bravery, sacrifice and service. Forced to register and take a loyalty test or questionnaire to participate in active military duty, Issei and Nisei adult men were asked to renounce allegiance to Japan. Many residents of Rohwer served in the 442 Regiment which was an all-Nisei unit. Some served in the 100

Battalion, an all-Nisei National Guard unit from Hawaii, which, according to Fremon (1996: 82), was 'known as the Purple Heart Battalion because of the many casualties it suffered'. The Rohwer Cemetery and monuments were built by the camp internees with the materials available, mostly concrete. While the camp was open, the cemetery was a personal space, used to bury camp residents who had died during internment and to memorialize the service of their fathers and sons who had died on foreign soil while serving America. Years after the closing of the camp in 1945, two new memorials were added to the Rohwer camp cemetery, funded by local groups, Japanese Americans, state and national institutions, in addition to the US Parks Service. The cemetery was not completely restored until 2011. Most likely a catalyst for the recent renovation, local historian and now Arkansas State University administrator, Dr Bill Smith, posted a video in 2010 which showed broken cement monuments and the neglected state of the cemetery. His video was a reminder to Arkansans to remember the words written in English, on the left side of the memorial obelisk. In a pattern invoking Japanese identity with an eastern orientation to vertical text reading (see Figure 6.4), the message from the internees of Camp Rohwer to the people of Arkansas was as follows:

> May the
> People of Arkansas
> Keep in
> Beauty
> And Re
> Verence
> Forever
> This
> Ground
> Where
> Our
> Bodies
> Sleep

Framing multilingual memorials with LL approach

Forgetting and remembering

In every society and culture there are rituals of practice to memorialize the dead and tell stories of past events which should not be forgotten. Significant as literacy events (Barton and Hamilton 2005), these practices of everyday life are not just objects of knowledge but they 'constitute an act of which they intend to mean' (de Certeau 1984: 80). As alluded to earlier in this chapter, often traumatic or shameful events are not remembered until years later. Connerton (2008) offered seven reasons for 'prescriptive forgetting' – one as a means of moving forward, beyond a crisis to return to a sense of normalcy. To illustrate the painful process of memorializing too soon after an event, in a study of the LL in the planned monument to commemorate the horrific shootings at the youth camp in Norway in 2014, Lanza and Røyneland (2015) commented on the resistance from some parents to this project. Other LL studies (Shohamy and Waksman 2010) expose the challenges and complexities of rewriting or reconstructing the past in the process of post-event memorialization, which is sometimes guided by memories that are often fragmented, multidimensional, emotionally connected to trauma, as in the case of post-memory (Hirsch 2008). Within the institutions of transmission of history (poetry, art, memorials, oral and written histories), archival photography is an important tool in that it fills in the gaps of traumatic recall and generational remove. Once it became clear that the LL at the cemetery site was built by multiple agents at different times, additional archival photographs became essential stabilizing references (Barthes 1964; Hirsch 2008). Photographs often expose details that were forgotten.

The LL, a geographically defined and inscribed place, is a classic venue for building collective public memory. Nonetheless, when reconstructing the past, the LL is often uneven, guilty of omission and erasure, and, as Guilat (2016) discovered, an opportunity ripe for creating a counter-narrative. In the time between forgetting and remembering, memory shifts as 'it is deployed and redeployed by different parties towards different political ends' (Houdek and Phillips 2017). However, purposeful forgetting is often at the expense of others who suffered and remembering 'means to grant both legitimacy and recognition to those who have suffered and a way to confront past wrongdoings' (Houdek and Phillips 2017). With the renovation of the site at the Rohwer Cemetery and the opening of the Japanese American Internment Camps Interpretation Center at McGehee, Arkansas has chosen to remember and attempt to right a wrong. How is this event being remembered? What does the LL at this cemetery communicate?

In the past twenty years, LL approaches and theories have developed multiple ways to systematically dig through layers of material artefacts and documents, to explore interactions between multilingual and multimodal texts and to understand the significance of spatial orientations in time and place. Scollon and Scollon (2003) articulate the processes of *geosemiotics* and lay out a step-by-step approach through the concepts of *indexicality* and *emplacement*. In order to approximate and index meanings of signs, symbols and icons, we must consider 'the world in the environment of the speaker' (Scollon and Scollon 2003: 31) and where and how the signs are placed in the world. Furthermore, Scollon (2001) provides the concept of *nexus of practice* as means to understand interactions within and the meditational power of the LL.

Indexicality, emplacement and materiality

In addition to the work of Scollon and Scollon (2003), this study heavily draws on Aboussnnouga and Machin's (2010) study of the discourses of war monuments. Their study describes the brief glance or casual look given to war monuments, 'these routine features of our everyday lives, as objects of collective mourning' (2010: 219), with the intention of looking deeper into the relationships between monuments, nationalism and militarism. Aboussnnouga and Machin (2010: 220) assert that semiotic devices in monuments have been employed 'to legitimize war and the idea of national unity in the face of evident exploitation and inequality'. They noted the shift in inscriptions on war memorials from discourses of 'God' and 'Country' in the early twentieth century to discourses that focused on 'those who never returned' and those 'who gave all for freedom' (Abousnnouga and Machin 2010: 220) in the mid-to-late-twentieth century. Interestingly, the latter two discourses were inscribed in these exact words on memorials at the Rohwer Cemetery. At the first level of their multimodal discourse analysis, Abousnnouga and Machin (2010: 221) ask what does an image or sign denote: 'Who or what is depicted here?' Wang and Heath (2011: 402) also note Barthes's contributions to a systematic theory of semiology that 'could enable any tangible objects to deliver meanings towards the public as signs, in which the built environment is certainly verified'. The analysis of connotations at this first level questions what ideas, identities and shared values are being communicated in the public signs. This level of indexicality presents unique challenges for researchers who are exploring discourses in a multilingual or multicultural site. Within this level of analysis site there are at least two systems of discourse meanings at work in a multilingual site. Although the act of memorialization is an everyday common ritual practice, the same habitus (Bourdieu 1981) – those invisible and unprinted rules or conventions of society – is not completely shared. Translation is necessary to associate and ascribe meaning to values, identities and activities. At the third, metaphorical level, Abousnnouga and Machin (2010: 222) explain how 'conventions can become buried for contemporary viewers' and that it is necessary to 'trace the meaning of form, objects and materials used in monuments to understand their cultural and ideological meanings' and the discourses connoted with choices of linguistic and visual signs and symbols. Their discussion of the meaning of form and materiality (height, size, angularity and solidity) that was also influential in developing an understanding of the ways the war monuments in the Rohwer Cemetery communicate to the visitors who travel to this site and how messages in physical features of monuments contribute meanings. This study proposes to look deeper and elaborate the messages communicated at the site and in particular, at what Chmielewska (2010) discusses as 'placing the gaze' at tourist sites. How is the LL at this site contributing to collective memory?

Agency, identity and citizenship in the LL

History is shaped by discourse practices, relationships and sociocultural constructs within speech communities. De Fina (2000: 133) contends that 'storytelling is one of these discourse practices, and as such it displays the same ability to reflect and change context'. The stories we tell of past events are subject to the identity and positioning of one telling the story. As expressions of identity in narratives, De Fina (2000: 134) posits:

> The telling of narratives allows people to present themselves and others in certain roles by placing themselves and others as characters in storyworlds, by negotiating social relationships and images, and by expressing, transmitting, or debating social values and belief systems to which they adhere or are opposed.

The cemetery in this study was created and designed by American internees of Japanese heritage operating under acute political constraints. As Huebner and Phoocharoensil (2017) noted, 'this monumental [was viewed] as social space' (108). Each object, icon and symbol represented a piece of this story – and a story in itself. Unlike traditional texts, the LL is dynamic and 'affords language actors new modalities for the enactment of identity' (Tufi 2016: 114) and agency. Texts and studies (Le Page and Tabouret-Keller 1985; Blackledge 2004; Pavlenko and Blackledge 2004; Cenoz and Gorter 2006; Hanauer 2011; Blackwood et al. 2016) have documented options and challenges in bicultural and multilingual identity construction and negotiation in the LL. Through the LL, the internees performed and negotiated identities through 'acts of citizenship' (Stroud 2016) in resistance to negative national narratives and state ideologies (Slobada 2009) and, at the same time, inscribed the space with sacred rituals of remembrance reflecting their heritage culture.

At each of the three stages or phases of development and renovation at the Rowher Cemetery site, principal actors with specific agendas inscribed the space. The first actors or agents were the residents of Rohwer. They were living in what Hoffman (2004) calls the 'era of memory' – they had a living connection to this history. The second group of inscribers represented the national, institutionalized, collective voice of war memorialization. When the Rowher Camp and Cemetery was listed on the National Register of Historic [American] Sites, two new war memorials were placed in strategic locations to emphasize sacrifice and service to the United States. Later, insistent voices of the remnant in the 'era of memory' and the postmemory generation rose to tell their stories. Hirsch (2008: 107) defines 'postmemory' in terms of 'descendants of survivors (of victims as well as of perpetrators) of massive traumatic events' with memories that 'were transmitted to them so deeply and affectively as to seem to constitute memories in their own right'. Hirsch's (2008) study of the 'Generation of Postmemory' looked at memory, family and photographs. The researchers in this study closely examine motivations of inscribers of memorials and the artefacts in LL – languages, icons, images and emplacement of monuments. The study of the Rohwer Cemetery is enhanced by archival documents, photography and brief responses or readership to the LL at this site. Placed during the renovation of the cemetery, there are clearly messages for the 'no-memory' generations who may read the LL at this site to learn the history of this place and space and to understand the lives of people who once resided in this community.

Methodology

Data collection

A qualitative ethnographic approach was utilized to explore and experience the LL as a tool of remembrance and memorialization, purposefully designed and constructed to tell the story of Japanese Americans in Arkansas during the Second World War. The methodology in this study was designed to document and systematically analyse all literacy objects in the LL at a multilingual memorial site that had been neglected but recently remembered and restored. The primary data was collected in February 2015 and in March 2016 in the form of digital photography. Again, the purpose of the study was to understand how the internment and relocation experience was represented by initial inscribers and remembered by interested stakeholders, and, ultimately, to consider how the LL at this site is presently informing and shaping collective memory of the Japanese American Internment Camp in Rohwer, Arkansas and military sacrifices of its residents during the Second World War.

A critical reflexive approach to examine the initial researcher's processes of selection and 'telling' of this event was maintained. Blommaert (2005: 395) articulated two difficulties for sociolinguists who attempt to attribute meaning to particular forms: the 'differential access to forms' (access to language varieties/codes) and 'differential access to contextual spaces' which present challenges in meaning-attribution and 'differential capacity to interpret'. Acknowledging the initial researcher's limitations, in the process of member-checking Japanese linguistic content and cultural symbols with a Japanese colleague, the informant became co-researcher and collaborator in this study. Thus, enacting inclusive research methodology, researcher and informant are repositioned as co-creators of new insights (Szabó and Troyer 2017).

To enhance understandings of the impact of the LL at this site, two focus groups viewed a PowerPoint presentation of the signage with an initial explanation of the historical context and significance of a Japanese American Interment Camps in Arkansas. After the presentation they were asked to write their immediate thoughts or impressions of the presentation. All participants in the focus group were university students over 18 and under 30. The responses were submitted in written form with only gender and hometowns identified. Names or other personal identifying information remain anonymous.

Analysis

The diagram below shows the placement of the memorial documents in the actual cemetery space. Objects (Items #1–7) are numbered according to the directional gaze of the researcher who was oriented to the site based on access and the placement of informational sign, Item #1. Also note, Item #7 is representative of multiple rows of grave markers, not all shown.

After initial analysis of the Japanese script on the obelisk, it became apparent that the present orientation based on recently added signage was not its original orientation. Therefore, for diachronic analysis of the spatial orientation of the cemetery, we consulted online resources and archival documents and photos of the cemetery and compared them to recent data collected, the digital photographs taken after the national statewide renovation projects. Secondary

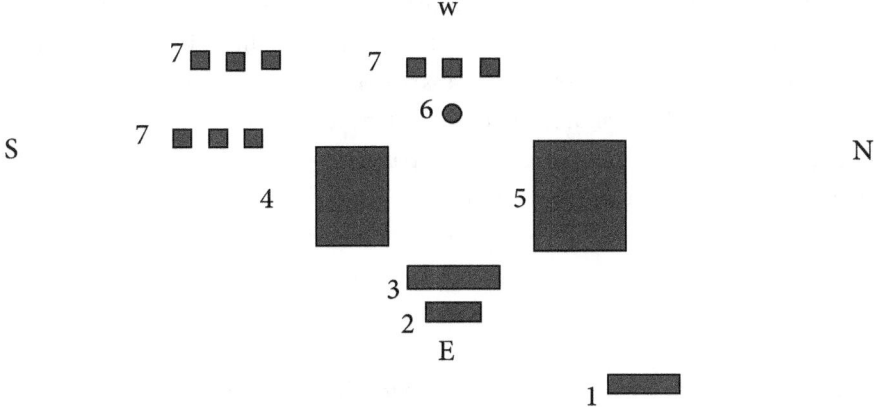

Figure 6.1 Placement of memorial objects in the Rohwer Relocation Camp Cemetery.

Table 6.1 List of memorial monuments analysed

Item #	Description	Figure	Detail
1	Orientational Sign	6.2	'We lived and died here', 2011
2	New marble marker	–	'Rohwer Japanese-American Relocation Center' National Historic landmark sign, 1992
3	New marble US War Monument	–	'Courage' US Fifth Army, 100 Battalion, 442 Regiment, 1992
4	Concrete US Army tank	6.3	100 442 monument with flag and star, 1945, 'In memory of our sons who sacrificed …'
5	Concrete obelisk	–	Japanese script and symbols, 1944
6	Obelisk on lotus	–	Japanese script, 1944/45
7	Concrete grave markers (× 23)	6.5	Inscriptions facing the west in rows on the left and back centre of Figure 1, placed 1943–5.

data included newspaper articles, blogs, websites, brochures, videos and two visits to the Interpretive Center in McGehee.

The responses from the focus groups were categorized by similarity and frequency of theme in the response and analysed based on referential, evaluative or emotional nature of sentential level responses (Garvin 2011). Gender and regional backgrounds were taken into consideration as possible factors or influence on responses. The focus groups' responses were used to provide a limited picture of the cognitive understandings of the historical event as represented in the LL and to briefly assess the emotional impact of the LL during the presentation of the photos. Also, important to note, the responses were not elicited by prompts or questions – participants were just asked to reflect on the presentation in a short written response.

Results

In this study, the first author visited the site for the first time with the purpose of experiencing, reading and documenting the LL in the order that it was presented to a first-time visitor. The signage was systematically documented beginning with directional signs on the highway marking the entrance road to the Memorial Cemetery and the site where the Rohwer Internment Camp was once located. On the road from McGehee to Rohwer, there is an official directional road sign on the right with an arrow signalling the entrance to 'Rohwer War Relocation Center National Historic Landmark'. There is a duplicate sign on the other side of the road for visitors who arrive at the site from the north. Placed low to the ground, a rectangle place-name sign is painted blue with white lettering, framed with iconic barbed-wire trim above and below the words, 'Rohwer Japanese American Relocation Center'. In between the turn off from the highway and the cemetery is an interactive mini-model of guard tower embedded with short audio recordings of internees' narratives, photographs and a map of the grounds. Looking from the guard tower, a grove of trees surrounding the cemetery is visible; however, all traces of the camp buildings have vanished. The walk from the guard tower is at least one hundred yards on a gravel drive that directs the tourist towards an orientational marker.

Item #1 faces the east, orienting the visitor's gaze from the east side of the cemetery (Figure 6.2). On this sign, the background is an archival photograph from 1940s that pictures on the left-hand side perhaps a former internee, an American child, standing in front of grave stones which can only be read by walking into the cemetery from the opposite side, entering from the west. You cannot see the child's face or expressions but his posture suggests reflection and respect. Based on the orientational sign, the visitor's gaze is directed towards the back or unmarked side of the gravestones. All language on the orientational sign (Item #1) is written in English with the heading 'We Lived and Died Here' in the largest font centred at the top. There are two smaller archival photos of

Figure 6.2 Orientational marker (Item #1) on the east side of the cemetery.

internees pasted on top of the larger photograph which serve as the background of the sign. One photograph shows a father facing the camera with a small child on his shoulders, thus evoking the familial forms of mediation postmemorials (Hirsch 2008), and the other is of three children playing in the dirt. Two of the children are facing the camera while the third seems unaffected. These photographs are the only representations of human forms at the site. Near the bottom right are two quotes (narratives) from self-described 'American Evacuees' written by residents of Rohwer Camp. One quote, written in slightly larger font than the other, encourages their children to keep hope during times of despair. The other narrative on the sign speaks of the humiliation, discrimination and the 'disastrous few years out of our life' while encouraging former residents to use this experience as a force 'towards building an enduring generation of finer Americans'. In the bottom right corner in small font are acknowledgements of funding for the project.

Resting on a marble slab, a marble rectangular place-name marker/monument (Item #2) stands about 4-feet high and is marked only on the side facing the east (see Figure 6.1 and Table 6.1). It is written in English only with the word 'Rohwer' in the largest font at the top, and 'Japanese-American Relocation

Center' in a slightly smaller font underneath it. In the centre of the monument is a square metal plate that is embossed with the name 'Rohwer Relocation Center Memorial Cemetery' and the words 'National Historic Landmark', the date of installation, 1992. Smaller text appears on the plate to acknowledge groups responsible for the new monument and funding. Below the metal plate inscribed on the marble are the words 'Made Possible By' and the list of supporters: Arkansas Historic Preservation Program, Japanese American Citizens League, Citizens of McGehee Arkansas and United States National Park Service.

Centred behind Item #2 is a tall, rectangular marble monument (Item #3) resting on what looks to be a large square block of marble (see Figure 6.1 and Table 6.1). Like Item #2, Item #3 was added later and was inscribed in English only. At the top of this monument the word 'Courage' appears in large font. In the second section of the monument from the top, the shield-like emblem of the 442 Regiment with the motto 'Go for Broke' at the bottom is inscribed in the stone. The third section of the monument has words of dedication to the patriotic Japanese American men from Rohwer Internment Camp who sacrificed their lives for America during the Second World War. Also, inscribed beneath the dedication are the US Fifth Army, 100 Battalion and 442 Regiment. The section of the monument below the dedication has the words 'Cassino' and 'Anzio', noting the important battles in Italy where lives were lost, on either side of an iconic image of a hand holding a torch, suggestive of Lady Liberty and/or her torch of freedom, a symbol often found on American memorials (Waldek 2018). On both narrow sides of the monument are iconic US military wreaths, a symbol of victory and redemption adopted into Christianity from ancient Greece culture (Abousnnouga and Machin 2010). Underneath the wreath are lists of Japanese American soldiers from the Rohwer Camp, their rank and the names of the countries where they died. Of the thirty-one soldiers who are listed (fifteen names on one side and sixteen on the other) seventeen died in France, thirteen in Italy and one in Germany. On the side of one section is the name Sam Yutaka Yada, 20 April 1905 to 19 April 1991, and the words 'In honor and memory of Sam Yutaka Yada who during his life in Arkansas 1942–1991 worked for the national recognition and the preservation and restoration of this cemetery'. The Yada family was the only Japanese American family who remained in Arkansas after their internment. On the opposite side of the monument facing west is the word 'Loyalty' in large font at the top. The next section is the actual oath of loyalty and a lengthy narrative explaining the reasons Japanese Americans were forced into relocation centres. Also inscribed are the executive order, the date the Rohwer Relocation Center was established and the number of internees. This is followed by a tribute to the

100 Battalion and the 442 Regiment that served with great valour. Inscribed in the narrative, near the bottom of the stone memorial, are other parts of the story. 'Ironically, the families of this unit remained interned' and there is also mention of the fact that it took over three decades after the war to release the records of Japanese Americans who served in military intelligence operations in the Pacific. This evidences some attempt to weave the harsh treatment of the internees within the national narrative of sacrifice and service.

Behind the 'Courage' monument (Item #3), on the left, is Item #4, one of the original concrete memorials designed by the Rohwer Camp evacuees (see Figures 6.1 and 6.3, and Table 6.1), which we refer to as the tank monument. The base of the monument is the shape of an American Army tank with the numbers '100 442' on bottom of the tank. Sitting on the tank is a large, tall rectangular block of concrete with an American flagpole and painted flag and the words 'In memory of our sons who sacrificed their lives in the service of their country. They fought for freedom. They died that the world might have peace'. Underneath this dedication is the name 'Edward B. Moulton, Assistant Project Director' and the date, 20 October 1945. Sitting on the top of the monument is a star. On the opposite side facing the west, there is an inscribed image of the symbolic American Eagle with its wings spread. Underneath the eagle are the names of Rohwer resident soldiers and the places they died. On the sides of the rectangle resting on the army tank are iconic inscriptions of wreaths at

Figure 6.3 Front and side views of the 'Tank' monument (Item #3).

the top and the months, days and years their fathers and sons fell listed below the wreaths. This war-like monument displays curvature, an interesting feature with different meaning potentials. This feature of angularity versus roundness was considered by Abousnnouga and Machin (2010) in their analysis of war monuments. As a war machine, the tank should perhaps suggest harshness and military strength. However, the curvature of the tank base of the monument, the flower-like representations of the wheels and the absence of a gun suggest something almost gentle, soft, emotional or fluid in contrast to aggressive connotations in more angular forms found on some war memorials.

The other large concrete monument built by the evacuees sits to the right of the tank when looking from the orientational sign (Item #1) and is referred to here as the obelisk (Item #5, see Figures 6.1 and 6.4, and Table 6.1). This multilingual monument is a tall obelisk, sitting on a lotus blossom (*Hasu*) that rests on three tiers of concrete platforms. The sides of the platforms are decorated with swirls, stars and freehand designs. Resting on the top of the obelisk is a ball, or sun disc (*Nichirin*) – a symbol of the Yamato people (*Minzoku),* the descendants of the Sun Goddess. The sun disc at the top of an obelisk is a traditional symbol in Japanese memorials; however, a three-legged crow (*Yatagarasu*), not an eagle, is often on the top. In this instance, there is an eagle with its wings spread. Interestingly, the eagle is facing the opposite side of the cemetery, based on Sign #1 and the researcher's initial eastern orientation to the LL. Below the eagle and sun disc, at the top of the obelisk is a flower. It appears to be the cherry blossom (*Sakura*), a symbol associated to the transience of life and appreciation for fleeting beauty in Japanese culture. Below the flower, written in formal, traditional Japanese characters is a message for the Yamato people, the state of Arkansas and all people. Figure 6.4 presents the Japanese text. Although not provided on the monument, the English translation of this text reads: 'In the 19th year/Of Showa Emperor/In the month of October/Wish for the peace/ Of the spirit of Yamato people/People who sleep/In the ground/For the state of Arkansas/Rohwer Camp/All the people.' In different places on the obelisk there is a distinction between *Yamato Minzoku* (大和民族 – the Yamato people) and *Damashi* (大和魂 – the Yamato spirit). Below this message demonstrating the hybridity of this particular monument are the words: 'Erected by the inhabitants of the Rohwer Relocation Center October 1944', written in English.

On one side of the obelisk is the message quoted earlier to remind the people of Arkansas to keep this ground in beauty and reverence. On the other side of the obelisk, at the top below the sun disc and facing the centre of the cemetery is a traditional Japanese icon, the three-comma tomoe (*Mitsudomoe*). This symbol is associated with the Shinto God of war and later, the Samurai. Underneath that symbol on this side are the names of the Rohwer Center Project Directors written in English. Interestingly hybrid, the panel below the names of the directors is filled with icons and images. There is a symbolic representation of the Yamato People/Spirit in the sunburst (*Taiyo* or *Hi*), an image of the crane (*Tsuru*) and one of the turtle (*Kame*) – traditional Japanese wishes for long life – 1,000 years symbolized in the crane and 10,000 in the turtle.

Inscribed on the 'back' side of the obelisk facing the western side of the cemetery is actually the title of the cenotaph monument (see Figure 6.4); however, unless you were familiar with Japanese monuments and could read Japanese script, you would not understand the words or meanings. Urns for flowers are also on this side. With an eastern orientation to text reading (Kress and van Leeuwen 1996),

Figure 6.4 The Japanese inscription on the obelisk, Item #5.

written from top to bottom in Japanese characters only are these words: 'Purity *Jyo* (浄)/Belief *Shin* (信)/Eternity *Kuon* (久遠)/To comfort *Nagusameru* (慰める)/Soul/spirit *Rei* (霊)/Cenotaph Stela *Hi* (碑). Underneath the title of the monument are the words written in English: To Him Who Sleeps/Eternally Here/ Descendant of/Glorious Yamato/Who Came in His/Prime with Hopes/And Ambitions/Heroic to Battle/The Fortunes of/Life Peace And/Bless Be Yours.' The poem-like blessing is followed by the date, 1944. This multilingual monument is the most ornate with designs that trim the edges, icons and images, as well as multilingual expressions of identity. The platforms are decorated with swirls, stars and free hand designs. It is this multilingual monument that reifies a bicultural identity through language, icons and symbols of ancient Japanese culture.

A US Flag on a silver flagpole (see Figure 6.1) is categorized as Item #6. The flag is positioned behind the tank (Figure 6.3) and obelisk. It is the tallest object in the cemetery and can be seen from all points of orientation in the cemetery.

There are twenty-three individual gravestones with names of people who were buried in this cemetery (Item #7, see Figures 6.1 and 6.5, and Table 6.1).

Figure 6.5 A gravestone (Item #7).

They are all uniform in shape, size and design and they are in rows located to the back left of the tank monument (Item #5) and behind the flagpole (Item #6). The inscriptions with names, written in English, and dates are facing the west boundary of the cemetery. There is a design at the top with an inscription or markings that have not been decoded; however, there appear to be two fish-like images, perhaps, representing fish/carp (*Koi*), a symbol of aspiration and perseverance from a Japanese legend. The gravestones are distinguished by a small iconic symbol above the name to represent religious or other cultural affiliations. On the gravestones are iconic options to denote religious identity: (1) a cross for Christians; (2) a flower, or possibly the sun, for the Shinto identity; and (3) in the case of the infants, a blank space.

Findings

After a close reading of the LL, there were three distinct voices in the LL at this site: (1) the personal voice of first-hand experience and postmemory, speaking in multilingual expressions of humiliation and hope, grief and pride, both Japanese and American; (2) an official unified national narrative of war memorialization; and (3) the collective voice or conscience of interested stakeholders – all the groups, institutions and organizations committed to remembering and addressing this injustice. Through LL analysis of the Rohwer Memorial Cemetery, this study identified competing narratives, multiple voices or 'ways of telling' the story. Entering the cemetery from the east, the emplacement of the new monuments enacts traditional US military rituals of memorialization and a unified narrative of nationality, military service and devotion to country. Names of funders and supporters of this project presented on various monuments remind visitors to the cemetery of the collective efforts of stakeholders and historical responsibility to remember this injustice. Nonetheless, we maintain that the unified national narrative at this site is contested by multilingual markers which importantly suggest bicultural national identity through articulation of both Japanese and American language codes and symbols. We also argue that this plurality of identity is perhaps diffused by the reorientation of this memorial space and inattention to the multilingual literacies.

Double articulation of identity

What is happening at this site is a double articulation of identity. Double focalization which occurs when an event or situation is presented in a narrative through two simultaneous perspectives. This is 'not the same as multiple focalization in which an event or situation may be presented a number of times from different perspectives' (Childers and Hentzi 1995: 89).

The monuments designed and inscribed by the Japanese American internees in both English and Japanese position this group as US citizens belonging to both worlds. This may be uncomfortable positioning for the host country based on what Pavlenko (2005) described as a negative attitude towards early twentieth-century immigrants which framed bilingualism [and mostly likely dual nationality] as an 'un-American' phenomenon. In some instances the identities represented in the LL at this site appear fused or hybrid. Although the tank monument clearly asserts American identity and patriotic service to country, the wheels of the tank appear as flowers and as some males in the focus group noted, the tank is strange because it is without the gun. Furthermore, while the obelisk/cenotaph is loaded with expressions of the Yamato people's spirit and identity – Japanese language as well as iconic cultural symbols – there are messages written specifically to American English-speaking audiences. In addition, an eagle, one of the most salient symbols of the American spirit, is on the top of the sun disc. In Japanese culture a three-legged crow is often placed above the round the ball-like sun on the top of the obelisk; but in this case, it is an eagle with its wings spread, suggesting a fusion of icons and identities. The sun (*Taiyo or Hi*), an iconic symbol of the Yamato people and Japanese characters were both inscribed on the obelisk; however, the chrysanthemum (*Kiku*), which is the official Japanese government seal and appears on the cover of all Japanese citizen passports, was not clearly documented at the site. The absence of the Japanese citizenship marker, perhaps, connotes a realignment of national loyalty, thus affirming a multilayered, bicultural identity that performed national citizenship and military service to the highest degree and at the same time embodied the Japanese cultural identity, spirit in the most adverse of circumstances. The LL provided a space to enact and perform a bicultural identity option (Hanauer 2011).

Reorientation of memorial space

After the camp's closure, the cemetery site was marked as a national war memorial and registered as a National Historic Site. Because of the placement of the orientation sign during the renovation which was completed in 2011, and in relation to previous additions of the new monuments after the camp had been closed, evidence from the photographs and messages on the obelisk suggest that the original orientation to the cemetery has been changed. In the processes of telling and retelling in the LL, there is potential for refocusing and diffusing intentions of original inscribers.

When the Rohwer Cemetery and Campsite was placed on the National Historic register and government institutions appropriated the story, the narrative subtly shifted to a more unified presentation. In the presentation of a National Historic Site, the new reorientation reinforces ways 'the state controls public spaces critical to the reproduction of dominant memory while marginalizing the counter-histories' (Low and Lawrence-Zúñiga 2005: 22). However, archival photographs of the LL at this site from the 1940s showed people looking at names on the grave markers and approaching the cemetery from the west, at the top of Figure 6.1, not the bottom. The names on the grave markers (Item #7) are not visible when approaching the cemetery from the east and the translations of the information written in Japanese on the obelisk clearly mark the front and the back of the monument which has been reoriented. Photographs from the past show people standing in front of and being photographed from what is now the backside of the obelisk. Hamilton (2005: 17) states, 'Photographs are particularly appropriate for documenting these aspects of literacy since they are able to capture moments in which interactions around texts take place'. In addition, other archival documents supported an awareness of the original orientation and allowed us to mark diachronic change that had occurred at the site over time. In the 1940s visitors were personally connected to the site, whereas now recent additions and renovations have given it a more unified national identity.

The ritual practices of war memorials and 'the military's indispensable role in building and maintaining a nation is an ideological principle that leaves few opportunities in the United States for debate and discussion' (Jenks 2018: 61). However, we argue that the current orientation to the site, which could be easily remedied with another sign on the west side, minimizes this double articulation of identity. Perhaps, the multilingual literacies and hybrid identity on the obelisk give us a clearer picture of what it means to be American.

Deane (1995: 356) asserts that 'culture, when it is propagated as a canonical system, always asserts its "monogenealogy," repressing its internal differences and hybrid origins'. In the case of the United States, this position confounds logic and compromises foundational principles. There should be a celebration of the plurality and diversity that define the United States. This multilingual memorial site reflects what it means to be a US citizen, part of a nation of immigrants with pieces of our hearts from other places.

All literacy objects in memorial spaces, their placement, material compositions, sizes and shapes contribute meaning. Some aspect of meaning is embedded in the features and relevant to understanding the significance of this historical site, the inscribers and/or the ones being remembered. Alonso (1988: 49) states, 'Meanings of the past define stakes of the present.' In public memorial spaces, the LL creates associations of place and space, connects the past with the contemporary moment. However, the process of memorializing in the LL is multidimensional, uneven and often guilty of omission and erasure. What happens in the time between forgetting and remembering? How does memory shift as 'it is deployed and redeployed by different parties towards different political ends' (Houdek and Phillips 2017)? LL research continues to develop new ways to answer these questions and in this study provides opportunities to go deeper to mediate new understandings of competing discourses.

Conclusions and implications

The LL is a powerful tool of remembrance that shapes, mediates and to a certain extent controls public history. More research of memorial sites is necessary to fully exploit the usage of LL approach as a tool for close readings of multilingual memorials and for evaluating the effectiveness and responses to public educational sites in general. As this study has shown, careful, critical observation and analyses of LLs at memorial sites strengthen accountability in representations; however, there is still a need for responsible awareness of the impact of the LL in shaping collective memory. The majority of the participants in the focus groups expressed genuine interest and sadness when presented with this aspect of Arkansas history; however, some of the participants expressed an understanding of the justification of the government's actions and the need for national security. Clearly, as in ways of telling, there were different ways of seeing (Berger 1972). Some participants in the focus group had no memory of this event and were learning about it through the visual presentation of the site for the first time. No one mentioned or seemed curious about the Japanese script or symbols on the obelisk. One participant was from Rohwer and was unaware that the cemetery existed. Virtual tours of LLs can be effective educational tools for communicating the past; however, like the LL, the researcher's gaze is subjective, selectively focused, and often full of omissions and gaps.

After periods of forgetting and remembering, in the process of 'telling' and 'retelling' through the LL, there are dangers of refocusing and diffusing messages and intentions of original inscribers or authors. Double vocalization of Japanese American identity was minimized in the transformation of the Rohwer Cemetery. This leads us to conclude and confirm Scollon and Scollon (2003) who argued that spatial organization and placement of signage contribute significantly to orientation of a site, resulting in nuanced understandings of meanings and messages expressed through individual and institutional practices of memorialization.

Another important, unexpected finding was the performance of the LL as a meditational tool. Perhaps, given the different voices or competing multilingual narratives at this memorial site, LL analysis provided a deeper understanding of the US voice and identity in the translations of the Japanese texts on the monument. The LL offers a dynamic space for the negotiation or re-negotiation of identity, unique from other types of texts. Expressions of bicultural Japanese American identity expressed at this site offer a deeper understanding of the lived experiences and performance of bicultural identities as presented in the LL at this time, in this place. More studies of US multilingual memorials are needed to appreciate the rich heritage of the people in this country. This plurality and multiplicity of cultures, religions and languages are and have always been this country's greatest strength and resource.

References

Abousnnooga, G. and D. Machin (2010), 'War Monuments and the Changing Discourses of Nation and Soldiery', in A. Jaworski and C. Thurlow (eds), *Semiotic Landscapes: Language, Image, Space*, 219–240, London: Continuum.

Alonso, A. M. (1988), 'The Effects of Truth: Re-presentations of the Past and the Imagining of Community', *Journal of Historical Sociology*, 1 (1): 33–57.

Barthes, R. (1964), *Elements of Semiology*, London: Jonathan Cape.

Barton, D. and M. Hamilton (2005), 'Literacy Practices', in D. Barton, M. Hamilton and R. Ivanič (eds), *Situated Literacies: Reading and Writing in Context*, 7–15, London and New York: Routledge.

Berger, J. (1972), *Ways of Seeing*, London: Penguin Group.

Berger, J. and Mohr (1982), *Another Way of Telling*, New York: Vintage International.

Blackledge, A. (2004), 'Constructions of Identity in Political Discourse in Multilingual Britain', in A. Pavlendo and A. Blackledge (eds), *Negotiation of Identities in Multilingual Contexts*, 68–92, Clevedon: Multilingual Matters.

Blackwood, R., E. Lanza and H. Woldemariam (2016), *Negotiating and Contesting Identities in Linguistic Landscapes*, London: Bloomsbury.

Blommaert, J. (2005), 'Situating Language Rights: English and Swahili in Tanzania Revisted', *Journal of Sociolinguistics*, 9 (3): 390–417.

Bourdieu, P. (1981), *Language and Symbolic Power*, Cambridge: Polity Press.

Cenoz, J. and D. Gorter (2006), 'Linguistic Landscape and Minority Languages', in D. Gorter (ed.), *Linguistic Landscape: A New Approach to Mulitlingualism*, 67–80, Clevedon: Multilingual Mattters.

Childers, J. and G. Hentzi (eds) (1995), 'Double-voiced Text', in J. Childers and G. Hentzi (eds), *Columbia Dictionary of Modern Literary Cultural Criticism*, 89–90, New York: Columbia University Press.

Chmielewska, E. (2010), 'Semiosis Takes Place or Radical Uses of Quaint Theories', in A. Jaworski and C. Thurlow (eds), *Semiotic Landscapes: Language, Image, Space*, 274–291, London: Continuum.

Connerton, P. (2008), 'Seven Types of Forgetting', *Memory Studies*, 1 (1): 59–71.

Deane, S. (1995), 'Imperialism/Nationalism', in F. Lentricchia and T. McLaughlin (eds), *Critical Terms for Literary Study*, 2nd edition, 354–368, Chicago: University of Chicago Press.

De Certeau, M. (1984), *The Practice of Everyday Life*, Berkeley: University of California Press.

De Fina, A. (2000), 'Orientation in Immigrant Narratives: The Role of Ethnicity in the Identification of Characters', *Discourse Studies*, 131–158, London: Sage Publications.

Encyclopedia of Arkansas History and Culture (2018), 'Japanese American Relocation Camps'. Available online: http://www.encyclopediaofarkansas.net/encyclopedia/entry-detail.aspx?entryID=2273 (accessed 18 December 2018).

Foucault, M. (2002), *The Order of Things: An Archaeology of the Human Sciences*, London and New York: Routledge.

Fremon, D. K. (1996), *Japanese-American Internment in American History*, Springfield: Enslow Publishers, Inc.

Garvin, R. T. (2011), *Emotional Responses to the Linguistic Landscape in Memphis, Tennessee: An Urban Space in Transition* (Doctoral dissertation, Indiana University of Pennsylvania).

Guilat, Y. (2016), 'Redefining the Public Space as a Semiotic Resourse through Institutional Art Events', in R. Blackwood, E. Lanza and H. Woldemariam (eds), *Negotiating and Contesting Identities in Linguistic Landscapes*, 163–179, London: Bloomsbury.

Hamilton, M. (2005), 'Expanding the New Literacy Studies: Using Photographs to Explore Literacy as Social Practice', In D. Barton, M. Hamilton and R. Ivanič (eds), *Situated Literacies: Reading and Writing in Context*, 16–34, London and New York: Routledge.

Hanauer, D. (2011), 'Non-place Identity: Britain's Response to Migration in the Age of Supermodernity', in D. Hanauer (ed.), *Identity, Belonging and Migration*, 198–217, Liverpool: Liverpool University Press.

Hirsch, M. (2008), 'The Generation of Postmemory', *Poetics Today*, 29 (1): 103–128.

Hoffman, E. (2004), *After Such Knowledge: Memory, History, and the Legacy of the Holocaust*, New York: Public Affairs.

Houdek, M. and K. R. Phillips (2017), 'Public Memory', *Oxford Research Encyclopedia of Communication*. Available online: http://oxfordre.com/communication/view/10.1093/acrefore/9780190228613.001.0001/acrefore-9780190228613-e-181?rskey=t3jl1P&result=1 (accessed 18 December 2018).

Huebner, T. and S. Phoocharoensil (2017), 'Monument as Semiotic Landscape: The Contested Historiography', *Linguistic Landscape: An International Journal*, 3 (2): 101–121.

Jenks, C. (2018), 'Meat, Guns, and God', *Linguistic Landscape: An International Journal*, 4 (1): 53–71.

Kress, G. and T. van Leeuwen (1996), *Reading Images: The Grammar of Visual Design*, London and New York: Routledge.

Lanza, E. and U. Røyneland (2015), 'Memorials, Multilingualism in Norway', Presentation at LL7, UC Berkeley, CA.

Le Page, R. G. and A. Tabouret-Keller (1985), *Acts of Identity: Creole-based Approaches to Language and Ethnicity*, Cambridge: Cambridge University Press.

Low, S. M. and D. Lawrence-Zúñiga (2005), *The Anthropology of Space and Place: Locating Culture*, Oxford, Blackwell.

Malinowski, D. (2009), 'Authorship in the Linguistic Landscape: A Multimodal Performative View', in E. Shomany and D. Gorter (eds), *Linguistic Landscape: Expanding the Scenery*, 107–125, New York: Routledge.

Pavlenko, A. (2005), *Emotions and Multilingualism*, Cambridge and New York: Cambridge.

Pavlenko, A. and A. Blackledge (eds) (2004), *Negotiation of Identities in Multilingual Contexts*, Clevedon: Multilingual Matters.

Scollon, R. (2001), *Mediated Discourse: The Nexus of Practice*, London and New York: Routledge.

Scollon, R. and S.W. Scollon (2003), *Discourses in Place*, London and New York: Routledge.

Shohamy, E. and S. Waksman (2010), 'Building the Nation, Writing the Past: History and Textuality', in A. Jaworski and C. Thurlow (eds), *Semiotic Landscapes: Language, Image, Space*, 241–255, London: Continuum.

Sloboda, M. (2009), 'State Ideology and Linguistic Landscape', in E. Shohamy and D. Gorter (eds), *Linguistic Landscapes: Expanding the Scenery*, 173–188, London and New York: Routledge.

Stroud, C. (2016), 'Turbulent Linguistic Landscapes and the Semiotic Citizenship', in R. Blackwood, E. Lanza and H. Woldemariam (eds), *Negotiating and Contesting Identities in Linguistic Landscapes*, 3–18, London: Bloomsbury.

Szabó, T. P. and R. A. Troyer (2017), 'Inclusive Ethnographies: Beyond the Binaries of Observer and Observed in Linguistic Landscape Studies', *Linguistic Landscape: An International Journal*, 3 (3): 306–326.

Tufi, S. (2016), 'Constructing the Self in Contested Spaces: The Case of Slovenian-speaking Minorities in the Area of Trieste', in R. Blackwood, E. Lanza and H. Woldemariam (eds), *Negotiating and Contesting Identities in Linguistic Landscapes*, 101–116, London: Bloomsbury.

Waldeck, S. (2018), *10 Monuments and Memorials That Changed America Forever*, Architectural Digest, 4 July. Available online: https://www.architecturaldigest.com/gallery/10-monuments-and-memorials-that-changed-america-forever (accessed 18 December 2018).

Wang, Q. and T. Heath (2011), 'Towards a Universal Language of the Built Environment', *Social Semiotics*, 21 (3): 399–416.

7

Sarajevo's War Childhood Museum: A Social Semiotic Analysis of 'Combi-Memorials' as Spatial Texts

Maida Kosatica

Introduction

Bosnia–Herzegovina (B&H) is usually represented as a multilingual, multifaith and multicultural post-war country. Divided by, inter alia, religion (Islam and Christianity–Catholic and Orthodox) and three official 'languages' (Bosnian, Croatian and Serbian), the country's constitutive peoples (Bosnian Muslims, Bosnian Croats and Bosnian Serbs), linguistically speaking, understand each other perfectly. However, when sorting out the story of what actually happened in the 1992–1995 war, who the victims are/were and where/how they should be commemorated, it seems as if the peoples of B&H speak completely different languages. This is particularly apparent in the country's memorial landscape. Whether we find them in golden plaques on façades, marble blocks, glass walls or simple white stones, memorials in the country are mainly reflected through the voices of victims, warnings and more experiential aspects. This comes as no surprise since the 1992–1995 war had no winners, and apart from recognizing the heroism of fallen soldiers, emotions associated with victory and a sense of closure are not as common. Sarajevo, in particular, the country's 'under-siege brand', delivers many sites of pain and trauma for citizens and foreign visitors alike. Such sites have generated a kind of 'dark tourism' (Lennon and Foley 1996) whereby memories of the war are commodified for consumers and war history is simplified for those who wish to gaze upon past violence. Memorial sites notably evidence contested and competing narratives rather than being signifiers of shared values and consensus. This is perhaps understandable considering these sites are often funded by higher political entities and elites or public agencies that inevitably privilege only one group's narrative. In this context, dark tourism thereby quickly morphs into merely 'hot tourism' (cf. Naef, 2012), offering visitors a very limited insight into the country's past and the impact of conflict in general (Volcic et al. 2014). Within Sarajevo's semiotic landscape, a different site emerges: the War Childhood Museum. Claiming to be the first museum ever to deal exclusively with the experiences of growing up during a time of war, this museum has a somewhat unusual story behind it; more precisely, a question. In 2010, a young Bosnian activist asked those who were children during the siege of Sarajevo – *What was a war childhood for you?* Over 1,000 received messages were published in the book *War Childhood* (Halilović 2013). As the author, and later the founder of the museum, realized that many of these messages relate to different personal objects, he asked people to donate these to, what at that point was, a museum in preparation. Containing 4,000 items, the museum was officially opened in January 2017 and awarded the 2018 Council of Europe Museum Prize.

Spontaneously working as a memorial and addressing violence unconventionally through the eyes of the innocent, the museum reconstructs the war exclusively within the framework of personal stories subsequently reproducing 'discourses of history, and part of a socially and institutionally mediated collective struggle with a painful, unsettling, and traumatic past' (Byford and Tileagă 2017: 104). What makes this museum even more different from other, usually contested sites, is its intent to recognize violence in ways which obviate heavily loaded associations with 'perpetrator' identities. Aiming to build a universal story of children's war experiences, the museum remains mindful of and oriented towards only those who did not play a protagonistic role in starting the war but have undoubtedly suffered its horrific consequences. Their traumatic experiences are especially imbued with the narratives of lost lives and the museum is thus directly invested in remembrance that is discursively constructed and promoted in the public sphere (Wodak and Richardson 2009). Remembering is, of course, a discursive act (Middleton and Edwards 1990) but one which is accomplished and communicated not only through/in speech and writing. As Ravelli and Heberle (2016) explain, space as well is an important communicative resource as sated with meanings as any written, spoken or visual text. Needless to say then, remembering is realized through/in the production of spaces, especially memorial spaces.

Keeping all of the above in mind, I organize this chapter around the following two approaches. First, I want briefly to situate my analysis in the context of museum studies, explaining some of what makes the War Childhood Museum distinctive and particularly special, conceptualizing it as a 'combi-memorial' – a third-generation post-war memorial project 'amalgamating elements of memorial, archive and exhibition' (Niven 2013: 78). I then turn to an empirical part in which I read the War Childhood Museum as a spatial text, that is, 'a complex, three-dimensional multimodal text constituted of a number of co-deployed semiotic modes – space, structure and movement – working together through the process of inter-semiotic transformation' (McMurtrie 2016: 23). As museums make meanings through a variety of semiotic resources and mediational means (Halliday 1978; Van Leeuween 2005) (e.g. artefacts, images, spaces, technologies) realized both discursively and physically (Ravelli and McMurtrie 2015), my interest here is directed towards the interplay of the spatio-interactional formats and semiotic modes organized into a complex 'assemblage' which produces a particular set of interactions (Pennycook 2017). By examining how meanings are generated through a specific selection/composition of different meaning-making resources, I aim to pinpoint a multimodal discursive organization of this specific spatial text. I am likewise interested in the embodied experiences of space created through movement and design choices (cf. Tzortzi 2007; Christidou and Diamantopoulou 2016) that affect the ways the exhibits are perceived and sensed (e.g. Leahy 2012). Ultimately, by engaging in gripping memories through multimodal performances of a commemorative dialogue, the museum represents a complex interplay of convention (normative) and innovation (countering). Regardless of its bilingual nature, the museum does not seem to be 'properly' or rather equally engaging local visitors, specifically the Bosnian Serbs. By omitting the Cyrillic script used exclusively by Bosnian Serbs, it prioritizes, perhaps inadvertently, Sarajevo's post-war language ideology and upholds the existing linguistic power of the capital. Yet, the museum does establish a truly different space for warning and reminding in a post-war B&H and produces new discursive practices which challenge our analytical approach to spatial texts.

Beyond counter-monuments: Museums as 'combi-memorials'

The twentieth century saw profound changes in the design of memorials particularly with regards to transformative processes of representation and interpretative agency. These transformations have blurred the boundaries between museums and monuments. The conceptualization of museums as memorials was primarily based on the architectural design which highlighted their monumental function. Their contemporary memorial character, however, is associated instead with emotion- and memory-focused narratives. Indeed, contemporary museums tend to establish themselves as sites of remembrance, representing social memory along with other spatial texts (e.g. cemeteries, galleries). That museums act as spaces inviting visitors to engage in the imagination of difficult experiences and memories aligns nicely with Arnold de-Simine's (2013: 1) notion of 'neogenesis': 'The ethical imperative to remember is taken to its literal extreme: visitors are asked to identify with other people's pain, adopt their memories, empathize with their suffering, reenact and work through their traumas'. By the same token, memorialization practices have thus taken a 'countering' turn which, as James Young (1992: 271) explains, creates 'brazen, painfully self-conscious memorial spaces conceived to challenge the very premises of their being'. In simple terms, the idea behind counter-memorials rests in the proposition that conventional forms are actually oppressive and abused for political purposes. However, not all counter-memorials succeed in disrupting the norms. Highly political examples which failed to escape clichéd representations and stimulate an expected public response have come under strong criticism for simply producing 'a new social formulation of re-memory' (Lupu 2003: 132).

Bill Niven (2013), too, offers a critique of counter-memorials' 'special' status, arguing that these aesthetically bolder forms do not represent a radical break with what came before. Regardless, in this chapter, I am less concerned with the issue of counter-memorials being just 'rhetorical gestures' (Niven 2013) addressing the same issues only more neatly. Instead, I am interested here in their potential to allow all three ethnic groups involved in the war to share one space without silencing or domination (Strakosch 2010), especially since the museum fully greets their participation despite excluding one of the country's official scripts. In order to identify what is reflected in/through the taxonomy of museums that is intrinsic to counter-memorials, I investigate the following features bound to the absence of conventional forms: an opposition to common beliefs and accepted truths, a rejection of traditional forms, the creation of intimacy with the audience and an invitation for visitors to make sense of the meanings they themselves (re)make (Stevens et al. 2012). Although acknowledging that contemporary indoor museums may adopt certain 'countering' features, they are still largely museum-like anyway; they are buildings, with entrances and exits, with exhibits and exhibitions, established objectives and tickets to sell. In this sense, I ultimately follow Niven's (2013) notion of 'combi-memorials' which through countering elements seek to integrate memorial, archive and exhibit in an act of interpretation, as well as to redefine the traditional elitist understandings of memorial art as the preserve of professionals. Countering features here constitute an innovation that affects the organization of space and thus they come to recognize the embodied and involved presence of visitors and interaction (between people, artefacts and space) which unfolds in complex ways. For example, in combimemorials we find new walking and looking methods, bodily responses and intense awareness of one's own empathy. By their very nature then, combi-memorials show how the complex blend of modernization and standardization creates the flux of museum-monument and public-intimate experiences. Therefore, combi-memorials as a new breed of post-war memorial and as a kind of elaborate and diffuse spatial text help in analytically approaching what Pennycook (2017) calls 'semiotic assemblages' as transitory arrangements in which things and people are brought together and function in new and messy ways.

Analysis: The museum as multimodal, spatial text

The approach underpinning the following analysis lies within the complementary framework of social semiotics and multimodality (e.g. Kress and Van Leeuwen 2001; Van Leeuwen 2005). In this regard, I focus on socially motivated signs realized through the interconnectedness of different modes combined to communicate and create meanings (Lindstrand and Isulander 2012). Inherently multimodal, museums are, as Ravelli and McMurtrie (2015) explain, best understood as spatial texts. They are realized in a range of representational, compositional and interactional meanings, modes and resources which simultaneously contribute to wider sociocultural contexts (Kress and Van Leeuwen 2001). These three meanings (or metafunctions) are adopted from Halliday's (1978) systemic functional theory proposing that all communicational systems must be able to simultaneously represent some aspects of the world (representational meanings), produce texts related to other texts within a certain context (compositional meanings) and construct social relations between the participants in communication (interactional meanings) (Kress et al. 2001). I use the three meaning systems for organizing my analysis of the museum's semiotic-spatial features, their symbolic values and the ways in which they constantly overlap.

Representational meanings: Children's stories

Positioned in an aesthetically unappealing narrow passage, the simple 'black & white' square-building lacks a bold architectural design and presents itself only with the prominent entrance signage: 'War Childhood Museum', in the local language(s) but Latin script only and in English, along with the juxtaposition of childhood and war – a boy and a girl holding a grenade balloon (Figure 7.1). The logo fixed to the façade is powerfully representative of the living conditions of children in war when death was an integral part of their everyday life. Moreover, it illustrates the way in which children adapt to such living conditions – armaments, shell fragments and bullet casings were indeed regular playthings. This logo also alludes to the main interior content and integrates well with the overall exhibition theme. The building was not designed for the museum specifically but was repurposed and allocated by the Old City Municipality

Figure 7.1 War Childhood Museum, entrance and façade, Sarajevo, 2017.

Council. As such, the architectural style itself tells us little about the museum. On the other hand, the choice of script may tell us more. With regards to B&H's language policy, three official languages correspond to the country's three main ethnic groups or constitutive peoples – Bosnian, Croatian and Serbian languages – and two scripts – Latin and Cyrillic. However, the so-called different languages are three varieties of one language referred to as Serbo-Croatian before the war. Thus, Bosnian, Croatian, Serbian and Montenegrin, respectively, are a single polycentric language (Kordić 2010). Bosnian Muslims and Croats use the Latin script exclusively, while Bosnian Serbs use both Latin and Cyrillic scripts, but mainly Cyrillic. On the one hand, it could be argued that the Cyrillic script is absent since Bosnian Serbs did not show interest in active participation in the museum (i.e. donating objects and/or recording video-testimonies). The 'War Childhood' project was initiated in Sarajevo, and a large number of objects were collected in the capital. Consequently, the exhibition reflects the demographic structure of the area (Bosnian Muslim majority). More recently however, the collectors have also been active in the areas with other ethnic groups as majorities (e.g. Mostar, Banja Luka) since the project's initial intention is openness to and inclusivity of all people who have experienced the war as children, regardless of the ethnic group they belong to. On the other hand, we could ask had the museum initially included the Cyrillic script, would that be a sufficient initial step in welcoming Bosnian Serbs to actively participate in the museum. As Shohamy and Waksman (2010) argue, the absence of one of the country's official languages at the sites of memorials, in this case a variety and a script, indicates exclusion of a group using that language/variety/script. Thus, the practice of omitting Cyrillic potentially indicates a greater ideological bias or the museum's aim at only Bosnian Muslims and Croats as the local target audience.

Representationally speaking, what we essentially see in the museum are different ways of depicting memory: personal stories, biographical objects, video testimonies and projected messages originally published in the book *War Childhood*. Visitors are initially presented with a collection of distinctive mementoes, consisting of common objects such as toys, food packaging, musical instruments, clothing, photographs, letters, diaries etc. The approach to the topic of childhood through these banal objects accompanied by intimate stories already represents a break with a more traditional way of schooling people about (the) war. Appearing to be silent, disposable objects, these 'biographical objects' (Hoskins 1998), as we shall see, present more than a visual-material experience – they are sensory resources (cf. Thurlow 2015, on sensuous materialities), the carriers of affect and the sources of imagination. Alongside the objects, visitors are also offered personal stories originally written in participants' native language and translated into English. These stories are much more than explanations of the objects they follow, playing an essential role in the production of both autobiographical and public memory. Unlike curators' interpretations, so-called label scripts, which typically accompany the artefacts, the stories contextualize objects and are an important part of the conceptualization and design of the museum. The founder of the museum himself explains, in an online video interview, 'personal stories give the objects particular significance, whereby the museum gives these stories collective and universal significance; it gives them a life'.[1] Stories often rich in detail and varying in length are displayed next to, below or above the objects. The exhibited content follows unusually distinctive stories which explain what the objects symbolize. Some stories are about suffering and hardship, loneliness or fear. Some revisit acts of bravery and playfulness – wittily, almost romantically. However, I specifically focus on the stories of loss symbolizing a very powerful form of personal memorialization which takes a fully public shape. The main reason I focus on these stories is because they counter and expand semiotic terrains in Sarajevo, and B&H in general, by being free from the 'blame game' as well as being presented in quite unexpected, incoherent ways. One such story is called 'Blue Bunny' positioned above the smiling stuffed toy, neatly displayed in a glass cabinet:

Extract 1. Blue Bunny

I don't remember my brother. He was only a little bit older than me. They took him from my mother's arms and killed him. We fled from our home without a chance to lock the door behind us. Then we lived in a refugee camp. This blue bunny was the only thing that brought me joy. Its colour and smile brightened the gloomiest days. I donated the rest of my toys, keeping only my bunny.

Other stories which are also a part of the exhibition we find in the video testimonies shown on a screen in the central part of the exhibition space (about 100 hours of interviews in which participants retell their personal war experiences) and short messages projected on the wall, originally published in the book *War Childhood*. Although they do not relate directly to any specific biographical objects, these are nonetheless powerful elements included in the production of thematic meanings. What becomes clear at this point is that these four methods of delivering war memories stand in a mutually complementary relationship. In the realm of this visual-verbal interaction, both written texts and visual objects whose meanings are indexed by/through each other offer the 'naturalistic' representation of war memory underlining real and 'authentic' experiences and producing an overarching discourse of loss.

Neather (2008) explains that a further complexity is added to bilingual museums since both target and source texts must operate within the same museum space and in relation to the same set of visual codes. All content in the War Childhood museum is translated into English – stories on placards, video testimonies, projected messages, audio tour. There is no significant expansion or reduction of textual information in the translations. English is explicitly meant for the foreign visitors who have an opportunity to hear the story of war in a completely different way than they are used to (i.e. free of explicit accusations and identification of perpetuators). Latin text in the local language is positioned above the English translation. Scollon and Scollon (2003: 158) argue that the positioning is a key means for expressing 'code preference'. However, the Cyrillic script is absent, and this is quite expected due to the status the Cyrillic script has in Sarajevo, as well as in other areas with Bosnian Muslims and Bosnian Croats as a majority. In simple terms, as this is the script used exclusively by Bosnian Serbs (and in Serbia), it is treated as the enemy's. Of course, Bosnian Serbs also use Latin so the omission potentially indicates the economy of space on the placards, or a resistance to the imposed post-war language policies on exclusivity of usage based solely on ethnicity. However, the prediction that all Bosnian Serbs will accommodate to Latin as the script of the dominant group in Sarajevo can in fact result precisely in their unwillingness to visit the museum. Thus, a script adjustment could signal an invitation for active participation of all ethnic groups, which is clearly crucial for B&H's memory landscape as it is currently already simplified and contributes to inter-group tensions.

Although the museum contains 4,000 items, the permanent exhibition displays fifty objects which rotate every three months. The founder of the museum indicates three practical reasons for such a sequence: (1) the protection of the artefacts from prolonged light exposure, dust, and people's touch; (2) all objects and stories from the collection must be displayed eventually; (3) the prevention of empathic numbing as it is difficult to absorb more than fifty personal stories which eventually become similar (Halilović 2017 – personal interview). Rotation certainly attracts the audience by offering new content and altering the exhibition space. In addition, a display with a smaller number of objects assumes greater significance (Coxall 1991). A psychological phenomenon labelled 'numbers and numbness' by Slovic (2007) relates to this effect. The relationship between imagery, affect and sensitivity to the number of people suffering suggests that the exposition to the individual stories increases our capacity to experience empathy. As humans naturally find statistics hard to process, big numbers fail to invoke emotions and motivate compassionate actions (Slovic 2007). Organizing collections into sets of fifty objects also implies that the curators create a specific message they want to convey. Indeed, as the founder of the museum explains, when selecting the artefacts for one rotation, the primary intention is to include as diverse a range of experiences as possible in order to illustrate the complexity of growing up in war. It has not been indicated whether the age and ethnic structure are considered relevant aspects when selecting artefacts. On the other hand, when it comes to their presentation, some of the participants themselves contributed to the formal appearance (i.e. arranging donated objects in cabinets). This adds to the 'authenticity' of the performance and potentially to the establishment of strong connections the visitors make between themselves and the objects/stories. It also shows how the museum accomplishes itself as a combi-memorial which, as Niven (2013: 84) explains, develops in the collaboration between professionals and donors, creating 'public art in a truly interactive sense'. Such interaction seems to be the result of a sort of 'singularization' (Kopytoff 1986) as the objects initially having emotional value only to individuals are musealized[2] and consequentially assigned a special status of unique artefacts valuable to the public. The process of musealization is particularly important as an object associated only with the original owner arrives in a completely 'raw' shape, and once it settles into the collection, its meaning and value are reordered as its uniqueness is remade. As Albano (2007: 18) explains, personal possessions which turn into artefacts gain broader sociocultural significance suggesting 'the evocative power of objects, whether imaginative or emotive, that enlists them as bearers of both the form and content of life narratives'. In this sense, once the personal objects and stories go through such mode of documentation and public delivery, they become 'performative narratives' (Schiffrin 2003). All this shows that people's material as well as reflective (experiential) contributions become documented and synthesized into an institutional archive (Legrady and Honkela 2002), establishing the process central to my theoretical framing: memory + archive + exhibition = combi-memorial.

Finally, the representational meanings operate along two dimensions and reveal a kind of inconsistency. Locally, the museum enhances the dark tourism identity of the city where around 1,600 children were killed during the siege. It archives and exhibits personal memories of survivors about the friends and family members they have lost, as well as confessions about how this affects these now grown-up citizens. Hagemann (2013: 135) notes that children in particular 'strengthen the impression of the vulnerability and the victim status of the city in general'. In this sense, the museum comes inevitably to reproduce and secure the epithet of an anguished city further amplifying the local competition for victimhood as a recognizable quality of the country's semiotic landscape. However, speaking in more global terms, the museum narrates a universal story of children in war and their ambiguous loss. Setting the process of remembrance in motion via fully 'authentic' and intimate content, it provides the space which, as we shall see, contributes to the depoliticization of the war. In this regard, the museum, challenging the post-war semiotic landscape, symbolizes a global anti-war message and an attempt to move beyond unsynchronized stories about the atrocities, perpetrators and victims.

Compositional meanings: 'Moving' shadows

In museums, compositional meanings are made through arranging the visual, spatial and material elements in a coherent whole. This section is thus concerned with identifying how coherence is produced through the relations which exist between various resources used to create a certain narrative. Here, I specifically focus on how the museum's elements are placed in relation to each other. In this sense, I start with a description of design choices that shows how the layout of space interacts with the layout of objects to realize a specific effect (Tzortzi 2007).

The exhibition space consists of one relatively small square gallery with two partitioned walls creating two corridor-like narrow, connected passages. In the first passage, we find artefacts displayed in glass showcases or on white pedestals, and the messages projected on the wall above the artefacts which can be clearly seen from the central section. The second narrow passage leads to the central exhibition section, containing objects stored in glass/wall cabinets or on pedestals, on-screen audio-video excerpts (for which headphones are available), objects fixed on the walls or hanging from the ceiling. The internal spatial cohesion is primarily achieved through design choices – we can see consistency in terms of size, colours, materials and the nature of artefacts. Artefacts are equally separated from each other. In each row, there are five to nine artefacts displayed. The order of the artefacts in different rows is determined by the nature of the objects being efficiently represented. Therefore, the 'hierarchy' is design-dependent. The way artefacts are displayed seems to be a result of practical considerations rather than anything else, and in this regard, display choices are size-dependent. Some objects hang down from the ceiling in the centre of the gallery because almost all objects found in this section are pieces of clothing which, unlike the paper-based objects (letters, diaries, photographs), are not too sensitive to touch. For example, it would be difficult to properly display a dress in a small glass cabinet. However, despite the practical nature of the design choices, the meanings are nonetheless extrapolated from the method of display (cf. Coxall 1991) as we shall see in the following examples encapsulating the museum's multimodal ordering.

Words which introduce the visitor to personal stories are brought via technological modes, projected above the artefacts displayed in the first passage. On the black wall, working as a slide layout, we find messages originally published in the book *War Childhood*. These are simply written, yet complex in meaning. Presented as enlarged and raised components they make a powerful impression; first, in a quantitative manner, and second, in a dynamic manner with the messages constantly interchanging in terms of both the content and language (local language in Latin script to English). We see that some words are bigger in font and more prominent, but such presentation appears to be rather random, similar to the way the messages are presented in the book *War Childhood*. Messages are unified with other modes precisely through the stories of loss, creating a sense of the spatial synchrony. They are instant, ephemeral, staged. Similar to the monument inscriptions, many of them work as intimate expressions of grief and commemoration of the loss of loved ones (Abosunnouga 2012) aiming to emphasize violent acts that cause sorrow and pain. However, the focus often seems to be on those who are remembering – we do not always get to know the victims' names or birth and death dates typically found on monuments. This notwithstanding, most people can strongly relate to and empathize with these messages as most of us can imagine what it would be like to lose parents, siblings and loved ones. Narrators make themselves especially prominent through strong expressions of affect representing the whole childhood period as marked by a singular event – *It killed my childhood*. Sentiments are sometimes expressed almost ironically as if a participant is asking the visitor 'What the war childhood could be like if not only pain and trauma?' Impersonalization is particularly common and accomplished through *instrumentalization* where social actors are represented by a reference to the instrument used to perform activities they are engaged in (Van Leeuwen 1996) – *A sniper killed my brother; A crush at school killed by a shell*. Such linguistic choices for avoiding the perpetrators are closely associated with implicit or mediated meanings (Coxall 1991) strategically generating resistance to the politicization of the war.

Projected messages offer an introduction to the stories of loss I am specifically interested in, followed by the artefacts presented in the May 2017 exhibition. These written recollections create complex performances of memorialization and illustrate how different resources work together, specifically how written language and other resources stand in a complementary relationship. Such stories of suffering, troubling memories and violent events focusing explicitly on the victims and suppressing the perpetrators' identities indicate another counter-monumental strategy the museum acquires (Stevens et al. 2012). Every story is unique indeed, but typically they all offer a kind of introduction, gradually getting stronger in affect through emotional components brought forward into space. Free from any accusations, stories warn of the worst consequences of war and help visitors understand the representational meanings of the exhibition. One such story is about a young girl's death:

> **Extract 2. My sister's drawings of Disney heroes**
> *My sister, Aida Mehmedagic, made these drawings when the war first started. It was dangerous to go outside, so we spent most of our time in either the house or the basement. She always had a book in her hands, or some colours. She loved to draw and was quite talented at it, too. It wasn't rare for a real masterpiece to emerge by the light of an oil lamp. Sometimes she wrote letters to her friends, but they were more a diary of sorts than anything else. Shortly after she wrote these letters and her seventeenth birthday, on a relatively peaceful night, someone knocked on our doors. It was one of my sister's friends. My sister stood in the wide doorway, and I went to the kitchen in hopes that I would join them soon. Suddenly there* was *a loud explosion, the whole house shook, and everything was covered in dust. I heard shouting and my dad's voice. I sat down, I couldn't move from the shock. Shortly after, my dad came into the room, lost out of his mind, and just grabbed a blanket. I never saw my Aida again.*
>
> Selma 1995, Sarajevo

The opening sentence informs the visitors how the donor and the producer of the artefacts are related. The first passage identifies and describes the girl the artefacts belonged to, capturing her innocence and introducing her to the visitor who is supposed to easily identify with the victim (the act of drawing) and imagine a human face to whom the drawings belonged. Such creation of intimacy produces familiarity, and this is important as empathy is invoked more easily towards those who become familiar (Bloom 2016). Details in the passage help the visitors understand the meaning of the artefacts and imagine the conditions under which they were created – exactly when and where. Powerfully inviting the reflections of visitors through the description of physical and mental conditions, the second passage describes the setting when the traumatic event took place. Here, the spatio-temporal framework is pivotal in constructing the sequential structure that illustrates rapid transitions from order to chaos (Schiffrin 2003). Such framework also plays an important role in structuring the story that delivers shifts from material/somatic to emotional:

Spatio-temporal references	*On a relatively peaceful night; my sister stood in the wide doorway; and I went to the kitchen, my dad came into the room*
Physical conditions	*Suddenly there was a loud explosion; the whole house shook; and everything was covered in dust; I sat down; and just grabbed a blanket*
Mental conditions	*I could not move from the shock; lost out of his mind*

Although this testimonial is surrounded by stories of other kinds of suffering, various referring terms that apply to the experiences of wartime children create a coherent set of 'labels' that enhance textual meanings of the museum. Lexical repetition of the spatial term *basement*, for example, that we find in other personal stories as well as in space, establishes indexical relationship with the content at display and powerful interplay with the overall design:

Extract 3. The safest hiding place in besieged Sarajevo
*Just before the war started my grandfather built a swing for me to play at our cottage. My swing remained in the mouldy **basement** where I spent the first years of my life instead of being surrounded by nature's beauty.*
Naida 1989, Sarajevo

Extract 4. Small Oven
*We lived in the **basement** and had not seen the sky, sun, nor rain for months. This small oven symbolizes the art of survival during the war.*
Sanja 1979, Sarajevo

At this point, we come to the construal of visitors who, organizationally speaking, are positioned as being central to the experience of the museum and to the negotiation of space (Ravelli and Heberle 2016). As Abousnnouga (2012: 343) explains, the visual components 'allow the viewer to feel the experiences metaphorically in a way which the written discourse alone cannot achieve'. The recurring term *basement*, for example, is reflected in and reinforced by the design of the exhibition space and visual components. The museum employs fragments or inherent properties of basements: confined space, dark colours and shadows. The two passages made by the partitioned walls in the exhibition gallery create a spatial sensitivity by simulating the narrowness of small spaces. When there are many visitors, such spatial composition invokes the physical experience of crowding (*There were always a lot of us in that small basement, sometimes as many as thirty people*). Here, the movement is possible in one direction only and this narrowness leaves us intimately engaged with the space as we are literally physically confronted with the densely concentrated artefacts.

This is exactly how the space, or more precisely the organization of space, creates an experiential dimension. The space closes up around the visitors affecting the way they feel (according to Ravelli and Stenglin 2008, powerless, uncomfortable and insecure).

This materialization of basement interchangeably invites feelings of intimacy and isolation. Indeed, the museum encapsulates this specific spatial moment determined by the nature of personal stories/experiences. The idea seems to be to make the visitors imagine and try to comprehend how it feels (for a child) to be 'captured' in a basement. In alignment with such ambience, cool tones prevail throughout the museum. Black walls and grey floors create a sense of a quiet, simple space, and add to the museum's dark tone and depth. Counter-monuments are generally dark forms (which recognize and warn of violent events), and such countering strategies are clearly visible here as well (Stevens et al. 2012). Compositionally speaking, the lighting of the space is equally significant. Whether displayed in wall or glass cabinets, white pedestals or hanging from the ceiling, the bright lights illuminate all the artefacts (Figure 7.2). As the cabinets and pedestals have a white background and the artefacts are additionally illuminated, there is a contrast between the background of the exhibition gallery and the artefacts which is immensely pronounced. Such composition visually limits distractions, intensifies the visual force of each element a visitor

Figure 7.2 Illuminated artefacts creating shadows.

encounters and fosters an intimate experience (Dickinson et al. 2006). Indeed, lighting design creates shadow patterns that add symbolic and emotional value to the objects and enhance textual cohesion (Kress and Van Leeuwen 2001) as these are fully representative in terms of the ways in which children were growing up – in the shadows of war.

Interactional meanings: Outside the glass

Speaking in spatial terms, meanings in the museum are made through the interactions between participants and their stances and attitudes towards the interior while they negotiate their feelings, attitudes and judgements (Ravelli and Stenglin 2008). Here, I start from the notion that our interactions unfold in response to the emplacement of the exhibition elements (how/where they are positioned). Being inspired by Radley's (1991) idea that objects are perceived morally (as well as aesthetically, functionally and nostalgically), I seek to illustrate how the specific display influences the way visitors interact with them while intensifying their imaginative and affective experience. In this section, I address the two aspects of embodied rhetoric – bodily movement and the imagination of embodiment 'read out' by means of a created display (Radley 1991).

The exhibition gallery is rather simple, ensuring easy movement for the visitors. Two narrow passages impose a route indicating we should move towards the central exhibition space – a very traditional, didactic model applied to the visitors. Yet, these passages enforce a significant proximity to the exhibits – a counter-monumental strategy. It could be argued that the simulation of confined space forms a desired affective moment as the visitors become emotionally responsive before the space becomes less linear. In this way, the gallery sections are delicately extending each other (Ravelli and McMurtrie 2015). How the artefacts are displayed in the central exhibition space affects their saliency and power to impress, as well as the ways visitors interact with them, which we shall see shortly. Here, they can create their own fields of movement (e.g. going straight, towards the front or the end of the central section, or even below the artefacts) while being encouraged to explore and go beyond simply gazing. Ten objects hanging from the ceiling are closing this section with story placards positioned between them, and the intended way to walk through this section, if wanted, is to crouch below them – a movement especially simple for children. Multiple patterns of movement facilitate agency and participation in terms of choice of what to read/observe/listen to. Visitors thereby can observe the objects and skip to watch video testimonies, consume all or only a few artefacts, controlling and thereby self-regulating their engagement with the content, as opposed to the narrow corridors where interaction is much more sequential. These alternative modes of movement, and subsequently of engagement, rely on a constant interplay between convention and innovation.

Some artefacts are conventionally stored in simple showcases, but this does not diminish their affect. The objects we stare at are only seemingly passive – they make relationships with the visitors, make us wonder, imagine and empathize. In Thurlow's (2015: 626) words, objects are 'communicative actions, ways of representing the world (or saying something about it), ways of interacting with users, and broader meta-communicative or textual accomplishments'. Clothing items especially, as Albano (2007: 20) explains, talk through their different physicality (shape, condition, texture, colour, smell) and 'literalize the notion of embodiment by showing the traces left by the body'. The features of the blue hat in a glass cabinet, for example, are not easily identifiable in a visitor's visual field after entering the central exhibition section (Figure 7.3). But once we approach the artefact, the object's quality changes. Here, the visitors use their movement as a semiotic resource to assign themselves various spectating and participatory roles within the installation (McMurtrie and Murphy 2016). As we move closer, the hat fills more of our visual field and we are then able to identify and 'read' different details. It is first our body, or more precisely, our movement, that determines the qualities of the artefacts and therefore their meanings.

Figure 7.3 'Adidas hat'.

Physical distance from or proximity to the object as 'embodied resources' (Iedema, 2003) modifies what the object is then telling us. Likewise, movement is an essential part and mode through which the visitors *see* the objects (Christidou and Diamantopoulou 2016). The text is thus produced for us as the spectators, but we also actively participate in its further production as our movement influences the way these objects talk to us. Sometimes, just one detail (a hole) of an object (the hat) creates an irresistible appeal and communicates much more than perhaps expected while forcing us to engage actively with other resources (written text). In this sense, only after approaching the Adidas hat closely enough, do we notice a white tear and the visitor is immediately invited to read its story (below is just an extract of it):

Extract 5. Adidas hat

On the right side of my head, my scalp, I felt a hole that fit two fingers. I started to panic, but my father found me then. Later, at the hospital, they stitched my wound up. The next day I learned that six of my friends, with whom I had been playing, had been killed, and five others had been wounded. The hole in my Adidas hat is a reminder of what happened.

Goran 1982, Sarajevo

Artefacts such as the Adidas hat thus function as tangible embodiments of personal stories that 'imbue the exhibition display with emotional and imaginative power within the exhibition context' (Albano 2007: 25). Similarly, artefacts function as objects of violence and 'tangible surrogates of the absent subjects' (Albano 2007: 20) making us imagine the victims and bringing back a memorial component to the exhibition that ultimately makes this combi-memorial a place of empathy and remembrance. In this sense, artefacts communicate to the visitors through traces of injury, consequently representing fully embodied objects reflecting and retrieving people's real experiences.

Examples of particular interest here are the artefacts outside the cabinets which show how, along with the visual perception, our movement as well (i.e. close approach) is a dominant aspect in gaining an affective sense of the objects. Indeed, as Ravelli and McMurtrie (2015) point out, the museum experience is not simply visual. In short, and to follow Christidou and Diamantopoulo (2016: 12), it is fully multimodal, 'entailing a series of embodied performances'. Take, for example, the vest in Figure 7.4 which disrupts boundaries and conventions and creates an evocative engagement by the countering display. It illustrates how the borderless presentation of the objects can make loss approachable and imaginable through sensory oriented encounters that establish intimate experiences. The vest hanging from the ceiling, apart from seeming to be more

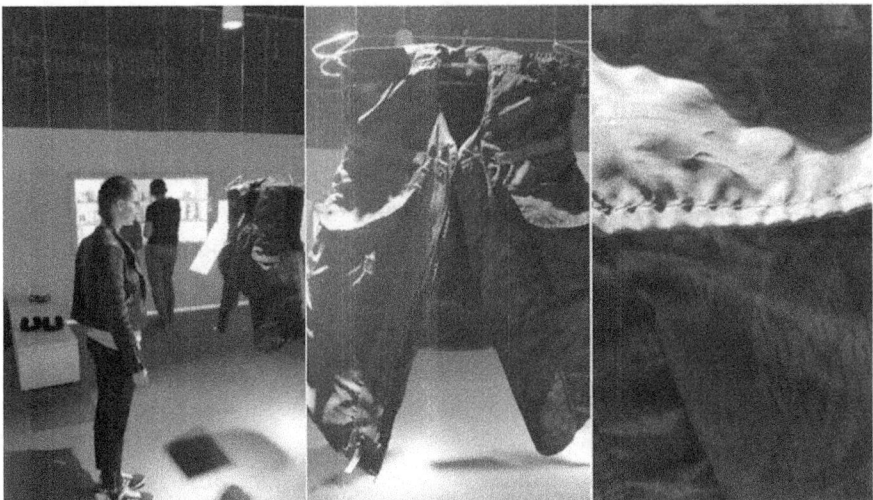

Figure 7.4 Bulletproof vest.

I was 16 years old when the war started, and overnight I had to replace my plastic and wooden toy guns with a real automatic. On that day, December 7, 1992, we were expecting a major armed attack. My neighbour, Mr. Nedžad, was one of the few lucky ones who owned a bulletproof vest. Right before we left for the front he convinced me to put it on and to tighten my helmet. Words can't describe the hell that my troop went through that day. Sadly, only one young woman and I managed to escape that hell alive, heavily wounded. Later they showed me the hole in my bulletproof vest that the shrapnel made on its way to my heart. My wounds took a long time to heal, and I was no longer the same, playful boy.

Alem 1975, Sarajevo

important due to its central emplacement, also creates an illusion of being more tangible 'evidence' inviting a complex bodily engagement. It is the 'borderless' presentation that enables the visitors to almost *feel* the texture and even smell the fabrics of that vest. Radley (1991: 74) explains how we sense the artefacts through spatial arrangements but also through their use, 'they are sensible in what they call out in us as we would touch, lift, wear, or stand upon them'. As we cannot *sense* the objects in such ways (although Halilović indicates that the visitors often cannot resist touching the artefacts), 'the body is a key feature of the perception' (Radley 1991: 74), or more specifically, an imagination of embodiment. As Latour (1991: 10) observes, 'things do not exist without being full of people', but they need embodied voices and a 'corporeal nature' in order to gain the power to function as 'primary evidence and incisive signifying devices' (Williams 2007: 31). Entwistle and Wilson (1998: 94) argue that the body and clothing are in a dialectic relationship to one another, where clothing is 'a crucial aspect of our experiences of embodiment since the body is a dynamic field, which gives it life and fullness'. Like any other personal items, clothes are 'fetishized' because they belong to someone who wore them (Albano 2007), and the borderless presentation attributes sensory values to them – we can get extremely close to the vest, see the damaged part where the shrapnel pierced it, imagine a teenager wearing it – imagine the sixteen-year-old Alem who lost his childhood overnight. In addition, this imagination of embodiment reminds us of the many absent bodies as well – those who were killed.

Conclusion: Spaces of remembering

In this chapter, I have illustrated how we might understand public remembrance being accomplished through a spatial text, specifically focusing on the multimodal organization of the War Childhood Museum in Sarajevo. With little attention paid so far to how remembering is accomplished semiotically, I believe my analysis contributes to the field of semiotic landscape studies, museum studies and discourse studies of memory/remembering. In this regard, I have offered a close reading – a social semiotic analysis – of a museum as a spatial text and as an example of an interior semiotic landscape or microscapes (see Juffermans 2018).

The War Childhood Museum's significance – in terms of its message and its importance – cannot be attributed to or explained only by representational practices. It is precisely the spatial compositional and embodied interpersonal meanings that are ultimately key. They show us that remembering as a discursive act is constituted through, and partly relies on, complex exchanges between visitors and the space that radically departs from convention not just through countering elements, but also through the disruption of well-established questions – *who is the enemy and who is guilty*? By this token, museums realized as combi-memorials are not just spatial texts, but rich spatial-embodied assemblages that obscure the borders between museums and monuments and allow us to see the importance of objects, the body and the place alongside the meanings of linguistic resources (Pennycook 2017). Ultimately, my analysis shows that remembering is both a communicative and a social act which is enacted through an autobiographical and participatory war discourse. This museum, acting as a combi-memorial and a powerful performative spatial text, produces a critical, self-reflectional war discourse realized through a story about remembering. Appeals to imaginative, affective and intimate experiences that support delicate mediation between 'private and public' are precisely the strategies that produce the resistance to the politicization of the 1992–1995 war and create narratives entirely independent of 'perpetrator' identity. Visitors are thus prompted instead to focus on children/childhood as a less charged way to relate these narratives to their own personal and meaningful experiences. The museum's openness to diverse interpretations of remembering calls for more introspective, and more critical and complex perspectives on historical events. It could be argued that those who read a story 'of a child' are free to empathize and be that child for a moment, while being free from ethno-centric and political baggage. It may not be realistic for this particular configuration of war-heritage to establish new forms of collective memory in B&H. However, by carrying a strong anti-war message, the museum challenges the grounded rituals of remembrance and symbolizes a nexus between all innocents regardless of the ethnic groups they belong to. These new ways of understanding the war and of remembering the victims challenge established meanings, conventional memorial topography and enrich contemporary semiotic landscapes.

Notes

1 Video interview with the museum's founder: https://www.youtube.com/watch?v=bINbTLfNSzw
2 Musealization can be defined as the process of extracting a real thing from its original, natural or cultural environment and conferring on it a new character as 'museum object' (musealia) (Mairesse 2004: 11).

References

Abousnnouga, N. G. (2012), 'Visual and Written Discourses of British Commemorative War Monuments', PhD thesis, Cardiff University.
Albano, C. (2007), 'Displaying Lives: The Narrative of Objects in Biographical Exhibition', *Museum and Society*, 5 (1): 15–28.
Arnold de-Simine, S. (2013), *Mediating Memory in the Museum: Trauma, Empathy, Nostalgia*, New York: Palgrave Macmillan.
Bloom, P. (2016), *Against Empathy: The Case for Rational Compassion*, New York: Harper Collins.
Byford, J. and C. Tileagă (2017), 'Accounts of a Troubled Past: Psychology, History, and Texts of Experience', *Qualitative Psychology*, 4 (1): 101–117.

Christidou, D. and S. Diamantopoulou (2016), 'Seeing and Being Seen: The Multimodality of Museum Spectatorship', *Museum and Society*, 14 (1): 12–32.

Coxall, H. (1991), 'How Language Means: An Alternative View of Museums Text', in G. Kavanagh (ed.), *Museum Languages: Objects and Texts*, 85–89, Leicester, London and New York: Leicester University Press.

Dickinson, G., B. Ott and E. Aoki (2006), 'Spaces of Remembering and Forgetting: The Reverent Eye/I at the Plains Indian Museum', *Communication and Critical/Cultural Studies*, 3 (1): 27–47.

Entwistle, J. and E. Wilson (1998), *The Body Clothed: 100 Years of Art and Fashion*, London: Hayward Gallery.

Hagemann, S. (2013), 'The Bomb and the City: Presentations of War in German City Museums', in W. Muchitsch (ed.), *Does War Belong in Museums? The Representation of Violence in Exhibitions*, 4, Edition Museumsakademie Joanneum.

Halilović, J. (2013), *War Childhood*. Sarajevo: Udruženje URBAN.

Halilović, J. (2017, May 28). Personal Interview.

Halliday, M. (1978), *Language as Social Semiotic*, London: Arnold.

Hoskins, J. (1998), *Biographical Objects: How Things Tell the Stories of People's Lives*, New York and London: Routledge.

Iedema, R. (2003), 'Multimodality, Resemiotization: Extending the Analysis of Discourse as Multi-semiotic Practice', *Visual Communications*, 2 (1): 29–57.

Juffermans, K. (2018), 'Micro-landscapes and the Double Semiotic Horizon of Mobility in the Global South', in C. Stroud, A. Peck and Q. Williams (eds), *Making Sense of People and Place in Linguistic Landscapes*, 201–222, London: Bloomsbury.

Kopytoff, I. (1986), 'The Cultural Biography of Things: Commoditization as Process', in A. Appadurai (ed.), *The Social Life of Things: Commodities in Cultural Perspective*, 64–92, Cambridge: Cambridge University Press.

Kordic, S. (2010), *Jezik i nacionalizam*, Zagreb: Durieux.

Kress, G. and T. Van Leeuwen (2001), *Multimodal Discourse: The Modes and Media of Contemporary Communication*, London: Arnold.

Kress, G., C. Jewitt, J. Ogborn and C. Tsatarelis (2001). *Multimodal Teaching and Learning: The Rhetorics of the Science Classroom*, London: Continuum.

Latour, B. (1991), 'The Berlin Key or How to Do things with Words', in P. M. Graves (ed.), *Brown Matter, Materiality and Modern Culture*, 10–21, Routledge: London.

Leahy, H. (2012), *Museum Bodies: The Politics and Practices of Visiting and Viewing*, Farnham: Ashgate.

Legrady, G. and T. Honkela (2002), 'Pockets Full of Memories: An Interactive Museum Installation', *Visual Communication*, 1 (2): 163–169.

Lennon, J. J. and M. Foley (1996), *Dark Tourism*, London: Continuum.

Lindstrand, F. and E. Insulander (2012), 'Setting the Ground for Engagement – Multimodal Perspectives on Exhibition Design', *Designs for Learning*, 5 (1–2): 30–49.

Lupu, N. (2003), 'Memory Vanished, Absent, and Confined: The Countermemorial Project in 19980s and 1990s Germany', *History and Memory*, 15 (2): 130–164.

Mairesse, F. (2004), 'La muséalisation du monde (The musealization of the world)', in F. Mairesse (ed.), *RTBF 50 ans. L'extraordinaire Jardin de la Mémoire*, Morlanwelz: Musée royal de Mariemont.

McMurtrie, R. J. and A. Murphy (2016), 'Penetrating Spaces: A Social Semiotic, Multimodal Analysis of Performance as Rape Prevention', *Social Semiotics*, 26 (4): 445–463.

McMurtrie, R. J. (2016), *The Semiotics of Movement in Space*, New York and London: Routledge.

Middleton, D. and D. Edwards (1990), *Collective Remembering*. London: Sage.

Naef, P. (2012), 'Travelling through a Powder Keg: War and Tourist Imaginary in Sarajevo', *Via@* (1).

Neather, R. (2008), 'Translating Tea: On the Semiotics of Interlingual Practice in the Hong Kong Museum of Tea Ware', *Meta*, 53 (1): 218–240.

Niven, B. (2013), 'From Countermonument to Combimemorials: Developments in German Memorialization', *Journal of War and Culture Studies*, 6 (1): 75–91.

Pennycook, A. (2017), 'Translanguaging and Semiotic Assemblages', *International Journal of Multilingualism*, 14 (3): 269–282.

Radley, A. (1991), 'Boredom, Fascination and Mortality', in G. Kavanagh (ed.), *Museum Languages: Objects and Texts*, 63–82, Leicester, London and New York: Leicester University Press.

Ravelli, L. and V. M. Heberle (2016), 'Bringing a Museum of Language to Life: The Use of Multimodal Resources for Interactional Engagement in the Museu da Lingua Portuguesa, Brazil' RBLA, *Belo Horizonte*, 16 (4): 521–546.

Ravelli, L. and R. McMurtrie (2015), *Multimodality in the Built Environment: Spatial Discourse Analysis*. London and New York: Routledge.

Ravelli, L. and M. Stenglin (2008), 'Feeling Space: Interpersonal Communication and Spatial Semiotics', in A. Gerd and E. Ventola (eds), *Handbook of Interpersonal Communication*, 355–396, Berlin, New York: Walter de Gruyter.

Schiffrin, D. (2003), 'We Knew That's It: Retelling the Turning Point of a Narrative', *Discourse Studies*, 5 (4): 535–561.

Scollon, R. and S. W. Scollon (2003), *Discourses in Place: Language in the Material World*. London: Routledge.

Shohamy, E. and S. Waksman (2010), 'Building the Nation, Writing the Past: History and Textuality at the *Ha'apala* Memorial in Tel Aviv-Jaffa' in A. Jaworski and C. Thurlow (eds), *Semiotic Landscapes: Language, Image, Space*, 241–255, London: Continuum.

Slovic, P. (2007), '"If I Look at the Mass I Will Never Act": Psychic Numbing and Genocide', *Judgment and Decision Making*, 2 (2): 79–95.

Strakosch, E. (2010), 'Counter-monuments and Nation-building in Australia', *A Journal of Social Justice*, 22 (3): 268–275.

Stevens, Q., K. A. Franck and R. Fazakerley (2012), 'Countermonuments: The Anti-monumental and the Dialogic', *The Journal of Architecture* 17 (6): 951–972.

Thurlow, C. (2015), 'Multimodality, Materiality and Everyday Textualities: The Sensuous Stuff of Status', in G. Rippl (ed.), *Handbook of Intermediality: Literature, Image, Sound, Music*, 619–636, Frankfurt am Main: De Gruyter.

Tzortzi, K. (2007), 'The Interaction between Building Layout and Display Layout in Museums', PhD thesis, University of London.

Van Leeuwen, T. (2005), *Introducing Social Semiotics*. New York and London: Routledge.

Van Leeuwen, T. (1996), 'The Representation of Social Actors', in C. R. Caldas Coulthard and M. Coulthard (eds), *Texts and Practices: Readings in Critical Discourse Analysis*, 32–70, London: Routledge.

Volcic, Z., K. Erjavec and M. Peak (2014), 'Branding Post-war Sarajevo', *Journalism Studies*, 15 (6): 726–742.

Williams, P. (2007), *Memorial Museums: The Global Rush to Commemorate Atrocities*. Oxford, UK: Berg Publishers.

Wodak, R. and J. Richardson (2009), 'On the Politics of Remembering (or Not)', *Critical Discourse Studies*, 6 (4): 231–235.

Young, J. E. (1992), 'The German Counter-monument', *Critical Inquiry*, 18 (2): 271–295.

Part Three

Memories

8

Remembering in Order to Forget: Scaled Memories of Slavery in the Linguistic Landscape of Rio de Janeiro

Branca Falabella Fabrício and Rodrigo Borba

Introduction: Remembering in order to forget

In 2011, the City Hall of Rio de Janeiro started investing in work to renovate the abandoned harbour area of the city. This ambitious redevelopment of a long-neglected historic site was part of the preparations for the 2016 Olympics. The re-urbanization programme, named *'Porto Maravilha'* (Marvelous Port), involved not only the improvement of the district's streets and squares but also the construction of two new museums – the Rio Art Museum and the Museum of Tomorrow. The latter, designed by Spanish architect Santiago Calatrava, is dedicated to technology, science and sustainability. Embedded in the larger revitalization plan, it explicitly projected Rio as a modern city looking ahead to a successful future.

This projection of Rio as a vanguard space is a scaling manoeuvre which retells the history of the city from very specific standpoints, as we will elaborate shortly. But it produced a clash. Despite its futuristic vision, the restoration venture ended up unveiling the region's connection to the Atlantic trade of enslaved Africans. As excavation work advanced in the waterfront quarter, they soon stumbled on the Valongo Wharf (*Cais do Valongo*), a nearby zone buried under a square and a parking lot, where 1 million African slaves arrived between the end of the eighteenth century and the beginning of the nineteenth century.

I am grateful to the National Council for Scientific and Technological Development (CNPq) for the grant which made this research possible (307157/2013-0).

Thanks are due to the Coordenação de Aperfeiçoamento de Pessoal de Nível Superior (CAPES) for the grant which allowed the development of this research (BEX00000.61/2017-04).

Considered one of the largest entry points of enslaved Africans in the Americas (Jordão 2015), the pier and its surroundings integrate a complex named 'Little Africa' (*Pequena África*), which includes a major slave market and, a few metres away, a slave cemetery whose history is saturated with tragedy, death, injustice and social annihilation.

This finding was celebrated by both entrepreneurs and authorities. Eduardo Paes, Rio's mayor at the time, asserted that he planned to build a museum to preserve the many objects found in the previously buried port. In a post on Instagram he was even more emphatic: 'I hope that the history of the Black diaspora will be remembered. That the origins of our country, of our background, and of our culture can mark our memory. That men's [sic] violence may be remembered to avoid being repeated.'[1] This kind of discourse led to some initial concrete actions committed to memorialization. One of them was the inauguration of the 'Historic and Archaeological Circuit to Celebrate the African Heritage' (*Circuito Histórico e Arqueológico de Celebração da Herança Africana*), which has both touristic and pedagogical aims. The itinerary comprises a two-hour walking tour around Little Africa that can be pursued on one's own, using a map specially designed for the activity, or with a local guide.

In 2017, UNESCO designated the Valongo sector a World Heritage Site in an important initiative towards the constitution of a permanent memorial to the suffering imposed on enslaved Africans. The area was thus placed on an equal footing with Auschwitz Concentration Camp and Hiroshima Peace Memorial – considered by UNESCO as world historic sites emblematic of humans' destructive power. In fact, the local signage provides a reminder of the 'intense criminal activity against humanity' put forth by colonialism. Although UNESCO's upscaling action potentially entails a sense of social awareness, its symbolic value has been continuously mitigated by practical actions concerned with the market rather than history, a common phenomenon in sites used for so-called dark tourism and the global market built around the 'fascination with visiting sites of death, disaster and atrocity' (Lisle 2007: 333) on which many cities capitalize. An ultra-developmental impetus triggered by a business-oriented mindset invested approximately $2.5 billion in real estate, transportation and corporate towers, at the expense of supporting the priceless archaeological heritage found in the port area. This kind of negligence is testimony to the fact that narrating the history of a city (or, indeed, of a nation) entails complex relations between remembering and forgetting[2] in order to (re)cast it into a positive forward-looking image. The proximity of the Valongo Wharf to the Museum of Tomorrow is representative of such motion.

In this sense, as Jordão (2015) illustrates, the mayor's actions towards the preservation of Little Africa were paradoxical. While the two museums were built and became operational in record time, the many objects of African origin found in the excavation works have been kept in containers where they still await the attention of expert studies. At the present moment, authorities say that there is no money to provide for further research on the sites. Consequently, the Institute of the New Blacks, a centre whose aim is to revitalize the history of the African diaspora in Brazil and which houses the historic cemetery, is about to be closed.[3]

It can thus be said that the celebratory public rhetoric resulted in empty discourse and unfulfilled promises. Although the 'discovery' of the Valongo Wharf and its transformation into a memorial were celebrated by many as a laudable effort to remember the city's history as one of the most important slave ports for the colonial enterprise, it materialized in practice as an exercise to forget, or as Jordão affirmed in an interview, 'It is a weird logic to remember while forgetting.'[4]

Such a scenario provides the backdrop against which we explore how memories of destruction, survival, resistance and identity are fathomed, that is, scaled, and communicated in contemporary Little Africa. Analysing the Linguistic Landscape (LL) of the area through the sociolinguistic notions of scale and indexicality, we probe three memorials which constitute Little Africa and their semiotic surrounds: the 'Valongo Wharf', 'Pedra do Sal' and the 'Cemetery of the New Blacks'. Approaching memorials as semiotic accomplishments, we understand that the scale work they do may simultaneously contribute to a sense of ethical responsibility and violent processes of alienation (Carr and Fisher 2016). Therefore, we pay close attention to the dynamics of remembering-forgetting that accompany memorialization practices and reflect on its meaning-effects. In order to understand how the LL around Little Africa performatively constructs the area at the intersection of a slavery past and Rio's allegedly cosmopolitan present, we resort to a decolonial perspective. Decolonial thinkers are critical of the colonial episteme based on the credo of racial superiority and inferiority. This dichotomy has produced many others involving racial classifications, followed by gender and sexuality taxonomies. In conjunction, they lie among the central parameters of intelligibility that constituted Eurocentric modernity (Quijano 2000; Mignolo 2006; Grosfoguel 2011). Making such orientations visible frames our overall discussion.

Linguistic Landscape: Politics of remembrance and regimes forgetfulness

LL research calls our attention to the fact that language is materially implicated in the public sphere. In its first stages, the field was concerned with the visibility and vitality of specific ethnolinguistic communities in the public realm (Landry and Bourhis 1997). However, the correlation between language varieties and their community of speakers circumscribed them within specific places and times. As Kallen observes, this analytical perspective tends to conceptualize public signage in a one-to-one relationship with the groups that inhabit a region and, as such, the LL is analysed 'as an *indicator* (in this case, of "ethnolinguistic vitality"), rather than as a form of discourse' (2009: 272 original emphasis). This being so, the investigation of public signage tended to be representational and synchronic, overlooking the fact that both signs and the places on which they are inscribed tell the histories of their own constitution (see, however, Spolsky and Cooper 1991).

More recently, though, researchers in the field have recognized that public signage is of a performative nature (Stroud and Jegels 2014) and, as such, its role in establishing how people make sense of place cannot be restricted to the linguistic realm or to a specific time period (i.e. the present). This epistemological movement has led scholars to broaden the analytical lenses to include all sorts of semiotic aggregates and their dynamic processes of inscription in the public realm (Peck and Stroud 2015; Milani and Levon 2016). In this strand of research, 'landscape' is not limited to the status of an *a priori* canvas on which dispassionate, impersonal, uninterested signs can be inscribed and 'linguistic' does not only refer to issues of language, strictly speaking. Rather, the meanings and functions of the public signage lie in the complex relations between diverse semiotic assemblages and their relations to pre-textual, contextual, sub-textual, intertextual and post-textual phenomena (see Pennycook 2010, 2018).

In this scenario, researchers have recently recognized that history and diachronicity are constitutive of the meanings and social effects of LLs (Pavlenko and Mullen 2015; Borba 2019). LL scholars argue that 'historicity is a critical tool that allows us to reframe linguistic landscapes in terms of complex regimes of past, present, and future constituted in material and (inter)textual spaces' (Train 2016: 227). As public places which are meant to bring the past into the present, memorials and other types of remembrance sites provide LL scholars with rich material to investigate the semiosis of history *and* place (Ben-Rafael and Ben-Rafael 2016; Guilat and Espinosa-Ramírez 2016; Train 2016; Woldemariam 2016) and, perhaps more importantly, of history *in* place. This insight is particularly useful for our purposes since it allows us to see memorials not simply as monuments that unproblematically pay homage to admirable deeds of the past or attempt to expurgate shameful acts. Instead, memorials are complex semiotic accomplishments which encapsulate conflicting layers of meaning and, thus, fracture history.

By retelling the past through present lenses, these monuments shape social memory through well-planned choices that involve not only who can authoritatively tell a part of history but also which languages will be used in such historical reconstruction. Although their most overt aim is to make us remember, memorials also help us forget since history is told selectively in these public places: who tells whose history from what point of view and in which language(s), after all? Which semiotic resources are employed (linguistic and non-linguistic)? Privileging a stretch of the past to be recast in the public realm necessarily entails the construction of a narrative which is shaped by the narrator's choices regarding the focus of the story, its plot and characters. In analysing memorials as constitutive parts of the LL, it is important to keep in mind that the elements brought to the fore will always push other aspects of history to the shadows. As semiotic accomplishments, memorials constitute politics of remembrance as much as they forge regimes of forgetfulness. As such, they are also privileged sites to observe the operation of indexicality, that is of the way signs are placed in the world and the social meanings they invoke (Scollon and Scollon 2003).

In this sense, the LL of memorials provides elements to problematize the history they tell. This can be done by taking into account the intricate semiosis of these public places which are constituted by multiple layers of meaning-making practices. The language(s) used (or erased) in the narratives memorials tell and reframe figure prominently in the production of these stories and the projection of effects onto those who visit these places. In order to understand the politics of remembrance and regimes of forgetfulness emplaced in the LL of Little Africa, we scrutinize the convoluted relations between several semiotic and linguistic aspects involved in memorialization practices. How is the history of the slave port told? Which languages are used to retell this history? What are their implications for the memory of the city? What are their relations to other semiotic resources available in the LL?

In the introduction, we highlighted how Rio de Janeiro (and, indeed, any city) can be narrated from different perspectives. Its history may be told through a narrative that emphasizes its role as a 'marvellous' cosmopolitan city which looks into the future[5] in detriment to a plot that remembers the huge numbers of enslaved Africans who came ashore on the Valongo Wharf (Moraes 2016). In the case of Little Africa, the semiotic and linguistic dynamics between remembering and forgetting depend on who tells the history of the Atlantic trade of enslaved Africans and how this harrowing past is told. In order to unpack the politics of remembrance and the regimes of forgetfulness the LL of Little Africa performatively produces, we joined the Historic and Archaeological Circuit to Celebrate the African Heritage. The analysis we develop in the remainder of this chapter is informed by our guided visit to Little Africa. We use the two-hour walk around the vicinities with a group of tourists and students as the methodological thread which intertwines the history of the place and the semiotic resources that performatively interpellate (Butler 1997) those who visit these memorials and shape their bodily-discursive (re)actions.

Memories of little Africa: Scales and indexicalities

On a rainy day in December 2017, a group of thirty people (mostly students) was led through the area by a female guide. She would stop at different sites and explain the relation between the so-called Little Africa and slavery. Gradually, the stories she told unfolded grim colonial memories. The cloudy skies added a sombre tone to the emergent historical reconstruction of persistent genocide practices against black people. In the area that housed the largest slave market in Brazil, millions of slaves reached their destination after an exhausting journey. They came from different African regions and spoke a variety of languages (Yoruba, KiKongo, KiMbundu and Bantu, to name but a few) which are completely absent from the signage. Despite their pedagogic purposes, the memorials in Little Africa tell the history of slavery only in Portuguese and English. Thus, besides erasing the huge influence African languages had in of the formation of Brazilian Portuguese (Mendonça 2012), they recycle the country's indifference to its shameful past. Drawing attention to the blending of languages would have been an important political stance. These memorials, however, may be seen as 'language graveyards' (Rumbaut 2009) that help support the hegemonic narrative of Brazil as a linguistically unified nation (see, however, Cavalcanti and Maher 2017).

As our walk around the circuit continues, we learn that, unloaded as cargo, Africans were deposited in warehouses where they waited for a dehumanizing fate, encompassing humiliation, ill-treatment, physical and moral violations, and even death. Like our guide, some historians describe facts which give us the dimension of these atrocities (Karasch 1987: 35–36):

> After anchoring offshore and undergoing legal formalities, the ships' crews were permitted to transfer the Africans to small lighters and row them ashore to the customhouse in the commercial district. The customs officials counted them by sex and noted the number of *crias* [children] who accompanied their mothers. After the importers had paid duties on all slaves above age three, the Africans were led in a group to the auction block. If enough buyers were present, they were immediately auctioned off near the customhouse, and their fates were quickly determined upon arrival. Those not sold that day were then led to houses to be restored to health [i.e. fattened] and prepared for sale. At the beginning of the century, Africans were disembarked as they travelled, that is, without any clothing. With nothing to cover their nakedness, they were subjected to a public auction and inspection by owners who crowded around to examine them closely (…) The travellers of that period describe the grotesque appearance of skeletal Africans, whose skin colour had turn a scaly grey from scurvy (…) Because of the rigors of the journey from Africa, they arrived almost invariably thin and emaciated with scrofulous skin afflicted with ulcers and skin rashes and scabies, not to mention the horrible poxes of smallpox. Small children had bloated bellies due to malnutrition and parasites. If an epidemic of ophthalmia has blinded many on board ship, dealers led columns of blind slaves stumbling one behind the other to the warehouses.

These appalling conditions also resulted in outbreaks of different diseases. Mortality rate was thus high. The following description narrates what happened to those who died (Karasch 1987: 39):

> In the middle of the cemetery was a 'mountain' of earth and decomposing naked bodies partially uncovered by the rains. The 'bad odour' was 'insupportable' (…) from time to time they burned the 'mountain of semi-decomposed cadavers'. The survivors were housed so close to the burial ground of their *malungos* (slave ship companions) that they, too, must have seen the corpses of their countrymen and women.

In view of such brutality, no wonder there are reports by travellers of pervasive melancholy and nostalgia among Africans. They are depicted as 'miserable, indifferent, dull, confused or disconsolate' (40). Many committed suicide. Those who survived had to go through further afflictions. At the final stage of the trade between slave dealers and buyers, besides 'parting from their slave ship companions', captives were branded with the signs of their new owners. A piece of heated tin burned a mark which caused the flesh to swell up (47). This mark was never to fade. After such dreadful ritual, many left the market in apathy – their suffering to be continued. Besides forced labour, punishments and minimal food on plantations, enslaved Africans were deprived of any sense of identity. Their homes were lost. So were their rights over their bodies. Their names, cultural background and languages were banished in the new land (the disregard to the survival of African languages in Brazilian soil is also prevalent in the LL of contemporary Little Africa). They were discouraged 'by means of threat and physical violence' (Karasch 1987: 215) from using their native languages and made to learn Portuguese. The process of rendering these languages invisible through violence, as a result, has contributed to the construction and dissemination of the widespread myth which portrays Brazil as monolingual (Cavalcanti and Maher 2017) and helps erase, in policy and everyday practices, the sociolinguistic complexity of the country.

Enslaved Africans were forced to have no human or political status, let alone linguistic identity. As we walk around Little Africa and are interpellated by these stories, a sense of loss and void takes us over. According to Mbembe (2003: 21), these multiple losses are 'identical with absolute domination, natal alienation and social death (expulsion from humanity altogether)'. Because of this sort of 'terror formation', Mbembe (2003: 22) considers slavery as a 'state of exception' which spread throughout the colonial world. This *modus operandi*, he says, is necropolitical in that it is entitled to 'define who matters and who does not, who is disposable and who is not' (27). Decolonial thinkers relate this extermination habitus in the Americas to the classification and ranking of nations, people, languages and bodies through the lens of race and ethnicity (Grosfoguel 2011). They contend that such practices have structured social existence in the West, having instituted the profound racism and social imbalance between whites and blacks we experience to this day. In Brazil, the anthropologist Ribeiro (2013: 91) points out that all Brazilians carry the scars of cruelty and torture in their souls 'ready to explode in racist and classist brutality'. As we look at the plaques and other signage in Little Africa that were supposed to remember this historical moment, we inevitably feel an indexical mismatch between the story our guide tells and that the LL of the area resemiotizes.

Our guide's oral recollection emphasized the cruelty perpetrated against blacks and the consequences of colonialism Brazilians have inherited. However, there was a flagrant narrative imbalance between what the guide and the signs on the memorials told us. The circuit's signage did not support the shocking historical content of her talk. The state of exception Mbembe alluded to could not be grasped from the public texts that help tell the history of Little Africa. On the contrary, they were quite minimalist, mostly including general and factual information. A staggering vacuum of memory is thus produced. The signs' 'effort to remember' in fact goes on silencing the incessant assaults on human bodies, languages, knowledges, cultures and identities.

Having recontextualized these erasure practices, we would like to argue that they constitute a recurrent scaling strategy that has characterized official discourses of memorialization in Rio, specifically, and in Brazil, more broadly. By aligning ourselves with Carr and Lempert (2016), we approach scales as a mode of perspectivizing and guiding perception. Comparing, measuring, classifying, qualifying, ranking, ordering, emphasizing, totalizing etc. are scalar manoeuvres that contextualize experience in space and time. Scales are assembled through a variety of sign systems – linguistic and non-linguistic. Together with the use of metaphors and analogies, they may render phenomena big or small, significant or unimportant, ancient or modern and, thus, contribute to forging various politics of remembrance and regimes of forgetfulness. These operations are inherently relational in that they rely on comparisons among events, people and activities (Gal 2016).

For the sake of illustration, let us focus for a moment on the revitalization plan of Rio de Janeiro's harbour zone. How has it been scaled? How has it foregrounded a remarkable future-driven city at the expense of its past? Certainly, multiple signs and linguistic resources are at play. By concentrating on some of them, we may shed light on the inextricability of scaling processes and semiosis. Think of the Museum of Tomorrow, which is located a few blocks away from Little Africa. It is a white hyper-modern construction of massive proportions, situated on the very edge of the dock. Besides projecting itself onto the sea, the huge building is reflected by a water mirror strategically integrated into its structure. Everything about it – size, location, design, name, colour, time references – magnifies the idea of a grandiose present-future. Moreover, wide-circulating texts do further scale work. For example, propositions such as 'The museum is at the pace of Tomorrow,'[6] 'Gigantic, colossal'[7] and 'Today we are a planetary force'[8] contribute to carve the impression of a marvellous-gargantuan-modern port. The undertaking is visibly analogical as both the city and the country are equated to the renovated harbour, in itself a metaphor for advancement and modernity.

This kind of semiotic bombardment both forges and stabilizes the grandiosity of the feat, which becomes a vantage point of calculus. In contrast to the sense of enormity, everything around the neighbouring area of Little Africa – the slave trade, enslaved blacks and barbarian acts –is made small and trivial. In this light, the downplayed signage and the many unexplored sites in the region also function as scaling techniques delineating, by comparison and contrast, a perception of indifference. This exercise can be said to be performative, having pragmatic and epistemological consequences. For instance, it may fashion social life in different directions as shown by the scalar tension we have just examined. One is expansionist and forms a unified semiotic block that moulds present-future time-space as central. The other emerges out of scarcer resources, amidst temporal-spatial losses and ruins that semiotize the 'Historic and Archaeological Circuit to Celebrate the African Heritage' as rather marginal.

All in all, 'competing scalar orientations' (Carr and Lempert 2016:14) are accomplished through intense semiotic labour that can either enhance or inhibit mobility in time and space. Thus, scalar endeavours are ideological, presupposing points of view and social positionings. This kind of understanding makes visible how some perspectives are favoured over others. The scalar distinctions we have highlighted above attend to a globalized neoliberal urban model based on the idea that cities and historic districts should be incorporated into touristic planning designed by large corporate companies. Their main interest is profitability. If the priority is business, the conservation of historic memory and collective identities of local communities is sidestepped and becomes secondary.

Relying on the rhetoric of 'rehabilitation' of degraded areas, authorities and entrepreneurs in Rio were granted safe-conduct for the removal of the local population, the eviction of original dwellers and the erasure of the city's foundational colonial past. Little Africa succumbs, incarnating as a mitigating device or as a concession to history. It is reduced to mere footprints on this long-celebrated route followed by the Museum of Tomorrow, which looms like a giant over the area.

This state of affairs is the outcome of particular scale-making processes that cannot be taken for granted, especially because (1) they constitute a persistent mode of necropolitics and (2) they can always be contested, transformed or reimagined outright. They, therefore, need close attention. Following this lead, in the remainder of this chapter we probe the pragmatics of scale by scrutinizing how the semiotic landscape around the Valongo Wharf, Pedra do Sal and the Cemetery of the New Blacks (re)anchors and (re)orients historic memories by flattening out their multilingual nature.

Scaling memories

In scaling early colonial memories, Brazilian official history has consistently excelled in forgetting the horrific experiences lived by enslaved Africans. This suppression is indexed by the 'signs in place' (Scollon and Scollon 2003) around Little Africa. However, defiance of silencing regimes has found different ways of expression, from the tragic to the artistic. Suicide, rebellion, escape, religious rituals, music and dance lie among the means employed by captives to their bleak fate. As we set out to analyse part of the signage in Little Africa, we privilege the unstable balance of remembrance and oblivion, which was particularly perceptible in the two-hour walk around the Historical and Archaeological Circuit to Celebrate African Heritage. As we will see in a moment, the modes of this celebration, however, eclipse important aspects of Rio's past and help shape its present with regards to how racism is disguised in memorialization policies and in the very semiotic fabric of the city.

Predatory upscaling: A black city with a white memory

Since its coming to existence as a sugar dock in the sixteenth century until its growth into a prosperous political-economic centre, Rio had frequently displayed concern with an ideal of magnitude. As the history of the port area synthetizes this sort of upscaling crusade, and the ideological underpinnings in which it is entangled, we find it worth dwelling upon its background for a while.

In 1763, Rio became the colonial capital of Brazil. At this time, the former sugar dock also began to ship off the abundant gold production of the country, which made the demand for slave labour rocket. The harbour district thus began to suffer successive interventions. The flourishing local elite that gathered there felt troubled by the increasing number of Africans disembarking in the pier, as well as by the slave business and the cemetery which served it. Besides being upsetting to the emergent bourgeois sensibilities, the landing of sick black prisoners was considered harmful to commerce and health. Therefore, in order to hide the wretched spectacle from public view, the unloading and trading of slaves, along with their burial ground, was transferred to a nearby wharf, the Valongo, which soon became the most important port of the Portuguese Empire and a major slave market of the colony.

After the Portuguese court moved to Brazil in 1808, different alterations took place at the quay. First, local warehouse owners called for the removal of the open slave graveyard. Later, the area was completely refurbished to receive

Princess Teresa Cristina, the future bride of the Emperor Dom Pedro II. By that time, the first anti-trafficking law had already been passed, and the slave market had been officially deactivated. In practice, however, slave-trading continued as a clandestine activity, away from the growing opposition to human trade. In view of such practices, authorities of the period did not want to run the risk of confronting the European Princess with any wrongdoing. Hence the original dock – and the human demise it represented – was completely concealed underground, entombed by large stones and renamed as the Empress's Wharf. Rebuilding and renaming the wharf were scaling projects with a view to downplay its recent history and give it a patina of bourgeois cosmopolitanism in order to welcome the princess.

When Brazil was proclaimed a Republic in 1889, Rio was the biggest city in the country, attracting many foreign businessmen and investors. Slavery had already been abolished by then, but its memory still hovered over everyday life. In comparison to European metropolises, Rio was considered a backward and lagging ex-colony. Inspired by the late nineteenth-century urbanistic reforms in major cities in Europe, Rio joined the transformational impulse as a way of reinforcing its new Republican profile. In 1903, the then-mayor Pereira Passos implemented a plan to remodel and beautify the city. In that reform, the two wharfs, one on top of the other, were collapsed under a landfill project, becoming a square. New buildings and a public garden were erected around it, in accordance with European architectural standards, which provided a 'civilizing' frame to the whole site.

This reform also came along with modification of a different nature. A Municipal Code of Conduct was passed, including the criminalization of vagrancy and of disorderly acts. According to the new legislation, African cultural and religious manifestations like Candomblé, Samba and Capoeira were considered insubordinate (Mussa and Simas 2010). In practical terms, this measure intended to control circulation in the region and avoid 'misdemeanours'. In the name of order and morality, citizens of African origins were inspected and removed from public view. The Empress' Wharf was thus 'whitened'.

The docks disappeared for over a century and with them the memory of the social, cultural and linguistic formation of Brazil. According to a scalar-sensitive approach, it can be argued that modernization, Europeanization, monolingualism and racial whitening are upscaling projects which conform to the ideal of a modern developing capital. Despite the advancements such reform may have brought, it simultaneously produced predatory effects concerning memorialization processes.

City embellishment may be said to be a scaling technique covering unpleasant recollections. In fact, the obfuscation of the city's inglorious past, and the saga of a host of Africans, their cultures and languages, is indexical of a pervasive scalar mode in Brazil. Doing so dilutes its profound social imbalance and structural racism. Moreover, it diminishes the importance of Brazil's African population in building the country and its cultural and linguistic identity. This unacknowledged legacy is shaken from time to time. The preparations for the 2016 Olympic venue, for instance, displaced the state of amnesia. When contractors were draining the area for the Marvellous Port Project, they encountered the Empress' and the Valongo Wharfs. In view of the long-hidden archaeological treasure, Rio's mayor attested his awe by saying enthusiastically, 'I'm going to build a square like in Rome. There lie our Roman ruins'.[9] Indeed, such scalar amplification of the site, and the World Heritage status it gained, set it on an international trajectory. Nonetheless, in view of the city's majestic itinerary in preparation for the 2016 Olympics, we could not help but see how the Little Africa circuit was made to look rather tiny. Together with the partially reconstructed wharf and the precarious signage on display, it shrinks scale to a disconcerting level (see Figure 8.1).

Figure 8.1 The Valongo Wharf memorial.

Besides the modest size of the memorial, the two explanatory signs available contain rather meagre information. On the one hand, the placard hanging on the Roman column limits itself to an informational scale. It reads (in Portuguese and in English): 'This place once housed the Empress' Wharf. In 1843, the former Valongo Wharf was widened and beautified to receive the future Empress Teresa Cristina, who would marry D. Pedro II'. On the other hand, the bilingual poster next to the archaeological site contains a vague narrative in Portuguese and English and an image painted by Johann Moritz Rugendas in 1835 (see Figure 8.2). Although this multisemiotic text invokes different scalable dimensions, it presents an ambiguous movement concerning memorialization. Our recontextualization below (with bold font added) makes this incertitude more visible:

Figure 8.2 Bilingual plaque in the Valongo Wharf memorial:

O SÍTIO ARQUEOLÓGICO DO CAIS DO VALONGO

O sítio arqueológico Cais do Valongo, **protegido pela Lei Federal 3924/61**, e considerado o mais importante **vestígio material fora da África** do tráfico atlântico de africanos escravizados, expressando material e simbolicamente um local que representa um registro de ação criminosa contra a humanidade. **Em 2013**, foi reconhecido como **sítio de memória do Projeto Rota do Escravo: Resistência, Liberdade e Patrimônio da UNESCO.**

Estima-se que, nos **mais de 300 anos de tráfico, cerca quatro milhões de africanos escravizados** desembarcaram em **portos brasileiros**, sendo **mais da metade pelo Rio de Janeiro**. Só **no Valongo**, calcula-se que **tenham passado cerca de um milhão**.

VALONGO WHARF ARCHEOLOGICAL SITE

The Valongo Wharf Archaeological Site, **protected by Federal Law** 3924/61, is considered the most important material **trace outside Africa** of the Atlantic trade of enslaved Africans. It expresses materially and symbolically a place that is a record of criminal activity against humanity. **In 2013**, it was recognized as **the Slave Route Project memory site – Resistance, Freedom and Heritage**, of **UNESCO**.

It is estimated that in **over the 300 years** of slave traffic about **four million enslaved Africans** arrived in the **Brazilian ports**, and **more than half in Rio de Janeiro**. Only **in Valongo**, the estimate is that **this number exceeds a million** enslaved persons.

Quantification highlights the great proportion of enslavement in Rio and in Brazil. Time-space references situate the length and scope of slavery. The appeal to authority brings to the forefront the 'material and symbolic' import of remembering 'criminal activity against humanity'. However, despite these amplifying projections, the story being recontextualized is significantly lessened in two different ways. First, its concision baffles the state of exception that spread in the colonial world – which produces life based on the social death of non-white bodies (Mbembe 2003). Second, the image framing the text belongs to a tradition of traveller-artists who depicted Rio as a tropical paradise and as 'a lovely small village' (Karasch 1987: 37). Responding to this environment, Rugendas's watercolour 'Disembarkation' romanticizes Valongo and scales it away from the terrifying reality it hosted. As such, the LL in the State-maintained Valongo memorial privileges a Eurocentric, Western narrative about Rio's African heritage and, hence, erases the history of a black city by retelling it through a supposedly dignifying white gaze.

Rescaling memories and the micropolitics of resistance

The meanings of the few signs anchored in the Valongo area index a peculiar space-time tension. It is as if history had broken down under the weight of the nearby 'Giant' (the Museum of Tomorrow) and the futuristic plot it conveys. However, as impressive as this grand narrative may be, it can be resisted and rescaled when signs 'out of place' index other voices. Their capacity to turn 'footnotes' into a main text becomes visible when we explore other sites of the historic circuit.

A case in point is the area that surrounds Pedra do Sal, a historical and religious monument situated at the symbolic centre of Little Africa. This area was the place where sugar, and later other products such as salt and coffee, arrived from the countryside to be later exported to the settler countries. Because of this intense commerce, the area was an important meeting place for enslaved Africans. In fact, on the Conceição Hill where Pedra do Sal stands today there used to be the Aljube Prison to which enslaved people and later quilombolas (i.e. the descendants of slaves) were sent if convicted of crimes (Corrêa 2016). Even after the abolition of slavery, large numbers of Afro-Brazilians worked and lived around Pedra do Sal.

At the end of the eighteenth century and the beginning of the nineteenth century, the Conceição Hill housed a handful of *zungu* houses, places where meals such as corn mush were made and sold. Importantly, these houses provided African individuals with places where they could meet and maintain some of their traditions such as religious practices, music and dance, which, as pointed out above, were later considered as 'misdemeanours' by the Pereira Passos administration and were fervently prosecuted in an attempt to 'whiten' the port zone and modernize Rio. Despite the surveillance, the areas surrounding Pedra do Sal became places of resistance and counter-cultural production so much so that *samba* and *carnival*, allegedly Brazil`s most famous cultural emblems, are believed to have been born in these premises (Mussa and Simas 2010).

Despite their historical links to the African diaspora, these areas have become the focus of a legal dispute as for their ownership. In the 1990s, the Catholic Venerable Third Order of St. Francis of Penance, which owns several properties around Pedra do Sal, started an eviction process which removed dozens of families from their residences in order to expand its educational and welfare projects. The residents, however, view this expansion project as opportunism since gentrification of the port zone has made prices skyrocket (Guimarães 2013). Faced with the possibility of being forced out of their houses, some families who were involved in social movements and political activism for the recognition of Afro-Brazilian culture and against structural racism spearheaded the creation of the Quilombo Pedra do Sal (Guimarães 2013). Their ethnic claims to the land have started a long and still ongoing process of anthropological and historical investigations which has temporarily halted the Order's expansion project. In order to challenge the Order's claim of land ownership, which is based on the fact that the St. Francis of Penance church has been in the area since 1733, the collectives that require the legal status of quilombo to Pedra do Sal highlight the ancestry of the African presence and its cultural importance to the region. This is accomplished through the juxtaposition of several space-time scales. According to the *Boletim Quilombola,*

> The Quilombo of Pedra do Sal is comprised of descendants of black slaves from Bahia and Africa. Saúde was the site of all the slave trade infrastructure during the 18th and 19th centuries. After slavery was abolished, blacks continued to live around Rio de Janeiro's Port Zone, and the area was appropriated as a social space for rituals, religious cults, drumming and capoeira. Popular culture flourished around Pedra do Sal and traditional samba artists drew inspiration from the community [...] The land was located by the sea and received its name because it was where the salt sold in the capital market was unloaded. In the same port zone, 'Brazil's Little Africa' was established, a refuge for blacks escaping Pereira Passos' 'bota abaixo' (tear it down), an urban renewal project in the first decades of the 20th century. (Cited in Guimarães 2013)

This is testimony to the fact that Pedra do Sal is at the intersection of different memorialization projects. On the one hand, the Order's claim of ownership intends to eclipse the African history and, mainly, the area's links to Afro-Brazilian religious practices such as that of *candomblé*, whose rites maintain several links to African languages and which had been violently impeded both by slave traders and by the Pereira Passos administration but nevertheless flourished in the shadows. On the other hand, the quilombolas' narrative highlights the ethnic connection of the premises with enslaved Africans and, more recently, to counter-cultural production, and, thus, revives Pedra do Sal as a place of resistance.

This historical conundrum is materialized in the signage of the area and allows for the 'investigation of how the LLs are actively deployed [...] to enhance local engagement, sense of belonging, or acts of resistance and to create conditions for new emotional geographies of place' (Stroud 2016: 4). In fact, political engagement and historical belonging constitute strategies of resistance which may be forged by rescaling semiotic manoeuvres that promote a shift in perspective and contest the official Eurocentric narrative. This is visible in the graffiti art that abounds around Pedra do Sal. Figure 8.3 demonstrates how the LL in the area jettisons the official scalar tropes projected

Figure 8.3 Graffiti at Pedra do Sal.

in the institutionalized signage at the Valongo memorial by refocusing and reimagining (i.e. rescaling) alternative memories of Little Africa and its history as a place of resistance.

In contrast to the institutionalized signage at the Valongo memorial, the LL around Pedra do Sal highlights the perspectives of those who have been directly affected by the Marvellous Port project through dislocation, removal, eviction or rising living costs (i.e. the descendants of enslaved Africans who first inhabited the region). The graffiti above shows the image of Zumbi, the former king of Quilombo dos Palmares who spearheaded a rebellion against slave owners in colonial Brazil and is now revered as a symbol of anti-slavery and anti-colonial resistance, defiantly looking ahead. In itself, the graffiti seems to project alternative space-time dimensions to Pedra do Sal: it situates the area in its slavery past while simultaneously projecting the presence of the African diaspora and its anti-colonial stance in the present – a semiotic move that challenges the official scalar project of the nearby Valongo wharf in which slavery seems to be almost forgotten on behalf of the future. By doing so, the graffiti rescales this narrative and recalibrates the power relations involved in the regimes of forgetfulness mobilized by the signage in the Valongo memorial.

Such rescaling is also importantly accomplished by the signs that surround the image of Zumbi, which juxtapose messages in Portuguese with a plethora of other semiotic resources such as stencil art, colours, shapes and music signs. In contrast to the bilingual LL of the Valongo Wharf in which Portuguese and English are used in ways that reframe (erase, even) Rio's black history through Western white eyes and narratives, the signage around Pedra do Sal tells this story through multiple assemblages of semiotic resources that are intertextually linked to the place's black history and culture. In this sense, while the institutional LL of the Valongo strategically downplays the importance of race and African cultures to the constitution of the city's memory, the highly saturated, multisemiotic walls at Pedra do Sal give this story a different racialized angle. The fact that African languages are absent in such an environment – whose purpose is to foreground the voices of those connected with Little Africa – is indexical of the way these languages have been silenced, to the point that city residents do not know them: they are not taught, used or seen.

In the graffiti shown above, on Zumbi's left-hand side, for example, two messages place the body at the centre of the memorialization project in the LL of Pedra do Sal. The poster on the top brings the imperative sentence: 'Don't allow them to privatize your public body' (*Não deixem privatizarem seu corpo público*). The stencil art at the bottom announces that 'black meat is for sale. Call 190' (*Vende-se carne negra. Tel.: 190*). While the former may be warning about the dangers of the privatization impetus encouraged by the government to modernize the area as part of the Marvellous Port project, the latter criticizes the institutionalization of racism by the police and, as an extension, the state, as 190 is the toll-free number for the police in Brazil.

Another fundamental memorialization feature of this graffiti are the music G-clef signs placed in the outer left area of the image above. These emplace Pedra do Sal's link to counter-cultural production, especially *samba* which is believed to have been created in this neighbourhood where important composers such as Donga and Pixinginha lived. Today, this memory is revived by the samba groups who play at the weekly parties in Pedra do Sal which are popular among the residents and a younger crowd with leftist political inclinations (as well as tourists). Importantly, the juxtaposition of these musical notes and the sign that reads 'black meat is for sale' intertextually connects the graffiti to a very popular song whose lyrics explicitly criticize structural racism in Brazil. Performed by Elza Soares, a singer who is an important representative for Brazilian black activism, the song denounces that 'the cheapest meat on the market is the black meat'.

The LL at Pedra do Sal, thus, does not take for granted the official scale project which lessens the state of exception slavery produced in colonial Brazil by romanticizing the area and moving it away from its harrowing past. In other words, it does not abide by state-sanctioned scaling manoeuvres. Rather, it rescales the official narrative by bringing the voices of Afro-Brazilians to the fore and, more importantly, placing Pedra do Sal at the centre of grassroots movements that defy the gentrification and the 'whitening' of the area. This type of 'guerilla memorialisation' (Rice 2012) rescales the Valongo Wharf memorial by transforming it into the official site for white regimes of forgetfulness while at the same time recasts Pedra do Sal as an unofficial zone for the production of bottom-up, localized, defiant black politics of remembrance. The anti-establishment nature of the LL and its multisemiotic character disavow the official bilingual Westernized signage of the Valongo memorial by retelling history through the voices of those whose ancestors lived, worked and died in Little Africa. Memorialization is rescaled to encompass the voices and bodies of the marginalized ones. Thus, the LL at Pedra do Sal materializes counter-memories.

De-escalating fear

The Cemetery of the New Blacks had been covered by twentieth-century urbanization and was thus lost from the cityscape. Its exact location had been unknown until it was found by chance in 1996, when, during the remodelling of their new home, a couple came across a large amount of human bones. The discovery finally revealed the place where thousands of captured Africans were precariously buried during the eighteenth and nineteenth centuries. It also unveiled the degrading conditions under which corpses were piled in a grave-like ditch and incinerated, showing no respect for traditional African religious rituals concerning funerals.

This sudden exposure of the heinous colonial *modus vivendi* led one of the house owners to preserve the space as an archaeological site dedicated to the memory of the many lives buried there and to communicating the intense slavery activity in the so called Marvellous City. This project involved a decade-long pursuit to inaugurate the New Blacks Institute (IPN) — a two-room facility in the Valongo neighbourhood. The IPN was the last stop in our tour around the historic circuit. According to information published on *RioOnWatch.org*,[10]

> The Institute serves as a museum, memorial and research center exploring the history of the cemetery and the Port Region, and celebrates Rio's black heritage (…) It is the only stop on Rio's Black Heritage Circuit where detailed historical information is exchanged and people are regularly available to answer questions and deepen the visitor's understanding of the tragic and dramatic history of the world's largest slave port.

Our experience in the institute confirmed this perspective. Despite its minimal dimensions, the memorial reconstructs the monstrous proportions of slavery. Indoor signage abounds. Bilingual leaflets, in Portuguese and English, and posters occupying most walls explain in simple language the story the official LL in the Valongo Wharf bypasses. Maps, photographs, interviews with experts, drawings, videos and historical artefacts reconstruct the port zone as 'a place of horrors' and of 'enormous violence'. No alleviating devices are employed. The story told by the IPN defies scales frequently associated with a sense of 'humanity', as kindness, brotherhood or bondage. Much to the contrary, the 'signs in place' there bluntly index colonial necropolitics, focusing on human's capacity for destruction. As such, they incite consternation and distress. As far as scaling practices are concerned, the perspective put forward by the IPN is not simply informational. It is mainly educational and political. This agenda becomes clearer when we attend to *de-escalation* which, according to Carr and Fisher (2016: 135), is produced when people forge 'intimacy out of fear, threat, and awe'. In the case at hand, the uneasiness visitors experience when interacting with the LL at the IPN may be transformed through different scalar logics that potentially change participants' perceptions on events, by engaging them affectively.

That involvement becomes palpable when we observed the interaction of people in our group with the overwhelming mortal remains of a young enslaved female who died at the beginning of the nineteenth century. Her well-preserved skeleton was found intertwined with other remains (broken bones, teeth). She was named Josefina Bakhita after the first African Saint in Catholic Church.

Bakhita lies in an open grave inside the IPN. Her name, her position in the room and the possibility of close inspection scale the whole scene as synecdoche.[11] To look at her is to feel an important chunk of Brazilian history. The genocide of millions of people is encapsulated in the remains of one woman. Her exposed bones are thus indexical of that tragedy. Scrutinizing them affects bodies in a particular way. As the image below indicates (Figure 8.4), people are made

Figure 8.4 New Blacks Institute and skeletal remains of Josefina Bakhita.

to bend and look down. This bowing position in itself suggests consideration and amazement. No wonder many people took their hands to their mouths or chins or kept them behind their backs. Some folded their arms. Such bodily performance that evokes a reverential quality can be seen as experience beyond language (Massumi 2002), illustrating the affective and embodied entanglements of public signage (Stroud 2016). There is thus symbiosis between signage, body and the past. It is this affective state that forges connections between individuals, the LL and historical space-times in as much as it enhances respectful deference for the suffering of millions of people. In short, it provides greater proximity with slavery. Thus scaled, Little Africa becomes big.

Conclusion: Forgetting in order to remember

As semiotic accomplishments, the Valongo Wharf, Pedra do Sal and the Cemetery of the New Blacks recreate memories very differently by forging conflicting politics of remembrance and their respective regimes of forgetfulness. We have made this process visible by exploring not only semiotic and linguistic phenomena but also the distinctive scaling modes that they engender and the performative meaning-effects they produce. Thus, the analysis foregrounds the importance of bringing a scale-sensitivity approach to the study of LLs. While available signage in the Valongo downscales a rich archaeological site and promotes ignorance of a horrid form of life through Eurocentric perspectives and languages which eclipses the African history of the city, memorialization practices in Pedra do Sal and the IPN bring to the fore the necropolitical ordeal of slavery and racism through the voices and bodies of those whose history is told.

Silencing practices are a type of scaling tactic that indexes the way Brazilian society deals with unpleasant memories: past, present and future ones. The foundational myth of Brazilian 'racial democracy' may well illustrate this effect. In very broad terms, this idea poses that the social relations between European colonizers and Africans did not develop into racial discrimination or prejudice against blacks in Brazil. Such scalar projection causes an important part of the country's history to sink into oblivion. This in turn deemphasizes and simplifies the vicious power struggles during the Colonial Period. Unfortunately, this handling of signs and languages entails specific ways with memories that attest to the instituted disregard of African legacy in Brazil. At the Valongo Wharf specifically, the latter has been 'historically constructed and reiterated via the resilience of racial ideologies that orient to whiteness as a social ideal to be met' (Jordão 2015: 11).

Nevertheless, scalar innovations are also cultivated. The signs 'out of place' in the other two sites produce contrasting scalar effects that suggest critical reflection about social life. Having been placed by residents, the semiotic resources employed transgress the official muting rhetoric by remembering the brutality of history and by speaking out for the misfortune impinged on millions of people. Put differently, part of LL in Little Africa trespasses the insidious scalar habits we have just highlighted. They do so by forgetting the city's commitment to strategic urban planning and by focusing instead on the recollection of an otherwise dim background, which has been central in the structuring of Brazilian society. These scaling processes have ultimately shown that memorials and their semiotic organization of experience are loci where resistance can be enacted micropolitically. Therefore, the conception of memorials should involve not only experts, but also the diversified voices and scaling imagination of those who have participated in the history that is being memorialized.

Notes

1 Available at https://oglobo.globo.com/rio/escavacoes-de-obra-de-drenagem-da-zona-portuaria-encontram-restos-dos-cais-da-imperatriz-do-2816387#ixzz55Dt1NXGR.
2 There is a body of literature dealing with the dialogue between remembering and forgetting. While pivotal theorists as Paul Ricoeur (1998) and Todorov (2000) focus on the ethics of remembrance and on rememoration-erasure acts, others cast doubt over memorialization practices. David Rieff (2017), for example, by exploring what he terms 'the culture of grievance', argues collective historical memories – of heroes, martyrs or innocent victims – may end up increasing resentment, exacerbating historical violence and leading to war rather than peace.
3 This fact testifies to the structural lack of government attention for the memorialization of the country's past. A recent example of this lack of care and funding is the fire that consumed *Museo Nacional* and its collection of 20 million items in September 2018. Because of the absence of government investment, the museum infrastructure had been crumbling for decades, which facilitated the rapid spread of the flames and the destruction of the most significant museological and research archive in Latin America.
4 Available at https://www.cartacapital.com.br/sociedade/o-porto-maravilha-e-negro.

5   *Cidade Maravilhosa* (i.e. the Marvellous City) is a carnival song composed by André Filho in 1935 which pays homage to Rio de Janeiro. After its huge success, it was officially recognized as the anthem of the city. Because of this, Rio became popularly known as the marvellous city of Brazil.
6   Available at https://odia.ig.com.br/noticia/rio-de-janeiro/2015-12-18/em-inauguracao-do-museu-do-amanha-dilma-comemora-vitoria-no-supremo.html.
7   Available at http://g1.globo.com/jornal-nacional/noticia/2017/12/museu-do-amanha-no-rio-comemora-2-anos-recebendo-vizinhos-para-festa.html.
8   Video projection onto a wall inside the museum.
9   Available at https://oglobo.globo.com/rio/escavacoes-de-obra-de-drenagem-da-zona-portuaria-encontram-restos-dos-cais-da-imperatriz-do-2816387#ixzz57masYOzt.
10 Available at http://www.rioonwatch.org/?p=35646.
11 Carr and Fisher make the very same point (2016: 147) when exploring the way a huge piece of floating concrete is scaled when it reaches Oregon's shores.

References

Ben-Rafael, E. and M. Ben-Rafael (2016), 'Schöneberg: Memorializing the Persecution of Jews', *Linguistic Landscape*, 2 (3): 291–310.

Borba, R. (2019), 'Injurious Signs: The Geopolitics of Hate and Hope in the Linguistic Landscape of a Political Crisis,' in C. Stroud, A. Peck and Q. Williams (eds), *Making Sense of People in Linguistic Landscapes*, 161–181, London: Bloomsbury.

Butler, J. (1997), *Excitable Speech. A Politics of the Performative*, New York: Routledge.

Carr, E. S. and B. Fisher (2016), 'Interscaling Awe, De-escalating Disaster', in E. S. Carr and M. Lempert (eds), *Scale: Discourse and Dimensions of Social Life*, 133–156, Oakland: University of California Press.

Carr, E. S. and M. Lempert (2016), 'Introduction: Pragmatics of Scale', in E. S. Carr and M. Lempert (eds), *Scale: Discourse and Dimensions of Social Life*, 1–21, Oakland: University of California Press.

Cavalcanti, M. and T. Maher (2017), *Multilingual Brazil: Language Resources, Identities and Ideologies in a Globalized World*, London: Routledge.

Corrêa, M. L. (2016), *Quilombo Pedra do Sal*, Belo Horizonte: FAFICH.

Gal, S. (2016), 'Scale-making: Comparison and Perspectives as Ideological Projects', in E. S. Carr and M. Lempert (eds), *Scale: Discourse and Dimensions of Social Life*, 91–111, Oakland: University of California Press.

Grosfoguel, R. (2011), 'Decolonizing Post-colonial Studies and Paradigms of Political Economy: Transmodernity, Decolonial Thinking and Global Coloniality', *Transmodernity: Journal of Peripheral Cultural Production of the Luso–hispanic World*, 1 (1): 1–38.

Guilat, Y. and A. Espinosa-Ramírez (2016), 'The Historical Memory Law and Its Role in Redesigning Semiotic Cityscapes in Spain: A Case Study from Granada', *Linguistic Landscape*, 2 (3): 247–274.

Guimarães, R. (2013), 'Urban Interventions, Memories, and Conflicts: Black Heritage and the Revitalization of Rio de Janeiro's Port Zone', *Vibrant*, 10 (1): 208–227.

Jordão, R. P. (2015), 'Uma descoberta anunciada: lembranças, apagamentos e heranças no mercado de escravos do Valongo no Rio de Janeiro', Ph.D diss., Pontifícia Universidade Católica do Rio de Janeiro.

Kallen, J. (2009), 'Tourism and Representation in the Irish Linguistic Landscape', in. E. Shohamy and D. Gorter (eds), *Linguistic Landscape: Expanding the Scenery*, 270–283, London: Routledge.

Karasch, M. C. (1987), *Slave Life in Rio de Janeiro: 1808–1850*, Princeton, NJ: Princeton University Press.

Landry, R. and R. Y. Bourhis. (1997), 'Linguistic Landscape and Ethnolinguistic Vitality: An Empirical Study', *Journal of Language and Social Psychology*, 16 (1): 57–76.

Lisle, D. (2007), 'Defending Voyeurism: Dark Tourism and the Problems of Global Security', in P. M. Burns and M. Novelli (eds), *Tourism and Politics: Global Frameworks Local Realities*, 333–345. Oxford: Elsevier.

Massumi, B. (2002), *Parables of the Virtual: Movement, Affect, Sensation*, London: Duke University Press.

Mbembe, A. (2003), 'Necropolitics', *Public Culture*, 15 (1): 11–40.

Mendonça, R. (2012), *A influência Africana na português do Brasil*. Brasília: Fundação Alexandre de Gusmão.

Mignolo, W. (2006), 'El desprendimiento: pensamiento crítico y giro descolonial', in N. Maldonado-Torres and F. Achiwy (eds) *(Des)colonialidad del ser y del saber: videos indígenas y los limites coloniales de la izquierda en Bolivia*, 11–22, Buenos Aires: Ediciones del Signo.

Milani, T. and E. Levon (2016), 'Sexing Diversity: Linguistic Landscapes of Homonationalism', *Language and Communication* 51: 69–86.

Moraes, R. (2016), 'A escravidão e seus locais de memória: O Rio de Janeiro e suas "maravilhas"', *Odeere*, 2 (1): 33–58.

Mussa, A. and L. A. Simas (2010), *Samba de enredo: história e arte*, Rio de Janeiro: Civilização Brasileira.

Pavlenko, A. and A. Mullen (2015), Why Diachronicity Matters in the Study of Linguistic Landscapes, *Linguistic Landscape* 1 (1/2): 114–132.

Peck, A. and C. Stroud. (2015), 'Skinscapes', *Linguistic Landscape*, 1 (1/2): 133–151.

Pennycook, A. (2010), *Language as a Local Practice*, London: Routledge.

Pennycook, A. (2018), *Post-humanist Applied Linguistics*, New York: Routledge.

Quijano, A. (2000), 'Colonialidad del poder y clasificacion social', *Journal of World-Systems Research*, Special Issue: Festschrift for Emmanuel Wallerstein, 6 (2): 342–386.

Ribeiro, D. (2013), *O povo brasileiro: a formação e o sentido do Brasil*, São Paulo: Global Editora.

Rice, A. (2012), *Creating Memorials, Building Identities: The Politics of Memory in the Black Atlantic*. Liverpool: Liverpool University Press.

Ricoeur, P. (1998), 'Memory and Forgetting' in M. Dooley and R. Kearney (eds), *Questioning Ethics: Contemporary Debates in Continental Philosophy*, 5–11, London: Routledge.

Rieff, D. (2017), *In Praise of Forgetting: Historical Memories and Its Ironies*, New Haven, CT: Yale University Press.

Rumbaut, R. G. (2009), 'A Language Graveyard? The Evolution of Language Competencies, Preferences, and Use among Young Adult Children of Immigrants', in T. G. Wiley, J. S. Lee and R. Rumberger (eds), *The Education of Language Minority Immigrants in the United States*, 35–71, Bristol: Multilingual Matters.

Scollon R. and S. W. Scollon (2003), *Discourses in Place. Language in the Material World*, London: Routledge.

Spolsky, B and R. L. Cooper. (1991), *The Languages of Jerusalem*, Oxford: Oxford University Press.

Stroud, C. (2016), 'Turbulent Linguistic Landscapes and the Semiotics of Citizenship', in R. Blackwood, E. Lanza and H. Woldermariam (eds), *Negotiating and Contesting Identities in Linguistic Landscapes*, 3–18, London: Bloomsbury.

Stroud, C. and D. Jegels (2014), 'Semiotic Landscapes and Mobile Narrations of Place: Performing the Local', *International Journal for the Sociology of Language*, 2014 (228): 179–199.

Train, R. (2016), 'Connecting Visual Presents to Archival Pasts in Multilingual California: Towards Historical Depth in Linguistic Landscape', *Linguistic Landscape*, 2 (3): 223–246.

Todorov, T. (2000), *Mémoire du mal, tentation du bien: enquête sur le siècle*, Paris: Editions Robert Lafont.

Woldemariam, H. (2016), 'Linguistic Landscape as Standing Historical Testimony of the Struggle against Colonization in Ethiopia', *Linguistic Landscape*, 2 (3): 275–290.

9

Cast in Iron: Remembering the Past in Penang

John Macalister and Teresa Ong

Introduction

This chapter focuses on memories of the past as presented through one element of the Linguistic Landscape (henceforth LL) in twenty-first-century Georgetown, on the island of Penang, in Malaysia. The past that is being evoked is that of Penang since the late eighteenth century and so, while acknowledging the millennia of human habitation that preceded it, the chapter begins with a brief overview of that more recent history. It follows with an overview of languages and language policy in Malaysia and a short discussion of the sociolinguistic situation in Penang in the twenty-first century, and the importance of tourism to the local economy, before introducing the study itself. At the heart of the study are thirty iron rod sculptures that form part of the tourist experience in Penang. They were installed in the historic centre of Georgetown after World Heritage Site status was conferred on the area by UNESCO in 2008.

The chapter explores two questions. Malaysia is a multi-ethnic, multilingual nation and one in which language continues to play a significant part in discussions of national identity and nation-building. The first question, then, is the way in which the multiple languages of Malaysia contribute to the memories of the past chosen to be conveyed through the sculptures. These sculptures have been installed in a vibrant urban area; they are not monuments, they are not set aside from the daily life of residents and visitors; they form part of a crowded LL. The second question that this chapter explores is the way in which the sculptures relate to the wider LL and the local language ecology.

A brief history of modern Penang

The establishment of modern Penang is linked with the resurgence of Thailand in the region in the late eighteenth century, and its ongoing struggle for regional dominance with Burma. The Sultan of Kedah, in whose domain the island sat, felt vulnerable to pressure and possible attack from either side. As a result, he offered to lease the island to the East India Company in the hope of gaining a degree of protection and so, in August 1786, Captain Francis Light 'took formal possession of Penang in the name of King George III of Britain' (Andaya and Andaya 2017: 115). Differing expectations and dissatisfaction marked the initial years, however, culminating in the Sultan of Kedah launching an unsuccessful attack on Penang in March 1791 which was followed by a successful counter-attack and the signing of a treaty that confirmed the British occupation of the island. 'Now the epitome of commercial success was represented ... by the British town of Penang' (Andaya and Andaya 2017: 117). Penang would go on to become one part of the Straits Settlements, formed in 1826 which also included Singapore and Malacca. Originally controlled by the East India Company, the Straits Settlements became a Crown colony in 1867 and remained such until 1946 when it became part of what would become modern Malaysia.

Commerce and trade are typically a trigger for population growth, and so Penang grew. Unrest and poverty in China contributed to a significant inflow of Chinese (Andaya and Andaya 2017: 125), although to say 'Chinese' suggests a homogeneity that did not exist. Keong (2006: 60) explains that the first to arrive were the Peranakan Chinese, 'the descendants of fifteenth-century Hokkien traders' (p. 59) who had settled in the region, and who Light saw as 'key to the success of his project – to make Penang the chief port for trade between India and China' (p. 60), at least in part because of their intercultural understanding and ability to act as linguistic bridges between communities. But the arrival of new migrants – initially Hokkien and Cantonese speakers – from China somewhat weakened the influence of the Peranakan Chinese in Penang. By the 1820s, the fourth group, the Hakkas, was also becoming a presence on the island (Keong 2006: 61).

The different dialect groups tended to be involved in different occupations (Andaya and Andaya 2017: 150) and divisions were further strengthened by the 'secret societies' which, in Penang, 'from the beginning had a reputation for fomenting dissent' (ibid). In broad terms, Hokkien speakers allied with the Peranakan Chinese, with whom they shared a common ancestry, whereas

Cantonese speakers remained separate and distinct from those two groups and maintained their traditional enmity with Hakka-speakers when they established themselves in Penang (Keong 2006: 61). No doubt the ties between Peranakan Chinese and the more recently arrived Hokkiens contributed to the fact that 'By the 1870s, the Penang Straits Chinese had become the largest dialect group in the colony' (ibid.: 62).

As well as Chinese migration, there was also migration from India. Like the Hokkien traders from whom Peranakan Chinese descended, Indian traders had had a presence in Malaysia since the fifteenth century, and had been in Penang 'as early as 1770' although before the arrival of the British in 1786 Penang 'was undeveloped and [...] only a transit point for small ships' (Mujani 2012: 1350). More Indian traders including Jawi Peranakan, the Indian equivalent of Peranakan Chinese, settled on the island once it began to be developed. The traders were from South India and Muslim, and, by 1822, 'Tamil Muslims comprised 36.25 per cent of the resident population' (Andaya and Andaya 2017: 145) in Penang, more than the Chinese population.

During the nineteenth and into the twentieth centuries the Indian population in Malaysia – and South East Asia generally – grew through two mechanisms. One was 'free' or voluntary migration, the other the system of indentured labour through which 'our colonial masters forcefully took away Indians to work in rubber, tea and coffee plantations' (Mukhopadhyay 2010: 997). There was, as a result, a distinction in the Indian population in Malaysia between the Hindu labourers in rural areas and the Muslim community which was 'more focused in urban areas in small businesses' (Mujani 2012: 1352).

Events in the late eighteenth and the nineteenth centuries can be seen, therefore, to have laid the foundations for a multilingual, multicultural society, but also the basis for ethnic and language tensions in modern Malaysia. This is the focus of the following section.

Languages and language policy in Malaysia

Since achieving independence from Britain in 1957, Malaysia has focused much on issues related to nation-building, national unity and the formation of the nation's identity. One important element for nation-building has been the implementation of national language policy (Gill 2014), which has resulted in a series of events that demonstrate the power struggle between different ethnic groups in the process of building an identity for Malaysians.

Prior to independence, Omar (2012: 57) claims, the different language communities existed in 'separate worlds'. Yet at the same time English played an important role as a language for communication. The Malay elite and wealthy Chinese and Indian families educated their children in English schools. These children had more opportunities to further their studies overseas or gain employment in the civil service. English also served as an economic language for those living in the urban areas. As a consequence of English being treated as 'the' language to gain economic and academic achievements, many Malays in rural areas felt neglected. This situation led to frustration among the Malays because they believed that economic and political power lay in the hands of those who spoke English (Kelman 1971). As a result, and as Chai (1977: 5) states, prior to independence the 'differences in language, religion and culture provided no natural basis for national integration'.

To overcome this unbalanced situation, in 1963, the Malaysian Federal Government decided to institute Bahasa Malaysia as the national and official language of Malaysia, including establishing it as the language of education and administration. This was accomplished through the passing of the National Language Act (Government of Malaysia 1963/1967). It was done with the hope of providing greater professional mobility (Gill 2005) and better education for the Malays through reducing the role and status of English, which was perceived as having provided more advantages to the non-Malays (Albury and Aye 2016). Bahasa Malaysia was chosen as the national and official language for several reasons: first, it was the main language spoken by the Malays and Indigenous people who made up the majority of Malaysia's population; second, it had always been the language of communication between various language groups in the Straits of Malacca, and on the coasts of Peninsular Malaysia, Sumatra and Borneo; and third, Bahasa Malaysia was used as the trading language among the kingdoms in the Malay Archipelago (Asmah 1987). The Chinese and Indian communities did not offer much resistance to the adoption of Bahasa Malaysia as the country's national and official language, because they were offered citizenship as a compensatory 'bargaining tool' (Gill 2005: 246). As Asmah (1979: 11) puts it, 'the institution of Bahasa Malaysia as the national and official language [...] was a barter for the acquisition and equality of citizenship for the non-Malays'.

National unity was not, however, achieved so easily. The federal election of 1969 was 'fought on the highly emotional issues of education and language [...] as each ethnic group sought to preserve its interests against the encroachment of others' (Andaya and Andaya 2017: 302). The election itself did not lead to any resolution and three days afterwards, on 13 May 1969, serious racial riots broke out. 'Bloody fighting, arson and looting' (ibid.: 303) lasted for four days, with the Chinese community suffering the most loss, including loss of life.

The conflict of May 1969 marked a low point in Malaysian history but the issues that triggered those riots have retained currency since independence and the relationship between Bahasa Malaysia and English has often been uneasy. While English remained the official language for ten years after independence, and today continues to play the role of unofficial second official language, it has been replaced by Bahasa Malaysia in some domains. In public schools, for example, the medium of instruction gradually switched from English to Bahasa Malaysia and even though English was a compulsory subject for all students to take, it was not necessary to pass (Asmah 1997). Many Malays were unsatisfied at the slow progress of the adoption of the national and official language, however, in particular at higher education sector. It took eighteen years for the medium of instruction at public universities to change from English to Bahasa Malaysia (Gill 2004), resulting in the transition from a bilingual to a monolingual system not being achieved until 1983.

The many efforts to establish Bahasa Malaysia as the national and official language in Malaysia and the main medium of instruction in the Malaysian national education system received something of a setback when there was another dramatic change in language-in-education policy in 2003. After forty years of promoting Bahasa Malaysia and enforcing it as the language of education and administration in Malaysia, the then prime minister of Malaysia, Tun Dr Mahathir Mohamad, announced that the medium of instruction for Science and Mathematics would be English (Gill 2014). The justification for this major change was that it was Malaysia's response to the influence of globalization and the need to develop a knowledge-based economy. Once again, English took its role as the language of instruction in the fields of science and technology. At the same time, there was pressure to ensure that Bahasa Malaysia has a place in the linguistic ecology of Malaysia.

The reintroduction of English as a medium of instruction for Science and Mathematics did not progress smoothly as many argued against it. Chinese educationalists strongly opposed the implementation as they feared the erosion of Mandarin Chinese in Chinese-medium schools. Tamil school principals objected. Bahasa Malaysia advocates were worried about the loss of their national and official language, and its status and role in defining the nation's identity. In addition, public examination results indicated poor performance in Science and Mathematics, particularly in rural areas where most of the Malays live. As a result of such opposition, the Malaysia Federal Government decided to revert to

Bahasa Malaysia for Science and Mathematics with more emphasis being placed on learning English. In 2010, the policy of 'Upholding Bahasa Malaysia and Strengthening English' was implemented (Ministry of Education Malaysia 2014). The policy was aimed at protecting the sovereignty of Bahasa Malaysia as the country's sole national and official language, as stated in the Federal Constitution of Malaysia, while making sure that Malaysians have good command of English to succeed in the world (Gill 2014).

English, then, remains important in Malaysia today. The importance attached to English was shown in a narrative study of pre-service language teachers (Macalister 2017). At the individual level, proficiency in the language provided life opportunities; in the family, the workplace and the wider community, proficiency engendered respect and success; while for the state English was seen as contributing to national development goals. Yet, despite this, English may sometimes still be regarded by Malays as *Bahasa penjajah* or *Bahasa imperialis*, the colonial or the imperialist language (Omar 2012: 60), and a threat to the construction of national identity along ethnic, religious and linguistic lines. By contrast, for speakers of other languages in the Chinese and Indian communities, the growth of Bahasa Malaysia is seen as a threat to their ethnolinguistic identities.

Penang in the twenty-first century

A sociolinguistic profile

As mentioned earlier, Chinese have played an important role in modern Penang since its establishment in the late eighteenth century. Today, Chinese remain one of the most important ethnic groups in the state. With a population of 1.76 million, Penang is composed of three main ethnic groups: Malays (42.3%), Chinese (39.4%), Indians (9.4%) and other ethnicities (8.9%). The population of Penang is characterized by a substantially higher proportion of Chinese than in Malaysia as a whole (23.2%) and of other ethnic groups (8.9% as compared with 1.0%), and a correspondingly lower proportion of Malays (Department of Statistics 2018).

Among the different Chinese dialect speakers, Hokkien speakers form the majority (approximately 64% – Department of Statistics 2010). As a result, many Chinese in Penang including other ethnic groups usually communicate in Hokkien (Wang 2017). Simultaneously, other Chinese dialects such as Cantonese, Hakka, Teochew and Hainan are also spoken by the Chinese community. Even though these dialects play important roles in daily life, they are not taught in national and private schools. The only Chinese language taught is Mandarin Chinese (Government of Malaysia 1996, as stated in Part I). Since Mandarin Chinese has become the medium of instruction in Chinese-medium schools, it is also used as a language of communication by many Chinese, in particular the younger generation in the home domain (Wang 2017).

Although Hokkien and other Chinese dialects are commonly spoken in Penang, the official language used for government administration, education and the legal system is Bahasa Malaysia – a system that aligns with the Malaysia Federal Government. All official government documents are also written in Bahasa Malaysia. English, by contrast, remains as a widely spoken language by many ethnic groups and serves as an unofficial language in Penang. It is taught in schools and used in many private sectors.

In summary, then, Penang is a linguistic mix – Bahasa Malaysia is the official language, English is the unofficial language, Hokkien is the main language of communication, and Mandarin Chinese and other Chinese dialects are also widely spoken.

Tourism and the economy

Penang has long had a reputation as a tourist destination but only in recent decades has tourism in Malaysia been the recipient of targeted promotion. Deliberate efforts can be tracked back to the establishment of the Ministry of Culture and Tourism in 1987 and subsequent substantial government investment in the sector (Teo 2003: 547). As elsewhere in the world, tourism in Malaysia has proven to be a growth industry; Ghaderi et al. (2012: 80), for example, report an increase from 5.5 million to 24.7 million in the number of international tourist arrivals to Malaysia from 1998 to 2011, with an even greater proportional increase in revenue over the same period. Penang is also, of course, a major destination for domestic tourism.

In Penang, tourism has been identified as one of two growth areas, the other being technology. As part of the shift to making Malaysia generally a centre for investment in hi-tech industry, the country has had 'to rescript its national identity away from the "Malay indigenist" discourse prominent in the postcolonial period to a multicultural identity' (Teo 2003: 553) which coincides with movements in tourist promotion. In Penang heritage is one 'of a few core tourism products' and 'the multicultural society of Penang is the highlight of this product' (ibid.: 555). One of the advantages of developing a heritage 'product' is that it is less susceptible to sudden change. Ghaderi et al. (2012: 82) report that 'the state authorities sought to encourage cultural and heritage tourism in the aftermath of the Indian Ocean tsunami [of 2004] which damaged some of Penang's beaches'. Diversification is key, it seems, to a sustainable tourism market. The iron rod sculptures of Georgetown, which are introduced in the following section, are one expression of this diversification and the threads of heritage tourism and national identity.

The iron sculptures

This chapter is about heritage, and the way in which the past is remembered. The focus of this investigation is on the historic centre of Georgetown, the capital of the state of Penang. The historic centre forms a relatively small area bordered on the north and east by roads following the shore, with, in the east, an active, commercial port; Jalan Transfer and Jalan Dr Lim Chwee Leong form the western and southern edges, respectively. This is the area that, in 2008, was awarded World Heritage Site status by UNESCO and is part of the island's heritage zone; the other zones are culture, agrotourism, nature and sun/sea (Teo 2003: 551).

One of the ways in which heritage is given the tourist treatment is through a series of iron rod sculptures that have been erected since 2009. Following the award of Word Heritage Status, the Penang State Government wanted to draw attention to the title and ran a competition inviting suggestions for creative uses of public space. This was won by a Kuala Lumpur-based design firm, Sculpture at Work, whose website describes the project thus:

> The Marking George Town is a collection of caricatures placed on historic streets of George Town. The concept is related to the history or characteristics of selected streets in George Town by using steel rod caricatures of local cartoonist. It makes the history of George Town interesting and easily grasped by the residents, the young and the old. The Marking George Town is the voices from the people that would reflect the unique character of each location through amusing caricatures and there are total 52 sets of sculpture. In September 2009, Sculptureatwork won the competition that organized by the Penang State Government to present George Town's listing as a UNESCO World Heritage Site. (http://sculptureatwork.com/project/marking-george-town/)

The data – photographs and field notes – for this investigation were generated over two days that involved a deal of walking, guided by a map that was then available online (http://www.stylebyasia.com/marking-george-town/). While the Sculpture at Work website mentions fifty-two sculptures, the map provides directions to only twenty-four. In the event, thirty-one sculptures were located and of these thirty were included in this study; one was excluded because, at the time of the data collection, it was largely obscured from public view by protective fencing.

Both linguistic and non-linguistic elements were taken into account in the analysis. Figure 9.1 is an example of, and exemplifies the features of, the sculptures. Immediately obvious is the dominating image, in this case three figures, a giant shoe and a sign. In this example, the only language directly linked to the image is on the sign (*Kedai Kasut*). In addition to the image, on every sculpture there are usually two other pieces of information. In upper case letters followed by the World Heritage emblem is information about the location; in this example, the information identifies the street (*Muntri*) and places it in a particular zone (*Buffer*) before reinforcing the World Heritage message. Additional information about the site is provided in cursive script; this script, while being arguably more important, is often difficult to read. In the discussion that follows a distinction will be made between location and site information. On most sculptures one

Figure 9.1 Jimmy Choo. Local information: Muntri Street, Buffer Zone, George Town World Heritage Site. Site information: 'This is the place where the famous shoe designer Jimmy Choo started his apprenticeship.'

additional piece of information is included – the name of the artist, in this case Baba Chuah.

All sculptures included location information, in English, and almost all included site information. Site information was predominantly in English but did include words or phrases from other languages, such as *tok tok mee* (Hokkien transliterated; a noodle dish with dumplings); however, other languages were mainly present through proper nouns – place names such as *Chowstra* (Indian) or *Gedung Rumput* (Bahasa Malaysia). Twice *hokkiens* was included and there appeared to be an equation of Chinese with Hokkien, rather than any of the other dialect groups.

Language was not present as part of around one-third of the images (as distinct from location/site information), but where it was again English was predominant. Figure 9.1 is an example of an image where language was present as part of the image although in this case the language present, *Kedai Kasut*, is Bahasa Malaysia (shoe store) rather than English. Understanding the image is not dependent on understanding the language, although interpreting it is. In other words, the viewer can see a happy family and shoes and conclude that they are cobblers, but the link to Jimmy Choo and the exact location becomes clear only through the additional linguistic elements of the sculpture.

In all but one of the images, people (and sometimes animals) are present. The people include Chinese, Malay, Indian and European/English, and while Chinese figures seemed to be the most common, no attempt was made to reinforce this impression quantitatively. A quantitative summary of ethnic representation was not done for it is not straightforward as (a) it is not always to clear to which ethnic group a figure belongs, and (b) some images included multiple minor or background figures which might skew any numerical categorization.

Although site information almost always referenced the past, not every image did. Two of the original twenty-four sculptures appeared to have more contemporary reference (*Kopi O*, see Figure 9.3, and *No More Plastic Bags*) as did one of the seven newer sculptures located during the two days of field work. This sculpture was linked to the operation of a pawn shop.

In summary, while the sculptures did link to the multilingual and multicultural nature of Malaysia, both past and present, they were strongly English-dominant in terms of language choice and tended to favour representation of Chinese over other ethnic groups. In the following sections the main themes identified in the thirty sculptures are discussed. These themes concern audience understanding, the role of humour and a focus on entertaining, and the erasure of awkward history.

Audience

As noted earlier, tourism is one of the major industries of Penang and tourism appears to have been a prime motivation for the commissioning and creation of these iron sculptures; they were a way of publicizing the city's World Heritage Status. It is perhaps no surprise, then, that linguistically the sculptures target an international rather than a local audience. The provision of site information on almost all the sculptures was in the nature of a mini-history lesson for the English-literate viewer. However, the non-linguistic elements of the sculptures ensured that the general message was being conveyed or, at least, that the images had meaning to the viewer. In the sculpture entitled *Labourer to Trader* (Figure 9.2), for instance, a non-literate viewer would see two near-identical male figures, identifiably Indian, one happy and one not. The unhappy figure may be feeling that way because he is carrying a load of rocks on his head. The other is not carrying rocks, which may explain his broad smile; perhaps his load is lighter. An English-literate viewer would connect the Indian figures with the

Figure 9.2 Labourer to trader. Local information: Chowrasta Market, Buffer Zone, George Town World Heritage Site. Site information: 'The early convict labourers were reputed to have built most of the government buildings in Penang. Some ex-convicts became petty traders and were the core group who started the Chowrasta Market.'

place name (*Chowrasta Market*) and also recognize that the unsmiling figure on the left represents a convict labourer, that on the left an ex-convict who became a trader. The meaning of the sculpture is enhanced through connecting the linguistic and the non-linguistic.

At the same time, however, elements of the images could on occasion be hidden without the appropriate linguistic knowledge. The English-literate viewer of this sculpture may not be able to decipher the inscription running long the right leg of the ex-convict; this reads: *Indian kuth seller*. *Kuth*, it transpires, is an Indian word for a cannabis-like plant. Possibly then the smile has more than one explanation.

Humour and happiness

Common to all the sculptures is that either humour or a projection of happiness – and often both – informs the narrative element, as can be seen in both Figures 9.1 and 9.2. There would seem to be a clear link between this feature of the sculptures and their intended tourist viewership. They are designed to amuse and entertain. Indeed, the firm that created them called them 'caricatures'.

In most of the sculptures the reference is to the past, but there are exceptions. Contemporary reference is found in a small number, such as *No More Plastic Bags* located in what the site information describes as 'a petty-trading neighbourhood' and which may reflect light-hearted advocacy of reusable shopping bags, and in Figure 9.3. Figure 9.3 is unusual as an instance of a sculpture having no explicit site information, and so its placement is not explained. It is, however, on a shop wall on a busy street where food and drinks are sold, and so not incongruously sited. The young man with the laptop orders a very modern form of coffee, the older man continues blissfully making coffee as he always has, and the central figure mediates between them, translating 'one tall double shot decaf espresso' into simple 'kopi-o-kau', a borrowing from Hokkien into Bahasa Malaysia for strong black coffee. The past, an old-style coffee stall, is being evoked in different ways such as the dress of the old man, the implements being used for making the coffee (including what appears to be an opened can of condensed milk on his right), and the woman loudly shouting the order to the old man. The humour can be guessed at by a non-Malaysian (similar to the viewer appreciation of Figure 9.2), and it is interesting that while the three figures are presumably Chinese, the language choices are English and Bahasa Malaysia.[1]

However, to make the point that humour is in the eye of the beholder, it might be noted that the first author found this sculpture amusing, the second author

Figure 9.3 Kopi O. Local information: Kimberley Street, Buffer Zone, George Town World Heritage Site. Site information: [none provided].

commented that 'I feel that it's a Malaysian joke' and a reviewer of this chapter noted that 'I didn't get the humour at all'.

Erased history

One consequence, however, of this light-hearted approach to remembering the past is the erasure of darker moments of history. This is to some extent apparent in Figure 9.2, where the use of indentured and convict Indian labourers is glossed over, but perhaps the best example is shown in Figure 9.4. Called *Win Win*, this shows two happy men, merchants probably, doing a very contemporary fist-bump as they greet each other in a mix of English and Bahasa Malaysia (*tauke* meaning *boss, orang kaya* being *rich man*). The basis for their relationship, and the source of their wealth, is alluded to by the word 'tin' on the boxes behind the Malay man. The site information explains that 'The tin merchants of Penang worked very closely with Ngah Ibrahim as Larut district was one of the major suppliers of tin at that time'. Nothing suggests that this was not a happy harmonious relationship.

Figure 9.4 Win Win. Local information: Muntri Street, Buffer Zone, George Town World Heritage Site. Site information: Muntri Street was named after the Orang Kaya Menteri of Larut, Perak, Ngah Ibrahim. The tin merchants of Penang worked very closely with Ngah Ibrahim as Larut District was one of the major suppliers of tin at that time.

The history books, however, suggest otherwise. As Andaya and Andaya (2017: 158–159) explain, Ngah Ibrahim (whose role and relevance are not explained by the sculpture) inherited the district in 1858 upon the death of his father and the next fifteen years saw three Larut wars, with control of the tin industry behind all three. The first, 1861–1863, began when two Hakka-speaking clans associated with different secret societies clashed over control of a waterway; Penang merchants weighed in, hoping to benefit not only from the tin mines but also from Larut's opium trade. The Chen Sang clan won the battle for the waterway, but not the war, for the Fei Chew clan sought Penang government support, resulting in the dispatch of a gunship and the payment by Ngah Ibrahim of compensation to the Fei Chew Hakka for their lost mines. This was not the end of the tension, however, with serious rioting occurring in Penang in 1867. Muslim societies allied with the Chinese parties were drawn in to the unrest, and the government response was to enforce registration of such societies as a way of maintaining control. Rising tin prices in the late 1860s may have paved the way for the third Larut war, 1871–1873, which saw five different Chinese societies fighting for control of the mines and waterways.

As the outline of the history ignored in Figure 9.4 hints at, secret societies played an important role in nineteenth-century Penang. In popular imagination, secret societies are linked with a criminal underworld but the reality is more complex for they also acted as mutual aid associations, as political forces and as a means for overseas Chinese to maintain links with China. In Penang, however, 'the societies from the beginning had a reputation for fomenting dissent' (Andaya and Andaya 2017: 150), and the response of the government following the second Larut war 'drove the societies underground' (ibid.: 158) where, conceivably, criminal activity could thrive more easily. The Chinese secret societies had parallels in the Red and White Flag societies, whose members came from Jawi Peranakan and Indian Muslim communities. The net result was that:

> In a monotonous and exacting life it was not uncommon for thousands of men to be sworn enemies because of an isolated dispute involving only a few society members over a woman, or rights to a watercourse, or because of some event as far away as Rangoon or Saigon.
>
> (Andaya and Andaya 2017: 151)

The sculptures do not completely ignore the existence of, at least the Chinese, secret societies, but their treatment is much as that of the tin mining industry in Figure 9.4. Their existence is acknowledged in two of the more recent of the iron sculptures. In one, two broadly smiling new migrants laden with baggage which includes a couple of chickens, a duck, a puppy and a goo-ing baby are welcomed to Penang; the site information informs the viewer that 'Yeoh kongsi was established in 1836 to look after the welfare of the newly arrived Yeoh clansmen'. The inclusion of the animals and infant adds a very domestic air to the scene being portrayed. In the other, the site information explains that 'To the dismay of parishioners of the Portuguese church there, Church Street also housed the headquarters of the notorious Gee Hin secret society'. A smiling clergyman raises an admonishing – or hushing – finger from an arched window as he looks down on two Chinese men engaged in a martial arts fight, the air between them replete with profanity symbols. Humour makes light of the history alluded to.

Linking to the streetscape

These sculptures are spread throughout the historic centre of Georgetown; it is a busy area in which they contribute just one component of the LL. As this section explains, they fit into the physical streetscape while competing to be noticed in a crowded LL and are, perhaps, in competition with other discourses.

The sculptures take advantage of and are reinforced by the streetscape in two ways. They gain meaning through their emplacement, which Scollon and Scollon (2003: 142) identify as 'the most fundamental issue of geosemiotics – where in the physical world is the sign or image located?' The first way in which emplacement works is shown in Figure 9.5, where the depiction of the escaping husband's precarious perch exploits the existing structure as he hides from the owner of the imaginary voice crying 'Where's my husband?' that comes from the real window. The voice, of course, is that of his wife.

In this the sculpture shares a characteristic with the wall murals that also decorate Georgetown. The first of these were commissioned from a Lithuanian-born artist for the Georgetown Festival in 2012, and they soon became favourites to visit because of their interactive elements, both the interaction with existing (or introduced) structures and the opportunity to become a part of the mural (as can be seen on http://thenextsomewhere.com/2017/07/11/walking-tour-street-art-in-penang/). Today painted art seems to be everywhere in Penang.

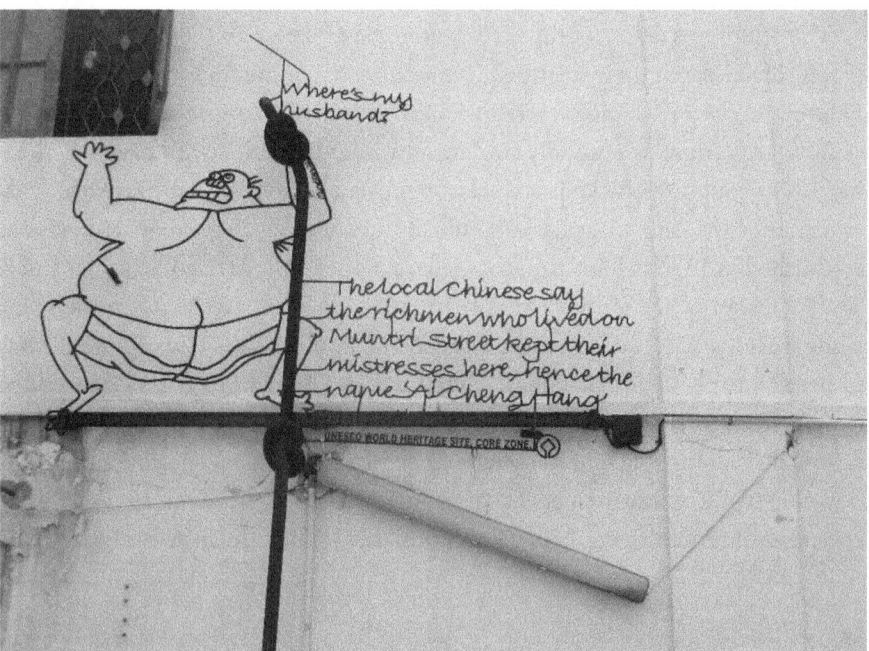

Figure 9.5 Escape. Location information: UNESCO World Heritage Site, Core Zone. Site information: The local Chinese say the rich men who lived on Muntri Street kept their mistresses here, hence the name 'Ai Cheng Hang' [or Love Lane].

In Figure 9.5 the site information links very clearly to the past; there is no obvious indication that rich men keep mistresses in houses in this street any more. At other sites, however, the history that is evoked at a site is still in evidence today. One such example is the Jimmy Choo site (Figure 9.1) which is near a (possibly closed) shoe store; a tri-lingual sign (English, Chinese, Bahasa Malaysia) declares the shop's function. Another site, *Limousine*, which recalls the manufacture of paper effigies for burning as part of funeral rites is opposite a vibrantly active temple, described below. Emplacement links past and present.

What is also the case, however, is that these sculptures are competing for attention in a crowded streetscape. They are not even the sole tourist-directed artistic features of Georgetown. Many of the tourists seem to be drawn by the street art painted on walls (see Figure 9.6), a fair number of which, as mentioned above, invite interaction from passers-by. This street art also features on T-shirts, bags, fridge magnets and postcards. The sculptures do not appear to have generated the same type of commercial interest.

Not only do they compete for tourist attention, but they also compete within a multilingual LL. Exploring this area, the impression is that Chinese and English are the dominant languages. Chinese, it seems, relates to the lives lived in the town, and not purely to commercial activity; on the first day of exploration, for

Figure 9.6 Learn Hokkien.

example, a temple ceremony was being conducted with accompanying noise and smells from braziers on the street. English, however, appears to be the language, the *lingua franca* of tourism; on the second day of exploration, for instance, a young couple on a motorbike pulled up to ask for directions – in English; they were tourists from Vietnam.

While Chinese and English appear dominant, they are certainly not the only languages in evidence. Bahasa Malaysia is clearly present, as are Arabic and Indian languages, most obviously in a part of historic Georgetown marked out as Little India where, during our visit, Diwali street stalls added another layer to the life of the town.

A good sense of the vibrancy of the LL and the roles different languages play can be gained from a snapshot examination, summarized in Table 9.1, of the seven signs closest to one of the sculptures (Escape, see Figure 9.5) at the corner of Lebuh Acheh and Lebuh Pantai. Two of the seven are monolingual – the language of the sculpture is English, of a road sign Bahasa Malaysia. Three of the signs feature two languages, with the first named of each being dominant – Bahasa Malaysia and English on a directions sign, Bahasa Malaysia and an Indian language on a street name sign, Chinese and English (the transliteration of the name) on a shop sign. A second shop sign has three languages – Bahasa Malaysia, English and Chinese – with the Chinese occupying the bottom third but the largest font and Bahasa Malaysia the top portion but the smallest font. This sign, incidentally, presents a challenge for any interpretation based on code preference (Scollon and Scollon 2003). Finally, an official sign providing historical information about the street is the most multilingual, featuring Bahasa Malaysia, English, Chinese (both Hokkien and Cantonese) and Tamil, with Bahasa Malaysia dominant. Apart from reinforcing the notion that the LL can be 'chaotic' (Ben-Rafael et al. 2006), the picture that emerges from this snapshot is of Bahasa Malaysia for official use in line with language policy (most obviously on the Stop and street signs), Chinese for commerce, English for tourism (the street directions sign, for instance, is intended to guide tourists towards sites) and others as a reflection of the local linguistic ecology. On that last point, it is worth noting that since 2008 Penang has adopted a policy of multilingual street signs; a sign would have the name in Bahasa Malaysia and one other language – English, Chinese, Tamil or Arabic. While the Bahasa Malaysia name would be dominant, the move still attracted legal action from language activists who perceived it as a threat to the status of the national language (Ng 2008).

But, it should be noted, these are not the only languages evident in Georgetown. Vietnamese, for example, appears on a new restaurant, and unusual combinations leap out – a restaurant advertising *Danish briyani*,² a stencilled sign advising *Teksi only*. The LL is most definitely multilingual, and the sculptures reflect this in some measure.

Yet there are clearly tensions at play here. These are overt at one location where a painted sign (Figure 9.6) exhorts the, presumably ethnic Chinese, viewer to learn Hokkien. The English in the speech bubble says *Teach you speak Hokkien*. The same message is conveyed above and below in pinyin and Chinese characters. However, it seems likely that the speech bubble represents, in Scollon and Scollon (2003)'s terms, an instance of transgressive semiotics, an addition of politically motivated graffiti to the original. While not necessarily the work of teenaged adolescents, it fulfils the function of protest, of challenge to the official discourse (Christen 2003; Pennycook 2009) that sees Mandarin Chinese being taught in schools.

Conclusion

The sites of the sculptures determined the nature of the memories of the past that were selected for representation. The selected memories were not grand moments in Georgetown's history, nor were they markers of tragedy; they are, rather, generally reminders of past daily life presented in a light-hearted manner and intended to entertain as much as they are to instruct. In recalling this past they draw on the multilingual and multi-ethnic nature of Malaysia, but with a strong code preference for English, which is explained by the intended tourist audience. Bahasa Malaysia, despite being the country's official language and being prominent on official signage (Table 9.1), plays a minor role on these sculptures. Among the other languages it is Chinese, specifically Hokkien, that has the greatest presence and the contribution of Chinese languages is nicely illustrated by the use of *kau* in the phrase *kopi'o kau* (Figure 9.3, Note 1). The Chinese presence is further heightened through the frequency of Chinese people's appearance on the sculptures, and is explained by their role in Georgetown's history, and their relative prominence in contemporary Penang. As mentioned earlier, this is not just a question of demography; a walk through much of Georgetown conveys a strong sense of being in a Chinese community.

The iron rod sculptures do present the past in a light-hearted way, and as their creators noted, they are intended as caricatures. This is neatly illustrated in the representation of European/English figures, who were, incidentally, always male. Historical representations sported a pith helmet and moustache;

Table 9.1 Languages on signs close to *Escape*

	Bahasa Malaysia	English	Chinese	Tamil	Originator of sign
Iron sculpture		X	As transcribed place name		Official
Road 'Stop' sign	X				Official
Street directions sign	X	X			Official
Street name sign	X			X	Official
Shop sign		As transliterated Hokkien	X		Local commercial
Shop sign	X	X	X		Local commercial
Blue plaque	X	X	X Both Hokkien and Cantonese	X	Official

contemporary representations were of backpackers. One consequence of this approach to depicting the past is that historic grievances and conflicts are erased (Figures 9.2 and 9.4). In a country where ethnic, linguistic and religious divisions persist, the decision to not draw attention to contentious issues could be thought of in terms of national unity, nation-building and identity formation. Far better, perhaps, to remember – or imagine – moments in history as shared and good-humoured than to recall occasions that might feed lingering, inherited resentment.

Whatever their purpose, the sculptures do compete for attention in Georgetown. Indeed, as their commodification indicates, the painted murals have greater tourist appeal than the sculptures do. But while the murals often reference past activities, such as children playing on a swing, they do not explicitly address heritage or language concerns. The sculptures are part of the LL and vie with Bahasa Malaysia, Chinese languages and, particularly in the area known as Little India, Tamil. Possibly, with their English dominance, they stand apart from other signs. They are not always easy to find, not always easy to read, but they are worth seeking out for the bites of history they reveal.

Notes

1 At a conference presentation in Kuala Lumpur in December 2018, an audience member suggested that *kau* (which she said was usually spelled as *kaw*) was a borrowing into Bahasa Malaysia from Chinese. Further investigation found it was a transliteration of the Hokkien, and that there is no standardized orthography for *kau/kaw*, which has the original meaning of 'thick'. Etymologically *kopi* also derives from Hokkien. Despite these origins, we have chosen to treat *kopi-o kau* as a Bahasa Malaysia term.

2 At the same conference in Kuala Lumpur in December 2018, it was suggested that *Danish* may in fact be a person's name, rather than referencing Denmark. A consequent web search revealed this to be the case: 'Danish cuisine? Hmm…. not quite. In fact, this place was named after the owner of the briyani house who happens to inherit the same name.' (https://www.foodadvisor.my/best-nasi-briyani-in-penang). The point remains, however, that to a non-Malaysian English speaker the immediate association of *Danish* is with Scandinavia, not India.

References

Albury, N. J. and K. K. Aye (2016), 'Malaysia's National Language Policy in International Theoretical Context', *Journal of Nusantara Studies*, 1 (1): 71–84.

Andaya, B. W. and L. Y. Andaya. (2017), *A History of Malaysia*, Palgrave: London.

Asmah, H. O. (1979), *Language Planning for Unity and Efficiency – A Study on the Language Status and Corpus Planning of Malaysia*, Kuala Lumpur: University Malaya Press.

Asmah, H. O. (1987, 6–8 September), *English in Malaysia: A Typology of Its Status and Role*. Paper presented at the 'Seminar on Language Planning in Multilingual Settings: The Roel of English', National University of Singapore, Singapore.

Asmah, H. O. (1997), 'From Imperialism to Malaysianisation: A Discussion of the Path Taken by English towards Becoming a Malaysian Language', in M. S. Halimah and K. S. Ng (eds), *English Is an Asian Language: The Malaysian Context*, 12–21, Kuala Lumpur: Association of Modern Languages, Malaysia and The Macquarie Library Pty. Ltd.

Ben-Rafael, E., E. Shohamy, M. H. Amara and N. Trumper-Hecht (2006), 'Linguistic Landscape as Symbolic Construction of the Public Space: The Case of Israel', in Durk Gorter (ed.), *Linguistic Landscape: A New Approach to Multilingualism*, 7–30, Clevedon: Multilingual Matters.

Chai, H. C. (1977), *Education and Nation Building in Plural Societies: The West Malaysia Experience*, Canberra: The Australian National University Press.

Christen, R. S. (2003), 'Hip Hop Learning: Graffiti as an Educator of Urban Teenagers', *The Journal of Educational Foundations*, 17: 57–82.

Department of Statistics (2010), *Population (Malaysian Citizen) by Ethnic Detail (Chinese) and State*, Kuala Lumpar: Government of Malaysia.

Department of Statistics (2018), 'Population Quick Info', *Government of Malaysia*. Available online: http://pqi.stats.gov.my/searchBI.php?kodData= (accessed 9 January 2019).

Ghaderi, Z., A. P. Mat Som and J. C. Henderson (2012), 'Tourism Crises and Island Destinations: Experiences in Penang, Malaysia', *Tourism Management Perspectives*, 2/3: 79–84.

Gill, S. K. (2004), 'Medium-of-instruction Policy in Higher Education in Malaysia: Nationalism versus Internationalisation', in J. W. Tollefson and A. B. M. Tsui (eds), *Medium of Instruction Policies – Which Agenda? Whose Agenda?*, 135–152, New Jersey, NJ: Lawrence Erlbaum.

Gill, S. K. (2005), 'Language Policy in Malaysia: Reversing Direction', *Language Policy*, 4, 241–260.

Gill, S. K. (2014), *Language Policy Challenges in Multi-ethnic Malaysia*, Netherlands: Springer.

Government of Malaysia (1996), *Education Act*, Kuala Lumpur: The Commissioner of Law Revision, Malaysia.

Government of Malaysia (1963/1967), *National Language Acts*, Kuala Lumpur: The Commissioner of Law Revision, Malaysia.

Kelman, H. C. (1971), 'Language as an Aid and Barrier to Involvement in the National System', in J. Rubin and B. H. Jernudd (eds), *Can Language Be Planned? Sociolinguistic Theory and Practice for Developing Nations*, 21–51, Honolulu, HI: The University Press of Hawaii.

Keong, N. K. J. (2006), 'Economic Change and the Emergence of the Straits Chinese in Nineteenth-century Penang', *Journal of the Malaysian Branch of the Royal Asiatic Society*, 79: 59–83.

Macalister, J. (2017), 'English and Language Teacher Education in Malaysia: An Exploration of the Influences on and Experiences of Pre-service Teachers', *RELC Journal*, 48: 53–66.

Ministry of Education Malaysia (2014), *Dasar Memartabatkan Bahasa Malaysia Memperkukuh Bahasa Inggeris (MBMMBI): Buku penerangan* [Policy of 'Upholding Bahasa Melayu and Strengthening English' (MBMMBI): Description book]. Putrajaya: Kementerian Pendidikan Malaysia.

Mujani, W. K. (2012), 'The History of the Indian Muslim Community in Malaysia', *Advances in Natural and Applied Sciences*, 6: 1348–1353.

Mukhopadhyay, J. (2010), 'Indian Diaspora in South East Asia: Predicaments and Prospects', *The Indian Journal of Political Science*, 71: 995–1002.

Ng, S-A. (2008), 'Multilingual Road Signs Put Up to Boost Penang's Tourism', *The Star*, 22 November. Available online: https://www.thestar.com.my/news/nation/2008/11/22/multilingual-road-signs-put-up-to-boost-penangs-tourism/#gP6joJH18QywS8gC.99 (accessed 10 January 2019).

Omar, A. H. (2012), 'Language, Politics and Education in Malaysia', in Wan Rafaei Abdul Rahman (ed.), *The Annual SAAD Lectures*, 55–70, Victoria Univerity of Wellington/Chair of Malay Studies: Wellington, New Zealand.

Pennycook, A. (2009), 'Linguistic Landscapes and the Transgressive Semiotics of Graffiti', in E. Shohamy and D. Gorter (eds), *Linguistic Landscape: Expanding the Scenery*, 302–312, Routledge: New York.

Scollon, R. and S. W. Scollon. (2003), *Discourses in Place: Language in the Material World*, Routledge: London.

Teo, P. (2003), 'Limits of Imagineering: A Case Study of Penang', *International Journal of Urban and Regional Research*, 27: 545–563.

Wang, X. M. (2017), 'Family Language Policy by Hakkas in Balik Pulau, Penang', *International Journal of the Sociology of Language*, 224: 87–118.

10

Instances of Emplaced Memory: The Case of Alghero/L'Alguer

Stefania Tufi

Of all things that are, the greatest is space, for it holds all things; the wisest, time, for it brings everything to light.

Thales of Miletus (as quoted in Diogenes Laertius, *Lives of the philosophers*, I, 35)

Introduction

Alghero/L'Alguer (pop. 44,000) is a multilingual town in north-western Sardinia (Italy), the second largest of Italy's island.[1] Local repertoires include Italian, Sardinian and Alguerese, a variety of Catalan which was introduced in the fourteenth century following the town's conquest by the Crown of Aragon and its subsequent repopulation with Catalan people. The presence of Alguerese characterizes the town as a linguistic island within an island and contributes to the complex linguistic make-up of Sardinia.

Surveys (see the section 'Theoretical background') have indicated that a shift to Italian is in progress and that intergenerational transmission has been compromised by a number of factors. Even though Alguerese Catalan enjoys protection under both regional and national legislation, widespread use of Italian (the national language) and Sardinian (also officially recognized and endowed with local prestige) competes with uses of Alguerese, which is therefore subjected to great pressure in spite of recent attempts at revitalization. However, the vitality and visibility of Catalan culture are ensured by literary production, employment of the language in the public space (e.g. place names/street signs) and in education, and promotional activities supported by local agents and by the wider Catalan cultural movement (Toso 2008).

This chapter is based on data gathered from the Linguistic Landscape (LL) of Alghero and, in keeping with the themes of the volume, discusses issues of spatial and linguistic organization of memory. The analysis focuses on place-naming as an exemplification of emplaced and manipulated memory and as a site of tension between rememoration (to try and capture the truth of the past) (Todorov 2003) and commemoration (to adapt the past to the needs of the present). This tension emerges from an observation of the intertextuality of multilingual street-name signs in the town centre which narrativize (Benjamin 2002) the city's linguistic and cultural history. In addition, the layering and juxtaposition of monolingual and multilingual street-name signs referring to different historical periods point to processes of spatial de-structuration (see the section 'Reconstructing the urban map'): meaningful spatial information indicating physical characteristics of streets and carried by place names has been lost, and celebratory discourses have replaced the earlier functional map over time. As a result, and within a dynamic view of memory as performative cultural practice, multilingual street names can be seen as memory acts (Hobuß 2013) constituting fluid memorial intertext. From this perspective, they enable the construction of a hypertext (a town map encompassing multiple spatial and historical references) which is able to return not only the physicality of three-dimensional space, but also a fourth element – time.

Street-name signs have been analysed within LL scholarship before, either as the main focus of discussion (e.g. Spolsky and Cooper 1991; Spalding 2013; Amos 2017) or as part of the empirical LL data presented in given publications (e.g. Cenoz and Gorter 2006; Blackwood and Tufi 2015).[2] In our context street-name signs are framed primarily as multilingual monuments both in an etymological sense (the Latin *monumentum* means both memorial/reminder and monument) and as discursive devices positioned at the intersection of memory and identity. From this perspective the selectivity of memory is particularly significant in reviving memorialization processes while forging identity, and in bringing to the fore the fact that both memory and identity are socially constructed.

In terms of the organization of the chapter, in the following section we provide background information with respect to the re-discovery of Alghero as a Catalan enclave and some data about current language practices. We then discuss the theoretical frameworks that have helped us shed light on Alghero street-name signs as instances of emplaced memory. These are followed by the presentation and analysis of the data, and the chapter closes with conclusive remarks.

The re-discovery of Alghero as a Catalan enclave

The fortified city of Alghero was most likely founded by the Doria family from Genoa between the twelfth and the thirteenth centuries, and kept under their almost uninterrupted rule until 1353, when the town was conquered by the Crown of Aragon (Meloni 1994). This event represented a watershed in linguistic terms: the city was repopulated with Catalan-speaking people and Alguerese, the local form of Catalan, has since developed as a distinct variety resulting from the contact between fourteenth-century Catalan and multiple Italo-Romance varieties (including Sardinian, Corsican and Genoese) over centuries of commercial, political and migratory exchanges (Argenter 2008).[3]

The union of the Crown of Aragon with Castile in the late fifteenth century marked the beginning of Spanish rule in Sardinia, which would last until 1720 when the Treaty of London sanctioned the passing of Sardinia into the hands of the Savoy dynasty, the future monarchs of the Kingdom of Italy. Under Spanish rule Alghero lost the privileges granted by the Aragon administration and its economic importance declined. For the purposes of this chapter, it is important to note that after 1720 contacts with Catalonia would only be sporadic.

The long period leading up to the second half of the nineteenth century therefore was one of progressive distancing from Catalonia. The re-discovery of Alghero as a Catalan enclave is usually attributed to the Catalan Eduard Toda i Güell, who served as a diplomat in Sardinia in 1887–1888 (Caria 2014). Barcelona at the time was in the middle of the Renaixença, a literary movement which lay the foundations for Catalan nationalism. In this context the intellectuals who flocked to Alghero searched for traces of a cultural heritage that could prove that the city was an integral part of the golden age of the Catalan nation and one that had preserved the core and unadultered essence of Catalanness (Farinelli 2014). Toda i Güell put Alguerese intellectuals in contact with the cultural circles of Barcelona and encouraged the publication of works in Alguerese in Catalan journals. An outcome of these activities was the creation of the *Centre Catalanista La Palmavera* (1906). This, however, was short-lived and similar initiatives were stifled by the onset of Fascism in Italy and subsequently franchismo in Spain, in that both regimes repressed linguistic and cultural diversity.

In the 1950s emigration from Alghero to mainland Italy and abroad was counterbalanced by immigration into the city from neighbouring towns and from peninsular areas such as Naples and Sicily to support industrial development and particularly tourism. The new social and linguistic mix, together with the socio-economic developments that affected the whole of

Sardinia and indeed Italy in its entirety, fostered a process of language shift to the detriment of Alguerese. As a result of these events, Alguerese came to occupy more of a niche position in the life of the town with folkloristic activities such as songs and amateur theatre. This situation remained unaltered until the 1960s, when a new relationship between Alghero and Catalonia started being developed. A key event marking the symbolic beginning of the re-discovery of Alghero as a Catalan enclave was the arrival in the town of the Catalan cruise ship *Virginia de Churruca* on 26 August 1960. The 139 passengers were warmly welcomed by the locals and this episode has since been remembered as *Lo Viatge del Retrobament* (the journey of rediscovery). As in other parts of Italy (and beyond), the 1960s and 1970s hailed the embracing of regional, minority and unofficial culture with an inclusive approach to linguistic heritage (see Tufi 2013 for an account of Sardinia). However, while a renewed attention was being given to previously stigmatized local languages and to the need to preserve them, standard language ideology had long taken root and dictated a change in family linguistic practices which increasingly privileged Italian. As a result, the initiatives introduced to raise the status of Alguerese were not being matched by language use. With respect to ethnolinguistic revitalization activities, Caria (2014) mentions, amongst other initiatives, the introduction of (experimental) Alguerese language teaching and the opening of the *Escola de alguerés Pasqual Scanu* (1985), the founding of the *Obra Cultural de l'Alguer* (1991) and, following increasingly intense links with (Iberian) Catalonia, the establishment of an office of the Generalitat de Catalunya (2009). The setting up of institutional links with Catalonia in fact dates back to 1972, when Alghero was twinned with Tarragona in Catalonia (*Alghero Eco* 2012) and has intensified ever since. The 1991 Municipal Statute laid the foundation for the promotion of Alguerese language and culture (*Comune di Alghero* 1991). Subsequently, two main pieces of legislation sanctioned the official status of Alguerese Catalan, one regional law (Legge Regionale 26/1997), which is inclusive of all languages in use in Sardinia, and one national law (Legge 482/1999) which singles out twelve minority languages in use on the national territory, including Alguerese Catalan. Local associations promote language maintenance via the organization of cultural activities, publications (including the press) and the training of teachers on a voluntary basis (Argenter 2008). A more systematic approach taking the timetabled teaching of Alguerese into schools was introduced in 1999 through the *Joan Colomba* project, but recent reports lament the decline of this type of initiatives.[4] In 2003 a written Alguerese standard was sanctioned by the

Institut d'Estudis Catalans (*Institut d'Estudis Catalans* 2003) – this relatively late development explains the current coexistence of different spellings, an aspect that emerges while observing LL.

Recent developments therefore point to an intensification of links between Alghero and Catalonia since the 1960s, which were further enhanced by the approval of the Statute of Autonomy of Catalonia in 1979 and by institutional initiatives, as well as the establishment of tourist connections both by sea and by air. Farinelli (2014) highlights, however, that the links between Alghero and Catalonia had become ever more tenuous over the centuries, and that the expectation that the people of Alghero would participate in promoting the political stances of pan-Catalanism has overall not been met by the wider population, due to their remaining peripheral to the nationalist movement. In this context, local language vitality is difficult to sustain due to both the absence of strong links with Catalonia and to the multiple pressures exercised by both Sardinian and Italian.

Information about local linguistic and cultural attitudes is provided in Argenter (2008), who discusses the peculiarities of identity formation and performance in Alghero. Generally, people claim a separate identity from Sardinians. This is present in local discourses of belonging by employing the term 'los algueresos' or, more recently, 'los catalans' (as a result of renewed links with Catalonia) as opposed to 'los sardos'. Argenter (2008: 212) highlights the relevance of these discourses in relation to the 'local politics of language' and to the deployment of verbal resources that either minimize or maximize the distance between standard Catalan and the Alguerese variety, depending on the ideological stance that speakers are keen to support. However, this type of language ideological alignment tends to be apparent in discursive constructions of identity and in the metapragmatic awareness of language agents, rather than through the actual use of Alguerese.

The three sets of data relating to language use in Alghero that we identified in available sources are reported in Tables 10.1–10.3. Tables 10.1 and 10.2 are very similar and were in fact carried out in the same period. Oppo (2007) was commissioned by the Sardinian regional authority (Table 10.1), while Table 10.2 reports information about Alghero as part of a wider survey about Catalan-speaking areas (*Generalitat de Catalunya* 2008).[5] Table 10.3 refers to a more recent survey by the *Generalitat de Catalunya* (2015).

Even though the 2015 survey (Table 10.3) does not provide information about other languages in use in Alghero, it is evident that Alguerese had been subjected to further erosion within the period 2007–2015.

Table 10.1 Language use in Alghero as reported in Oppo (2007)

	First language	Habitual language
Italian	64.9%	83.3%
Alguerese Catalan	22.8%	13.9%
Sardinian	12.3%	2.8%

Table 10.2 Language use in Alghero as reported in Generalitat de Catalunya (2008)

	First language	Habitual language
Italian	59.2%	83.0%
Alguerese Catalan	22.4%	13.9%
Sardinian	12.3%	2.8%
Other	6.1%	0.3%

Table 10.3 Language use in Alghero as reported in Generalitat de Catalunya (2015)

	First language	Habitual language
Alguerese Catalan	17.5%	9.1%

In what follows we shall outline the main theoretical frameworks which have informed our interpretation of Alghero's street-name signs as instances of emplaced memory before discussing the data.

Theoretical background

As mentioned in the Introduction, the paper builds upon existing scholarship on memory and memorialization practices,[6] and the following discussion foregrounds aspects that we consider relevant in uncovering the dynamics at play in the naming practices of Alghero's historic map. Key aspects such as commemoration and rememoration emerge in varying forms in authors and works that we have taken into consideration. One such author is Walter Benjamin and his influential reflections on the concept of history.

Two main aspects of Benjamin's *œuvre* provide a useful perspective on the present context. The first is in relation to Benjamin's critique of historicism as summarized in the quote 'Articulating the past historically does not mean recognizing it "the way it really was". It means appropriating a memory as it flashes up in a moment of danger' (Benjamin 2004–2006: 391). The quote needs to be framed within Benjamin's critique of historicism and its rhetoric of objectivity whereby constructions (and reconstructions) of the past in the present always reproduce certain configurations of power (de Wilde 2009: 186). On the contrary, Benjamin's images of the past are endowed with a disruptive force, or are unsettling (ibid., 192), and as a result they escape attempts to appropriate and instrumentalize the past on the part of political positionings. Benjamin's politics of remembrance is therefore to be distinguished from practices of commemoration, where historical happenings are transformed into official monuments and serve given interests.

The second aspect of Benjamin's work with which we wish to engage is central to *The Arcades Project* (2002). While discussing the multiple constructions of Paris as a revolutionary city, Benjamin (2002: 840) refers to the city as a linguistic cosmos and highlights the close interconnections between space and naming practices in urban environments, and the role of language in narrativizing the city via multiple intertextual references. Names, in particular, appropriate space and construct place. We thus observe that on the one hand, and for the purposes of this chapter, to name is to materialize identity. On the other hand, this very operation opens the possibility of contestation and of transforming space into material events which cannot be choreographed by a single entity and where a multiplicity of actors and actions have left traces.

Todorov (2003) builds on the concept of commemoration as suggested in Benjamin (2004–2006) and establishes a distinction between commemoration and rememoration. Commemoration practices simplify history in that they single out individuals to worship as heroes or to detest as enemies (ibid., 133). In addition, and in line with Benjamin's perspective, commemoration consists of the appropriation and instrumentalization of the past for present purposes, while rememoration is to try to grasp the truth of the past. In Todorov's discussion historical truth is relativized through a positive view of revisionism in its literal sense, whereby history is always subject to revision and not sanctified, a characteristic pertaining to the discourse of commemoration.

Todorov (2003: 127) also discusses memory as being a (partial) forgetting as well as a remembering. This idea suggests the forging of a dialectical interaction between the two processes and highlights the selective nature of human memory, a feature that is indispensable to making sense of the past and, we would add, of the present. The selectivity of memories and their materialization via familiar landscapes is pointed out in Mitchell (2003), for whom forgetting is a corollary of memory and both are hegemonically produced by hierarchies of power. This process is made more visible by the aestheticization of politics via, amongst other aspects, the creation of monuments. This concept was first introduced by Benjamin (2008), too, in relation to fascist regimes and their conceiving of life (and of the endeavours of the living) as innately artistic, therefore creating the premises for viewing politics as an art form. Mitchell (2003: 443–444) comments on the spectacular memorial event, usually created at the scale of the city, where architecture, monuments and rallies represent a classic case for the complete aestheticization of politics. Mitchell (ibid., 446) highlights that it is necessary to analyse and dissect the archaeology of power, that is, the historical layering underpinning memory construction, in order to uncover its polymorphous nature and replicability, an aspect that monuments share in that they can be moved to different sites, removed and replaced. Ensuing processes of resemioticization ensure that hegemony over memory is never complete or unchanging – this aspect will also account for Alghero's LL and open invisible spaces of memorial agency. Mitchell (ibid., 445) incorporates references to Nora (1989) into her discussion. In particular, Nora's *lieux de mémoire* (places of memory) provide the conceptualization for 'conflated spaces, where geography, history, identity and memory run into and through each other and are captured (and put to work) in specific sites' – a concept similar to what Rothberg (2010) would call memory knots. In the discussion, however, these local spaces contribute to the linking with and legitimization of national discourses. Thus Mitchell, too, points out that commemoration practices have the role of bringing closer together different memorialization scales. In the case of Alghero, the places of memory represented by multilingual street-name signs actualize multiple linkings of the locality with different entities, including a transnational element, as will become evident over the course of the chapter.

Commemoration as a fundamental aspect of memory-making is also central to the discussion in Gillis (1994), who investigates developments in both national and post-national contexts. For instance, in Western discourses the 1960s are identified as a turning point in the re-discovery of minority culture and of marginalized or annihilated histories. New emancipatory discourses on the part of new nations and ethnic groups were legitimized by the identification of usable pasts to put in relation with new claims. In Gillis (1994: 13–14) monuments are identified as being very effective in concentrating time in space and in conjuring up commonalities in groups, regardless of the physical or social distance between their members.

This leads us to another aspect that we wish to foreground for our context – space cannot be separated from time in memory-making processes and indeed we would like to suggest that space can be conceptualized as a *sequence of happenings*. The impossibility of disentangling space from time is aptly encompassed in Bakhtin's (1981: 7) theorization of chronotopes, which are defined as:

> Points in the geography of a community where time and space intersect and fuse. Time takes on flesh and becomes visible for human contemplation; likewise, space becomes charged and responsive to the movements of time and history and enduring character of a people [...] Chronotopes thus stand as monuments to the community itself, as symbols of it, as forces operating to shape its members images to themselves.

Street-name signs therefore provide spatial anchoring to narrated events so that understanding place and landscape is indispensable for the creation of the self (Basso 1996).[7]

However, the creation of the self is a relational process and a result of the dialectical co-construction of identity as social practice. Drawing upon performative theories of meaning-making practices, Hobuß (2013: 14) highlights that contexts of uses cannot be fully controlled by single individuals in intentional ways and borrows Derrida's concept of the 'iterability' of signs (Derrida 1988) to point out that signs become endowed with meaning only if they are re-iterated, that is, repeated, reused and quoted. In addition, a continuous slippage of meaning characterizes all signs so that it is impossible to control their future resignification and recontextualization. This applies to cultural memory acts as well – memory practices need to be relativized in relation to their changeable contexts and are not controllable once and for all. However, contextual aspects make certain readings possible. In our setting, the multiglossic characteristics of the material environment are decoded via ongoing conversations with the historical and societal positions of LL agents. In line with theories of performativity, while habitual mediation practices (among which language occupies a privileged position) create the possibility of communication, the inherent slippages of meaning provide the possibility for change. Hobuß clarifies, however, that the performance of memory is closely linked to the degree of social authority that individuals and groups can exercise (namely Mitchell's archaeology of power cited above). As a result, visual and textual descriptions (or representations) need to be analysed as instances of 'technology of power' (Paulus 2007: 279, quoted in Hobuß 2013: 16), a notion indebted to Foucault's theory of productive power whereby illustrations and descriptions are not to be taken as a more or less accurate rendering of reality. In this perspective, multilingual street-name signs in Alghero (and their peculiar arrangement) are not just narrativizing the city, to use Benjamin's words – they are to be observed as dynamic objects producing a given reality in that the practices of their illustration will help unfold the power that produced them.

The analysis of street-name signs, therefore, cannot be separated from the analysis of ways of producing and executing a specific reality (the street-name signs themselves). The practices of illustration themselves will reveal much about the complex web of competing hegemonic discourses and the tensions between them.

Reconstructing the urban map

Street-name signs in the historic centre of Alghero display peculiar characteristics in terms of linguistic distribution, emplacement and employment of different material for their execution. We were unable to retrieve documents which allowed a direct reconstruction of the displayed layering of the signs, except for the latest version of the local municipal statute which, as in the original 1991 text, mentions historical toponyms and the commitment to preserve them in Article 9 (*Comune di Alghero* 2000). Caria (1993), however, provides both contextual information about the spatial organization of the city and a reconstruction of place names based on three land registers, allowing us to acquire a backdrop within which to situate our data and analysis.

Caria (1993) discusses, amongst other aspects, typologies of place names, which are often linked to the geological characteristics of an area (*Alghero* itself seems to have originated from a type of algae which is typical of this coastal site; see also Blasco Ferrer 1984) and provides a historical reconstruction of the city after the Catalan conquest. The scholar highlights the increasingly multi-ethnic composition of the urban fabric following the repopulation of Alghero with Catalan people, including Jews moving from Mallorca and Occitan and Provençal areas, Sardinian groups from different areas of the island, Neapolitan and Ligurian adventurers [*sic* in Caria 1993: 30], and finally incomers from the Piedmontese administration after Italian unification in 1861. The developments which characterized the city between the XVI and the XIX centuries were accomplished by a multilingual and multicultural population, and toponyms carry the traces of this linguistic mix (ibid.: 30–31). The peculiar characteristics of Alguerese Catalan are therefore a result of the social history of the city. Place names reconstruct the original map of walled Alghero – the current Piazza

Civica, for instance, was the *Placa Reial*, positioned at the centre of a larger quadrangle accommodating the local establishment and hosting institutional, economic, military and religious activities. The spatial distribution of social groups (e.g. the fishermen's dwellings in the port area, or the farmers' homes on the *Carrer de les Arjoles* – Street of the Farmyards) changed over time, however, and the attraction exercised by the privileged status of Alghero as a kind of city-state explains the migrations from other Sardinian and peninsular Italian areas. Caria (1993: 32) also explains that, given that three-quarters of the urban perimeter were surrounded by the sea, the compact urban structure allowed the rapid movement of inhabitants from one side of the city to another in the case of threats coming from the sea. It was therefore essential that the urban configuration was familiar to the people of Alghero and that they could rely on consolidated place names (passed on orally primarily, it should be added, like most events in the life of the city). As a result, the local language also acted as a defence mechanism, a safety code to be deployed among neighbours and urban allies in the presence of danger. In current times, the legacy of past orientations and life maps is encompassed in the presence and iterativity of place names (however contradictory to some extent) on the street-name signs of the historic centre. This contributes to articulating and safeguarding core Alguerese identity and provides a choreographic palimpsest of cultural and linguistic survival.

Caria (1993: 33) reports about changes in street names observed when studying three land registers (from 1827, 1871 and 1876, respectively). The documents show the reduction in place names between the XVI and the XIX centuries (showing a trend in the process of simplification of the urban map – a metasemiotic symptom of the selectivity of memory), but place names relating to towers, churches, streets, convents, wells and key personalities, events and activities of local importance were maintained, indicating that Benjamin's narrativization of the urban fabric is integral to the city's social continuity.

The 1876 land register shows the addition of official place names (the Italian ones which are still in use today) and a simplification of previous maps, where different blocks along the same street were named in different ways. By simplifying the urban map, the 1876 land register deleted meaningful historical space from local memory – a forgetting, in Todorov's (2003) terms. This operation also actualized a process of spatial de-structuration which disconnects lived experience (Lefebvre 1991) from memory and produces (the geographical coordinates of) a bi-dimensional map – terms conveying spatial information such as *carrer* (street/road), *carreró* (lane), *devallada* (road going down – slope), *muntada* (road going up – rise) etc. became simply *via* (street or road) in Italian. In addition, whether a street was steep, narrow, broad etc. had an impact on daily life in terms of accessibility, physical effort, transport etc. so named spatial characteristics facilitated the planning of daily activities. As an example of this transformation, *Via Roma* (Figure 10.1) has lost all connections with *Muntada del Campanil* (Bell Tower Rise) (Figure 10.2), which on the one hand encompasses information such as 'you need to go up the hill to reach the bell tower (which stands for the cathedral)', and on the other hand it desacralizes the directory leading to a spiritual dimension, both literally and metaphorically. On the contrary, and using Lefebvre's model of space production, naming a given spatial trajectory *Muntada del Campanil* encapsulates the three elements of lived, conceived and perceived space, therefore maintaining the memorialized integrity of a given space.

Spatial de-structuration is also enacted via the replacement of the functional map with celebratory discourses. This entails the reference to both national (Italian) personalities and sites, and figures of local importance. In addition to the example quoted above (Figure 10.1, Via Roma), the Italian sign Via Principe Umberto (one of the Savoy kings of Italy) replaced a different local name (*Carrer del Bisbe*, Street of the Bishop) which was closely linked to spatial orientation

Figure 10.1 Via Roma – Italian-only sign.[8]

Figure 10.2 Example of spatial de-structuration: Muntada del Campanil/Via Roma.

and the ability to establish a relational nexus between physical and mental maps. Another important aspect that emerges from Caria's (1993) diachronic reconstruction of the changes in place names is that, by comparing the lists from 1827, 1871 and 1876 with our data, the current street-name signs are not an accurate reflection of this reconstruction and therefore they emphasize the commemorative intention of restoring the emplacement of memory objects to its memorial landscape. An example of this is provided in Figure 10.3.

The Catalan sign includes two place names: *Carrer de la Carneceria Vella* (Street of the Old Butcher's/Abattoir), previously *Carrer de la Pretura* (Street of the Magistrate's Court – this is in brackets on the sign therefore indicating that the street was previously named Carrer de la Pretura). The Italian sign, *Via Columbano*, is named after a member of the local nobility. In his reconstruction, however, Caria (1993: 65) lists *Carrer de la Carnisseria Nova* (Street of the New Butcher's/Abbattoir) as the older toponym, which was later replaced by *Carrer del Mercat* (Market Street) and subsequently named *Via Columbano*. In keeping with Caria's reconstruction, *Carrer del Mercat* is more generic than *Carrer de la Carnisseria Nova* – this type of change started implementing the simplification of the urban map, a material enactment of the selectivity of memory.

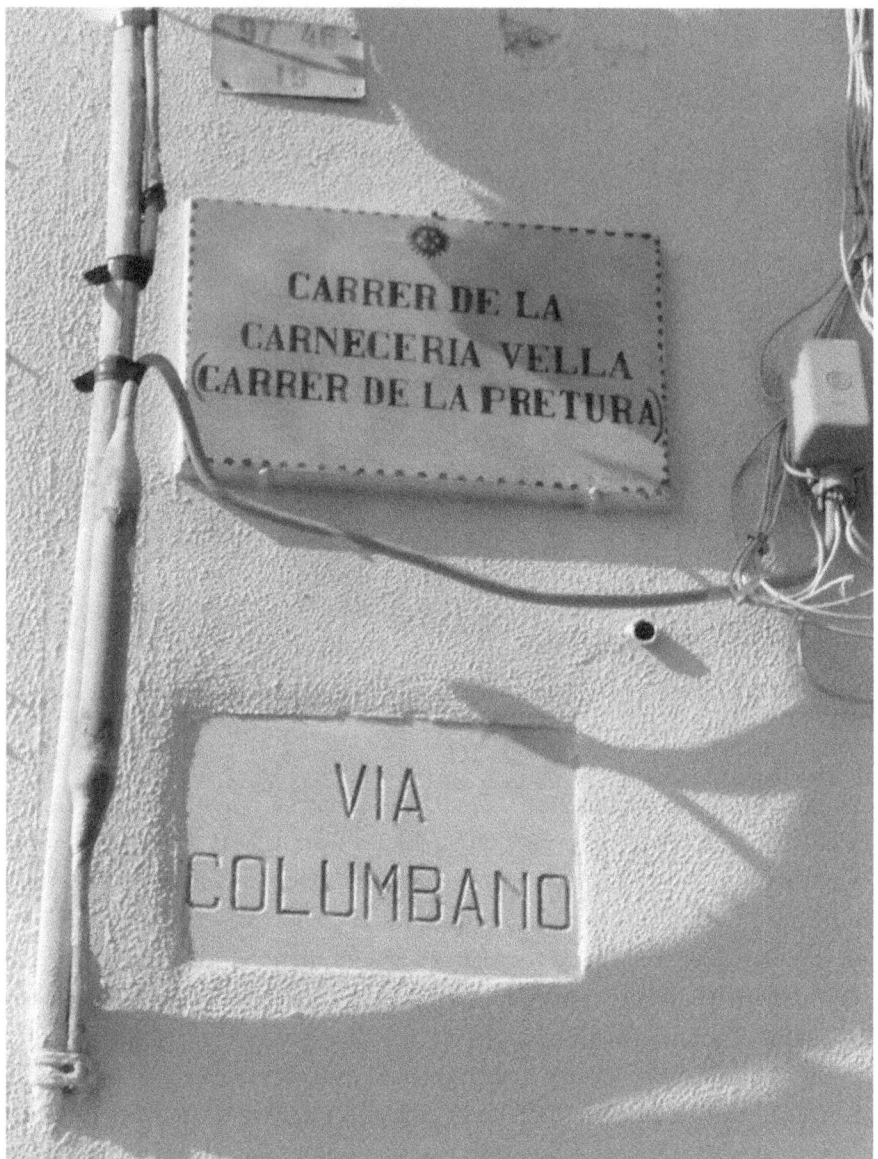

Figure 10.3 Example of inaccurate reconstruction of successive street names.

The above example foregrounds another feature of the Alguerese street names: the different spelling between *Carneceria* and *Carnisseria*. The corpus includes other examples of spelling inconsistencies that point to the arbitrary reproduction of forms of orality which were prevalent until recent times and to the absence of a unified orthography which was only introduced as recently as 2003, the time of the commissioning of the monolingual Alguerese street-name signs. From our perspective, however, the displayed and juxtaposed inconsistency of street name reproduction addresses local needs of personalization of memory (Nora 1989). This allows local memory processes to blur the dichotomy between public and private memory-making by allowing a dialogic dimension between memorialization practices that co-construct each other.

The data

Surveys in Alghero historic centre (which corresponds to the walled city) were carried out between 2016 and 2017. The corpus consists of 159 street-name signs. In terms of linguistic distribution, Table 10.4 illustrates a breakdown of signs according to language combination:

Unlike in Amos (2017), who provides an analysis of typologies of signs in Toulouse, it seems impossible to identify given functional aspects of different signs and/or correlations with language distribution. Italian-only signs were of three types. The first type (31 items) included the majority of them (31/37 items) and consisted of embedded marble plaques (e.g. Figure 10.1 – Via Roma) which shared the same dimensions and font, and engraved lettering which was mostly discoloured – they represent the oldest set. The second type (two items) were supported marble signs placed on the surface of walls which again shared dimensions and font, but where the engraved lettering was still partly visible. These signs most likely replaced older signs or were added for practical purposes. The third type (four items) were embedded ceramic signs with blue lettering against a white background. They, too, represent later additions to fulfil civic requirements.

Table 10.4 Breakdown of signs according to language combination

Languages displayed	Items
Alguerese/Italian	81
Monolingual Alguerese	37
Monolingual Italian	37
Italian/Alguerese	4
Total	**159**

Figure 10.4 *Lo Portal Nou* (New Gate).

All the Alguerese-only signs share the same characteristics: they are all ceramic plaques with place names in blue against a white background and a painted frame which is also blue (Figure 10.4).

The Alguerese-only signs were an initiative of the local Rotary Club, and a wheel, the Club's symbol, is painted on each of them. Occasionally they are signed *Silecchia*, the name of a local designer. They are made of glazed terracotta and have a distinctive artisan, handcrafted aspect to them – a visual element that can be understood as 'traditional' (as opposed to industrially produced) and decoded as a material bond with authentic Alguerese identity. The local Rotary Club is proactive in the promotion and dissemination of local language and culture, and they were actively involved in the setting up of the twinning of Alghero with Tarragona (Catalonia) in 1972. These plaques were erected in 2003.[9]

In Figure 10.5 the Alguerese sign identifies the street as the location of the old postal service. In this instance the sign is placed below the Italian sign, but this is not the norm. In addition, Figure 10.5 shows one of the existing modalities of street name evolution, with the Italian name bearing no resemblance to the Alguerese one and belonging instead to celebratory discourses generated by either national or local institutional actors. In this instance Ardoino was the name of a nineteenth-century bishop of Alguerese origins and therefore local celebratory discourses prevail over national ones on this occasion.

The bilingual Alguerese-Italian signs were commissioned by the municipality and placed in 1995 – the year 1995 appears next to the signature *Pobega* on some

Instances of Emplaced Memory 253

Figure 10.5 Monolingual Catalan sign (literally Road of the Old Postal Office) coexisting with Italian sign.

of the signs. They, too, are made of ceramic, with a blue frame and blue letters on a white background, but the lettering and the execution suggest mass-produced items rather than handcrafted ones. In Figure 10.2 (*Muntada del Campanil/ Via Roma*) it can be noted that on bilingual signs the Italian names tend to be more prominent in terms of font. However, the dominant position of Alguerese in the vertical order of the signs and the fact that, due to the additional information, the Alguerese names tend to occupy more space ensure the foregrounding of the Alguerese place names. This type of visual prominence is further enhanced by the monolingual Catalan signs positioned in the proximity of the bilingual signs.

Given that place names are mentioned explicitly both in the 1991 Municipal Statute and in the 2000 version, the signs reflect the local authorities' decision to make the original Alguerese place names visible again. To illustrate this point, consider the sign placed in the square featuring the nineteenth-century theatre which is presented as *Plaça del Bisbe* in the upper position (Alguerese: Square of the Bishop) and *Piazza Teatro* beneath (Italian: Theatre Square). The Alguerese name *Plaça del Bisbe* (Square of the Bishop) is due to the fact that the palace which became the bishop's residence in the sixteenth century overlooks the square (factual information of this type was provided on the tourist plaques available in the proximity of the buildings/monuments). By having the local sequence of happenings restored, the square incorporates different memorialized narratives and generates historical bodies which contemporary memory has obliterated. In addition, by naming the *Bisbe* into existence, LL engenders the deconstruction of both spatial and cultural-linguistic resemioticization and in so doing it reinstates a rememoration mechanism that adds meaning to place.

The linguistic distribution of the Italian/Alguerese signs (four items) is not systematic. In Piazza Antonio Sanna (an Alguerese officer who died during the war in 1943) and Piazza Pasqual Scanu ('scholar') (Figure 10.6), only 'Piazza' is provided in Alguerese as well (*Placa*), but the additional information is in Italian. On the contrary, in Piazza Pasqual Gal ('Alguerese singer-song writer')

Figure 10.6 Bilingual sign displaying the Alguerese translation only of *Piazza/Placa* (Square).

the additional information is bilingual Italian/Alguerese and in Via Don Giuseppe Sanna ('author of the dictionary of Alguerese Catalan') the additional information is in Alguerese.

The emplacement of street-name signs seems to be random as well. On long streets signs appear more than twice (not a rarity in itself), but both the modalities of their display and the linguistic composition vary. Both bilingual and monolingual signs are visible, either in isolation or together, and either in vertical or horizontal orderings with no apparent hierarchy. An example is Via Principe Umberto (one of the Savoy kings of Italy) mentioned above, where previous names reported in Catalan include *Carrer de Bonaire* (lit. 'Street of good air', with reference to a Catalan-built sanctuary in Cagliari, the regional capital, now called *Bonaria*), *Carrer del Bisbe* ('Street of the Bishop', leading to the Bishop's palace) and *Carrerò de Ritxo* ('Street of the Portico', with reference to local architectural details).

In our view this lack of a pattern contributes to the peculiar characteristics of Alghero's named map and provides a metasemiotic reading of different sets of discourses. In the attempt to name places of identity and belonging into existence, however, the visual reconstitution of historical spaces has been carried out by an extreme operation of memory selection which has erased the voices of those subjectivities that have in fact been instrumental in shaping Alghero as it is today – Sardinian is conspicuous by its absence and in a way it has been assigned the role of stone guest.[10] It is nowhere to be seen, but it is perceived as a threat and pushed off the city walls in the awareness that both the status and the vitality of Sardinian are much stronger on the island, and that Sardinian is endowed with political power, unlike Alguerese.

Conclusion

Alghero street-name signs are an interesting example of multilingual memorials and we propose that in the local memory landscape the commemorative aspect dominates elements of rememoration. Because a multiplicity of actors has been involved in the initiation, execution and placement of street-name signs, however, the productive powers, in Foucault's terms, have, paradoxically, created the conditions for an integration of those disruptive forces that Benjamin (2004–2006) advocated in his criticism of historicism and that have spatially enacted a multidirectionality of memory which is best understood via the metaphor of memory knots (Rothberg 2010). Even though the knot metaphor highlights the entangled nature of memory, and Alghero LL demonstrates that memory processes are far from linear, in our context the concept also encompasses unresolved relationships with complementary and intersecting narratives of collective memory which have de facto been diluted or removed *tout court* from spatial representation.

The complete eclipsing of Sardinian from Alghero street map uncovers spaces of identity annihilation that elsewhere we have called *visual silence* (Tufi 2013: 400). We know that Sardinian has contributed, together with other languages, to the peculiar configuration of the Alguerese variety (Caria 1993) and that historical linguistic accounts demonstrate the extent to which Sardinian varieties brought into the city via multiple contacts over the centuries have had an impact on local linguistic developments (Blasco Ferrer 1984). However, non-Alguerese elements that have left traces in current place names are not transparent to the contemporary resident, tourist or passer-by and therefore the erasure of Sardinian is noteworthy. Sardinian varieties are dominant on the island (Oppo 2007) and are in use by a sizeable group in Alghero (around 12 per cent of local inhabitants, see Tables 10.1 and 10.2). In addition, Sardinian is officially recognized as a minority language both nationally and regionally, therefore representing a threat to the maintenance of Alguerese language and culture. This phenomenon, observable in peripheral areas, has been termed fractal recursivity (Irvine and Gal 2000), that is, the creation of a new centre within a periphery and of a new periphery within each centre – Sardinian has been marginalized to an extent that it has been deleted from the town map.

It could be argued that the grand narrative permeating street-name execution and emplacement is simply explained by considering Alghero's historic map as a space managed by institutional actors. As a matter of fact, the municipality allows (or even encourages, depending on the political orientation of local administrations) the preservation and employment of historical place names alongside the Italian ones in keeping with official deliberations. The local Rotary Club is another institution endowed with both local and international prestige and status, and a primary agent in the promotion of Alguerese language and culture. The Club has also been instrumental in the re-establishment of close relationships with Catalonia via initiatives (as discussed above) that have also served the contemporary logic of pride and profit (Duchêne and Heller 2012) with the inevitable commodification of local authenticity and exoticism, a process that small, peripheral sites have increasingly deployed (Pietikäinen et al. 2016) to be able to survive in contemporary globalized forms of the marketization of everything. A third institutional actor is the *Generalitat de Catalunya*, which has promoted a pan-Catalan identity and provided the (missing) discourses of neo- and trans-nationalism, thereby contributing to a refunctionalization of displayed Alguerese.

A close examination of the LL of historic Alghero, however, has showed that LL allows the construction and preservation of additional constituencies of memory via the original and non-normative deployment of memory details, represented by the spaces of inconsistency created through alternative spellings, and the written eclipsing of Sardinian (and other identities) enacted through the deafening visual silence of language(s) that are (and have been) inextricably intertwined in the social, linguistic and cultural fabric of the city.

Rather than an integral part of commemorative monuments, these spaces of inconsistency and erasure are in our view the most dynamic memory acts (Hobuß 2013) performed via LL in Alghero. Their role is one of rememoration and chronotopic actualization of the past as a result of meaningful social practice. As such, these non-normative spaces are particularly susceptible to reinterpretation, recontextualization and resignification, they make future understandings of personal and collective memory trajectories more elusive and difficult to control, and generate spaces of potentiality in the landscape of minority memory. To use Derrida's (1988) concept, the material re-iteration of street-name signs contributes to both the consolidation and the re-creation of memorial meaning.

In identifying the peculiarity of multilingual memory acts in a minoritized setting we have therefore extended both Benjamin's (2002, 2004–2006) and Todorov's (2003) insights by highlighting the role of LL in the plural dimension of memory-making and emplacing. The data has shown that LL in the given context enables the enactment of multiple, changeable and contradictory narrativizations of the city. This process in turn engenders the possibility of grasping the *truths* of the past, therefore challenging hegemonic attempts of memory construction, selection and preservation, and enabling memorial agency.

Notes

1   Throughout the paper we use *Alghero* for ease of exposition and because this is how the city is known internationally. *Alguerese* will be used to refer to the local variety of Catalan, as explained above, and as an adjective.

2 To our knowledge, the most recent LL contribution is Järlehed (2017), to whom the reader is referred also for a sketch of the main LL studies on street-name signs and their perspectives on the topic.
3 See also Blasco Ferrer (1984) and (2001), and Bolognesi and Heeringa (2005) for analyses and descriptions of the local linguistic set-up.
4 See for example the newspaper article 'Catalano di Alghero, patrimonio dimenticato.' *La Nuova Sardegna*, 13/6/2017.
5 The *Generalitat* is the devolved form of government of the Autonomous Community of Catalonia (within the country of Spain) and equivalent to the *Regione* in the Italian context. All twenty Regioni in Italy have a degree of devolved political power, but more so those regions, like Sardinia, which were granted a special status (and have elaborated a Special Statute) according to the 1948 Italian Constitution.
6 The reader is also referred to the 2016 special issue 2(3) of the journal *Linguistic Landscape*, which highlights the currency and relevance of memorialization practices as enacted in LL.
7 For a recent discussion of chronotopes within sociolinguistics, see Blommaert and De Fina (2017).
8 All images in this chapter are the author's own.
9 The local Rotary Club provided the information relating to monolingual Catalan and bilingual signs as outlined above via a telephone conversation.
10 Based on a seventeenth-century play by Tirso de Molina and made famous by the homonymous play by Pushkin (1830), the stone guest has been used in literary and musical works to refer to a disturbing but invisible presence that everybody is aware of but nobody talks about (= names), and which is perceived as a threat.

References

Alghero Eco (2012), Alghero e Tarragona: Gemellaggio di 40 anni. 21 September. Available online: http://www.algheroeco.com/alghero-e-tarragona-40-anni-di-gemellaggio/ (accessed 9 April 2018).

Amos, H. W. (2017), 'Regional Language Vitality in the Linguistic Landscape: Hidden Hierarchies on Street Signs in Toulouse', *International Journal of Multilingualism*, 14 (2): 93–108.

Argenter, J. A. (2008), 'L'Alguer (Alghero), a Catalan Linguistic Enclave in Sardinia', *International Language of the Sociology of Language*, 193/194: 205–217.

Bakhtin, M. M. (1981), *The Dialogic Imagination: Four Essays by M.M. Bakhtin*. Translated by C. Emerson and M. Holquist, Austin: University of Texas Press.

Basso, K. H. (1996), *Wisdom Sits in Places: Landscape and Language among the Western Apache*, Albuquerque: University of New Mexico Press.

Benjamin, W. (2002), *The Arcades Project*, Translated by H. Eiland and K. McLaughlin, New York: Belknap Press.
Benjamin, W. (2004–2006), 'On the Concept of History', in H. Eiland and M. W. Jennings (eds), *Walter Benjamin: Selected Writings. Vol. 4*, 389–400, Cambridge, MA: Belknap.
Benjamin, W. (2008), *The Work of Art in the Age of Mechanical Reproduction*. Translated by J. A. Underwood, London: Penguin.
Blackwood, R. and S. Tufi (2015), *The Linguistic Landscape of the Mediterranean: French and Italian Coastal Cities*, Basingstoke: Palgrave Macmillan.
Blasco Ferrer, E. (1984), *Grammatica storica del Catalano e dei suoi dialetti con speciale riguardo all'Algherese*, Tübingen: G. Narr.
Blasco Ferrer, E. (2001), 'Il dialetto catalano di Alghero', in J. Carbonell and F. Manconi (eds) *I catalani in Sardegna*, 3rd reprint, 167–170, Cagliari: Consiglio Regionale della Sardegna.
Blommaert, J. and A. De Fina (2017), 'Chronotopic Identities : On the Spacetime Organization of Who We Are', in A. De Fina, I. Didem and J. Wegner (eds), *Diversity and Superdiversity: Sociocultural Linguistic Perspectives*, 1–15, Washington, DC: Georgetown University Press.
Bolognesi, R. and W. Heeringa (2005), *Sardegna fra tante lingue. Il contatto linguistico in Sardegna dal Medioevo a oggi*, Cagliari: Condaghes.
Caria, R. (1993), *Toponomastica algherese. Vol. II*, Sassari: EDES.
Caria, M. (2014), 'Alghero – L'Alguer, o i catalani d'Italia', *Bollettino dell'Atlante Linguistico Italiano*, 38: 75–90.
Cenoz, J. and D. Gorter (2006), 'Linguistic Landscape and Minority Languages', *International Journal of Multilingualism*, 3 (1): 67–80.
Comune di Alghero (1991), *Statuto Comunale 1991*. Available online: http://www.comune.alghero.ss.it/.galleries/doc-amministrazione/statuto_comune_alghero.pdf (accessed 20 May 2018).
Comune di Alghero (2000), *Statuto Comunale 2000*. Available online: http://www.comune.alghero.ss.it/.galleries/doc-amministrazione/statuto_comune_alghero.pdf (accessed 20 May 2018).
Costituzione della Repubblica Italiana (1948), Available online: https://www.cortecostituzionale.it/documenti/download/pdf/Costituzione_della_Repubblica_italiana.pdf (accessed 23 March 2018).
Derrida, J. (1988), *Limited Inc*, Evanston, IL: Northwestern University Press.
de Wilde, M. (2009), 'Benjamin's Politics of Remembrance: A Reading of "Über den Begriff der Geschichte"', in R. J. Goebel (ed.), *A Companion to the Works of Walter Benjamin*, 177–194, Woodbridge: Boydell and Brewer.
Duchêne, A. and M. Heller (eds) (2012), *Language in Late Capitalism: Pride and Profit*, New York: Routledge.
Farinelli, M. A. (2014), 'The Invisible Motherland? The Catalan-speaking Minority in Sardinia and Catalan nationalism', *Studies on National Movements*, 2: 1–29.

Generalitat de Catalunya (2008), 'Sociolinguistic Situation in Catalan-speaking Areas'. Available online: http://llengua.gencat.cat/permalink/7c8aed03-5386-11e4-8f3f-000c29cdf219 (accessed 4 December 2017).

Generalitat de Catalunya (2015), 'Language Policy Report'. Available online: http://llengua.gencat.cat/web/.content/documents/informepl/arxius/IPL-2015-ang.pdf (accessed 4 December 2017).

Gillis, J. R. (1994), 'Memory and Identity: The History of a Relationship', in J. R. Gillis (ed.) *Commemorations: The Politics of National Identity*, 3–24, Princeton, NJ.: Princeton University Press.

Hobuß, S. (2013), 'Memory Acts: Memory without Representation. Theoretical and Methodological Suggestions', *ISTME Working Papers*, 1. Available online: http://www.transculturalmemoryineurope.net/Publications/Memory-Acts-Memory-Without-Representation-Theoretical-and-Methodological (accessed 9 February 2017).

Institut d'Estudis Catalans (2003), 'El català de l'Alguer: un model d'àmbit restringit'. Barcelona: Institut d'Estudis Catalans. Available online: https://publicacions.iec.cat/repository/pdf/00000040/00000028.pdf (accessed 3 August 2017).

Irvine, J. T. and S. Gal (2000), 'Language Ideology and Linguistic Differentiation', in P. V. Kroskrity (ed.), *Regimes of Language*, 35–83, Santa Fe, NM: School of American Research Press.

Järlehed, J. (2017), 'Genre and Metacultural Displays: The Case of Street-name Signs', *Linguistic Landscape*, 3 (3): 286–305.

La Nuova Sardegna (2017), 'Catalano di Alghero, patrimonio dimenticato', 13 June. Available online: http://ricerca.gelocal.it/lanuovasardegna/archivio/lanuovasardegna/2017/06/13/nazionale-catalano-di-alghero-patrimonio-dimenticato-37.html (accessed 9 April 2018).

Lefebvre, H. (1991), *The Production of Space*, Oxford: Basil Blackwell.

Legge regionale 15 ottobre 1997, n.26 (1997), *Promozione e valorizzazione della cultura e della lingua della Sardegna*. Available online: https://www.regione.sardegna.it/documenti/1_19_20091130171706.pdf (accessed 2 October 2017).

Legge 15 dicembre 1999, n.482 (1991), *Norme in materia delle minoranze linguistiche storiche*. Available online http://www.camera.it/parlam/leggi/99482l.htm (accessed 2 October 2017).

Meloni, G. (1994), 'Alghero tra Genova, Arborea, Milano, Catalogna. Nuovi documenti', in *Atti del convegno su Alghero, la Catalogna, Il Mediterraneo, Alghero, 30 ottobre – 2 novembre 1985*, 59–74, Sassari: Gallizzi.

Mitchell, K. (2003), 'Monuments, Memorials, and the Politics of Memory', *Urban Geography*, 24 (5): 442–459.

Nora, P. (1989), 'Between Memory and History: Les Lieux de Mémoire', *Representations*, 26, 7–24.

Oppo, A. (2007), *Le lingue dei sardi. Una ricerca sociolinguistica*. Available online: https://www.regione.sardegna.it/documenti/1_4_20070510134456.pdf (accessed 16 September 2017).

Pietikäinen, S., A. Jaffe, H. Kelly-Holmes and N. Coupland (2016), *Sociolinguistics from the Periphery: Small Languages in New Circumstances*. Cambridge: Cambridge University Press.

Rothberg, M. (2010), 'Introduction: Between Memory and Memory: From lieux de mémoire to nœuds de mémoire', *Yale French Studies*, 118/119: 3–12.

Spalding, T. (2013), *Layers: The Design, History and Meaning of Public Street Signage in Cork and Other Irish Cities*, Dublin: Associated Editions.

Spolsky, B. and R. L. Cooper (1991), *The Languages of Jerusalem*, Oxford: Oxford University Press.

Todorov, T. (2003), *Hope and Memory: Lessons from the Twentieth Century*, Princeton, NJ: Princeton University Press.

Toso, F. (2008), *Le minoranze linguistiche in Italia*, Bologna: Il Mulino.

Tufi, S. (2013), 'Shared Places, Unshared Identities: Vernacular Discourses and Spatialised Constructions of Identity in the Linguistic Landscape of Trieste', *Modern Italy*, 18 (4): 391–408.

11

Appropriation and Re-appropriation: The Memorial as a Palimpsest

Christian Bendl

Introduction

Urban historic sites are related to discourses which are inseparable from the history of a city or even a nation.[1] On the one hand, the semiotic landscape and architecture of such places might give the impression of representing a stable and unified meaning of a place. On the other hand, the variety of differing spatial practices at these places and the discourses (re-)activated by these acts challenge a definite and one-sided interpretation of the place, history or meaning. Sociolinguistics, then, is confronted with the dynamics of a public act and – additionally – with the complexity of social space.

In the case of acts of commemoration at historic sites and memorials, these partly perceivable, partly concealed semiotic and discursive layers may even have a significant impact on society. At these *spatial palimpsests* traditionalized acts of commemoration possibly constitute (national) identities and the meanings of a place by applying selected discourses about history and 'memory', and by leaving others aside (cf. Uhl 2008; Wodak et al. 2009: 26).

The Viennese *Heldenplatz* ('Heroes' Square') is a perfect example for a place that is used in many ways and that – additionally – inherits several different discursive layers in its semiotic landscape. As a huge square which is surrounded by various buildings and institutions that index social and political discourses of Austrian history, it has also hosted historically significant events such as Hitler's proclamation of Austria's 'annexation' in 1938, and both in 1993 and 2015 demonstrations by hundreds of thousands of people protesting against xenophobia and redefining the place. Besides these and other salient events that constituted Austria's history and identity, daily routines highlight other characteristics of the square, for instance offering considerable space for a range of events.

This contribution aims to discuss all these different aspects of appropriation of a historical site from an interdisciplinary perspective. Thereby, the focus will be on the interrelatedness of time and space, and on their perceptibility not just in the acts themselves but also in the material place itself. As these acts or (re-)appropriations are dynamic processes that are driven by actors/bodies, semiotics/language-use and discourses/knowledge, all three aspects need to be considered to further allow a methodological discussion and an empirical analysis. The concept of the 'production of space', outlined by Lefebvre ([1974] 2016), offers philosophical and sociological arguments about these aspects and will therefore be discussed in greater detail. As some of the concepts, such as 'space' and 'time', are fundamental parts of everyday communication and social life they cannot be covered in their entirety in this single contribution. Instead, they are considered in an explorative manner and by relying on sociolinguistic and discourse analysis concepts which aim to offer a replicable research design.

To illustrate the dynamic constituting of meanings, and discursive memories in public space, this chapter focuses on a single commemorative act which takes place on Austria's National Day on the *Heldenplatz*. At first, we discuss the interrelatedness of acts in space, discourses about space and symbolizing by space. This is followed by an exploration of the concepts of 'space', 'time' and 'memory' in the context of a *spatial palimpsest*. In the concluding analysis, the communicative (re-)appropriation of a multilayered space and its semiotic and discursive contexts will be considered.

The appropriation of space

Research into the interactions in, and the constituting of, social space in disciplines as diverse as geography, sociology or linguistics, *inter alia*, is grounded in the 'spatial turn'. The spatial turn is, in short, a new perspective on space: space is no longer seen as a (material) 'container' that gets filled by fixed meanings, but as a dynamic (social) expression of power, ideologies and individualistic projections that is constantly negotiated in everyday social life. This distinction is partly done by differentiating 'space' from 'place'. 'Space' is often related to the French *espace* (German *Raum*) which is understood as the global concept of having or being a locality; in other words, this means having the feature of spatiality. 'Place', by comparison, is often related to the French *lieu* (German *Ort*) which is a distinct 'made' area or locality that allows interaction.

Bachmann-Medick (2016: 216) points out that 'nearly all the approaches associated with the spatial turn have a common reference point', namely that of Lefebvre ([1974] 2016). Although other influential French thinkers in the second half of the twentieth century, such as Bourdieu (1989), de Certeau (1988: 91–130) and Foucault (1984), also played a tremendous part in this paradigm shift, Lefebvre's concept of the 'production of space' was and still is a landmark point of reference. One reason for the interest in this concept lies in the social functions of space that he describes: amongst other functions, space can be consumed, politically instrumentalized, and is inherently connected to ideologies, hierarchies and power relations (cf. Lefebvre [1974] 2016: 349). Another reason for this popularity might be – as will be discussed shortly in more detail – that the production or (re-)appropriation of space can be analytically divided in three spatial dimensions,[2] namely 'spatial practices', 'representations of space' and 'spaces of representation', as well as into three experiential dimensions: the perceived, conceived and lived space. Though having distinct characteristics on their own, we consider these dimensions as inherently interrelated. From an analytical point of view, we suggest that whichever dimension is privileged, the concept still retains its wider context and the other elements of the triad in sight.

The dimensions of the triad are sketched by Lefebvre in a tentative and poetic manner and, as such, any details given in the following are always part of an interpretative co-construction of the concept which explains the partly differing observations in (linguistic) studies (e.g. Jaworski and Thurlow 2010; Busch 2013, 2015; Huebner and Phoocharoensil 2017; Purkarthofer 2018).

- Spatial practice consists of the totality of everyday, routinized and traditionalized acts *in* space (such as sightseeing, commercial activities, manifestations, commemorations). These are acts of constitution and perception and therefore of the first experiential aspect of the triad: the perceived space.
- Representations of space consist of regulatory texts, plans and expert knowledge that represent discourses *about* a place. They are institutionalized by actors who are, according to Lefebvre, privileged to talk about 'space', like architects, city planners, politicians or scientists. Its complementary bodily aspect is the conceived space.

- Spaces of representation are vivid symbolic expressions by space which represent the way in which spaces are experienced, appropriated and transformed by subjects as the lived space. The meaning of this 'third space' is hard to grasp when observed isolated from the others. But in the combination with the other two 'spaces' Lefebvre's concept becomes more tangible: The lived space is constituted by acts that deal with the objects in a place, by the discourses and ideologies pointed out in the conceived space and by practices and the spatial context that are related to the everyday practices of the perceived space. In other words, the lived space consists of positionings towards and experiences of what was and is discursively said (second dimension) and spatially done (first dimension).

Besides the appealing simplicity of a concept that connects acts, discourses and symbolic representations, a few points of criticism of this triad should be considered, one of which concerns the difficulties in referring to the concept of Lefebvre, although he avoids describing a model with distinct functions. His concept is part of a 'project' (Lefebvre [1974] 2016: 419) that is inherently open to adaptions, but is at the same time 'an intensely political document' (Harvey 2016: 431), namely by having a Marxist agenda. Furthermore, 'the production of space' is, despite Lefebvre's scattered reflexions on the use of language in space, *not* a linguistic concept, but is deeply rooted in the philosophy of Hegel, Marx and Nietzsche and offers primarily a sociological standpoint. However, from a linguistic perspective an application of this specific interpretation can be outlined as in the following.[3]

1. The spatial practice consists of, first, any form of communicative acts at a specific place, hence it is not limited to everyday acts alone. In sociolinguistic terms, the implementing of genre (Briggs and Bauman 1992) leads to the following research questions that are applied in this paper: Which forms do acts have? Do they occur repetitively? And are they 'challenged' in a confronting, opposing or imitating manner? Second, spatial practices can be found 'through the deciphering of its space' (Lefebvre [1974] 2016: 38), meaning the perceived space in which they occur. The semiotic landscape and the spatial context in general are therefore the favoured sources for finding spatial practices in and communicative negotiations of space.
2. Representations of space resemble concepts about a conceived space which anyone – not just a specific set of privileged actors – can discursively

construe. These concepts are part of discourses that consist of language ideologies (cf. Irvine and Gal 2000) that regulate which languages are of a specific value at a place and which are not. In a broader sense, representations of space refer at the same time to the constituents of discourses: actors, space-time relations, power and ideologies.
3. Spaces of representation consist of the multimodality in space and of discourses insofar as a place is symbolically represented or indexed. The 'third space' thereby echoes the actors' stance and their social positioning towards the symbolized space and to other actors (cf. Du Bois 2007; Spitzmüller 2015), forming, finally, the lived space.

Overall, Lefebvre's approach to space and language can be implemented in interdisciplinary research in different ways,[4] be it a source of inspiration, a preferred political agenda or a framework for data collecting. In this chapter, the interrelatedness of space and time and their communicative representations will be discussed primarily from the point of sociolinguistics and without a specific political aim, although the author has a personal connection to this set of data (for details, see the section 'Research design, methodology and data').

Palimpsests and polyhistoricity

The Viennese *Heldenplatz*, like other public places in cities, is a social space in which all dimensions of the production of space are negotiated by a variety of actors in differing communicative modalities that then form a spatial palimpsest. Comparable to some (ancient) manuscripts that consist of several layers of different texts, 'urban palimpsests', as Shep (2015) points out, consist of 'ghost signs' of preceding time frames that are sometimes not visible any longer. Whenever a semiotic and discursive layer is added, another one is likely to be forgotten as the visual perceptibility of the former layers is diminished or even prevented.[5] Overall, palimpsests 'expose the coextensive temporal and spatial dynamics of urban identity politics and the readings that engage with and bring them to life' (Shep 2015: 215). This is also true for museums and memorials or for buildings that are thought to combine both, such as the Mauthausen Memorial, a former concentration camp of the Nazi era (cf. Busch 2016a). Applying the three dimensions of the production of space such a place might be described as consisting – from a chronological point of view – as of various different (third dimensional) layers of past experiences (e.g. of tortured/killed prisoners), (second dimensional) planning strategies which change over time (e.g. establishing a museum) and (first dimensional) acts in actual space (e.g. commemorations).

Social spaces, one can conclude, are grounded in processes of change and overwriting, as space is intrinsically connected to time by spatial practices of a past. Since their beginning, studies on linguistic and semiotic landscapes have been concerned with changes in the Linguistic Landscape (LL) and therefore with temporal dynamics in general (e.g. Spolsky and Cooper 1991; Backhaus 2005; Pavlenko 2010; Blommaert 2013) and with monuments and historic sites in particular (e.g. Sloboda 2009; Abousnnouga and Machin 2010; Huebner and Phoocharoensil 2017). What these and comparable studies show is that traces of time, that is, the phenomenon of historicity, shine out communicatively in the linguistic and semiotic landscape. For the purposes of this chapter, we understand historicity as a condition of having a time-relatedness which is semiotically and discursively (re-)activated (cf. Kämper et al. 2016: 3). Regardless of whether there are references to the past, present or to the future, communication is always related to various discursive time frames or 'layers of historicity', as Blommaert (2005: 130) names them. These layers are time-references that are interpreted relative to the ('cultural') discursive knowledge of the actors and to the actual context given (Silverstein 2013). Texts, discursive events and, one can add, the semiotic landscape are inter- and intradiscursively related in various time frames (cf. Silverstein 2005).

In some settings, several layers can even conflate by referring to several times within a single communicative act. These layers inherit specific functions by constituting ideologies about history and events that have a time-related value. For example, we are likely to find cues of historicity[6] in political speeches in the context of a commemorative act. There, a multitude of time references occur within a short period of time, signalling a polyhistoricity that is related to places, discourses and actors, e.g. when a 'dark' past is opposed to a 'bright' future which, finally, can be accomplished by a certain behaviour in the present. It can be assumed that the reference to this range of different ideologies and knowledge about these differing times can have a specific function, especially in the production of historic sites (Lefebvre [1974] 2016: 116–117).

Discourses of memory in social space

A monument 'as a site of social, political, and economic changes' (Pavlenko and Mullen 2015: 129) plays a decisive role in the constitution of social spaces.

Such places are locations that (re-)produce (collective) memory that transports cultural values (Lefebvre [1974] 2016: 120–121). Depending on how such events are experienced by different subjects (in the spaces of representation) and how the subject is positioned by and positions him- or herself vis-à-vis these events, the site gives rise to differing associations, meanings and emotions. Donohoe (2006, 2009) states that memories in place are narratives that connect temporarily with the narratives of other actors in a place. This philosophical approach can be adopted for sociolinguistic needs, when an act of commemoration is considered as an individualistic *and* a collective act reflecting both the knowledge of a single actor and of a social group. Considering this, we intend to reflect on 'memory' (in the sense of 'public' or 'national memories') via a specific discourse that highlights ideologies of and about a certain time. In this chapter, we take discourse to mean a 'thematically constrained ("virtual") text corpus' (Spitzmüller and Warnke 2011: 76) that refers to the knowledge of a group of actors and, at the same time, to acts that constitute these forms of knowledge. Hence, several memories equal several layers of discourses that interfere or challenge each other.

Besides the more permanent material and visual aspects, it is a variety of communicative acts that constitute memories *and* the meanings of a place. Huebner and Phoocharoensil (2017: 109) point out: 'The power of monuments rests in the histories they create. They do this both verbally and visually.' 'Memorization' (Train 2016), which labels this communicative negotiation of memory in public space, includes the linguistic and semiotic landscape and 'their attendant discourses, ideologies, practices, and policies' (Train 2016: 226). This concept holds, on the one side, the diversity of memories in a 'collective memory' and, on the other side, the phenomenon of 'counter-memorizations', which unveils differing or opposing memories. Finally, the variety of functions that commemorations inherit is outlined by Reisigl (2018: 368): 'Commemoration is a multimodal semiotic (including verbal) practice and – with respect to its purpose – an important political activity that serves the formation, reproduction and transformation of political identities.' Commemorations and their constituting elements (space, time, actors, language choice etc.) are therefore a relevant part of society as they form an aspect of 'memorization'.

Research design, methodology and data

The data discussed here is drawn from a larger project on the discursive constituting of the *Heldenplatz* in public media. This data (over 1,100 media reports ranging from 2015 to 2017) constitutes the context for this study and is analysed linguistically (cf. Spitzmüller and Warnke 2011) with the help of the QDA software *Atlas.ti*.

Spatial acts, in general, are highly dynamic and short-timed (cf. Kitis and Milani 2015) and they index at the same time macro-discourses of places, actors and history (cf. Stroud and Jegels 2014), thereby making analysis a fairly complex task. Therefore, commemorative acts at the *Heldenplatz* will be discussed in three distinct but inherently connected analytical steps that rely on the adapted spatial triad: the act's (a) spatial and historic context, (b) its discursive appearance and (c) the communicative act in social space itself. Methodologically, these dimensions will be applied thus:

First, spatial practices are (non-)verbal acts *in* places that constitute genres of acts. Ethnographic observations at different situations and over a longer period of time (2015–2017) permitted the collection of different data (photographs, videos, notes) of public acts and the place itself. Although the sheer presence in public space is appropriative in nature, no observation was conducted in an active supportive manner for or against any political or other actor that has been observed ethnographically.

The ethnographic approach also allows repeated reflection on my own positioning towards the data and the research question in general, which became an important task since most recorded acts have political implications. In short, my personal relation to this place, as an Austrian, has been discursively formed from an early age, especially by teachings in school. As an adult these experiences were extended by having a workplace at the *Heldenplatz* and, some years later, by reaching the University of Vienna often by crossing the square.

Second, representations of space are, from a sociolinguistic perspective, the hegemonic discourses that constitute ideologies. In the following, the goal is to set linguistic expressions of 'ideologically constructed representations of linguistic differences' (Irvine and Gal 2000: 37) in relation to discursive and semiotic layers of historicity that might be implicitly or explicitly made relevant, that is, *contextualized*. Gumperz's (1992) notion of 'contextualization' offers, in essence, a linguistic starting point for describing how actors, space and time form communicative acts. He points out that the interpretation of co-constructed communicative acts is based on shared knowledge which is (re-)activated by means of 'contextualization cues'. Methodologically, these cues can be found in any communicative element in space that indexes communicative relevance and that is perceivable (texts, signs, typography etc.). As a palimpsest also holds layers of meaning that are not visible in plain sight but still are of discursive relevance, again, the context and an interdisciplinary approach that heavily, but not solely, draw from historical research (cf. Reisigl 2018) are carefully brought in.

Third, spaces of representation are expressed *by* space and its semiotic and discursive layers. The 'third space' is a temporal communicative act consisting of discourses and ideologies (representations of space) and of genres (spatial practices) conducted in bodily actions. Because the theoretical and methodological aspects would have to be broadened vastly (e.g. by discussing phenomenological and narrative aspects), individual experiences, biographical aspects and actors' existing knowledge about signs and places are not considered in this study, even though they are valuable (cf. Pavlenko and Mullen 2015: 117; see for methodological discussions Busch 2016b; Purkarthofer 2018). Nonetheless, the dynamics of bodily movements in appropriations of space are captured in a way that photographs, videos, ethnographic observations and texts about these acts are brought together to make the context and the act itself perceivable. Hence, the photographs in the following analysis are not analysed according to the composition of the image or the discursive powers of media but as 'frozen' snapshots of a multifaceted communicative act.

The main points of interest in the data are spatial, historical and social aspects of the Viennese *Heldenplatz*. The square itself is placed in the centre of Vienna, right beside the parliament, several important museums, the Austrian National Library and the *Hofburg* (Figure 11.1).

The history of the square begins after acts of war in the early nineteenth century, which led to the destruction of buildings and to extensive renovations and the redesigning of the square. The then so-called *Promenadenplatz* ('Square of Promenades') offered green areas and an open design which facilitated social activities. In the mid- and late-nineteenth century, additional buildings and two statues of two (then popular) leading military men[7] constituted a discursive layer of heroism and led to the renaming of this place to *Heldenplatz*. In the early twentieth century, the square was repeatedly chosen for military parades, especially by the National Socialist German Worker's Party (NSDAP) of Nazi Germany, but also by the occupying forces after 1945. Since 1955, finally, several annual acts of commemoration, yearly festivities for the Austrian National Day and a military parade have made the *Heldenplatz* a much frequented place that prominently reflects parts of Austrian history.

As an extraordinarily remarkable act of commemoration in Austria that is embedded in daylong festivities, the focus of this paper will be set on parts of a wreath-laying ceremony on the Viennese *Heldenplatz* that has taken place annually since 1955 on Austrian National Day (26 October). Austrian National

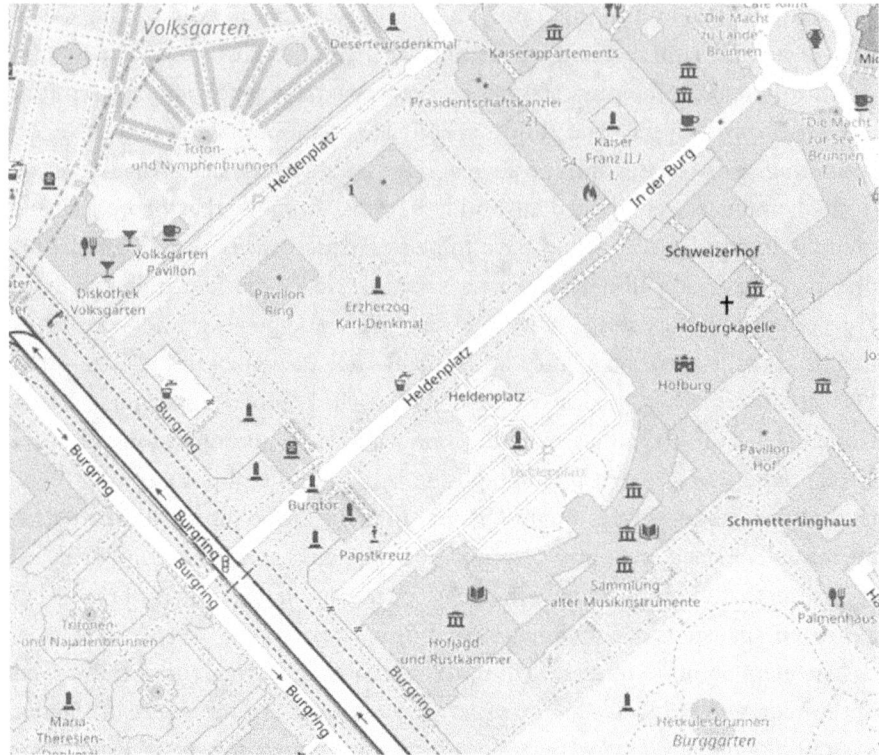

Figure 11.1 Aerial view of the *Heldenplatz* (structural map) © OpenStreetMap contributors.

Day marks the declaration of 'permanent neutrality'. Traditionally, the vice-chancellor (i.e. the deputy of the Federal Chancellor) as well as the minister of defence and other high-level officials participates in several parts of the festivity.

(Re-)Appropriations of the Viennese *Heldenplatz*

Spatial practices of everyday life and commemoration

Ethnographic investigations done over three years (2015–2018) allow the definition of the spatial practices at the Viennese *Heldenplatz* partly by everyday routines, like crossing the place by foot, car or, less frequently, by carriage (the Viennese *Fiaker*) and partly by the semiotic landscape. In the summertime, visitors or passers-by often take a rest at the exposed stairs of the Austrian National Library (in the southeast) or at the Outer Castle Gate (*[Äußeres] Burgtor*, in the southwest) by the main road. Also, seasonal markets and major events like the celebrations of Austrian National Day, acts of commemoration, public concerts or protests take place temporarily. From 2017 to 2020, changes in the bodily movements of tourists and others can be observed: two administration buildings (in contemporary architectural style and with several informative inscriptions) of the Austrian Parliament have been constructed at the *Heldenplatz* for the period of the renovations to the historic buildings of the Austrian Parliament. As the analysis of the media reports via QDA software suggests (cf. the section 'Research design, methodology and data'), these traditionalized or dynamically changing spatial practices are what the media are currently most interested in when discussing the *Heldenplatz*.

A central place for acts of commemoration is the Outer Castle Gate. It was erected in 1824 in memory of the Battle of Leipzig (1813), which was a giant battle of joint forces against the Emperor Napoleon I. Two large inscriptions – Latin words in golden letters – were placed on the upper part of the building: one praises Francis II, the Holy Roman Emperor, facing away from the *Heldenplatz*, and one – facing the inside of the square – names the emperor's motto (in capitals): '*Iustitia regnorum fundamentum*' ('Justice is the foundation of sovereignty') (Figure 11.2).

Figure 11.2 Inscription on the Outer Castle Gate.

Using Latin for inscriptions in this period of time and for this type of buildings is not uncommon. In fact, the LL of the surrounding area reveals that imperial buildings (in Vienna) often have mottos and plaques that mention historically relevant actors and dates in Latin.[8] The representations of this space (i.e. the values and ideologies that are indexed by the chosen language, font and height of emplacement) will be analysed below.

Nearly a hundred years after the erection of the Gate, a donation campaign in honour of the soldiers of the First World War was initiated. Contributors could have their name or that of a soldier inscribed on a metal laurel leaf (see Figure 11.2, beneath the motto). Several famous contributors took that opportunity, amongst them the Emperors of Austria-Hungary, the German and the Ottoman Empires, whose laurel leaves are gilded and placed on the outer side of the building.

In summary, spatial practices of bodily movements and architecture have a palimpsest-like character, meaning that acts as well as actors and the main spatial objects consist of several semiotic and discursive layers. Ethnographic observation reveals that each practice has its own time; that is, it is conventionalized by the genres of everyday life.

The discursive representations of space

Discourses about the *Heldenplatz* vary over time and depend heavily on spatial practices. Mostly these (re-)appropriations of space are political in nature and highlight the history of the place or of its actors. For example, protests that were conducted in 2015 and 2017 by the *Identitarian Movement* (IBÖ), a right-wing youth movement, appropriated the space by semiotically and discursively referring to events of an idealized heroic, military and non-Islamic past of Austrian history that is long gone (approximately 400 years ago). This discursively constructed past is represented by the statue of Prince Eugene of Savoy (noted above) and then iconically reused on T-shirts, banners etc. by these actors (Bendl 2018).

Furthermore, politicians add discursive layers to this spatial palimpsest: for example, since 2017 politicians, journalists and public figures have demanded a discussion about renaming the *Heldenplatz* ('Heroes' Square') to *Platz der Demokratie* or *Platz der Republik* ('Democracy Square' or 'Square of the Republic'). They contend that it is no longer suitable at this place to still refer to battles and heroes. It does not come as a surprise that these ideas were opposed, especially by actors with conservative views. Other recent attempts to redefine this place centre on the Museum of Austrian History, the spatial conditions for its establishment and its orientation regarding Austrian history.

Concerning commemorations, the Outer Castle Gate is the primary spatial resource for acts of state, although the most salient inscription does not explicitly refer to it (cf. Figure 11.2). On the one hand, its language choice indexes a linguistic competence that was and still is only in the hands of an elitist minority. On the other hand, interpreting the typography itself depends 'on the social group and the knowledge of this group, but also on the context (including place and its local history) and the context expectations' (Spitzmüller 2015: 133). The language ideology of the font refers to Roman ideals (in case this cultural knowledge is immediately available for the viewers; cf. Silverstein 2013). In addition, the material representation, namely the shiny gold letters as well as the emplacement of the inscription and plaques at the upper part of the (high) building, underline the high value of the contextualized ideologies. This ensemble finally forms the discursive 'face' of the Gate and partly of the *Heldenplatz*.

In the yearly acts of commemoration, the discursive layers indexing heroism and military history re-appropriate the *Heldenplatz*. For example, from the 1990s to 2012, *Burschenschafter* (members of student fraternities regarded as politically conservative or right-wing) commemorated the fallen soldiers of the Second World War on the day of the surrender of the *Wehrmacht* of Nazi Germany, 8 May. Elsewhere in Europe, this day is largely celebrated as 'Victory in Europe Day'. These and other commemorative acts, like the wreath-laying ceremony on the Austrian National Day (discussed below), occur at the central memorial of the Outer Castle Gate (built in the early 1930s) which consists of two military memorials.[9] One is at the rooftop of the Gate to commemorate the troops of the Habsburgs and is not open to the public, and the other is in the interior crypt of the west wing, which was initially erected for the fallen of the First World War. This crypt contains a large lying sculpture, representing the 'unknown soldier' who wears the uniform of a German soldier of the First World War, and an altar with a golden cross on an elevated position at the back for the Roman Catholic Mass which is, nowadays rarely, celebrated there (Figure 11.3). Candleholders on both sides refer to Christian discourses, as they hold the *Christogram* (consisting of the first two Greek letters in the word *Christos, Chi* and *Ro*) at the top. At the back an inscription – in capital letters – immediately draws one's attention as it is emplaced at an elevated position and illuminated from beneath: '1914 | 1939 Den Toten des Weltkrieges 1918 | 1945' ('For the dead of the World War' – this was completed after the Second World War).

Figure 11.3 Entering the Crypt at the Outer Castle Gate.

Using German at war memorials is rooted in the discursive constituting of European nations (Schreiner 2001). Also, German is, from the standpoint of language policy, still the dominant language in Austria. This second point highlights the (political) functions of language choice and use at this place, suggesting that these discourses of war and (religious or physical) sacrifice need to be easily comprehensible to the general public. In total, the language ideology establishes the identification with unnamed actors ('the dead', the statue) who are related to a 'Germanness' of a former time period (uniform, language choice).

In 2012, the statue of the 'unknown soldier' was raised for repair work and two messages, one from the sculptor and the other from his assistant were found in a small time-capsule. These findings were not unexpected for historians, as the sculptor – Wilhelm Frass – left hints about the messages during his lifetime. Moreover, leaving messages in statues or salient places of buildings is not uncommon (cf. Jarvis 2002). However, the messages contained two different comments on the sculpture and the political circumstances of its modelling, one that appears to be '*völkisch*' (i.e. nationalistic), the other (of the assistant) has a pacifist tenor. These discoveries led to a huge media response and to changes in prevailing predominant culture of remembrance: after the commemorative act of the *Burschenschafter* in 2012 was interrupted and heavily criticized (including by politicians), the fraternities no longer met there. Instead, soldiers have held silent vigils there since 2013. In addition, each year a concert (*Fest der Freude*, or 'Festival of Joy') is held by the Austrian Mauthausen Committee and the Vienna Symphony, attracting a great number of visitors.

This appearance of buried discourses led, in turn, to the partial cover-up of other historical representations of space in this spatial palimpsest: the wreath-laying ceremony on Austria's National Day was thenceforth no longer conducted *in* the crypt, but outside it, leaving the sculptors' discourses behind closed doors. Instead, these acts now take place in front of a plaque that is meant to commemorate the wounded and fallen soldiers of the Austrian Armed Forces and which was placed next to the entrance in 2002. These soldiers were not institutionally part of the armed forces of the Third Reich, and the now excluded discourses of the crypt.

The changes in the commemorative acts at the Outer Castle Gate also led to the redacting of the name of a war criminal listed in a book of fallen soldiers which was placed in the crypt. This and other books were removed, leaving the room empty.[10] Today, folders which inform the visitor about these changes are displayed in the crypt. Photographs hang in the empty side room of the crypt and document the changes. These artefacts serve, in this sense, as an 'archive' of acts of past spatial appropriations that individuals can no longer experience. At the same time, these discourses are not re-activated in the acts of commemoration that are publicly far more highlighted, namely the wreath-laying ceremonies on Austrian National Day.

In short, the representations of space of the Outer Castle Gate consist of several layers of historicity that are communicatively made relevant or are buried, hidden or kept away from immediate visibility. Here, the discursive concepts of 'history' and 'memory' are changed in a way that architectonical, discursive and knowledge-based layers of a certain past are no longer contextualized and therefore not easily perceivable in communicative acts. Yet, discourses of and ideologies about various timeframes are the main representations of space at this place.

The commemorative space of representation

In comparison to the spatial practices, which inherently refer to the linguistic and semiotic landscape and the whole spatial context, the spaces of representation are formed by the actual constituting or implementation of symbolic objects. As a consequence, the 'third space' includes the other two constituting dimensions. In other words, the spatial practice (e.g. an act of commemoration) enables a positioning towards representations of space (i.e. discourses and ideologies).

The spatial representation of a wreath-laying ceremony at the Austrian National Day, which is organized by the Austrian Armed Forces, is an example for this 'third space' (see Figure 11.4).

The wreath-laying ceremony is embedded in a daylong commemoration that includes speeches, the swearing-in of recruits and a military parade. It is conducted twice and in both cases similarly, so that the president of Austria (as Head of the Austrian Armed Forces) is the first to commemorate, followed by the vice-chancellor together with the minister of defence (see Figure 11.4). After the opening acts, which consist of salutes and music by the military band, soldiers lay a wreath in front of the plaque which commemorates soldiers of the Austrian Armed Forces (see the section 'The discursive representations of space'). Then, political representatives of the state adjust the ribbon of the wreath and position themselves, side by side with high-ranking officers, in front of it. In this sequence, the 'third space' is constituted as an aligning to a symbol of conventionalized

Figure 11.4 The wreath-laying ceremony (26 October 2017). Photograph: Ulrike Hütter (with kind permission).

acts of commemoration in public space. Again, music is played by the military band and the Federal Chancellor (with some others) signs the memorial book and others as the ceremony which lasts about fifteen minutes in total comes to an end. Approximately five minutes of that time is spent in front of the crypt alone.

Despite the brevity of this act, it is of high symbolic value in Austrian history. Its symbolic expressiveness is grounded in the physical positioning towards semiotics and discourses of the place that index polyhistoricity (the plaque, the wreath and the Outer Castle Gate). The non-verbal acts of standing still, kneeling and saluting are further salient contextualization cues of polyhistoricity, as they are connected to the traditional genre of (martial) commemorating and simultaneously refer to the spatial practices of this specific day. Both the materiality of the place and the acts refer to other discursive events and traditionalized acts at the place or even beyond, when considering the symbolic use of wreaths at acts of commemoration worldwide. However, in comparison to acts that took place before 2012, the discourses that are immediately touched upon here relate solely to the commemoration of the fallen soldiers of the Austrian Armed Forces. Contrary to the soldiers that the inscriptions and sculptures in the Gate refer to, these soldiers served the Republic of Austria of the post-world war and Nazi era, as the Armed Forces were established in 1955.

Acts of commemoration, like these, indexically point to Austrian history (via the chosen space-time) and to institutionalized and hegemonic power relations, but they do so in a limited manner, relative to the richness of discursive cues at the Gate. Most of the history of the place, all the discourses about war and the cleansing of semiotic and discursive layers of this palimpsest (cf. 'whitewashing', Shep 2015) remain untold here and are subject to discursive pre-existing knowledge.

However, one might politically evaluate the shift from commemorating fallen soldiers from the two world wars towards solely commemorating soldiers of present times, the spatially contextualized ideologies imply an exclusion of discourses of a specific past. The contextualization does not explicitly refer to the palimpsest as a whole, namely the crypt and its discourses that hold ideologies and positionings to two world wars and various acts of re-appropriation (as presented in the earlier analytical stages). Equally, the colossal architecture, the visibility of the linguistic and semiotic landscape of a past and the repeating acts of commemoration ('tradition') on this place are still partly perceivable, as one would expect from a spatial palimpsest, but they are subject to pre-existing knowledge about the place and parts of Austria's history when they are not explicitly contextualized.

Conclusion

The Viennese *Heldenplatz* is a place with a multilayered profile and meaning, being a palimpsest in nature. A spatial palimpsest consists of a variety of forms expressed in the semiotic landscape, in the daily acts of routine and in the spatial discourses and experiences. Although this potentially is true for each space (e.g. important crossroads), a historic site, like the Outer Castle Gate, supposedly receives its 'historic' significance by the constituting of it as such. This constituting can be traced in the LL, the material multimodality and in acts of appropriation which hold cues of polyhistoricity.

Applying Lefebvre's ([1974] 2016) triad of the production of space for linguistic needs gives a theoretical and even methodological structure, although each dimension is intertwined with the others. This is extremely valuable in the case of a spatial palimpsest that consists of various different semiotic and discursive layers that are partly covered. However, not only the (dividing) analytical steps but also the (unifying) interpretation of the data are structurally guided and simplified by the adapted triad.

The analysis shows that with each step, each dimension needs to be included in the discussion. This means that the analysis of the discursive representations of space relies on the explicit mentioning of spatial practices of the current point of interest. As a consequence, the analysis of the space(s) of representation needs to consider the interrelatedness of the preceding constituting dimensions, and still carefully accentuate its own (symbolic) character.

In the case of acts of commemoration, the analysis has shown that the bodily positioning in the lived space towards the spatial materiality *and* the discourses of a past, that is, the representations of a historic space, defines the temporarily valid production of space. However, as this act is repeated periodically, thereby re-constituting already existing discourses about history and identity, it is of social relevance and thereby utilizable for political and other activities.

Overall, the (re-)appropriation of a spatial palimpsest consists of overlapping semiotic and discursive layers that are (a) situational (space-time) and (b) selectively constituted in spatial acts. Thereby, they embed the contextualized semiotics and discourses of a place in already existing discourses that are represented by the genre of the act, ideologies and social positionings. The perceiving actors, as being part of the contextualization, then, are included in these (re-)appropriations and potentially position themselves. Finally, further identity-building and normative strategies are likely to be applied in certain (political) acts. As a consequence, historic sites are by default part of a dynamically negotiated memory and therefore of political positionings, negotiations and identity-establishing discourses.

Notes

1. The author wants to thank everyone who gave feedback on presentations of early versions of this chapter, especially at the 8th Linguistic Landscapes Workshop in Liverpool and the Sociolinguistics Symposium 21 in Murcia, and Brigitta Busch, Mi-Cha Flubacher and the three anonymous reviewers in particular.
2. It is crucial to take here the concrete constitution of space into account so that these dimensions are not (only) spaces but acts constituting specific spaces.
3. Schmid (2010: 234–245) traces the roots of the 'spatial triad' in a 'semiotic triad' (Lefebvre 1966) consisting of a symbolic, paradigmatic and syntagmatic dimension. A closer look reveals that these triads are two different concepts with a strong structuralistic outline and – concerning the 'semiotic triad' – share only few aspects of Linguistic Landscaping (such as an ethnographic approach).
4. Lefebvre ([1974] 2016) also follows an holistic approach that implemented historic data, the symbolics of places and the considering of actors and social networks.
5. This is partly comparable with the concept of layering (Scollon and Scollon 2003: 137) that describes multilayered signs (in space).
6. Compare with the notions of 'signals for historicity' (Spitzmüller and Warnke 2011: 87; orig. emphasis) in discourses and 'graphic indicators of historicity' ('graphische Historizitätsindikatoren', Spitzmüller 2013: 259).
7. These were Prince Eugene of Savoy, known as 'defender of Vienna' during the Siege of Vienna by Ottoman Turks 1683, and Archduke Charles, who inflicted Napoleon's first setback on a battlefield in 1809.
8. The author remembers being part of school excursions to Vienna in the context of history and Latin lessons. The pupils appropriated Austrian (imperial) history by visiting the Hofburg and other important buildings and by translating the Latin inscriptions of the LL.
9. Another place of commemoration was introduced in 1965 and lies in the southeast of the Gate. It is a place to commemorate the victims of the resistance of the era of National Socialism.
10. From time to time exhibitions are displayed in the crypt, like 'Final Sites before Deportation', an exhibition dealing with deportation collection camps in Vienna during the 1940s, open to the public from November 2016–November 2017 (extended).

Bibliography

Abousnnouga, G. and D. Machin (2010), 'War Monuments and the Changing Discourses of Nation and Soldiery', in A. Jaworski and C. Thurlow (eds), *Semiotic Landscapes. Language, Image, Space*, 219–240, London/New York: Continuum.

Bachmann-Medick, D. (2016), *Cultural Turns. New Orientations in the Study of Culture*, Berlin/Boston: De Gruyter.

Backhaus, P. (2005), 'Signs of Multilingualism in Tokyo – A Diachronic Look at the Linguistic Landscape', *International Journal of the Sociology of Language*, 175/176: 103–121.

Bendl, C. (2018), 'Protest als diskursive Raum-Zeit-Aneignung. Das Beispiel der Identitären Bewegung Österreich', *Zeitschrift für Angewandte Linguistik*, 68: 73–102.

Blommaert, J. (2005), *Discourse. A Critical Introduction*, Cambridge/New York: Cambridge University Press.

Blommaert, J. (2013), *Ethnography, Superdiversity and Linguistic Landscapes. Chronicles of Complexity*, Bristol/Buffalo: Multilingual Matters.

Bourdieu, P. (1989), 'Social Space and Symbolic Power', *Sociological Theory*, 7: 14–25.

Briggs, C. L. and R. Bauman (1992), 'Genre, Intertextuality, and Social Power', *Journal of Linguistic Anthropology*, 2: 131–172.

Busch, B. (2013), 'The Career of a Diacritical Sign. Language in Spatial Representations and Representational Spaces', in S. Pietikäinen and H. Kelly-Holmes (eds), *Multilingualism and the Periphery*, 199–221, Oxford: Oxford University Press.

Busch, B. (2015), 'Linguistic Repertoire and Spracherleben', the Lived Experience of Language', *Working Papers in Urban Language & Literacies*, 148: 1–16.

Busch, B. (2016a), 'Überschreibungen und Einschreibungen. Die Gedenkstätte als Palimpsest', in D. Allmeier, I. Manka, P. Mörtenböck and R. Scheuvens (eds), *Erinnerungsorte in Bewegung. Zur Neugestaltung des Gedenkens an Orten nationalsozialistischer Verbrechen*, 181–198, Bielefeld: transcript.

Busch B. (2016b), 'Methodology in Biographical Approaches in Applied Linguistics', *Working Papers in Urban Language & Literacies*, 187: 2–12.

de Certeau, M. (1988), *The Practice of Everyday Life*, Berkeley/Los Angeles/London: University of California Press.

Donohoe, J. (2006), 'Rushing to Memorialize', *Philosophy in the Contemporary World*, 13: 6–12.

Donohoe, J. (2009), 'Where Were You When …? On the Relationship between Individual Memory and Collective Memory', *Philosophy in the Contemporary World*, 16: 105–113.

Du Bois, J. W. (2007), 'The Stance Triangle', in R. Englebretson (ed.), *Stancetaking in Discourse. Subjectivity, Evaluation, Interaction*, 139–182, Amsterdam/Philadelphia, PA: John Benjamins.

Foucault, M. (1984), 'Of Other Spaces, Heterotopias', *Architecture, Mouvement, Continuité*, 5: 46–49.

Gumperz, J. J. (1992), 'Contextualization and Understanding', in A. Duranti and C. Goodwin (eds), *Rethinking Context. Language as an Interactive Phenomenon*, 229–252, Cambridge/New York: Cambridge University Press.

Harvey, D. (2016), 'Afterword', in H. Lefebvre, *In the Production of Space*, 425–434, Malden/Oxford/Victoria: Blackwell.

Huebner, T. and S. Phoocharoensil (2017), 'Monument as Semiotic Landscape: The Contested Historiography of a National Tragedy', *Linguistic Landscape*, 3: 101–121.

Irvine, J. T. and S. Gal (2000), 'Language Ideology and Linguistic Differentiation', in P. V. Kroskrity (ed.), *Regimes of Language: Ideologies, Polities, and Identities*, 35–84, Santa Fe: School of American Research Press.

Jarvis, W. (2002), *Time Capsules. A Cultural History*, Jefferson: McFarland.

Jaworski, A. and C. Thurlow (2010), 'Introducing Semiotic Landscapes', in A. Jaworski and C. Thurlow (eds), *Semiotic Landscapes. Language, Image, Space*, 1–40, London/New York: Continuum.

Kämper, H., Warnke, I. H. and D. Schmidt-Brücken (2016), 'Diskursive Historizität', in H. Kämper, I. H. Warnke and D. Schmidt-Brücken (eds), *Textuelle Historizität*, 1–8, Berlin/Boston: De Gruyter.

Kitis, E. Dimitris and T. M. Milani (2015), 'The Performativity of the Body. Turbulent Spaces in Greece', *Linguistic Landscape*, 1 (3): 268–290.

Lefebvre, H. (1966), *Le langage et la société*, Paris: Gallimard.

Lefebvre, H. ([1974] 2016), *The Production of Space*, Malden/Oxford/Victoria: Blackwell.

Pavlenko, A. (2010), 'Linguistic Landscape in Kyiv, Ukraine: A Diachronic Study', in E. Shohamy, E. Ben-Rafael and M. Barni (eds), *Linguistic Landscape in the City*, 133–150, Bristol: Multilingual Matters.

Pavlenko, A. and A. Mullen (2015), 'Why Diachronicity Matters in the Study of Linguistic Landscapes', *Linguistic Landscape*, 1: 114–132.

Purkarthofer, J. (2018), 'Children's Drawings as Part of School Language Profiles: Heteroglossic Realities in Families and Schools', *Applied Linguistics Review*, 9 (2–3): 201–223.

Reisigl, M. (2018), 'The Semiotics of Political Commemoration', in R. Wodak and B. Forchtner (eds), *The Routledge Handbook of Language and Politics*, 368–382, Oxon/New York: Routledge.

Schmid, C. (2010), *Stadt, Raum und Gesellschaft. Henri Lefebvre und die Theorie der Produktion des Raumes*, Stuttgart: Steiner.

Scollon, R. and S. W. Scollon (2003), *Discourses in Place. Language in the Material World*, London: Routledge.

Schreiner, K. H. (2001), 'Tote – Helden – Ahnen. Die rituelle Konstruktion der Nation', *Historische Anthropologie*, 9 (1): 54–77.

Shep, S. J. (2015), 'Urban Palimpsests and Contending Signs', *Social Semiotics*, 25: 209–216.

Silverstein, M. (2005), 'Axes of Evals: Token versus Type Interdiscursivity', *Journals of Linguistic Anthropology*, 15: 6–22.

Silverstein, M. (2013), 'Discourse and the No-thing-ness of Culture', *Signs and Society*, 1 (2): 327–366.

Sloboda, M. (2009), 'State Ideology and Linguistic Landscape. A Comparative Analysis of (Post)communist Belarus, Czech Republic and Slovakia', in E. Shohamy and D. Gorter (eds), *Linguistic Landscape. Expanding the Scenery*, 173–188, New York/London: Routledge.

Spitzmüller, J. (2013), *Graphische Variation als soziale Praxis. Eine soziolinguistische Theorie skripturaler 'Sichtbarkeit'*, Berlin/Boston: De Gruyter.

Spitzmüller, J. (2015), 'Graphic Variation and Graphic Ideologies: A Metapragmatic Approach', *Social Semiotics*, 25: 126–141.

Spitzmüller, J. and I. H. Warnke (2011), 'Discourse as a 'Linguistic Object': Methodical and Methodological Delimitations', *Critical Discourse Studies*, 8: 75–94.

Spolsky, B. and R. L. Cooper (1991), *The Languages of Jerusalem*, Oxford/New York: Clarendon Press.

Stroud, Ch. and D. Jegels (2014), 'Semiotic Landscapes and Mobile Narrations of Place. Performing the Local', *International Journal of the Sociology of Language*, 228: 179–199.

Train, R. (2016), 'Connecting Visual Presents to Archival Pasts in Multilingual California. Towards Historical Depth in Linguistic Landscape', *Linguistic Landscape*, 2 (3): 223–246.

Uhl, H. (2008), 'From Discourse to Representation: 'Austrian Memory' in Public Space', in S. Berger, L. Eriksonas and A. Mycock (eds), *Narrating the Nation. Representations in History, Media and the Arts*, 207–221, New York/Oxford: Berghahn Books.

Wodak, R., De Cillia, R., Reisigl, M., Rodger, R. and Liebhart, K. (2009), *The Discursive Construction of National Identity*, Edinburgh: Edinburgh University Press.

Conclusions

The memorials, or memory places, explored in the preceding chapters have been drawn from five continents, plus Australasia, and range from the grand to the domestic, from the *Heldenplatz* in Vienna to the birthplace of the Scottish poet Robert Burns. They include museums and monuments, sculptures and street name signs, linguistic and non-linguistic makers of meaning. They have been explored from different theoretical and methodological perspectives, and yet for all the diversity they represent a number of commonalities unify them. These themes are identified and discussed in this final chapter. They relate to the intention behind the creation of the memory place, the ways in which memory can change and be contested and the challenges in interpreting the memory place. However, before considering these themes we begin these concluding thoughts with our response to the question posed when we positioned this book, namely the meaningful contribution that Linguistic Landscape (LL) research can make to the study of the interface of memorialization and multilingualism.

Linguistic landscapes, memory, memorialization and multilingualism

The contribution that LL research makes to the study of memory, memorialization and multilingualism can be determined in part by the way in which LL research is conceptualized. Our contention that LLs have the potential to inform the study of memory, memorialization and multilingualism is predicated on the breadth, innovativeness and openness of LL research. Its creative methodologies, which consider multiple semiotic resources (Shohamy and Gorter 2009) and a broad range of approaches to interrogating a LL, are exemplified in the chapters contained in this volume. Questions of language in a narrower sense are privileged to different degrees by the contributors here, who may in turn give greater attention to such questions as geographic placement or people's interaction with the space or comparisons between older records and the contemporary setting. It is when multiple semiotic resources are considered that LL research contributes most richly to the reading of a place. Language is, however, always present in some form.

The memory places explored in this volume do raise questions for LL research. These include questions about how languages are represented in public spaces. Should the primary language be used, or is transliteration appropriate? What standards of correctness and adherence to norms apply to the display of language? What is the relationship between the historical use of written language and its presentation in contemporary times? And how is the non-appearance of languages to be interpreted? The inclusion or absence of languages cannot be easily interpreted as representing specific ideologies for particular times, and this is one dimension where the complex tools deployed in LL research contribute meaningfully to debates on visible multilingualism. Contemporary research in this field, involving the range of contributors to the emplacement of language in the public space, highlights the shortcomings of conclusions drawn from one perspective alone. From language choice in Livingstone, for instance, the reification of some kind of postcolonial Zambian language beliefs could be inferred by the exclusion of local languages. However, as the examination of the Livingstone Museum in this volume demonstrates, more practical, less ideological factors are in play. Curators responsible for recording and identifying flora relied on their own language skills and those of the communities where they worked to name plants and subsequently present them back to the visiting public. The array of LL approaches adopted by contributors to this volume highlights the capacity for this kind of research to reach more profound conclusions on the absence of some languages and the presence of others. Indeed, questions of remembering and forgetting permeate the themes of this volume. These we now identify and discuss.

Memory places are deliberate constructions

None of these memory places were created by accident. Each was a result of decisions made at either a macro-, meso-, or micro-level of society to commemorate a memory of the past. There are examples of all three in the preceding chapters. In New Zealand, for instance, the national government made the decision to create a war memorial park for the 100th anniversary of the ill-fated Gallipoli landing during the First World War whereas in Malaysia it was the state government that chose to commission a series of sculptures to celebrate the award of World Heritage Site status to Georgetown. In Sardinia, at the micro-level, the local Rotary Club decided to install Alguerese-only street name signs in Alghero. Behind these decisions was intention; the memory places that resulted had intended meaning.

As part of the process of creation choices needed to be made about what to include, and what to exclude. This is to be expected; resources are finite, and memory places must be fit for purpose. But as a result, and as Blair et al. (2010: 9) remind us, memory places are partisan, the memories represented partial. Thus, for example, one set of choices to be made concerns the memories of the past to be remembered, and the way in which they are to be remembered. In Georgetown, for example, the trade in tin would be recalled in an iron rod sculpture but not the wars that accompanied them.

Yet here we are not concerned with memory alone. In this volume we have set out to explore the way in which language contributes to the inevitable partiality of public memorials. Another set of choices, then, relates to the languages used to recall the memories. The Rotary Club's preference for Alguerese-only street name signs was a straightforward reflection of its wish to promote local language and culture. On the signs they sponsored, therefore, Italian and Sardinian were absent. A rather different example is found in Sarajevo, where the absence of Cyrillic script in the War Childhood Museum links to it being the written language of Bosnian Serbs. In another era, the architects of Vienna's *Heldenplatz* chose to emplace Latin, not German, in the prestigious position above the square on the Outer Castle Gate; the values identified with Latin at that time conveyed exactly the kind of ideology that the Emperors of the Austro-Hungarian Empire wished to impose on this prominent public space. Yet this is not to say that inclusion/exclusion choices are always necessarily deliberate or conscious. At Pukeahu, for instance, the decision to give prominence to the Māori language at the site was no doubt deliberate; the fact that other languages – Asian, Pacific, New Zealand Sign Language – are absent may not have been a conscious omission. It may have been, however, that the inclusion of other languages was not considered as they would have confused the message of the site. This is a reminder of the forgetting/remembering debate, and the fact that absence cannot be equated with forgetting; as Connerton (2008) made clear there are at least seven reasons for appearing to forget when viewed from a socio-historical perspective (psychologists would approach forgetting and remembering differently, as Erdelyi (2008) pointed out in a response to Connerton).

In the memory places explored in this volume, three of Connerton's seven reasons for absence or omission would appear to operate[1] with the most common being forgetting/remembering 'that is constitutive in the formation of a new identity'. It is clear that the motivation for creating memory places is very often linked to statements of who we are, or how we would like to be seen. Memory places might, then, be viewed as identity statements, formed not only by determining the memories to be remembered and the way in which they will be remembered, but the languages used to recall them. For, as we noted in the introduction, the relationship between languages on monuments and memorials is in and of itself 'a means of social construction' (Abousnnouga and Machin 2013: 29). The 'remembering' of te reo Māori, of Alguerese, of modern Scots all speak to statements of new identity.

Yet when it comes to language choice in the memory places considered in the preceding chapters, there is a strong tendency for dominant languages to push more local languages to the periphery. English, in its current role as global *lingua franca* and as the language of tourism, is evident almost everywhere. It is there in the War Childhood Museum in Sarajevo, on the streets of Georgetown, in the Livingstone Museum in Zambia, on the walls of the Robert Burns Birthplace Museum. Other languages – modern Scots, Tonga, Nyanja, Bemba, Lozi, Tamil, Chinese and even Bahasa Malaysia, the national language – become peripheral. Similarly, with the Landowski and other monuments to Franco-Moroccan friendship, French plays the dominant role, with the presence of Arabic often seen as symbolic only. Elsewhere we find the linguistic legacy of the people whose history is being recalled by a memory place – the African slaves transported to Brazil, the Irish migrants fleeing famine – is invisible.

These absences, these acts of forgetting, may be viewed as examples of another of Connerton's proposed reasons, that of 'forgetting as humiliated silence' which can be understood as 'the collusive silence brought on by a particular kind of collective shame' (2008: 67). He illustrates this, eloquently, with examples from Europe after the two world wars. For many years after 1918, '10 million mutilated survivors still haunted the streets of Europe', and yet:

> Every year, the war dead were ceremonially remembered and the words 'lest we forget' ritually intoned; but these words, uttered in a pitch of ecclesiastical solemnity, referred to those who were now safely dead. The words did not refer to the survivors. The sight of them was discomforting, even shameful. They were like ghosts haunting the conscience of Europe. (2008: 69)

At the same time as forgetting 'as humiliated silence', however, the war monuments of those inter-war years 'were deliberate attempts by governments, terrified of rising socialism during and just after World War I, to give a sense of meaning to the war, to distract from issues of social class and exploitation' (Abousnnouga and Machin 2010: 219) and 'were meant to be everyday semiotic devices to legitimize war and the idea of national unity in the face of evident exploitation and inequality' (2010: 220). They were also, therefore, 'constitutive in the formation of a new identity'. Memory places, we can see, are complex creations.

Memory changes, memory places are not immutable

If a memory place is a deliberate construction, it follows that it emerges from a specific time and place and that its construction will reflect that time and place, that it will be 'activated by concerns, issues, or anxieties of the present' (Blair et al. 2010: 6). As a result, memorials that are created, tangible and physically constructed are fixed at their time of production.[2] These monuments are inevitably, therefore, anchored at a specific point in time, somewhere around their conception, their design and their construction, but before their emplacement in the public space. LL research permits an examination of the relationship between the use of written language(s) at a given time (some of which, as we have noted, stretch back centuries) and contemporary language ideologies. LL research is particularly rich when it synthesizes the (usually conflicting) language ideologies of different eras, even if those periods are counted in decades rather than centuries. The tensions highlighted at the Robert Burns Birthplace Museum between shared understandings of how a language (or 'dialect') such as Scots can appear in places of prestige and social value (such as museums and monuments) attest to the potential of LL research to address difficult issues that are fixed in the public gaze by the very nature of memory places. An LL approach to reading and critiquing a Japanese-American internment camp memorial invites us to appraise the subtle shifts in how multilingualism is arranged visually for public consumption.

The present is not constant, of course. The concerns, issues and anxieties that shaped a memory place will change. Diachronic shifts in remembering the same event are likely, therefore, and have been illustrated in a number of the preceding chapters. Changes in the conducting of the Austrian National Day wreath-laying ceremony at the Outer Castle Gate in Vienna are a direct result of present concerns. At times, the physical nature of the memory place may alter. New additions to the Japanese-American Internment Camp Memorial Cemetery in Rohwer, Arkansas, have provided opportunities for re-telling the story of the camp. Elsewhere changes over time in the remembering of a given event have resulted in the use of different linguistic resources. In the most recent monument commemorating the Franco-Moroccan friendship, for example, Arabic plays a far more significant role than it did in monuments from earlier times, just as the absence of the Māori language at the Wellington Cenotaph is not repeated at the recently opened Pukeahu National War Memorial Park in the same city.

The examples from Austria and Arkansas suggest a third of Connerton's reasons, 'prescriptive forgetting', may be at play. This may best be understood as choosing to forget for the greater good, or, as Connerton put it speaking of the Ancient Greeks, 'they were acutely aware of the dangers intrinsic to remembering past wrongs because they well knew the endless chains of vendetta revenge to which this so often led' (2008: 61). At the Internment Camp Memorial Cemetery the monuments that speak to the sacrifice and patriotism of Japanese Americans, that emphasize their commitment to America and American values, seem to urge forgetting of the harsh treatment meted out to the internees. Similarly, changes in the acts of commemoration held in Vienna since 2012 would seem to be a deliberate attempt to de-emphasize militarism and Austrian involvement in the Third Reich with its unpalatable connotations and, indeed, memories.

In some ways these more recent developments present a challenge to the memory places of the past, but contestation occurs synchronically as well as diachronically. If, drawing on the traditional dichotomy in LL research between top-down and bottom-up signs (Ben-Rafael et al. 2006), the creation of a memory place can be treated as a top-down process, then the synchronic contestation can be seen as emerging from the grassroots. The graffiti wall at Pedra do Sal brings the African legacy in Rio de Janeiro into focus, as the fading wreath at the Wellington Cenotaph reminds the viewer of a conflict that is not otherwise remembered. In such cases, the intended meaning of the memory place is being challenged.

Nor should we overlook the fact that synchronic contestation can occur through studies such as those in the preceding chapters. In questioning the dominance of English and the reduced role played by Tonga, Nyanja, Bemba and Lozi in the Livingstone Museum and at the Victoria Falls area (as well as the absence of Zambia's many other indigenous languages), a challenge is offered and a new Zambian identity is imagined. By drawing attention to downscaling practices at the Valongo wharf, an alternative history to the Eurocentric version on display is revealed, a different history that remembers the barbarous and brutal slave trade that enabled the one on display.

Interpretation of memory places is personal

One of the shifts that have broadened LL research in recent years has been from the quantification of signs and languages visible in the site under investigation to a consideration of the experiencing of the LL. As an obvious example, the experience of being a part of a walking tour through Little Africa added new layers of meaning to the history of slavery in Brazil that this memory place explained. In Sarajevo, the victims of the Bosnian war have their own interpretation of memories emplaced alongside a cap or a bulletproof vest; voice here is given to those whose lives and losses are remembered, even when they are not physically present to engage with the visitor to the museum.

The advantage of joining a tour such as that through Little Africa is that elements of the memory place that may be hidden are explicated, although it is important to note that such input can only provide another partial perspective on the memorialization. All the same, such explication may be increasingly important for more recent memory places where 'complex references and cultural heritage markers' are more likely to be found (Abousnnouga and Machin 2010). A statue of David Livingstone, whether standing forcefully upright or gazing bravely forward, is relatively straightforward to read. The meaning of the designs on the cloak of the statue Hinerangi, by contrast, is not.

Intriguingly, in multilingual, multicultural settings it may be that the non-linguistic meaning-makers are more open to reading than the linguistic. The patterns on Hinerangi's cloak may not be easily understood, but they function successfully as explicit markers of Māori culture. The shamrocks on a fence surrounding the Black Rock in Montreal are fairly obviously indexing Ireland and, by association, the Irish typhus victims. The sunburst and the crane on the obelisk in the Internment Camp Memorial Cemetery are reasonably clearly referencing Japan rather than the United States. In the same way, perhaps it is not going too far to suggest that for the non-Arabic speaker, the Arabic script on the Landowski monument and others is perceived as decorative rather than meaningful, simply as serving to symbolize the Moroccans who fought and died. However, when Māori text is offered without translation, or humour relies on understanding a phrase from Bahasa Malaysia, meaning is not so easy to grasp.

Language use which can be broadly described as 'symbolic' has been considered in several of the contributions to this volume. On occasion, this symbolism tends to equate to some kind of diminished role in memory-making, where given languages are included for the sake of inclusion, and to perform multilingualism without necessarily activating meaning. In other words, the use of – for example – Arabic on the Landowski monument renders the statue multilingual, but not in the sense that it communicates in more than one language. Not only are its various audiences (in Morocco and, unintended, in France) unlikely to be able to read Arabic (given literacy rates, access to formal codes such as Modern Standard Arabic, and subsequently the language practices of the residents of Senlis, north of Paris), but the 'Arabic' inscribed on the plinth is not a code that Arabic-speakers can or could understand. In this respect, the symbolic use of language can come to serve not as authentic but rather as decorative, to signal an openness to including other codes, but not for the actual purposes of addressing other speech communities.

It is no surprise then that memory places are open to variable interpretation, that the intended meaning is not always that received. Is the figure on horseback atop the Wellington Cenotaph a figure of hope or despair? Are the two soldiers shaking hands in Landowski's statue agreeing on peace, achieving reconciliation or treating each other as equals? Interpretation depends on the schemata that the viewer brings, and, indeed, on the theoretical and methodological frameworks that the contributors to this volume have employed. In Vienna, Montreal and Wellington there is an added dimension that results from personal engagement. The memory places investigated in these cities all form part of the fabric of the researchers' daily lives, as opposed to being sites deliberately selected for investigation of multilingual memories. This, arguably, allows space for reflexivity, for developing an appreciation of how the memory place is used and experienced and for understanding of the memory place to evolve over time. But it is also a reminder of the fact that even in the familiar much can be hidden. In each of these three cases, the authors acknowledge that the research presented in their respective chapters has, at the very least, changed their interpretation of the memorial, and as a result prompted reflection on the memories that commissioners, designers and architects sought to evoke.

We can see then that memory places are multilayered and multidimensional and their polysemy is further complicated by the extent to which they are presented multilingually. They are seldom – if ever – open to a fixed interpretation, no matter what the intention animating their creation. Imposing – unintentionally or otherwise – a preferred reading by the use of more than one named language increases rather than limits the scope for personal engagement and understanding of the message(s) conveyed by these memorials. This opening up of meaning-making emerges only in part from the unquestionable lack of exact symmetry between languages. The partial and uneven use of more than one named language offers an unintended commentary on the intentions and ideologies of those responsible for the design of the memory places discussed here. It also prompts new and varied responses from those who encounter these memory places. Multilingualism makes memories.

Notes

1. It is perhaps worth noting that while 'erasure' is mentioned in a number of the chapters in this volume, Connerton's 'repressive erasure', at least in its more overt forms, does not seem to be operating in these memory places.
2. The exception is digital texts as memory places, which can be easily and subsequently modified, but there are no examples of those in our wide-ranging exploration.

References

Abousnnouga, G. and D. Machin (2010), 'War Monuments and the Changing Discourses of Nation and Soldiery', in A. Jaworski and C. Thurlow (eds), *Semiotic Landscapes: Language, Image and Space*, 219–240, London/New York: Continuum.

Abousnnouga, G. and D. Machin (2013), *The Language of War Monuments*, London: Bloomsbury.

Ben-Rafael, E., E. Shohamy, M. H. Amara and N. Trumper-Hecht (2006), 'Linguistic Landscape as Symbolic Construction of the Public Space: The Case of Israel', in D. Gorter (ed.), *Linguistic Landscape: A New Approach to Multilingualism*, 7–30, Clevedon: Multilingual Matters Ltd.

Blair, C., G. Dickinson and B. L. Ott (2010), 'Introduction: Rhetoric/Meaning/Place', in G. Dickinson, C. Blair and B. L. Ott (eds) *Places of Public Memory: The Rhetoric of Museums and Memorials*, 1–54, Tuscaloosa: University of Alabama Press.

Connerton, P. (2008), 'Seven Types of Forgetting', *Memory Studies*, 1 (1): 59–71.

Erdelyi, M. H. (2008), 'Forgetting and Remembering in Psychology: Commentary on Paul Connerton's "Seven Types of Forgetting" (2008)', *Memory Studies*, 1 (3): 273–278.

Shohamy, E. and D. Gorter (eds) (2009), *Linguistic Landscape: Expanding the Scenery*. New York and London: Routledge.

Index

Alghero 5, 7, 237–57, 257 n.1, 287
Alguerese 237, 239–41, 246–7, 250–7, 257 n.1, 287–8
Ancient Order of Hibernians (AOH) 43, 45, 50, 52
Anglican Church 42–3, 46, 48
ANZAC 21, 24
Anzac Day 18, 22
appropriation of space 264–7, 271, 274, 277, 280
Arabic 6, 63, 67, 69, 71–82, 230, 288, 290–2
audience 3–4, 17, 29, 77, 128, 154, 164, 167, 169, 222–4, 231, 233 n.1, 292

Bahasa Malaysia 216–19, 222, 224–5, 229–32, 233 n.1, 288, 291
bicultural identity 14, 142, 152–4, 157
Black Rock 5, 35–57, 57 n.1, 291
Bosnian 7, 161–3, 167, 169, 287, 291
Braille 32 n.4

Catalan 7, 237–42, 246, 249, 253, 255, 257, 257 n.1
Catalonia 239–41, 252, 256, 258 n.5
Cemetery of the New Blacks 189, 196, 206, 208
Cenotaph 5, 15, 17–20, 22–4, 26–31, 151, 154, 290, 292
Charter of the French language 37
Chinese 27, 93, 214–19, 222, 224, 226–32, 233 n.1, 288
Chinese dialects 218–19
chronotope 245, 258 n.7
citizenship 67, 142–3, 154, 216
clan 226
combi-memorial 7, 161–81
commemoration 7, 13–31, 36, 50, 55, 67, 77, 81, 90, 94, 172, 238, 242–4, 263, 268–9, 271–5, 277–80, 281 n.9, 290
competition 35–6, 40, 56–7, 117, 170–1, 220, 228

compositional meaning 165, 171, 180
contextualization 4, 96–9, 270, 279–80
Croatian 161, 167
Cyrillic 163, 167, 169, 287

decoloniality 31, 81, 189, 194
defunctionalisation 117
diachronic change 6, 144, 155, 249, 289–90
diachronicity 190
diaspora, African 188–9, 202, 204
diaspora, Irish 43–5, 47, 50
discourse 5, 7, 15, 36, 55, 70, 122, 128, 136–7, 141–2, 156, 162, 168, 174, 180, 188–90, 195, 219, 228, 231, 238, 241, 243–4, 246, 248, 252, 255, 257, 263–71, 274–81
division marocaine 64–5, 72, 74–5
double articulation 153–5

embodiment 3, 90, 108, 176–80
emplacement 92, 124, 130–1, 136, 141–3, 153, 176, 179, 228–9, 246, 249, 255–6, 274–5, 286, 289
English 6, 13–14, 16–17, 23–7, 29–30, 36–7, 41–2, 45–8, 50, 54–7, 75, 91, 95, 98–102, 108, 113–15, 119–20, 123–6, 128–31, 136, 139, 146–8, 150–4, 166, 168–9, 172, 192, 200, 204, 206, 216–19, 222–5, 229–32, 233 n.2, 288, 290
erasure 35–6, 48, 50, 57, 57 n.2, 89–91, 97, 103–8, 110, 140, 156, 195–6, 222, 225, 256–7, 293 n.1
Expo'67 47

Fever sheds 39–41
Fever ships 38
first responders 39–40
First World War. *See* World War 1
France 6, 63–82, 148, 292
French 6, 20, 31 n.1, 32 n.3, 36–7, 39, 41–3, 45–6, 48, 50, 55–6, 57 n.1, 63–82, 83 n.2, 95, 264–5, 288

Gallipoli 13, 24, 286
genre 126, 266, 270–1, 274, 279–80
Georgetown 7, 213, 220, 227–32, 286–8
Georgetown Festival 228
geosemiotics 3, 63, 76–7, 141, 228
German 58 n.10, 74, 79, 148, 264–5, 271, 274–6, 287
goums mixtes marocains 65, 79
graffiti 72, 203–5, 231, 290
Grand Trunk Railroad 43
Great War. *See* World War 1
Grey Sisters 39–41, 58 n.12
Grosse Île 35, 38–40, 45, 58 n.9

happiness 224–5
Heldenplatz (Vienna) 7, 263–4, 267, 269–80, 285, 287
heritage elites 36, 45, 55–6
heritage politics 19
heritage tourism 220
heritage, African 100, 188, 192, 196–7, 201
Hinerangi 26, 28–9, 31, 291
historicity 90, 96–7, 99, 102–5, 107, 109–10, 190, 268, 270, 277, 281 n.6
Hokkien 214–15, 218–19, 222, 224, 229, 231, 233 n.1
humour 121, 222, 224–5, 227, 232, 291

identity formation 232, 241
identity politics 267
identity, national 5, 13–15, 17, 27, 29–31, 153, 155, 213, 215, 217–20
ideology 2, 36, 55, 71, 94
immigration 39, 58 n.6, 137, 239
indexicality 5, 7, 141–2, 189, 191
Indian 215–16, 218, 220, 222–5, 227, 230
interactional meaning 165, 176–80
intertextuality 92, 238
Irish Famine 35–7, 43, 48, 50–1, 56–7, 58 n.6
Italian 237, 240–1, 246–9, 251–6, 258 n.5, 287
Italy 7, 79, 148, 237, 239–40, 248, 255, 258 n.5

Japanese 6, 135–40, 142–57, 289–90

Landowski, Paul 6, 63, 67–75, 77, 288, 291–2
language planning 124

language policy 1, 100, 108–9, 118–19, 121–3, 125, 128, 130, 167, 213, 215–18, 230, 276
Latin 166–7, 169, 172, 238, 273–4, 281 n.8, 287
learning 4, 20, 24, 113, 117–18, 123, 127, 156, 218
Lefebvre, Henri 118, 247–8, 264–9, 280, 281 nn.3–4
lieux de mémoire 75–6, 244
linguistic divisions 46, 232
linguistic landscape (LL) 1, 14, 31, 35, 58 n.4, 65, 94, 114, 116–18, 135, 187–209, 213, 238, 268, 285–6
linguistic regimes 2, 55, 57, 190–2, 195, 239
Little Africa 7, 188–9, 191–7, 199, 202–6, 208–9, 291
Livingstone Museum 6, 89–91, 94, 96–104, 106–10, 286, 288
Livingstone, David 89–91, 96–7, 103–8, 291
Lyautey, Maréchal 64–5, 67–71, 79

Malaysia 7, 213–19, 222, 231, 286
Maori language 13–14, 24–7, 31 n.1, 32 n.3, 287, 290–1
material culture 90–5, 98–9, 103, 124
material ethnography 91–3
materiality 89–110, 137, 141–2, 279–80
memorial agency 244, 257
memorialization 1, 3, 5–6, 17, 36, 42–3, 45, 47, 50, 137, 140–1, 143, 153, 157, 164, 168, 172, 188–9, 191, 195, 197–8, 200, 203, 205–6, 208, 209 nn.2–3, 238, 242, 244, 251, 258 n.6, 285–6, 291
memories 1–3, 5–7, 45, 47, 81–2, 89–90, 97, 99, 101, 105, 109, 140, 143, 161, 163–4, 168, 170, 173, 187, 189, 192–7, 201–6, 208, 209 n.2, 213, 231, 243, 264, 269, 287–8, 290–3
memory act 7, 238, 245, 257
memory constituency 7, 143, 163, 165, 188–9, 191, 195, 238, 257, 269, 287–9
memory knot 244, 255–6
memory landscape 57, 161, 169, 249, 255, 257
Mills, John 39, 51
minority memory 257
Montreal 5, 35–7, 39–48, 50–7, 58 n.5, 291–2

Montreal, history of 53, 55–6
monument 1–3, 5–7, 16–17, 22–3, 27–9, 35–6, 42, 44–6, 48–52, 55, 63, 66–82, 99, 136, 139, 140–3, 145, 147–55, 157, 163–5, 172–3, 175–6, 180, 191, 202, 213, 238, 243–5, 254, 257, 268–9, 285, 288–92
Morocco 5–6, 63–82, 292
multilingual memory 1–3, 63–83, 89–110, 139–43, 155–7, 255, 257, 292
multilingual monuments 152, 238
museum 1, 3, 5–7, 20, 24, 26, 30, 68, 89–91, 94, 96–104, 106–10, 113–31, 136, 161–81, 181 nn.1–2, 187–9, 195–6, 202, 209 n.3, 210 n.8, 267–8, 271, 275, 285–91
Muslim soldiers 76–8
Muslim war graves 75–7

narrative 6, 22–3, 27, 36, 47, 55, 57, 65, 82, 89–99, 101–3, 105, 107, 110, 136–7, 140, 142, 146–9, 153, 155, 157, 161–2, 164, 170–1, 181, 191–2, 194, 200–5, 218, 224, 254, 256, 269, 271
narratives of place 36, 57, 102, 110, 269
national unity 4, 136, 141, 215–16, 232, 289
nation-building 213, 215, 232
New Zealand Sign Language (NZSL) 14, 27, 287

objectification 117
oral remediation 95
orphans 40–1, 51

patrimoine national 63, 82
Pedra do Sal 189, 196, 202–6, 208, 290
Penang 7, 213–33
Penang, history of 214–15
place-naming 55, 103–5, 107, 238, 243, 271, 274
politics of remembrance 57, 190–2, 195, 206, 208, 243
polyhistoricity 267–8, 279–80
Portuguese 95, 192, 194, 197, 200, 204, 206, 227
postmemory 136, 143, 153
post-war memorial 161, 163, 165
Pukeahu 5, 15, 17–31, 31 n.1, 32 nn.3–4, 287

quarantine 35, 38–9, 45, 58 n.9
Quebec 35–8, 41, 45, 47–8, 50, 55–7, 58 n.4, 58 nn.8–9

race 46, 138, 189, 194, 198, 204–5, 208–9, 216
regimes of forgetfulness 190–2, 195, 204–5, 208
religious divisions 232
remembrance 7, 18–19, 46, 49, 57, 66, 96, 108, 135, 143, 156, 162, 164, 171, 178, 180–1, 190–2, 195, 197, 209 n.2, 277
rememoration 209 n.2, 238, 242–3, 254–5, 257
representational meaning 165–71, 173
resistance 7, 16–17, 65, 140, 142, 169, 172, 181, 189, 201–6, 209, 216, 281 n.9
re-urbanization 187
rhetoric 15, 23–4, 28, 164, 176, 189, 196, 209, 243
Rhodes, Cecil 103, 107
right-wing [youth] movement 274–5
Rio de Janeiro 7, 67, 187–209, 210 n.5, 290

Sardinia 7, 237, 239–40, 258 n.5, 286–7
Sardinian 5, 237, 239, 241, 246–7, 255–7, 287
scale 7, 66, 77, 79, 103, 105, 107, 187–209, 210 n.11, 244
Scotland 6, 114–15, 118–19, 121–2, 124, 126, 128, 130–1
Scots 6, 113–31, 131 n.1, 288–9
script 75, 102, 144, 151, 156, 163, 166–7, 169, 172, 221, 287, 291
Second World War. *See* World War 2
secret societies 214, 226–7
semiotic landscape 6, 15, 89–110, 162, 171, 180–1, 196, 263, 266, 268–9, 272, 277, 279–80
Serbian 161, 167
social class divisions 36, 42, 55, 289
social hierarchization 36, 47, 65, 265
social positioning 196, 245, 267, 280
social semiotic 161–81
space-time 201, 203–4, 208, 267, 279–80
spatial destructuration 238
spatial orientation 140, 144, 248

spatial palimpsest 7, 263–4, 267, 274, 277, 279–80
spatial text 161–81
spatial turn 264–5
standard language 78, 100, 120–2, 128, 240–1
street-name sign 238, 242, 244–7, 249, 251, 255, 257, 258 n.2
streetscape 227–31
symbolic space 5, 36–7, 266–7
synchronic change 16

Tamil 215, 217, 230, 232, 288
Tonga 90, 98, 100–2, 105, 288, 290
tourism, dark 50, 116, 161–2, 170, 188
tourism, hot 162
transgressive signs 30
Treaty of Waitangi 13–14
typhus victims 35–57, 58 n.12, 291

UNESCO 188, 200–1, 213, 220
unknown soldier 275–6

unknown warrior 24, 26, 30
USA 5–7, 37, 45, 50, 56, 58 n.6, 135–9, 143, 148, 155, 290–1

Valongo Wharf 7, 187, 189, 192, 196–7, 199–208, 290
Victoria Falls 6, 89–91, 94, 96–9, 103, 105–7, 109, 290
Vienna 7, 271, 274, 281 nn.7–8, 281 n.10, 285, 287, 289–90, 292

war memorial 1–2, 5, 13, 16, 20, 24, 26, 29, 30, 63–7, 70, 74–5, 135–6, 141, 143, 150, 153–5, 163, 165, 276, 286, 290
working class 37, 42, 48, 55–6, 66
World Heritage Site 188, 199, 213, 220, 266
World War 1 13, 18, 20, 24, 46, 63–7, 69, 73–4, 76, 78–9, 81–2, 274–5, 279, 286, 288
World War 2 6, 16, 18, 22, 25, 28–9, 63, 65, 77, 79, 82, 135–57, 275

www.ingramcontent.com/pod-product-compliance
Lightning Source LLC
Chambersburg PA
CBHW070016010526
44117CB00011B/1600